# AUTONOMOUS AGENTS

# AUTONOMOUS AGENTS

## From Self-Control to Autonomy

ALFRED R. MELE

Review
in
J. of Phil
February 1999

**OXFORD**
UNIVERSITY PRESS

# OXFORD
## UNIVERSITY PRESS

Oxford   New York
Athens   Auckland   Bangkok   Bogotá   Buenos Aires   Cape Town
Chennai   Dar es Salaam   Delhi   Florence   Hong Kong   Istanbul   Karachi
Kolkata   Kuala Lumpur   Madrid   Melbourne   Mexico City   Mumbai
Nairobi   Paris   São Paulo   Singapore   Taipei   Tokyo   Toronto   Warsaw

and associated companies in
Berlin   Ibadan

First published in 1995 by Oxford University Press, Inc.
198 Madison Avenue, New York, New York 10016

First issued as an Oxford University Press paperback, 2001

Oxford is a registered trademark of Oxford University Press, Inc.

Library of Congress Cataloging-in-Publication Data
Mele, Alfred R., 1951–
Autonomous agents : from self-control to autonomy / Alfred R Mele.
p.   cm.
Includes bibliographical references and index.
ISBN 0-19-509454-9; 0-19-515043-0 (pbk.)
1. Self-control.   2. Autonomy (Philosophy)   I. Title.
BJ1533.D49M45   1995
128'.3—dc20   94-32890

1  3  5  7  9  8  6  4  2

Printed in the United States of America
on acid-free paper

*For my parents, Alfred and Rosemary*

# Preface

This book explores two related topics: self-control and individual autonomy. 'Self-control,' as I use the term, denotes roughly the contrary of *akrasia* (want of self-control, incontinence, weakness of will) in Aristotle's Greek. Conceptions of self-control *as* autonomy (e.g., Dennett 1984) do not *compete* with mine; it is self-control *as* (roughly) the contrary of *akrasia* that concerns me. My examination of self-control is guided by two concerns: first, to understand *it* and its bearing on human behavior; second, to see what light a proper understanding of self-control and behavior manifesting it can shed on personal autonomy and autonomous behavior. My discussion of self-control goes beyond what is strictly required by my second concern; but a proper understanding of self-control is worth having in its own right.

The root idea of autonomy, which comes from *autos* (self) and *nomos* (rule or law), is self-rule or self-government. Taking etymology seriously, my efforts to understand autonomous agency are efforts to understand the agency distinctive of self-ruled or self-governed individuals. 'Autonomy,' as I shall use the term, is in the family of metaphysical freedom terms: 'free will,' 'free action,' and the like. However, just as there is no need to postulate the existence of *the will* in arguing for the reality of what is sometimes called "weakness of will" (Mele 1987), there is no need to postulate it in arguing for the reality of autonomous agency.

My interests in personal autonomy are traditional ones. I want to understand what it is to be an autonomous person and to act autonomously and whether autonomous agency is open to us. However, my approach is in some ways untraditional. My tack is to develop a conception of an ideally self-controlled person, to argue that even such a person can fall short of personal autonomy, to ask what may be added to such a person to yield an autonomous agent, and to offer an answer—or, rather, *two* overlapping answers, one for compatibilist believers in human autonomy and one for incompatibilist believers (i.e., libertarians). I do not try to settle the issue between compatibilists and incompatibilists about autonomy—that is, between theorists who hold that autonomy is compatible with determinism and theorists who deny this. (This will undoubtedly upset some readers.) I do argue, however, that the belief that there are autonomous human agents is better grounded than the belief that there are not.

I completed the first draft of this book during my tenure of a 1992–93 Jessie Ball duPont Fellowship at the National Humanities Center and a 1992–93 Fellowship for College Teachers from the National Endowment for the Humanities. Work continued during a sabbatical leave in the fall of 1993. I am grateful to the granting agencies and to Davidson College for their support and encouragement. Bob Connor and his marvelous staff made the National Humanities Center an ideal setting for research and writing.

Parts of this book are based on published journal articles of mine. Chapter 2 derives from "Akratic Action and the Practical Role of Better Judgment," *Pacific Philosophical Quarterly* 72 (1991). Chapter 4 incorporates material from a pair of articles: "*Akrasia*, Self-Control, and Second-Order Desires," *Noûs* 26 (1992) and "Errant Self-Control and the Self-Controlled Person," *Pacific Philosophical Quarterly* 71 (1990). Material written expressly for chapter 5 is the core of my "Self-Control and Belief," *Philosophical Psychology* 7 (1994). Chapter 6 is a revision of "Akratic Feelings," *Philosophy and Phenomenological Research* 50 (1989). I am grateful to the editors and publishers for their permission to use material from these essays.

I owe a special debt to Paul Moser and Randy Clarke. Paul provided helpful written comments on an early draft of the entire manuscript; Randy did the same for part II. For comments on various chapters or sections, I am indebted to Maynard Adams, Robert Audi, Simon Blackburn, Michael Bratman, Rachel Cohon, Richard Double, Irwin Goldstein, Ishtiyaque Haji, John Heil, Thomas Hill, Brad Hooker, Robert Kane, Tomis Kapitan, Paisley Livingston, Roderick Long, Ruth Lucier, Bill Lycan, Scott MacDonald, Ruth Marcus, Robert Noggle, David Pugmire, Piers Rawling, Andrews Reath, Jay Rosenberg, Geoff Sayre-McCord, Harry Silverstein, Lance Stell, Galen Strawson, Bill Throop, Bob Ware, and Michael Zimmerman, and to audiences at McGill University, Stanford University, the Triangle Ethics Group, and the University of North Carolina at Chapel Hill.

I am grateful, as always, to Connie and to our children—Al, Nick, and Angela— for everything. My parents, to whom this book is dedicated, have been a constant source of inspiration and encouragement.

*Davidson, North Carolina*                                    A.R.M.
*January 1995*

# Contents

# PART I

# 1

# Introduction: Self-Control and Personal Autonomy

This book is divided into two main parts. Part I advances a view of self-control, the self-controlled person, and behavior manifesting self-control. Part II does something comparable for personal autonomy, the autonomous person, and autonomous behavior. It is commonly held that personal autonomy encompasses self-control, and the two topics are quite naturally treated together.[1] The root notion of autonomy (from *autos* and *nomos*) is self-rule or self-government, and there is at least a superficial link between self-rule (or self-government) and self-control. Of course, whether the common view about their relationship is correct depends on what self-control and personal autonomy are.

The terms 'self-control' and 'autonomy' are used in a variety of senses in the literature. To avoid confusion, some guidance should be offered at the outset about my employment of these terms in this book. I understand self-control as, roughly, the contrary of *akrasia* (want of self-control, incontinence, weakness of will). By autonomy, taking etymology seriously, I mean, again roughly, self-rule or self-government. Joel Feinberg usefully distinguishes among four "meanings" of the term 'autonomy' as applied to individual persons: "It can refer either to the *capacity* to govern oneself . . . or to the *actual condition* of self-government . . . or to an *ideal of character* derived from that conception; or . . . to the *sovereign authority* to govern oneself" (1986, p. 28). My concern in this book is with autonomy as an actual condition of agents.

As the word is sometimes used, 'autonomy' names a property that is, by stipulative definition, possessable only by "moral agents," agents who engage in moral conduct. I make no such stipulation. In his *Nicomachean Ethics*, Aristotle mentions hypothetical gods for whom the moral virtues are otiose (bk. 10.7). Perhaps we can imagine, in the same vein, a universe whose only sentient inhabitants are self-sufficient, divine beings who devote their lives to various solitary intellectual activities, as they judge best, and want nothing from one another. Having no need or desire whose satisfaction requires interaction with other beings, they act in total isolation from one another. Such gods may be self-ruled or self-governed individuals. Even so, they may also be utterly *amoral*, on some conceptions of morality. Now it might turn out that there is an acceptable conception of morality according to which even beings of the imagined kind engage in moral conduct. Perhaps any such being has moral duties to itself, for example, and it may discharge those duties or fail to do so. I leave this issue open.

3

'Autonomy,' as I use the term, tags self-rule or self-government (or at least a species thereof). Whether all possible self-ruled or self-governed beings engage in moral conduct is a substantive issue, an issue that hinges on the outcome of substantive disputes about the nature of morality. I have no theoretical need for a sense of 'autonomy' that stipulatively limits the possession of autonomy to "moral agents."[2]

Autonomy, as I understand it, is associated with a family of *freedom*-concepts: free will, free choice, free action, and the like. In some of the philosophical literature that I will examine, the discussion is framed in terms of freedom rather than autonomy; but we are talking about the same thing, or at least aspects of the same thing.

## 1.   Self-Control and the Self-Controlled Person

Common acceptance of the idea that individual autonomy encompasses self-control may be more nominal than substantive, depending on the extent to which its proponents share a conception of self-control. The account of self-control that I will advance has its roots in an ancient explanatory project, the project of explaining intentional behavior, including *continent* and *incontinent* behavior. Aristotle asks, in chapter 7 of *De Motu Animalium* (701a7–8), "How does it happen that thinking is sometimes followed by action and sometimes not, sometimes by motion, sometimes not?" A proper answer requires that we understand how it happens that we sometimes act in accordance with our judgments about what it would be best to do and sometimes fail even to *attempt* to do so, pursuing instead a course of action at odds with what we judge best. Aristotle's question has attracted considerable attention both in philosophy and in psychology. Typically, the most fruitful work addresses *both* sides of the issue, attending not merely to rational action in accordance with one's evaluative judgments or, *instead*, to irrational departures therefrom. Psychiatrist George Ainslie asks, like Aristotle, not only why we sometimes pursue "the poorer, smaller, or more disastrous of two alternative rewards even when [we] seem to be entirely familiar with the alternatives" (1975, p. 463), but also why we seek the better or larger reward when we do. Psychologist Walter Mischel and his colleagues ask the same question in a series of studies standardly classified under the rubric "delay of gratification." Ainslie's and Mischel's work proved quite useful to me in *Irrationality* (Mele 1987, ch. 6), and I shall have occasion to return to some of it later in this book.

The recent psychological literature on self-control is extensive, as one would expect.[3] Psychological work on the topic is motivated both by broadly theoretical concerns and by the need for solutions to pressing practical problems. Any comprehensive theory of motivation must seek either to explain or to explain away behavioral phenomena associated with self-control or a want thereof—delayed gratification, impulsive conduct, and the like. To identify sources of practical interest in self-control, one need only consider a partial list of topics linked with it in the psychological literature: alcoholism, drug abuse, eating disorders, phobias, smoking, and spending. Theory informs practice and is in turn informed by observations of the results of practical applications. Emphasizing the former connection at the end of a chapter entitled "Self-Control," B. F. Skinner writes: "An . . . analysis of the *behav-*

*ior* of control should . . . improve the procedures through which society maintains self-controlling behavior in strength. As a science of behavior reveals more clearly the variables of which behavior is a function, these possibilities should be greatly increased" (1953, p. 241). This suggests, of course, that a partial test of the adequacy of "an analysis of the behavior of control" is its fruitfulness in this connection.

In philosophy, things are different. Peter Geach, in a book on the virtues, describes temperance as "a humdrum common-sense matter," adding that the considerations that recommend the trait "are not such as to arouse enthusiasm" (1977, p. 131). Some readers might have come to this book with a similarly dim view of self-control. However, the most general theoretical issues addressed in the psychological literature on self-control—issues about the motivational springs of action and the place of cognition in the explanation of motivated behavior—are also traditional philosophical issues. Further, some challenging philosophical problems about *akrasia*, problems that have exercised philosophers since Socrates' time, are mirrored by equally challenging problems about self-control, as will become evident in subsequent chapters.

What Aristotle called *akrasia* is, very roughly, a trait of character exhibited in uncompelled, intentional behavior that goes against the agent's best or better judgment—that is, a judgment to the effect that it would be best to do *A*, or (instead) better to do *A* than to do *B*. *Enkrateia* (self-control, continence, strength of will) is, again roughly, a trait of character exhibited in behavior that conforms with one's best or better judgment in the face of temptation to act to the contrary. (For stylistic reasons, I will often use 'better judgment' in a broad sense that includes best judgments, as well.) The akratic person, Aristotle writes, "is in such a state as to be defeated even by those [pleasures] which most people master," while the self-controlled person is in such a state as "to master even those by which most people are defeated" (*Nicomachean Ethics* 1150a11–13).

I will follow Aristotle in understanding self-control and *akrasia* as two sides of the same coin. On the view to be defended—and at this point I offer nothing more than a slogan—self-controlled individuals are agents possessed both of significant motivation to conduct themselves as they judge best and of a robust capacity to do what it takes so to conduct themselves in the face of (actual or anticipated) competing motivation. Akratic individuals, conversely, suffer from a deficiency in one or both of these connections. Human beings *wholly* lacking self-control are at the mercy of whatever desires happen to be strongest, even when the desires clash with their better judgments.

To avoid confusion, it should be observed that on a traditional conception of *akratic action*, not every instance of the phenomenon need manifest *akrasia*. Consider someone who is considerably more self-controlled in a certain sphere of life than the great majority of people. In a particularly taxing situation, such a person might succumb to temptation in that sphere, *A*-ing intentionally and in the absence of compulsion, although he judges it best not to *A*. Such behavior is standardly counted as akratic or incontinent, even if it manifests, not *weakness* of will or the possession of subnormal powers of self-control, but only an associated imperfection (Mele 1987, p. 4). Similarly, an agent who suffers from *akrasia* may successfully exercise his modest powers of self-control, on some occasions, and act continently.

I will distance myself from Aristotle on a number of counts. Aristotle limits the sphere of *enkrateia* and *akrasia*, like that of temperance and self-indulgence (*Nicomachean Ethics* 3.10, 7.7), to "pleasures and pains and appetites and aversions arising through touch and taste" (1150a9–10).[4] On the conception of self-control that I will defend, its sphere extends well beyond the bodily appetites. Indeed, in my account, agents may exhibit self-control not only in (overt) actions that accord with their evaluative judgments—including judgments having nothing to do with bodily appetites—but also in their acquisition or retention of *beliefs*. Just as agents can *act* akratically, they can *believe* akratically, as in some cases of self-deception (Mele 1987, ch. 8). By the same token, in successfully resisting actual or anticipated motivation to the contrary, agents may believe *continently* and manifest self-control, as I argue in chapter 5. In chapter 6, I argue that the sphere of self-control—and of *akrasia*—extends, as well, to which emotions we have or lack at a particular time: not only do we sometimes have control over how or whether our emotions manifest themselves in our behavior, we sometimes have control over which emotions we have or lack. In chapter 7, the sphere of self-control is extended even further—to our assessment, revision, and acceptance of values and principles.

I also depart from Aristotle on a metaphysical matter. He views the continent or self-controlled agent as a person whose "desiring element" is "obedient" to his "reason" or "rational principle," though less obedient than the virtuous person's (1102b26–28). A person "is said to have or not to have self-control," Aristotle writes, "according as his reason has or has not the control (*kratein*), on the assumption that this is the man himself" (1168b34–35). Given his contention that "reason more than anything else is man" (1178a7; cf. 1166a17, 22–23; 1168b27ff.; cf. Plato, *Republic* 588b–592b), Aristotle's identification of self-control with control by one's "reason" is predictable.

My own view of human beings is more holistic, as I will explain in due course. The *self* of self-control is not properly identified with reason. It is, rather, to be identified with the *person*, broadly conceived. Even when one's passions and emotions run counter to one's better judgment, they are not plausibly seen as alien forces.

A conception of self-controlled individuals as, roughly, people who characteristically are guided by their better judgments even in the face of strong competing motivation does not commit one to viewing emotion, passion, and the like as having no place in the self of self-control. Self-control can be exercised in support of better judgments partially based on a person's appetites or emotional commitments. In some cases, our better judgments may indicate our evaluative ranking of competing *emotions* or *appetites*.

Self-controlled individuals need not be Stoic sages. Their feelings, emotions, and appetites can inform their conceptions of the good life and their systems of values. The better judgments that self-control serves in a particular self-controlled person may often rest, for example, on a principle of practical reasoning that measures the importance of the interests of others on the basis of his emotional bonds with them. A thoroughly self-controlled person may even have as his goal in life the enjoyment of epicurean delights, and he will judge and act accordingly. The traditionally tight connection between self-control and better judgment in the self-controlled person leaves room for a great variety of lifestyles. What we judge best (or better) depends significantly on what we want, value, and enjoy; and most consistent collections of "pro-attitudes" can be well served by self-control.

To the extent that a better judgment derives from the agent's own desires, it has a motivational dimension. That helps to explain why many have regarded akratic action as theoretically perplexing. How, they wonder, can the motivation associated with a judgment of this kind be outweighed by competing motivation—especially when the competing desires have been taken into account in arriving at the judgment?

Much of *Irrationality* was devoted to answering this question (Mele 1987). A brief summary of my answer is in order, since it provides a partial basis for understanding how self-control can function at a certain crucial location in the generation of continent action. My answer rests partly on two theses, both of which I defended.

1. The motivational force of our desires is not always in line with our evaluation or assessment of the "objects" of our desires (i.e., the desired items).

2. Typically, decisive better judgments are formed, in significant part, on the basis of our evaluation or assessment of the objects of our desires.

If both theses are true, we should not be surprised that sometimes, judging it better to *A* than to *B*, we are more strongly motivated to *B* than to *A*.

Thesis 1, as I explained in *Irrationality* (1987, ch. 6), enjoys considerable empirical support. It is confirmed as well, I argued, by common experience and by various thought experiments (1987, chs. 2, 3). Desire strength is influenced not only by our assessment or evaluative rating of the objects of desires, but also by such things as the perceived proximity of prospects for desire satisfaction, the salience of desired objects in perception or in imagination, and the manner in which we attend to desired objects. (I will return to these points in subsequent chapters.)

Thesis 2 is a major plank in a standard conception of practical reasoning. In general, when we reason about what to do, we inquire, not about what we are most motivated to do, but rather about what it would be best, or better, or "good enough" to do. When we ask such questions while possessed of conflicting desires, our answers typically rest significantly on our assessments of the objects of our desires, assessments that need not be in line with the motivational force of those desires.

In *Irrationality*, I described a number of strategies of self-control, many gleaned from the psychological literature. Here is a modest sample. "An agent can . . . refuse, at the time of action, to focus his attention on the attractive aspects of the envisioned akratic action and concentrate instead on what is to be accomplished by acting as he judges best. He can attempt to augment his motivation for performing the action judged best by promising himself a reward (e.g., a night on the town) for doing so" (p. 23). In addition, an agent can picture a desired item as something decidedly unattractive to him—for example, a chocolate pie as a plate of chocolate-coated chewing tobacco (p. 26)—or imaginatively transform it into something that simply is not arousing. (Walter Mischel and his colleagues, in a series of studies, had children "cognitively transform" such treats as pretzels and marshmallows into logs and clouds, with significant results in their delay of gratification. For discussion of these studies, see *Irrationality*, pp. 88–93. I return to them in ch. 3, sec. 4.)

Self-control can be exercised in the face of present motivation (as in some of the scenarios just envisaged) and of anticipated motivation. Anticipating numerous urges to smoke at the office, a woman who has resolved to reduce her smoking brings only three cigarettes with her to work. A man who is afraid of flying embarks on a program of desensitization a month in advance of a scheduled plane trip.

Self-control, as I understand it, may be either regional or global, and it comes in degrees (cf. Rorty 1980a). A scholar who exhibits remarkable self-control in adhering to the demanding work schedule that he decisively judges best for himself may be "weak-willed" about eating. He is self-controlled in one region of his life and weak-willed in another. Further, some self-controlled individuals apparently are more self-controlled than others. Agents possessed of global self-control—self-control in all regions of their lives—would be particularly remarkable, if, in every region, their self-control considerably exceeded that of most people.

Self-control and its opposite can figure in the etiology of action at a variety of junctures. Suppose with Aristotle, for illustrative purposes only, that the generation of intentional action is roughly divisible into four stages: assent to the major premise of a practical syllogism, assent to a minor premise, assent to a conclusion, and action.[5] Amelie Rorty (1980b) has observed that *akrasia* may break in at any of these locations, manifesting itself, for example, in an agent's endorsement of a certain major premise, or in a failure to draw a warranted conclusion. Similarly, self-control may be exhibited, for example, in an agent's keeping a proper premise in focus, or in an agent's drawing a warranted practical-syllogistic conclusion (Mele 1987, ch. 4). Further, as I have mentioned, it also may be exhibited well beyond the sphere of action and practical reasoning, in our nonevaluative beliefs and in our emotions.

Looking even beyond assent to the "major premises" of some Aristotelian practical syllogisms, we notice that agents may accept principles concerning the acceptance, rejection, and modification of their beliefs, emotions, values, preferences, or desires. Acceptance of such a principle may take the form of one's holding a better judgment. For example, an agent may judge it best to assess his desires and preferences from an impartial perspective and to identify with or modify them accordingly; an agent may judge it best to monitor his values on a regular basis with a view to keeping them in line with those of his spiritual leader; and so on. People who are self-controlled in these spheres will conduct themselves in accordance with the principles they accept.[6]

## 2.  Personal Autonomy and Control

The root notion of autonomy, again, is self-rule or self-government, and autonomy as an actual condition of agents centrally involves self-rule. Not surprisingly, spelling out just what autonomy amounts to has proved difficult—both in the case of individuals, which is my concern, and in the case of groups. Part of the problem is that theorists have had quite different theoretical uses for a notion of individual autonomy.[7] When an account of a concept is developed for a particular theoretical purpose, it can easily fail to suit other purposes. A possible tack is to construct a characterization of autonomy with the end in view of accommodating *all* plausible theoretical demands that have been placed on something so named. However, the theoretical workload would then be enormous, and one may take comfort in the suggestion that no *one* specific concept is at work in all of these connections (Dworkin 1988, p. 6). Individual autonomy has been viewed as a necessary condition of moral responsibility, as a conduct-guiding ideal of rational beings, as a partial foundation for basic principles of justice, as a firm basis for the possession of rights, and so on. Perhaps no single concept can do all this work.

My own strategy concerning autonomy in this book is easy to state. I will argue that being a self-controlled person, in the robust, quasi-Aristotelian account to be developed, is insufficient for being an autonomous person. I will then ask what may be added to self-control to yield individual autonomy and offer an answer. Of course, the answer ought to be sensitive to some view or other of the theoretical work that autonomy, or a concept of it, is supposed to perform. But in putting together an account of autonomy, it is not necessary to *start* at the lofty level of identifying theoretical aims. Commonsense judgments can do some of the initial work, as the remainder of this section indicates.

It is a platitude that autonomous agents (if there are any) possess and exercise some degree of control over their lives. This platitude lies near the heart of an old and still lively debate between compatibilists and incompatibilists about freedom of action and freedom of the will. One way to see the debate is in terms of *control*: incompatibilists contend that determinism is incompatible with our having the control over ourselves required for free will and free action (or for *autonomy*, in my sense), and compatibilists deny this. A familiar argument against incompatibilists who hold that (some) human beings enjoy this freedom—that is, against *libertarians*—can be crudely framed as follows: freely willing and freely acting require that agents exercise control over their "willings" and their actions, but control is a causal phenomenon and causation requires determinism; so free will and free action *depend* on determinism.[8]

Unfortunately, it often is not made clear exactly what deterministic thesis is supposed to be required for causation. Determinism has been understood in a variety of ways, and quite distinct deterministic theses have prompted philosophical debate. Consider Peter van Inwagen's (orthodox) definition of 'determinism' as "the thesis that there is at any instant exactly one physically possible future" (1983, p. 3). It is determinism in this sense that van Inwagen argues to be incompatible with free will. But thus construed, determinism is probably false anyway. It clashes with leading interpretations of quantum mechanics; and there are implications for "personal" futures. For dramatic effect, imagine that an indeterministic trigger has been constructed for a personally significant event: whether the triggering event will occur is causally undetermined, but its occurrence would generate an event of personal importance. For example, "a tiny bit of radioactive substance" has been rigged to a bomb in my house—a bit "so small, that *perhaps* in the course of one hour one of the atoms decays, but also, with equal probability, perhaps not."[9] If, within one hour, any of the atoms decays, the causally undetermined decay event will detonate the bomb. If, alternatively, no such decay occurs in the specified period, the bomb will not explode. Assuming that the radioactive substance has more than one physically possible future, so do I. (Of course, it is difficult to see what I could possibly gain in the way of freedom or autonomy by someone's wiring the device to my house; but that is another story, one reserved for ch. 11.)

The coherence of this story indicates that causation (i.e., there being instances of causation) does not depend on the truth of the deterministic thesis that "there is at any instant exactly one physically possible future," nor on the truth of any thesis expressing a completely universal determinism. So even if it is granted—as I believe it should be—that freedom requires agential control and that control is a causal phenomenon, those who want to argue, along the lines sketched, that freedom requires determinism have their work cut out for them. They must identify the kind(s) of determinism required.

Setting aside the issue of determinism, some theorists have viewed free will or free action as incompatible with *caused* willing or acting, on any standard construal of causation. However, if freedom of these kinds requires agential control, and control is a causal phenomenon, these theorists face a variant of the antilibertarian argument just sketched. Roderick Chisholm, Richard Taylor, and others have adverted to "agent causation" in this connection. As Taylor describes it, this is the "causation of events by beings or substances that are not events" (1963, p. 52). Chisholm claims, similarly, that we have agent causation only when "there is some event, or set of events, that is caused, *not* by other events or states of affairs, but by the man himself, by the agent" (1966, p. 17). "On this view," Taylor writes, "it is a man himself, and not merely some part of him or something within him"—for example, "desires, choices, acts of will, and so on" (p. 49)—"that is the cause of his own activity" (p. 51). The view supposedly has the dual advantage of circumventing the control problem, "by conceding that human behavior is caused," and blocking determinism, by placing agents at the beginning of causal chains issuing in actions: "Some . . . causal chains, on this view, have beginnings, and they begin with agents themselves" (Taylor 1963, p. 52; cf. Chisholm 1966, Clarke 1993, Taylor 1966, and Thorp 1980, chs. 6 and 7).[10]

Although Taylor sees agent causation as required for freedom (1963, p. 50), he grants both that it is "so different from the usual philosophical conception of a cause that it should not even bear the same name" and that "one can hardly affirm such a theory of agency with complete comfort . . . and wholly without embarrassment, for the conception of men and their powers which is involved in it is strange indeed, if not positively mysterious" (p. 52). In fact, it is hard not to interpret what Taylor is driving at as *noncausal* control; and one may be excused for finding such control mysterious. Sometimes we may have to settle for mysteries—if we can do no better. Whether we can do better than agent causation in characterizing or understanding autonomy remains to be seen.

At any rate, that control is a causal phenomenon is difficult to deny. Try to imagine one being controlling another in the absence of any causal connection between them—Zeus controlling Prometheus, say. If there is no causal connection between them, Zeus has no *effect* on Prometheus. And if he has no effect on Prometheus, Zeus is not controlling Prometheus: one does not control a being on whom one has no effect. (Of course, one may *have the power* to control a being on whom one in fact has no effect; one may consistently refrain from exercising that power, perhaps because the being's conduct happens to accord with one's desires. But that is another matter.)

We can make some headway in understanding what sort of control over one's life is required for autonomy by asking what acting autonomously on a particular occasion requires. On election day, Ann voted for the Republican presidential candidate by pulling lever $x$. Whether she *autonomously* voted for the Republican candidate depends on further details. Suppose that Ann intended to vote for the Democratic candidate and mistakenly believed that lever $x$ designated that candidate. Then she did not *intentionally* vote for the Republican candidate, much less autonomously do so.

Autonomous $A$-ing (normally) is intentional $A$-ing.[11] And intentional $A$-ing, I have argued elsewhere, requires that the acquisition of an appropriate "proximal" intention (an intention for the specious present) play a causal role of a certain kind in the production of the $A$-ing.[12] This commits me to rejecting any account of autonomous (or free) action according to which such actions are uncaused—assuming that we sometimes act autonomously (or freely). Here, I treat the commitment as a provisional one. In *Springs of Action*, I develop a straightforwardly causal view of the explanation of intentional actions and argue that the most detailed competing anticausal theories fail (Mele 1992a). However, if it were to turn out that autonomous action must be uncaused, this would constitute grounds for reconsidering my arguments. These issues are examined in part II.

In cases of "overt" intentional action—intentional action essentially involving peripheral bodily motion—the agent is, at least to some degree, in control of the motions of his body. But how can this be so unless events in the agent figure in the production of relevant bodily motions? If no agent-internal events were at work in this way, his bodily motions would seem not to be controlled by him—any more than Prometheus's bodily motions were controlled by Zeus, in my earlier noncausal scenario.

One avenue open to the "anticausalist" is to give agents causal control over bodily motions of theirs, to treat overt actions as combinations of bodily motions and certain agent-internal events that figure in their production, and to hold that the combinations themselves, when they constitute autonomous actions, are uncaused. On such a view, your autonomous action of voting Republican by pulling lever $x$ might be composed of your "willing" to vote Republican by pulling lever $x$; certain bodily motions caused by that willing; and the motion of the lever, caused by those motions, that generates a Republican vote. If the "willing" is uncaused, you might have autonomously voted Republican, on an anticausal view of autonomous action.

Here, again, the anticausalist is faced with a problem. If events in you do not figure causally in the production of your willing, how can your willing be under your control? If you are a conscientious voter, then your decision to vote Republican rests on your deliberation about the merits of the candidates, their platforms, and so on. You decide for *reasons*, and your "willing" at $t$ to vote Republican by pulling lever $x$ at $t$ is presumably explained in part by your decision, typically one that you made long before entering the voting booth. But what is it to decide *for* a reason (or a collection of reasons)?

Three decades ago, Donald Davidson issued a challenge to proponents of anticausal theories of intentional action (i.e., anticausal theories of the *nature* of intentional action and of the *explanation* of such action). Bluntly put, it was this: Since you hold (like Davidson) that when we act intentionally we act for reasons, you should provide an account of acting *for* reasons that does not treat (our having) the reasons for which we act as figuring in the causal production of the associated actions (Davidson 1963). In *Springs of Action* (Mele 1992a), I argued that the most detailed attempts to meet Davidson's challenge fail, and I developed a causal account of acting for reasons. The point to be made here is that essentially the same challenge may be raised concerning *decisions*. Often, at least, we decide *for* reasons. Someone who holds that autonomous decisions are uncaused should be willing to provide an account of *deciding for reasons* that does not treat (our having) the reasons for which we decide as figuring in the causal production of the decision (i.e., of the deciding event).[13]

Typically, at least, our chief reasons for deciding to $A$ are reasons for $A$-ing.[14] A second voter, Beth, has a reason for voting for the Republican presidential candidate: she wants a certain governmental post and she believes both that she will get it if and only if the Republican candidate is elected and that her voting Republican will contribute to his election. If Beth does decide to vote Republican, do we have here a sufficient condition of her having so decided for the reason just identified? Plainly not. Beth might refuse on principle to allow purely self-interested considerations to influence her voting decisions; her decision to vote Republican might have rested on other grounds entirely. The reasons for which agents decide to $A$ are reasons that help to *account for* their so deciding. And it is difficult to see how reasons can help to account for an agent's deciding to $A$ if those reasons (or the agent's *having* them) do not play a causal role in the production of the decision.[15]

Here, again, the point can be put in terms of control. Autonomous agents are viewed as being, at least to some degree, in control of what they decide to do. And control, again, is a causal phenomenon. If an agent's reasons (or his having them) were causally irrelevant to his decisions, in what sense could his decisions be under his control?

Return to Ann. Suppose that she *intentionally* voted Republican. Is that sufficient for her having autonomously voted Republican? No. Her intention to vote Republican might have issued from a posthypnotic suggestion. What Ann is missing in this scenario, to put it simply, is control over what she intends.

What does such control require? One plausible requirement is the capacity or ability to intend to act as one judges it best to act—or the capacity or ability to intend on the basis of one's relevant evaluative judgments. Imagine a scenario not involving hypnosis. Instead, Ann carefully deliberated about the candidates' merits; formed, on that basis, the judgment that it would be best to vote Republican; intended, accordingly, to vote Republican; and executed that intention. Is *that* sufficient for her having autonomously voted Republican?

Again the answer is *no*. Just imagine that the values of Ann's that played a decisive role in her deliberation were products of coercive brainwashing. The Republican candidate's platform features cutting aid to the needy by fifty percent, tripling the military budget, making abortion unconditionally illegal, and so on—all measures to which Ann had been firmly opposed prior to brainwashing. In light of her new values, she views these features of the Republican platform as providing excellent grounds for voting Republican, and she judges, intends, and acts accordingly. Ann satisfies all of the conditions at issue; but she does not autonomously vote Republican.

In this scenario Ann's voting autonomously apparently is blocked by her lacking control over her values. What control in this domain requires is a complicated issue. It is reserved for subsequent chapters.

A brief review of the path just traversed—but in reverse order—will prove useful later. Full-blown, deliberative, intentional action involves (1) some psychological basis for evaluative reasoning (e.g., values, desires, and beliefs); (2) an evaluative judgment that is made on the basis of such reasoning and recommends a particular course of action; (3) an intention formed or acquired on the basis of that judgment; (4) an action, $A$, executing that intention. An agent who lacks control at any of these junctures does not *autonomously A*.

## 3.  Preview of Part I

The account of self-control to be developed in part I of this book centrally involves a notion of *evaluative judgment*. Chapter 2 advances a view of the causal bearing of what I term *decisive better* (including best) *judgments* on intentions and, less directly, on intentional actions. Chapter 3 takes up a problem about motivation to exercise self-control in a certain kind of case in which, judging it best to $A$, an agent wants more to perform an action $B$, even though he recognizes that his $B$-ing precludes his $A$-ing. Chapter 4 addresses a collection of threats to traditional, judgment-involving conceptions of self-control, the self-controlled person, and action exhibiting self-control (or continent action) and refines those conceptions. The remaining chapters examine the bearing of self-control on beliefs (ch. 5), on emotions (ch. 6), and on agents' collections of values and principles (ch. 7)—items influencing intentional behavior. More direct connections between exercises of self-control and overt intentional action were examined at length in *Irrationality* (Mele 1987, chs. 4–7). They will not be given similarly detailed attention here; but enough of my view on these matters will have emerged by the end of chapter 7 that a robust conception of a self-controlled individual will then be in place. In light of that conception, we can begin to see how, in certain circumstances, even an *ideally* self-controlled person is not autonomous. Identifying what such a person might lack provides a clue to important requirements for personal autonomy.

## Notes

1.  For the view that autonomy encompasses or requires self-control, see Audi 1991; Benn 1988, ch. 10; Feinberg 1986, ch. 18; Haworth 1986; Lindley 1986, ch. 5; and Young 1986.

2.  On the assumption that the hypothetical agents at issue are autonomous, the following claims from Kant's *Groundwork of the Metaphysic of Morals* jointly place these agents, or their "wills," "under moral laws": "a free will and a will under moral laws are one and the same"; "freedom and the will's enactment of its own laws are indeed both autonomy" (pp. 98, 104). As Onora O'Neill observes, Kant's conception of autonomy is by no means standard in twentieth-century literature on autonomy (1989, pp. 53–54, 66, 75–76). Readers are forewarned that it is not part of my aim to explicate a specifically Kantian notion of autonomy.

3. Psychological work on the topic is reviewed in Logue 1988. See also Ainslie 1992.

4. For other restrictive features of Aristotle's notion of *enkrateia*, see Charlton 1988, pp. 35–41.

5. In Mele 1984b, I argue that, for Aristotle, the conclusion of a practical syllogism is *not* an action. References to the literature advancing the opposing interpretation are provided there.

6. For an interesting discussion of the role of principles in overcoming temptation, see Nozick 1993, ch. 1.

7. Indeed, some theorists have used autonomy as a theoretical *foil* (e.g., Wolf 1990).

8. For more sophisticated versions of this argument, see Ayer 1954; Bergmann 1977, pp. 234–35; Hobart 1934; Nowell-Smith 1948; and Smart 1961; cf. Hume [1739] 1975, bk. 2, pt. 3, sec. 2; Hume [1777] 1975, sec. 8.

9. The quoted words are from Schrödinger 1983, p. 157. On triggering cases of this general kind, see also Anscombe 1981, pp. 144–47; Lewis 1986, p. 176; Sorabji 1980, p. 28; and van Inwagen 1983, pp. 191–92.

10. Bishop 1983 defends a related brand of agent causation, motivated largely by problems that causal deviance poses for the project of providing an "event-causal" analysis of intentional action. For such an analysis of intentional action that accommodates causal deviance, see Mele and Moser 1994.

11. Unbeknownst to Bob, who intends to vote Democratic, the Democratic lever in his voting booth is attached to a randomizing device. The only way for him to vote Democratic is to pull that lever, but pulling the lever yields only a 0.001 chance of producing a Democratic vote. Luckily, Bob succeeds in registering a vote for the Democratic candidate. Some would hold that his producing that vote was too lucky to count as an intentional action, even though that is what he intended to do (e.g., Mele and Moser 1994). Some who take this line may also coherently hold (depending on other features of the case) that Bob *autonomously* (or freely) produced a Democratic vote. Hence, the inclusion of the modifier "normally" in the text.

12. On proximal intentions and their role in the etiology of intentional action, see Mele 1992a, ch. 10. For arguments against "anticausalism" about action, see Mele 1992a, ch. 13.

13. 'Decision' has at least three senses: "(1) the act of deciding; (2) the immediate issue of the act, a decision *state*, a state of being decided upon something; and (3) *what* we decide, as in 'Her decision was to *A*'" (Mele 1992a, p. 158).

14. For resistance to this claim, see Pink 1991. See Mele 1992b for a reply, and Mele 1992c for discussion of an atypical case.

15. On two conceptions of reasons for action—one as abstracta and the other as states of mind—and two associated reason vocabularies, see Mele 1992a, pp. 104–5, 115. My own view on the etiology of decisions, intentions, and actions can be expressed in either vocabulary.

# 2

# Better Judgment: Nature and Function

The quasi-Aristotelian account of self-control advanced in part I of this book features a species of evaluative judgment. Suppose that an agent judges that his doing *A* would be morally (or aesthetically, or economically) better than his doing *B* and yet, in the absence of compulsion, intentionally does *B* rather than *A*. In doing *B*, he need not be acting akratically; for at the same time he may also judge, for example, that *all things considered*, his doing *B* would be better than his doing *A*. In doing *B*, he may be acting *continently*, in accordance with the latter judgment. Akratic action, in traditional cases, violates what I elsewhere termed a *decisive* best or better judgment (Mele 1987, pp. 5–6). A judgment made or held by an agent is a decisive best or better judgment, in my sense, if and only if it settles in the agent's mind the question what (from the perspective of his own desires, beliefs, etc.) it is best or better to do given his circumstances—and best or better, not just in some respect or other (e.g., financially), but *simpliciter*. (For stylistic reasons, I will normally use "decisive better judgment" as shorthand for "decisive best or better judgment.")

Sometimes deliberation issues in a decisive better judgment; sometimes it does not. Deliberation may issue in judgments of other sorts instead, and it may simply be incomplete. Even when deliberation does issue in a decisive judgment, an agent can akratically act against the judgment, if a central species of akratic action is a genuine possibility; and this can happen even when an agent decisively judges it best to *A straightaway*. However, for reasons that will emerge in subsequent sections, some theorists have sought a species of better judgment whose instances are immune to *akrasia*—immune in the sense that as long as such a judgment is present, an agent cannot act akratically against it. If there are judgments of this kind, then although an agent may exercise self-control in forming such a judgment, or in retaining such a judgment in the face of motivation that urges an akratic change of mind, there is no place for an exercise of self-control in mastering motivation that threatens to issue in akratic action performed while the judgment is present.

In the present chapter, I argue that no such *nonartificial* species of evaluative judgment is to be found, and I make a case for my own conception of better judgment and of the place of better judgment in the production of action. If, as is generally thought, the evaluative judgments of self-controlled and autonomous agents play a major role in their behavior, we would do well to understand that role. However, my objective here goes further. One of my aims in this part of the book is to display the breadth of self-control's potential sphere of operation. The segment of the etiology of intentional action on which this chapter focuses is a relatively small, but important, part of that sphere.

## 1.  Strict Akratic Action and Two Perspectives on Action Explanation

The alleged species of akratic action that has received pride of place in the literature is uncompelled intentional action that, as the agent recognizes, is contrary to a decisive better judgment that he consciously holds—or what I elsewhere termed *strict akratic action* (Mele 1987, p. 7). The occurrence of strict akratic actions seems to be an unfortunate fact of life. Unlike many such (apparent) facts, however, this one has attracted considerable philosophical attention for nearly two and a half millennia. A major source of the interest is not far to seek: strict akratic action, if it is a genuine phenomenon, raises difficult questions about the connection between thought and action, a connection of paramount importance for any theory of the explanation of intentional behavior that accords thought an explanatory role.

Matters are complicated by our having—in the philosophy of action, moral psychology, and ordinary thought—a pair of perspectives on the explanation of intentional action, a *motivational* and an *intellectual* one. Central to the motivational perspective is the idea that what agents do, when they act intentionally, depends on what they are most strongly motivated to do at the time. This perspective is taken on *all* intentional action, independently of the biological species to which the agents belong. If, for instance, cats, dogs, and human beings act intentionally, the motivational perspective has all three species in its sights. The intellectual perspective applies only to intellectual beings. Minimally sufficient conditions for inclusion in the class of intellectual beings are none too clear. But practical intellect, as it is normally conceived, is concerned (among other things) with weighing options and making judgments about what it is best, better, or "good enough" to do. Central to the intellectual perspective is the idea that such judgments play a significant role in explaining intentional actions of intellectual beings.

Many philosophers have sought to combine our two perspectives into one in the domain of intentional human action. One tack is to insist that, in intellectual beings, motivational strength and evaluative judgment always travel hand in hand. Socrates is commonly interpreted as advancing this view in connection with his rejection of the thesis that people sometimes knowingly do wrong (Plato, *Protagoras* 352b–358d). Theorists who take this tack can go several ways. For example, they can hold that judgment causally determines motivational strength, that motivational strength causally determines judgment, or that judgment and motivational strength have a common cause. They can also try to get by without causal determination or causation, seeking to find purely conceptual ground for the thesis at issue.

The apparent occurrence of strict akratic actions constitutes a problem for this general tack. The motivational perspective is well suited to akratic action: when acting akratically, one presumably does what one is most strongly motivated to do at the time. But the intellectual perspective is threatened (more precisely, certain interpretations of, or theses about, that perspective are challenged). In threatening the intellectual perspective while leaving the motivational perspective unchallenged, akratic action poses apparent difficulties for the project of combining the two perspectives into a unified outlook on the explanation of intentional human action. That is a primary source of perennial philosophical interest in akratic action.

The motivational and intellectual perspectives have much to recommend them, and a plausible combination is theoretically desirable. To some theorists, the threat that full-blown akratic action poses to a unified, motivational/intellectual perspective has seemed so severe that they have rejected such action as logically or psychologically impossible.[1] Many others have sought to accommodate akratic action in a unified perspective.

A proper tale of the two perspectives must mention various alleged intermediaries between motivation and judgment, on the one hand, and intentional action on the other—choice, decision, and intention, in particular. These items are featured in various versions of *both* perspectives, a fact that may be taken as grounds for hope that the perspectives may be plausibly combined. We can say, somewhat misleadingly, that the motivational and intellectual perspectives on the explanation of intentional human action converge not only on intentional action, but also on choice, decision, and intention. Appreciating *why* this way of putting the point is misleading reinforces the point. Deciding and choosing *are actions* (more precisely, action types), and in deciding or choosing to do something, one forms an intention to do it.[2] Further, the thesis that choosing and deciding are *unintentional* or *nonintentional* activities is difficult to sustain (McCann 1986a). It is not as though the perspectives, in *addition* to converging on intentional action, *also* converge on the named "intermediaries."

Aristotle claimed that choice (*prohairesis*), "the origin of action—its efficient, not its final cause," is "either desiderative reason [*orektikos nous*] or ratiocinative desire [*orexis dianoetike*]" (*Nicomachean Ethics* 1139a31–32, 1139b4–5). On one reading, Aristotle could not make up his mind whether choice belongs to the genus *judgment* or the genus *motivation*. On another, choice is a hybrid: it is judgment *cum* motivation, and perhaps judgment *cum* proportional motivation.[3] Donald Davidson holds, in a similar vein, that an "unconditional" better judgment is an *intention*; and R. M. Hare, as I understand him, maintains that assenting to a value judgment that one ought to *X* entails *intending* to *X* (in the guise of assenting "to the command 'Let me do *X*'").[4] But if these claims are correct, it is difficult to understand how someone might choose, decide, or intend akratically; and if akratic actions are possible, so, apparently, are akratic choices, decisions, and intentions. Seemingly, one may decisively judge it best to *A* and yet, owing to weakness of will and recalcitrant desires, choose (or decide, or intend) to *B*, knowing full well that his *B*-ing precludes his *A*-ing.

One moral is that those who seek to accommodate full-blown akratic action in a combined motivational/intellectual perspective on the explanation of intentional action should be wary of pursuing a simple solution at the level of choices, decisions, and intentions. If the two perspectives are in tension with one another at the level of *overt* intentional action, one should not be surprised to find a related tension at the level of such mental action as choosing and deciding.

Davidson, in "How is Weakness of the Will Possible?," a paper that shaped subsequent discussion of the topic, set out the problem of the possibility of akratic action in terms of three principles:

*P1*. If an agent wants to do *x* more than he wants to do *y* and he believes himself free to do either *x* or *y*, then he will intentionally do *x* if he does either *x* or *y* intentionally.

*P2*. If an agent judges that it would be better to do *x* than to do *y*, then he wants to do *x* more than he wants to do *y*.

*P3*. There are incontinent actions. ([1970] 1980, p. 23)

*P1* and *P2* entail a tight connection between better judgment and intentional action—a connection that *P3* seems to contravene. Davidson's aim was to show that, despite appearances, the principles form a consistent set.

Even if *P1* and *P2* are both false, there are, presumably, *some* notable connections among what we want, what we judge best (or better), and what we do intentionally. So, at least, we commonly suppose. Something *like P1* is bound, it seems, to be true.[5] And, surely, our better judgments are not wholly devoid of practical significance. As Davidson notes, "it is easy to interpret *P2* in a way that makes it false"; but perhaps, as he adds,

> [I]t is harder to believe that there is not a natural reading that makes it true. For against our tendency to agree that we often believe we ought to do something and yet don't want to, there is also the opposite tendency to say that if someone really (sincerely) believes he ought, then his belief must show itself in his behavior (and hence, of course, in his inclination to act, or his desire). (1980, p. 27)

This opposite tendency posits some dispositional, functional, or conceptual connection (the 'or' is not exclusive) between better judgment and intentional action, perhaps by way of wanting more or most. There is a real danger that in attempting to make conceptual and causal space for full-fledged akratic action one might commit oneself to the rejection of genuine ties between evaluative judgment and intentional action.

Supposing, if only for the sake of argument, that there are akratic actions, the possibility is left open that there is a *species* of judgment whose functional or conceptual connection to intentional behavior precludes there being akratic intentions and actions against its instances. Davidson and Hare purport to identify such a species of judgment. So might Aristotle, on one possible reading. The present chapter explores the putative possibility of there being judgments of this kind. My aim, in part, is to undermine the thesis that there is a nonartificial *akrasia*-proof species of evaluative judgment and to show that rejecting the thesis leaves intact the idea that our evaluative judgments bear importantly on what we intend and do.

This aim may be described more broadly. In a recent paper, Philip Pettit and Michael Smith address (among other things) the question how the motivational and intellectual perspectives on the explanation of intentional action can be squared with each other (1993, pp. 53–54). The motivational perspective links motivation to intentional action, as does *P1*; and the intellectual perspective links practical reasoning and evaluative judgments to intentional action—typically, by way of intention, decision, or choice, as a variant of *P2* might do. Whereas Davidson seeks to square *P1* and *P2* with the occurrence of incontinent actions (*P3*), Pettit and Smith employ their understanding of the difference between our two perspectives "to generate a systematic taxonomy of the different types of failure that we may expect to find in practical reason" (p. 53). In Davidson's paper, our two perspectives are viewed as constituting a relatively tidy package for which akratic action poses an apparent difficulty. In Pettit and Smith's paper, the perspectives are presented as being in tension with each other in a way that illuminates akratic action and other forms of "practical unreason." (I take the basic source of tension to be the point that the motivational force of a desire or want is sometimes out of line with the agent's evaluation of the desired item.)[6] In the present chapter, the tension is acknowledged, and it is accommodated in a manner that accords deliberative judgments a significant role in the etiology of intentions and intentional actions while leaving appropriate room for desire-influenced irrationality.[7]

## 2. Best Judgment*

It is easy enough to define a species of best judgment whose members are such that strict akratic action against them is impossible. Let us say that an agent consciously holds, at $t$, a *judgment** that it is best to $A$ at $t'$ if and only if, at $t$, he both consciously holds a judgment, in some standard sense of the term (take your pick), that it is best to $A$ at $t'$ *and* consciously *intends* to $A$ at $t'$. Thus, if, at a time, $t$, an agent consciously holds a judgment* that it is best to $A$ straightaway, he intends to $A$ straightaway. He has an intention for the specious present, a *proximal* intention.

Now, the presence of proximal intentions does not guarantee their successful execution, or even an attempt. Someone who intends to answer straightaway the phone on the desk at which he is working may be distracted by a gunshot outside his window—or, alternatively, be shot to death—even before he has time to move his hand toward the receiver. Occasionally, a proximal intention may be overturned or dissolved owing to weakness of will. A biology student, John, moving a needle toward his left index finger with the proximal intention of pricking himself to draw blood for an experiment, may, owing to a natural (but defeasible) aversion, intentionally stop short, the intention to prick having been supplanted by another intention.[8]

On the natural assumption, however, that an agent cannot intentionally do an $A$ *while* intending to do something else that he knows full well is incompatible with his $A$-ing, John cannot akratically fail to prick his finger while his proximal intention to prick it remains in place. If that is right, then as long as John's best judgment* stands, he cannot akratically act against it, since the presence of that judgment requires the presence of the proximal intention to prick. This would distinguish best judgments* from any conscious best judgments whose presence throughout $t$ does not preclude one's acting akratically against them during $t$. If, even while he was aborting the attempt, John consciously held a judgment (*sans* *) that it is best to prick his finger, he might have acted akratically against *that* judgment.

Perhaps, then, I have identified a kind of best judgment—best judgment*—so constituted that, as long as one continues consciously to hold it, one cannot act akratically against it. However, since the intention component of the judgment is doing the work, the notion is not likely to evoke enthusiasm. Best judgment* is just best judgment (on some reading of 'judgment') *plus* a corresponding intention. What *would* be interesting is a notion, *not* arrived at by stipulative augmentation, of a kind of best judgment that is *akrasia*-proof. Can we locate a species of best judgment that is tightly, but nonartificially, linked to intention?

## 3.   Some Putative Connections: Hare and Davidson

R. M. Hare contends that agents who assent to a value judgment that they ought to do $X$ "must also assent to the command 'Let me do $X$'," and that "it is a tautology that we cannot sincerely assent to a command addressed to ourselves, and *at the same time* not perform it, if now is the occasion for performing it, and it is in our (physical and psychological) power to do so" (1963, p. 79).[9] Treating talk of self-commands as metaphorical talk about intentions, and focusing specifically on *proximal* intentions, we get the following view: judging that one ought to $A$ entails intending to $A$, and, without exception, agents who proximally intend to $A$ do $A$, if they can. The second conjunct is too strong, since even agents who can execute a (nonaborted) proximal intention sometimes fail to do so: tennis pros intending to make easy shots that are well within their power occasionally miss. But it is the first conjunct that concerns me.

Is there a nonartificial species of ought-judgment so constituted that one who makes a judgment of that kind must intend accordingly? That is, is there a notion of "ought-judgment" so linked to intention, but *not* as a consequence of beefing up some other notion of ought-judgment simply by conjoining intention to it?

Hare tells us that "one of the characteristics of moral terms, and one which is a sufficiently essential characteristic for us to call it part of the meaning of these terms, [is] that judgments containing them are, as typically used, intended as guides to conduct" (1963, p. 67). Indeed, what renders ostensible akratic action theoretically problematic, in Hare's view, is "the fact that moral judgements, in their central use, have it as their function to guide conduct" (p. 70). Let us suppose that a necessary condition of a species of judgment's having a conduct-guiding function, in the pertinent sense, is that its instances can serve as springs of action. This would distinguish a relatively robust sort of guidance from, say, the sort of guidance that is offered by a recipe or a blueprint. Further precision should be gained by honest toil, not supposition.

If the essential conduct-guiding function of first-person, moral ought-judgments required the truth of the claim that anyone who judges that he ought (morally) to $A$ intends to $A$, we would have made significant headway. But the idea of a conduct-guiding function is too thin to bolster such a claim. Presumably, prudential judgments, judgments of etiquette, and the like, are standardly intended as guides to conduct. Few, however, would seriously entertain the suggestion that the conduct-guiding function of judgments of etiquette depends on its being true that anyone who judges that he ought, from the perspective of etiquette, to $A$ must intend to $A$. Additionally, if ought-judgments made from the perspectives of specific institutions or categories of value all required for their conduct-guiding work a tight connection of this sort to intending, we would often find ourselves possessed of intentions that we know cannot jointly be executed. This is a consequence at which even the credulous would balk. Surely, if I judge that, aesthetically, I ought to A now, but judge as well that, financially, I ought not to A now, it does not follow that I both intend to A now and intend not to A now.[10] Still, even in the absence of a strong intention-condition on ought-judgments of these kinds, aesthetic and financial ought-judgments can function as guides to conduct in an important sense, perhaps partly in virtue of their being tied to a motivational state like wanting (where wanting is understood, as it standardly is, as permitting an agent simultaneously to harbor wants that he knows cannot be jointly satisfied).[11]

Someone may insist that *moral* ought-judgments differ from the rest in being overriding (see Hare 1981, p. 53). Indeed, some will claim that the moral "ought" is just whatever sort of "ought" is overriding. Overridingness merits attention in any case.

Even if it is true that moral value is preeminent in some sense, the *sort* of preeminence enjoyed is relevant to an attempt to derive an "intend" from an "ought." If God told us—truly, let us imagine—that moral ought-judgments are the most authoritative, in the sense that they evaluatively outweigh any competing ought-judgments, it would not follow that judging that one ought morally to A entails intending to A. Perhaps, in light of the information, we would embrace a principle of the following sort: it is always best (*period*) to intend to do what you judge you morally ought to do. But that is another matter.

"Always intend to do what you judge it best, all things considered, to do," looks promising as a normative principle of intention formation (or intention acquisition). Further, judgments that it is best (or that one ought), *all things considered*, to A are candidates for bearing a sort of overridingness that guarantees the presence of intentions to A. A theorist might suppose that if, on the basis of everything an agent takes to be relevant, and from the perspective of the agent's own collection of values, he judges it best to A, there can be no internal obstacle to his intending to A. How, one might rhetorically ask, could an agent fail so to intend under these circumstances?

Here a Davidsonian note of caution is in order, a note that will lead us back to his triad of principles, *P1–P3*. A judgment that it is best to A differs at least superficially from a judgment that it is best, *all things considered*, to A. There is at least a difference of content or content-expression: one expression includes a modifier that the other lacks.

A much more fundamental alleged difference between these judgments is central to Davidson's proposed resolution of the "logical problem" that *akrasia* poses for *P1* and *P2*. These principles jointly imply the following one:

*P\**. If an agent judges that it would be better to do $x$ than to do $y$, and he believes himself free to do either $x$ or $y$, then he will intentionally do $x$ if he does either $x$ or $y$ intentionally.

Now, *P\** might appear to preclude the possibility of akratic action. However, akratic action, as Davidson defines it, clashes with an *all things considered* better judgment—not a better or best judgment *simpliciter* (1980, p. 22). The akratic agent intentionally does *B* while judging it better, all things considered, to do *A*, a competing action. But he does not, at the time, judge it better (*simpliciter*) to do *A*. Hence his action does not falsify *P\**. On a closely related point, Davidson remarks:

[T]here is no (logical) difficulty in the fact of incontinence, for the akrates is characterized as holding that, all things considered, it would be better to do *b* than to do *a*, even though he does *a* rather than *b*. . . . The logical difficulty has vanished because a judgement that *a* is better than *b*, all things considered, is a relational, or [*prima facie*], judgement, and so cannot conflict logically with any unconditional judgement. (1980, p. 39)

This is bound to seem a little mysterious. When an agent has judged that, all things considered, it is best to *A* (or better to *A* than to *B*) what, one wonders, is the point of his judging, *additionally*, that it is best to *A* (or better to *A* than to *B*)? And what would be added to his mental condition by the latter judgment? A lot, on Davidson's view; for, as becomes clear in subsequent work of his, the latter judgment is understood as an *intention* (1980, ch. 5; 1985a, p. 206). Thus, Davidson is denying that the presence of all-things-considered judgments is sufficient, logically or causally, for the presence of a corresponding intention.[12] However, as long as a better judgment *simpliciter*, in Davidson's sense, is present, akratic action against it is impossible, for reasons that I identified earlier concerning intentions. This, apparently, exhausts the logical commitments vis-à-vis akratic action of those who propound *P1* and *P2*.

Some readers will feel uneasy about the identification of intentions with better (or best) judgments. The alleged identification has received penetrating criticism in recent years, and Davidson himself has since said that he is "happy to give up the word 'judgement'."[13] Unfortunately, this leaves us without the species of *judgment* for which we have been looking—one inextricably linked to intention. All is not lost, however: there is a moral in the offing. But let us first return to Hare.

Hare occasionally speaks of the "down-grading" of an "ought." In some cases, he says, "an 'ought' does not have to be withdrawn but only down-graded. It no longer carries prescriptive force in the particular case" (1963, p. 80; cf. Hare 1992). In the same vein:

Even if we are at our most moral when we say that we ought to be doing such and such a thing (getting up, for example), and fully intend to set about doing it there and then, we know only too well that if our moral strength were to fail us at the last moment, and we did not get up, we could still go on saying that we thought we ought to be getting up—and saying it, though in a way in an attenuated sense, without in another way departing from the meaning of the word as we used it all along; for all along the meaning of the word was such that we *could* backslide in this way. (1963, p. 76)

Suppose . . . that we fail to do the required action. . . . Has the expression 'think that I ought' changed its meaning for us? We have, indeed, accepted, as exemplifying the state of mind called 'thinking that I ought', something less robust than formerly; but then from the start the expression 'think that I ought' had the potentiality of such a decline. . . . There are, indeed, many ways in which it can lose its robustness without, in a sense, departing from its original meaning. (1963, p. 77)

When an ought-judgment in favor of one's *A*-ing loses its prescriptivity for an agent, the agent loses his intention to *A*. In some sense, apparently, the judgment remains the same, on Hare's view. In another sense, it has changed: its prescriptivity is gone. Now, 'judgment'—like 'belief,' 'desire,' and 'intention'—has at least a double sense. It may mean *what* is judged, a content (e.g., "I ought to *A*"), or alternatively, a content together with the attitude toward it. This suggests one construal of downgrading: the *content* of the judgment that one ought to *A* remains the same while the *attitude* toward that content is downgraded from one incorporating intending to *A* to a less robust attitude not inclusive of intending.

In any case, once it is granted that ought-judgments can be "downgraded," one is entitled to wonder whether the alleged essential prescriptivity of the initial judgments comes to anything more than the essential "intendingness" built into my artificial notion of best judgment* in section 2 of this chapter. This is not to insist that there is *no* interesting, nonartificial connection between judgments that it would be best (or that we ought) to *A* and intentions to *A*, but I shall get to that soon enough.

On the present point, surprisingly perhaps, Davidson and Hare are not far apart. Consider Davidson's distinction between "all-things-considered" better judgments and better judgments (*simpliciter*) in light of Hare's remarks on the downgrading of "oughts." (Henceforth, unmodified uses of "better (or "best") judgment" should be read as "better (or "best") judgment *simpliciter*.") Suppose that an agent moves from an all-things-considered better judgment to a better judgment and then, while attempting to execute the relevant intention (an intention to *A*), loses his nerve—and his intention. In some such cases, the agent still holds a judgment in favor of *A*-ing, even though he intentionally terminates the attempt to *A*. Davidson (at least the earlier Davidson) will have to say that the agent no longer judges it best to *A*, since such a judgment is an intention to *A*. So what does he judge? Has the judgment been downgraded, perhaps, to an all-things-considered judgment in favor of *A*-ing?

There is no evident need to suppose that the content of a judgment has changed (devolved), or that there is now a new and distinct judgment whose content features (something properly expressed by) "all things considered," or that the current judgment is the agent's initial all-things-considered better judgment. Rather, the agent may retain his judgment that it is best to *A* while no longer intending to *A*.[14] What has changed, arguably, is his attitude toward *A*-ing: it is no longer one of intending. Why, then, should we suppose that the intending attitude was ever encompassed in the agent's holding a best judgment favoring his *A*-ing? The suggestion that the change in attitude entails the agent's no longer judging it best to *A* has the ring of artificiality. This entailment relation holds for judgment*; but we are not impressed.[15]

## 4. More Putative Connections: Aristotle

Aristotle asserts, in the *Nicomachean Ethics*, that the person possessed of practical wisdom (*phronesis*) is not subject to *akrasia* (1152a6–8, cf. 1146a4–9). He also maintains, on one reading, that human nature is such as to preclude the possibility of our acting akratically against a conscious best judgment made on the basis of deliberation explicitly addressed to the promotion of our *eudaimonia* or happiness (our "complete," "self-sufficient," and "highest" end), as long as the judgment continues to be held on those grounds. (For lack of a better name, I dub such a judgment a "*eudaimonia*-based" judgment.) Can we find in these claims a foundation for an in-teresting conception of a species of best judgment that is *akrasia*-proof?

It is worth noting that, for Aristotle, possessing practical wisdom requires pos-sessing all the moral virtues (1144b31–32, 1145a1–2), and having one of the vir-tues, temperance, requires the absence of all "evil" and "excessive" desires of the sort with which *akrasia*, on Aristotle's view, is concerned (1152a1–3). Thus, that the best judgments of practically wise agents are indefeasible by *akrasia* might sim-ply be a consequence of the agents' lacking desires that run contrary to their best judgments. In that case, there would be no need to suppose that the immunity to *akrasia* of these judgments is to be accounted for by some special internal feature of the judgments themselves. For example, it is not required that these judgments *en-compass* intentions. It might instead be the case, for instance, that, there being no motivational resistance to the best judgments of practically wise agents, the judg-ments uniformly *issue* in corresponding intentions. This is a moral to bear in mind.

A related observation applies to the claim that *eudaimonia*-based best judgments are immune to *akrasia*, in the sense that as long as one holds such a judgment one will not akratically act against it. Suppose that the claim is true. Even then, *eudaimonia*-based best judgments, rather than differing *internally* from other best judgments in their content or in the attitude that they encompass toward that content, might differ from the others only in their respective grounds and in noninternal ways associated with the differences in their grounds.[16] Perhaps, as Aristotle maintains on one read-ing, human beings are so constituted that they are always most motivated to pursue what they explicitly believe to be most conducive to their *eudaimonia*. But that itself would explain why *eudaimonia*-based best judgments are immune to *akrasia*—and explain it in a way that does not depend upon such judgments' differing internally from other best judgments. Our eudaimonistic desires might be so strong that com-peting motivation simply is incapable of carrying the day. There are, plainly, a vari-ety of routes to judgments that it is best to *A*; even for Aristotle, not all best judg-ments are explicitly based on considerations of *eudaimonia*. However, from the fact that the routes are different, it obviously does not follow that the judgments them-selves differ internally—either in their content or in the attitude toward that content.

The preceding remarks indicate, among other things, that we can take advantage of *relational* features of best judgments (where the relata include items external to the judgments themselves, such as the causal history and motivational setting of a judg-ment) in identifying *akrasia*-proof species of judgments. Here is one species: best judgments unaccompanied by motivation to act to the contrary. Here is another: *A*-favoring best judgments accompanied by preponderant motivation to *A*. But we knew all along that such judgments—provided that they continue to be so (un)accompanied —are *akrasia*-proof. The trick is to find (as Hare and Davidson attempted to do) strictly internal features of a kind of best judgment in virtue of which judgments of that kind are immune to *akrasia* and to do so without artificially tacking on to judgments of another kind intending, preponderant wanting, or the like.

I am skeptical about our prospects of accomplishing the trick. If there are strict akratic actions, then at least some decisive best judgments are defeated by compet-ing motivation. As yet, we have not encountered good grounds for holding that these judgments differ *qua* judgments (or internally) from decisive best judgments on which agents act—or good grounds for holding that some nonartificially construed, effective, decisive best judgments are by their very nature (as opposed to their nature plus accompanying circumstances) *akrasia*-proof. We have every reason to believe that best judgment plays an important conduct-guiding role, to use Hare's expression. And this point about guidance figures centrally in attempts to motivate acceptance of an interesting notion of best judgment that is linked to action in such a way as to preclude the possibility of akratic action against its instances. But, as I have argued, the idea of being a conduct guide is too thin to bear this weight. In the following section, I contribute to the case for this claim by sketching a plausible view of the functional connection between best judgments and intentions in virtue of which such judgments, as a class, are capable of filling a realistic conduct-guiding role. Once we see that the capacity of best judgments to play a significant role in the production of intentional actions does not depend on the existence of a nonartificial, *akrasia*-proof variety of best judgment, we will be less inclined to suppose that there is such a species.

## 5.   From Judging Best to Intending

Intentions, it would seem, are one thing and evaluative judgments another. Still, the frequency with which we intend and act in accordance with our better or best judgments is far too great to be written off as mere coincidence. How, then, is this salutary frequency to be explained? In particular, what bearing does judging best have on intending?

An important point of Hare's about moral judgments may be reformulated as a point about evaluative judgments generally: the chief practical function of evaluative judgments is to guide conduct. The conduct at issue, for the most part at any rate, is *intentional* conduct; and intentional conduct, on a popular view, depends for its occurrence on the presence of intentions.[17] However, attributing an action-guiding function to evaluative judgments, as I have argued, does not commit one to supposing that the judgments are themselves *logically* or *causally* sufficient for the presence of corresponding intentions.

So what is the connection, if neither of these? Perhaps the *ideal* connection between best judgments and corresponding intentions is causal sufficiency. Often, however, human beings, unlike Hare's angels, are stuck with second-best or worse. One can say, of course, that our best judgments are capable of *influencing* intention formation even though they do not uniformly give rise to intentions. This may be true, but it offers little illumination. We want to know, for example, what it is about our best judgments and ourselves in virtue of which the judgments influence intentions. Focusing on the judgments themselves, it may seem that we have just two things to work with—the *contents* of the judgments and the judging *attitude* toward those contents.

There is no motivational magic in the thought *content* "My *A*-ing would be best." An agent may have a variety of attitudes toward that content. He may doubt that it is true, hope that it is false, wish it to be true, believe that it is true, fear that it is true, and so on. Thus, the motivational dimension of a judgment that one's *A*-ing would be best cannot be lodged exclusively in its content (at least if that content is construed in such a way as to permit it to be the content of other attitudes of the kinds mentioned).

Does the judging-best *attitude* toward a prospective *A*-ing of one's own carry motivation to do, or to intend, an *A*? Robert Dunn, in a careful critical study of alleged grounds for the impossibility of akratic action, argues that "all-out present tense summary evaluative thinking about one's own [prospective] action is wholly theoretical and nonvolitional" and that a best judgment can be "completely dissociated" from an agent's motivation (1987, p. 124; cf. p. 83). But can such a judgment properly be counted as a *practical judgment*, in any interesting sense? Or, to avoid initiating what can easily become a merely verbal dispute, is a best judgment cut off in this way from motivation a best judgment of the sort violated in garden-variety instances of akratic action that involve motivational conflict?

Here we may, somewhat artificially, distinguish between a *belief* that one's *A*-ing would be best and a corresponding *judgment*, as follows. "Best belief" is the genus; best judgment is a species. Specifically, a judgment that one's *A*-ing would be best, in this stipulated sense of "best judgment," is what I will call a *type-B* belief that one's *A*-ing would be best: a *type-B belief* is, by definition, a belief nondeviantly formed as a conclusion of first-person *practical evaluative reasoning*, such reasoning being understood as an inferential process, involving evaluative premises, driven by motivation to settle upon what to do.[18] (Some readers might deny that all first-person practical reasoning is motivated in this way. However, some practical reasoning plainly is so motivated, and I stipulatively reserve the expression "practical evaluative reasoning" for it.) Best judgments, in the sense just defined, differ essentially from other beliefs that one's *A*-ing would be best: they differ in their etiology and in anything entailed by that difference. In this way, one might seek to locate a genuinely practical notion of best judgment, or, at any rate, a notion of best judgment that is well-suited to a popular phenomenology of akratic action.

Insofar as best judgments (in the sense just identified) essentially involve an etiology of the specified kind, agents will be disposed, in the presence of such judgments, to intend accordingly—at least at the moment at which the judgments are formed.[19] The motivation that drives practical evaluative inference, as I have characterized the latter, is also motivation to intend in accordance with the evaluative conclusion. Thus, all best judgments, in the sense at issue, have a motivational dimension, one grounded in the etiology of the judgments. Here we locate an important feature of best judgments (nondeviantly issuing from practical evaluative inference) in virtue of which they are fit to function in the production of intentions. Further, best judgments *rationally commit* agents to action, in that agents who hold such a judgment in favor of *A*-ing cannot consistently believe that they have better reasons not to *A* than to *A*. Akratic action against such judgments would, by the agents' own lights, be irrational.[20] Notice also that many normal agents may have a *generic*, standing desire to act as they judge best. They may desire, generically, to do *whatever* they judge best. Such a desire would dispose them to intend in accordance with their better judgments.

None of this implies, however, that the formation of a best judgment, in the sense identified, *ensures* the formation or acquisition of a corresponding intention, and for familiar reasons. The motivational condition of an agent who arrives at a best judgment in favor of *A*-ing partly on the basis of his evaluation of the objects of pertinent wants may be such as to thwart a transition from best judgment to intention. The motivational force of an agent's wants may be out of line with his evaluative assessment of the wanted items. Consider a man who, on the basis of an assessment of reasons for and against his continuing to smoke, has judged it best to kick the habit and has resolved to do so. Such a man may occasionally have a desire to smoke whose motivational force does not accord with his low assessment of the merits of his satisfying that desire. In some such cases, the agent's judging it best not to smoke a cigarette may, owing partly to the strength of his competing desires, fail to issue in a corresponding intention; and, succumbing to temptation, he may intend instead to smoke and proceed to execute that intention.[21]

The fact that *x*'s do not always issue in *y*'s does not, of course, show that *x*'s never issue in *y*'s, or that there is no systematic causal connection between *x*'s and *y*'s. Consider *default* procedures in computing—for example, a standard procedure in common word-processing programs for the spacing of text. When authors create new files, any text they type will be displayed (and, later, printed) single-spaced, unless they preempt this default condition by entering a command for an alternative form of spacing. When authors do not issue a preemptive command and their programs and machines are working properly, entering a new file systematically has the identified result. Similarly, in the absence of preemptive conditions (e.g., recalcitrant desires) in normally functioning human beings, their judging it best to *A* might systematically issue in an intention to *A*. Forming a best judgment in favor of *A*-ing might figure importantly in the production of an intention to *A* in particular cases, even if the transition from such judgments to such intentions sometimes is blocked—even if the disposition to make that transition is defeasible. A common route from decisively judging it best to *A* to intending to *A* might be a *default* route. Elsewhere, I have argued that this *is* a common route (Mele 1992a, ch. 12).

The basic idea is that "normal human agents are so constituted that, in the absence of preemption, judging it best *simpliciter* to *A* issues directly in the acquisition of an intention to *A*" (Mele 1992a, p. 231). In simple cases involving little or no motivational opposition, the transition from judgment to intention is smooth and easy. In such cases, having reached a decisive best judgment in favor of *A*-ing, agents have no need to reason, or even think, about whether to intend to *A*; nor, given the agents' motivational condition, is there a need to exercise self-control in order to bring it about that they intend to *A*. No special intervening effort of any sort is required. The existence of a default procedure of the sort at issue in normal human agents would help to explain the smoothness and ease of the transition. Indeed, we should expect an efficient action-directed system in beings who are capable both of making deliberative judgments and of performing akratic actions to encompass such a procedure. Special energy should be exerted in this connection only when one's decisive judgments encounter significant opposition. When one akratically fails to intend in accordance with one's decisive judgments, opposition is encountered: something blocks a default transition; something preempts the default value of the judgment.

We may distinguish among three kinds of case in which one's decisive best judgment is opposed by competing motivation: (1) a default process unproblematically generates a continent intention even in the face of the opposition; (2) a continent intention is formed even though the default route to intention is blocked by the op-position; (3) the motivational opposition blocks the default route to intention and figures in the production of an akratic intention. What is needed is a principled way of carving up the territory. In Mele 1992a, I suggested that making a best judgment gives rise *by default* to a corresponding continent intention, as opposed to doing so via a distinct causal route, when and only when (barring causal overdetermination, the assistance of other agents, science fiction, and the like) no intervening exercise of *self-control* contributes to the production of the intention (p. 233). (Sometimes opposing motivation is sufficiently weak that no attempt at self-control is called for.) If the move from best judgment to intention does not involve a special intervening effort on the agent's part, the intention's presence typically may safely be attributed to the operation of a default procedure.

Self-control also figures importantly in explaining why, when a default route from best judgment to intention *is* blocked, we sometimes do, and sometimes do not, intend on the basis of our best judgments. Barring the operation of higher-order de-fault processes, overdetermination, interference by intention-producing demons, and so on, whether an agent intends in accordance with his best judgment in such cases depends upon his own efforts at self-control. In simple cases of self-indulgence, he makes no effort at all to perform the action judged best, or to form the appropriate intention. In other cases, judging it best to $A$, he might attempt in any number of ways to get himself to do $A$, or to intend to do $A$. He might try focusing his attention on the desirable results of his $A$-ing, or on the unattractive aspects of his not $A$-ing. He might generate vivid images of both, or utter self-commands. If all else fails, he might seek help from a behavioral therapist. Whether his strategies work will depend upon the details of the case; but strategies such as these *can* have a salutary effect, as empiri-cal research on delay of gratification and behavior control amply indicates.[22]

I have introduced a technical notion of best judgment that gives its instances essential historical features. A best judgment, in the sense at issue, is a "best belief" that is produced in a certain way. Some things do have essential historical proper-ties, of course—sunburns and genuine U.S. dollar bills, for example. A burn is a sunburn only if it resulted from exposure to the sun, and a bit of paper is a U.S. dol-lar bill only if it was produced by the United States Treasury Department. So essen-tial historicity, in itself, is not worrisome. But perhaps some best beliefs *not* produced by practical evaluative inference are no less "practical" (no less fit for the "guidance" of action) than best beliefs so produced. Like what I have termed best judgments, they would be distinguishable from best beliefs "completely dissociated," in Dunn's words, from the agent's motivation. This suggests that the practical nature of best judgments might not be capturable in its entirety by reference to their etiology.

Here, one may be tempted to speak, with Davidson, of someone's "really (sin-cerely)" believing that one ought (or that it would be best) to $A$, or, with Hare, of "robust" ought-judgments. Again, the robustness—and obviously the sincerity—of a best belief is not a function of its content alone: the attitude toward that content is crucial. Perhaps any *practical* attitude toward the content of a best belief encompasses something more than the mere "thinking true" involved in motivationally dissoci-ated best beliefs. In attacking the idea that there is a nonartificial species of best judgment whose attitudinal component encompasses intending, I have not rejected more modest internalist suggestions about practical evaluative attitudes. Indeed, the most promising way to see what is distinctive of that sort of attitude might be to examine best beliefs that issue nondeviantly from practical evaluative inference, beliefs generated by an essentially practical process driven by motivation to settle upon a course of action. In any case, however we choose to speak, practical best beliefs not so produced will be no more tightly tied (as a class) to intention and intentional action than are best judgments, in the sense defined.

Attempts to construct an *akrasia*-proof notion of best judgment run the risk of artificiality identified earlier. Again, it is easy enough to arrive at such a notion simply by *adding* intention (or preponderant wanting, or the absence of competing motivation) to some other notion of judgment. But what we want is an account of the connection between a nonartificial variety of best judgment and intentions that illuminates the capacity of best judgments to play their conduct-guiding role. An account grounded in the partly motivational etiology of best judgments (or a species thereof) promises to fit the bill.

Why do people reason about what it would be best to do? Sometimes, at least, because they are concerned to *do* what it would be best to do and have not yet identified what that would be. (At other times, agents may settle—even rationally settle— upon the first alternative that strikes them as good enough: for example, when they take little to be at stake and suppose that the cost required to identify the best alternative would probably outweigh the benefits.) In such cases, if things go smoothly, best judgments issue in corresponding intentions. And it is no accident that they do, given what motivates the reasoning that issues in the judgments.

Of course, if common sense can be trusted, things do not *always* go smoothly: people can identify the better and—owing partly to the influence of recalcitrant desires—intend the worse. This shows, not that best judgments have no role to play in the etiology of intentions and intentional behavior, but rather that, in human beings as they actually are, the formation of a best judgment does not ensure the formation of a corresponding intention. In *Irrationality* (1987), I attempted to explain *how* this can be true, how best judgments may be rendered ineffective by competing motivation. My positive aim in this chapter has been to show that the assumption that it *is* true is compatible with best judgments' having an important function to fill in the production of intentions and, hence, intentional actions, and that their having such a function in no way depends upon there being a nonartificial, *akrasia*-proof species of best judgment.

It is tempting to speculate about how a default procedure of the sort that I have sketched might have emerged in us, but this is not the place. Suffice it to say that any speculation about how agents like us come about—agents who, often enough, reason about what it would be best to do with a view to settling upon what *to* do and then settle and act on the basis of their decisive better judgments—should attend to the emergence in such agents of what mediates between judgment and action. Agents like us would be well-served by a default procedure of the kind sketched: a procedure of this kind conserves mental energy, obviating a need for a special effort or act, in each case, to bring it about that, judging it best to *A*, one also intends to *A*.

Special efforts would be required only under special circumstances. I have suggested that we *are* served by a procedure of this kind and that, because we are, there is no need for an *akrasia*-proof species of better judgment in an acceptable theory of the connection between practical evaluative thought and intentional action.

Decisive better judgments, on the view just defended, are subject to defeat by opposing motivation. By the same token, they are, in principle, supportable by exercises of self-control. Faced with motivation that threatens to render his decisive better judgment ineffective, an agent might do his best to bring it about that he intends and acts as he judges best. It is to self-control that I now turn.

## Notes

1. Socrates is not alone in this. See Hare 1963, ch. 5.

2. See Mele 1992a, pp. 141, 156, 231. Some intentions, in my view, are not products of mental actions (Mele 1992a, pp. 141, 162, 184, 213, 231).

3. On various interpretations of Aristotle's notion of choice, see Mele 1984c, pp. 152–55.

4. Davidson 1980, ch. 5; 1985a, p. 206; Hare 1963, p. 79. I return to these claims in sec. 3.

5. I defend a significantly modified version of *P1* in Mele 1992a, ch. 3.

6. On this point, see Mele 1987, pp. 37–39, 84–95, and Smith 1992, pp. 330–31. I return to the point in sec. 5.

7. Elsewhere, I have attempted to establish and account for the possibility of akratic behavior, and I have advanced a conception of the connection between evaluative upshots of practical reasoning and intentions. Here, I try to hit my announced mark largely independently of this earlier work—especially, Mele 1987 and 1992a, ch. 12. I have defended elements of the interpretation of Aristotle suggested in sec. 4 of this chapter in Mele 1981 and 1985. In the present chapter, Aristotle's seminal work on *akrasia* is used primarily for illustrative purposes.

8. For discussion of this possibility, see Mele 1987, pp. 34–44.

9. Hare quotes this material from his 1952 book, pp. 20, 168.

10. Even on a rather modest conception of intention, an agent who intends at $t$ to $A$ then will at least *try* at $t$ to $A$ then, provided that he has the requisite ability. Since one cannot simultaneously try to $A$ and try not to $A$, this modest conception would not permit the simultaneous possession of competing intentions of the sort envisaged—on the assumption that possessing such intentions neither renders the agent unable at $t$ to try to $A$ then nor renders him unable at $t$ to try not to $A$ then.

11. Jackson 1985 argues for a conception of wanting or desire that does not permit this. For a response, see Mele 1992a, ch. 3, sec. 1.

12. I offer support for this denial in Mele 1992a, ch. 12, sec. 2.

13. For criticism, see Bratman 1985; Mele 1983; Mele 1987, ch. 2, sec. 1; Peacocke 1985; and Pears 1984, ch. 9. Davidson's considered view is clarified in his 1985a, especially pp. 211, 220.

14. I argue for this in Mele 1987, ch. 3.

15. Again, for detailed arguments against the identification of intentions with better judgments (construed *as judgments*), see the work cited in n. 13 above. My point here is that the identification at issue is no more promising than the identification involved in my artificial notion, judgment*.

16. Notice that reference to *eudaimonia* need not enter into the *content* of a *eudaimonia*-based best judgment. Based on considerations of *eudaimonia*, an agent may judge that *it is best to A* (*simpliciter*).

17. This is not to say that every intentional action must itself be intended. For discussion of this point, see Mele 1992a, ch. 8. An analysis of intentional action is offered in Mele and Moser 1994.

18. The nondeviance condition addresses the possibility that what is initially a process of practical inference degenerates into purely theoretical reasoning that issues in a judgment that it would be best to *A*. I am not supposing, I might add, that all genuinely practical best judgments must issue from inference.

19. Allowance should be made for downgrading. Although a best belief was formed in a way requisite for its counting as a best judgment, the agent may, at some future time, hold the belief on other grounds entirely. At such a time the belief may be, in Dunn's words, "completely dissociated" from the agent's motivational condition.

20. I return to this point in ch. 4, sec. 3.

21. The idea sketched in this paragraph is developed in Mele 1987, chs. 3, 6.

22. Parts of this paragraph and the preceding two are borrowed from Mele 1992a, pp. 231–34. For a discussion of the practical potential of strategies such as these in effective self-control, and of pertinent empirical literature on the topic, see Mele 1987, pp. 23–24, chs. 4–6. (I return to some of this literature in ch. 3.) For more on intentions by default, see Mele 1992a, ch. 12.

# 3

# Exercising Self-Control:
# A Motivational Problem

On a popular view, self-control can be exercised both against *anticipated* temptation and against *present* temptation. Anticipating a powerful desire to throw himself into the sea should he hear the Sirens' song, Odysseus has himself bound to the mast in advance. He seeks to thwart anticipated temptation by altering his external situation. In other cases, agents prepare themselves for anticipated temptation without preparing their environment. A woman whose relations with her brother have never been cordial fears that predictable remarks of his at a scheduled family reunion will seriously tempt her to quarrel with him. Preferring not to make a scene, she attempts in advance to steel herself for the encounter and devises various mental strategies for retaining her composure. For the resistance of *present* temptation, we learn numerous techniques—some homespun, others quite sophisticated. Children are taught to count to ten as a strategy for resisting the pull of anger.[1] More recently they have been taught, with remarkable success, to transform tempting items into nonarousing objects in their imaginations, a matter briefly taken up in section 3 of this chapter. Strategies of self-control against anticipated and present temptation range from those requiring considerable skill to something approaching brute resistance or sheer effort of will.[2]

My concern in the present chapter is *orthodox* exercises of self-control—that is, exercises of self-control in the service of a decisive better judgment. (Unorthodox instances are examined in ch. 4.) I am concerned, more narrowly, with orthodox exercises that serve a decisive best or better judgment about *overt* action, action essentially involving peripheral bodily movement.[3] Sections 1 and 2 provide some taxonomical and conceptual background. Section 3 develops a problem about the scope of our prospects for self-control, a threat to the reality of the robust powers of self-control that folk wisdom attributes to many human beings. Sections 4 and 5 disarm the threat. Section 6 draws a moral about akratic action. Section 7 addresses a worry about motivational explanations of behavior.

## 1. Taxonomy

Self-control scenarios may be distinguished along a pair of dimensions, temporal and motivational.

*Scenario 1.* S holds a decisive judgment at *t* that it would be better to A later than to B later.[4] At *t*, S is more strongly motivated to A later than to B later; but, thinking that as the time for action draws nearer he may become more strongly motivated to B than to A, he exercises self-control at *t* in support of his A-ing later. For example, at *t*, a man decisively judges it better to start an exercise program tomorrow than not to do so, and his relevant desires are aligned with his judgment. But thinking that, tomorrow, he may be severely tempted to procrastinate, he seeks at *t* to arrange things in such a way as to promote his chances of acting tomorrow as he judges best today. He announces to his family and close friends (at *t*) that tomorrow will be the first day of his new exercise program, thinking that his desire not to lose face will help him to resist temptation.

In this scenario, exercising self-control is, in principle, theoretically unproblematic. The man may be more motivated at *t* to take the measure just described than not to do so; he may act accordingly at *t*; and his so acting may be instrumental in his not succumbing to a temptation to procrastinate when the time for action comes.

*Scenario 2.* S holds a decisive judgment at *t* that it would be better to A later than to B later. However, S's motivational condition at *t* favors his B-ing later over his A-ing later. Recognizing this, he exercises self-control at *t* in support of his A-ing later. For example, at *t* an agoraphobe decisively judges it better to attend his daughter's wedding (in another city) next month than to miss the wedding; but he realizes that his long-standing fear of leaving his house is so strong and so deeply entrenched that he will not leave home unless he first does something about his fear. As he recognizes, the motivational power of his fear—a fear that he possesses *now*— is such that he will intentionally remain at home on the wedding day, unless he starts taking ameliorative measures soon. The man embarks upon a program of desensitization at *t*, hoping to attenuate his fear so that he can attend the wedding.

Here, too, an exercise of self-control is theoretically open. Although, at *t*, the agoraphobe's fear is such that, unless it is diminished, he will intentionally remain at home on his daughter's wedding day, he may nevertheless be more motivated at *t* to begin taking steps designed to enable him to attend the wedding than not to do so. And he may act, at *t*, as he is more motivated to act then.[5]

*Scenario 3.* S holds a decisive judgment at *t* that it would be better to A now than to B now. At *t*, S is more motivated to A then than to B then; but thinking that his motivational condition may shift in a B-favoring direction even as he is embarked upon A-ing, he exercises self-control in support of his A-ing. For example, a man who wishes to conquer his fear of heights judges it better to continue climbing a ladder than to stop climbing now, and he is more motivated to continue climbing than to stop. However, he has become frozen with fear under similar conditions in the past; and fearing that this may happen to him even in the midst of the step in progress, he attempts to prevent it from happening. Recalling his therapist's advice, he closes his eyes and imagines himself on the bottom rung (while continuing to climb).

This is, essentially, a variant of scenario 1 in which "later" is replaced by the specious present. The agent is more motivated at *t* to continue climbing than to stop. He may be more motivated, as well, at *t* to seek to prevent this motivational balance from shifting than not to do so. At *t*, he may act—on both counts—as he is more motivated to act.

*Scenario 4.* *S* holds a decisive judgment at *t* that it would be better to *A* now than to *B* now. At *t*, he is more motivated to *B* then than to *A* then; nevertheless, he exercises self-control in support of his *A*-ing then. (Is this possible?)

The fourth scenario provides the focal question for the bulk of this chapter. It raises a significant problem about the very possibility of exercising self-control under certain motivational conditions. Before that problem is addressed, something should be said about *temporally mixed* self-control scenarios—scenarios in which an agent holds a decisive judgment that it would be better to *A* later than to *B* now, or a decisive judgment that it would be better to *A* now than to *B* later. Scenarios of the former sort have been studied under the rubric "delay of gratification," and many familiar illustrations of self-control are instances of such delay. Adults sometimes resist the temptation to eat another appetizer now in order not to spoil the pleasure of eating dinner later; children sometimes eschew purchasing an attractive toy now in order to save money for a later purchase of a bicycle; and so on. On other occasions, agents apparently succumb to present temptation at the expense of greater but more remote gratification.

Imagine that, at *t*, *S* judges it better to *A* later than to *B* now and takes his *B*-ing now to preclude his *A*-ing later. Imagine also that *S* is more motivated at the time to *B* then than to *A* later. If it is supposed that, under these conditions, *S* exercises self-control at *t* in support of his *A*-ing later, we have a problem of the sort raised by instances of scenario 4. Given *S*'s motivational condition at *t*, how can an exercise of self-control be motivationally open to him at the time? How can he be sufficiently motivated at *t* to exercise self-control in support of his *A*-ing later, given that at *t* he is more motivated to *B* then than to *A* later? Cases of this kind require their own entry in a complete taxonomy, but they raise no special motivational problem of their own (i.e., no problem not raised by some instances of scenario 4). The same is true of related cases featuring the judgment that it would be better to *A* *now* than to *B* *later*: for example, the judgment that it would be better to give one's paycheck to one's spouse now than to bet it at the racetrack later. If an agent currently wants more to bet his check at the track later than to give it to his wife now, how can he be sufficiently motivated at the time to exercise self-control in support of his handing over the check? Even though the betting desire's target is prospective behavior beyond the specious present, the agent is possessed of that desire *now*; and possessing it now, he is tempted *now* to hold onto his check.

## 2.   An Interpreted Motivational Perspective

The primary theoretical setting of this chapter's focal problem is what I earlier called the "motivational" perspective on the explanation of intentional action (ch. 2, sec. 1). Some may take certain features of that perspective to show that scenario 4 is impossible. Others may view the scenario as possible and as undermining the motivational perspective, or at least as calling for radical revision. My own view is that our commonsense motivational perspective accommodates scenario 4, appearances to the contrary notwithstanding.

Sally now is more strongly motivated to insult an offensive colleague as soon as he completes his tasteless remark than to refrain from so doing; but she judges it best not to do so, she gets a grip on herself, and she refrains from uttering an insult. Did Sally's so refraining conflict with what she was most strongly motivated to do at the time? A predictable answer from the motivational perspective is *no*. How one elects to support that answer depends upon one's position on such matters as the role of higher-order motivation in the explanation of action, the individuation of motivational states, and the nature of self-control. It may be urged, for example, that while being more strongly motivated to insult her colleague than to refrain from so doing, Sally was also more strongly motivated to bring her first-order motivation into line with her judgment than to allow her first-order motivational condition to persist. If she succeeded in changing her motivational condition in the "right" direction, then when, a moment later, she refrained from insulting her colleague, she was more strongly motivated to do that than she was to insult him.

Whether the motivational perspective can accommodate scenario 4 depends, of course, on what that perspective amounts to. Although the perspective plainly is a common one, exactly what adopting it commits one to is less than plain. One modest commitment is to the thesis that every case of intentional action is a case of motivated action.[6] But this thesis certainly leaves it open that one may act against one's strongest motivation. If the motivational perspective comes to no more than this, it amounts to very little.

Some elementary observations about motivation are in order. Although there is controversy in the psychology of motivation about the precise manner in which motivation is to be understood, it is widely accepted that what distinguishes species capable of motivated behavior from other species is "flexibility" of behavior.[7] For example, rats can learn a variety of alternative strategies for getting food (e.g., pressing levers or running mazes in an experimenter's lab) and flies cannot (Toates 1986, pp. 22–23). Feeding behavior in flies, but not in rats, is "stimulus-bound." "To infer motivation," Philip Teitelbaum writes, "we must break the fixed reflex connection between stimulus and response" (1977, p. 12). Once the connection is broken and motivation is accorded a place in the explanatory scheme for (some of) an animal's behavior, so is a capacity to identify means to goals. Thus, at least a *proto*-belief/desire psychology is postulated.

There is a simple way of viewing the flexibility criterion for warranted attribution of motivational states to an entity. If an entity's behavior is not influenced by means even of the most carefully designed attempts at positive and negative reinforcement, that is evidence that there is nothing the entity wants or desires—in short, that the entity is devoid of motivation. The entity might fly and drink, as a fly does; but not because it *wants* to. Rather, these activities are direct, mindless responses to nonmental stimuli. However, if efforts to "reward" (positively reinforce) a certain kind of behavior increase the frequency of behavior of that kind and efforts to "punish" (negatively reinforce) a certain kind of behavior decrease its frequency, that is evidence that there is something the entity wants. Using an animal's desires as a lever, we get it to learn strategies for satisfying its desires. Notice that accepting this criterion gives us an easy answer to the question why we should not attribute motivational states to present-day chess-playing computers, robots, jets on automatic pilot, and the like. Their behavior is not modifiable by reward or punishment. (Rather, it is modified by altering software or hardware.)

Imagine a human being, $S$, with no motivational states. Lacking such states, $S$'s behavior will not be modified by positive or negative reinforcement—either of an intentionally administered or a naturally occurring variety. $S$ might mindlessly twitch and fidget, as a fly does; but in the absence of motivational states, $S$ will never get beyond that point. Having no motivation, $S$ lacks what is required for learning strategic behavior. Normal human beings plainly meet the flexibility criterion for attribution of motivation. To the extent to which the criterion is acceptable, normal human beings may safely be attributed motivational states.

Motivation is required specifically for *intelligent* or *learned* behavior, not for behavior in general (e.g., the mating behavior of flies). Via positive reinforcement of bar-pressing behavior, rats may learn a strategy for making water available to themselves. Such learning, on the present view, requires motivation. Further, once a rat has learned a strategy of this kind, our evidence that the rat has pressed a bar in order to make water available is evidence that the rat had a relevant desire and a relevant belief—a desire to drink water, we may say, and a belief to the effect that pressing the bar would make water available. Many motivational psychologists are happy to attribute mental representations to rats.[8] They are considerably less concerned than philosophers of mind about a precise specification of the content of particular mental representations. As yet, there is no twin-earth literature in motivational psychology about "water" thoughts in rats.

Imagine that an entity $S$ has a property $P$ such that $S$'s possessing $P$ is sufficient for $S$'s being subject to behavior modification by means of reward or punishment of its behavior. On the present view, at least some state of $S$, as imagined, is a motivational state. Motivation is required for the possession of a capacity to learn strategic behavior via reward or punishment. However, not everything required for this is motivation. An entity with no capacity for memory cannot learn. A rat with no memory may be consistently rewarded for pressing a bar; but that will have no effect on the frequency of its bar-pressing behavior. This indicates that it is in principle (conceptually) possible for there to be a being with motivational states that nevertheless does not satisfy the behavioral flexibility criterion for warranted attribution of motivation. However, that does not undermine the criterion. The criterion is not offered as a statement of necessary and sufficient conditions for the presence of motivation in a being; rather, it is offered as a criterion for the warranted *attribution* of motivational states to a being. A motivated being may nevertheless be a being to which we are not warranted in attributing motivation (as an agent guilty of a crime may be a being we are not warranted in deeming guilty).

Even so, the flexibility criterion is suggestive about the nature of motivation. Motivation is required for a capacity to learn strategic behavior by way of reward and punishment of the being's behavior. Memory is required, as well; but memory is distinguishable from motivation. Memory enables a being to form and retain an associative link between behavior of a particular kind and its rewarding or punishing consequences. Motivation inclines or disposes a being to seek consequences of some kinds and to seek to avoid consequences of other kinds.

As motivation is commonly conceived, both in motivational psychology and in popular thought, it varies in *strength*. An alleged connection between motivational strength and behavior is elegantly expressed in the following principle: "The act which is performed among a set of alternatives is the act for which the resultant motivation is most positive. The magnitude of response and the persistence of behavior are functions of the strength of motivation to perform the act relative to the strength of motivation to perform competing acts" (Atkinson 1957, p. 361).

Donald Davidson gives voice to the motivational perspective in a related principle mentioned earlier:

> *P1*. If an agent wants to do $x$ more than he wants to do $y$ and he believes himself free to do either $x$ or $y$, then he will intentionally do $x$ if he does either $x$ or $y$ intentionally. (1980, p. 23)

Here, "wants to do $x$ more than he wants to do $y$" may be read as "is more strongly motivated to do $x$ than to do $y$." There are other uses of 'wants more,' as has often been noted, but they need not concern us, for present purposes.

A familiar criticism of *P1* misses its mark. It is sometimes claimed that our intentional behavior is occasionally at odds with what we want most to do, because we are occasionally moved to act, not by our wants, but rather (for instance) by our moral judgments. However, someone who is moved to A by a judgment plainly is *motivated by* the judgment, in which case the judgment has a motivational dimension. In a suitably broad, Davidsonian sense of 'want,' an agent who is moved by a judgment is moved by a want.[9] As I use the verb 'want,' to want to A is to have some motivation to A, the content of which features a representation of the agent's (current or prospective) A-ing. I use the noun 'want' in a correspondingly broad sense. Distinctions blurred by this usage can be recaptured by differentiating among types of wants or desires—for example, appetitive versus nonappetitive wants, egoistic versus altruistic wants, affective versus nonaffective wants. I use 'want' and 'desire' interchangeably.[10]

Elsewhere, I showed that *P1* is false (on several counts); but I also advanced a replacement principle (Mele 1992a, ch. 3). The replacement provides a partial interpretation of our motivational perspective on the explanation of intentional action. I will motivate the replacement here, with a view to developing a conceptual context for the discussion in subsequent sections.

Attention to a certain defect in *P1* yields needed background for a proper understanding of the replacement. Consider the following case. Fred, a golfer, is faced with the choice of entering either a driving contest or a putting contest. The winner of the former (the contestant who hits the longest drive) will receive five thousand dollars, whereas the winner of the latter (the contestant who sinks the longest putt) will receive one thousand dollars. No player can compete in both contests. Given his utterly mundane financial preferences, Fred naturally wants to hit the longest drive more than he wants to sink the longest putt. But he is much better at putting than at driving, as he knows; and, after looking over the field of contestants, Fred judges that he has about a two percent chance of hitting the longest drive, should he enter the driving contest, and about a twenty percent chance of sinking the longest putt, should he enter the putting contest. So although Fred wants to hit the longest drive in the driving contest more than he wants to sink the longest putt in the putting contest, he also wants (good Bayesian that he is) to putt in the putting contest more than he wants to drive in the driving contest. Further, Fred wants to hit the longest drive in the driving contest more than he wants to putt in the putting contest: if he could choose between hitting the longest drive in the driving contest and putting in the putting contest, he would choose the former.

Our layout, then, includes the following pair of points:

> *W1*. Fred wants to putt in the putting contest more than he wants to drive in the driving contest.

> *W2*. Fred wants to hit the longest drive in the driving contest more than he wants to putt in the putting contest.

Fred believes that he is free to do each of the things mentioned. What will he do?

The conjunction of *W1*, *P1*, and the fact (*F*) that Fred has the relevant "freedom" beliefs implies:

> 1. Fred will intentionally putt in the putting contest, if he either intentionally does that or intentionally drives in the driving contest.

Further, *W2*, *P1*, and *F* jointly imply:

> 2. Fred will intentionally hit the longest drive in the driving contest, if he either intentionally does that or intentionally putts in the putting contest.

Make the following two assumptions:

> *A1*. Fred either intentionally putts in the putting contest or intentionally drives in the driving contest, but he does not do both.

> *A2*. Fred intentionally hits the longest drive in the driving contest only if he intentionally drives in the driving contest.

The conjunction of 1 and *A1* implies:

> 3. Fred intentionally putts in the putting contest and does not intentionally drive in the driving contest.

The conjunction of 2 and 3 implies:

> 4. Fred intentionally hits the longest drive in the driving contest.

Further, the conjunction of *A2* and 4 implies:

> 5. Fred intentionally drives in the driving contest.

So, given 3 and 5, Fred both does and does not intentionally drive in the driving contest. Something has gone wrong! What?

The argument in the preceding paragraph is valid, and assumptions *A1* and *A2* are acceptable. Further, Fred's relevant freedom beliefs plainly are possible beliefs. So the problem must lie somewhere among *W1*, *W2*, and *P1*. *W1* is unproblematic, and it is compatible with *W2*, which also is unproblematic. Although, for good Bayesian reasons, Fred wants to putt in the putting contest more than he wants to drive in the driving contest, we can well understand his wanting to hit the longest drive in the driving contest more than he wants to putt in the putting contest. After all, the payoff for hitting the longest drive in the driving contest is considerable, and there is no prize merely for putting in the putting contest: the prize in that contest is for sinking the longest putt. The problem is with *P1*.

An approximate diagnosis of the problem is that *P1* permits—indeed encourages—an illegitimate "double-counting" of wants. Fred's desire (*LD*) to hit the longest drive in the driving contest plays out its hand in its contribution to the strength of Fred's desire to participate in the driving contest, which latter desire is weaker than Fred's directly competing desire (*P*) to participate in the putting contest instead. A theorist who pits *LD* not only against Fred's desire to sink the longest putt in the putting contest, but also directly against *P*, counts *LD* *twice* in his motivational calculus. A successful variant of *P1* must preclude illegitimate double-counting. Fred can want to putt in the putting contest more than he wants to drive in the driving contest—and he can act, intentionally, on the former want—even though, at the same time, he wants to hit the longest drive in the driving contest more than he wants to putt in the putting contest. This point must be accommodated by an acceptable successor to *P1*.

My own successor principle involves a distinction between what I call "buffered" and "buffer-free" wants: roughly, a distinction between wants whose contribution to intentional action would depend on their contributing to the strength of other wants that are potentially more intimately related to action and wants that are not like this (Mele 1992a, pp. 59–61). It is only buffer-free wants that my principle addresses. One part of the principle reads as follows:

> *P1a.* If, at *t*, an agent takes himself to be able to *A* then and wants to *A* then more than he wants to do anything else that he takes himself to be able to do then—where the wants at issue are buffer-free—he intentionally *A*-s then, or at least tries to *A* then, provided that he acts intentionally at *t*. (p. 60)

This may be explicitly framed in terms of motivational strength:

> *P1m.* If, at *t*, an agent takes himself to be able to *A* then and is more strongly motivated to *A* then than to do anything else then that he takes himself to be able to do then—where the motivation at issue is buffer-free—he intentionally *A*-s then, or at least tries to *A* then, provided that he acts intentionally at *t*.

Sometimes agents simultaneously perform independent intentional actions. At the same time, an agent may be driving home from work, planning his evening's activities, unknotting his tie, and inspecting his new haircut in his rearview mirror. He need not have a single conjunctive want for the combination of all four activities; separate desires may simultaneously motivate separate activities. More robust versions of *P1a* and *P1m* would apply to each of the various independent intentional actions performed in such cases. Such versions may be arrived at with the assistance of the following three notions (Mele 1992a, p. 66).

*N1*. An action $A$ is *subjectively open* at $t$ for an agent $S$ if and only if, at $t$, $S$ takes himself to be able to $A$ then.

*N2*. $S$'s intentional $A$-ing and $S$'s intentional $B$-ing are *mutually independent actions* if and only if they are not parts of the same intentional action, neither is identical with nor part of the other, and neither is performed as a means to the other.

*N3*. $S$'s intentionally $A$-ing at $t$ *competes\** with $S$'s intentionally $B$-ing at $t$ if and only if either $S$ takes himself to be unable to do both $A$ and $B$ (i.e., the conjunction) or $S$'s doing either would make his doing the other sufficiently unattractive that he would neither intentionally do nor try to do each.

With these notions in place, *P1m* may be conjoined with the following principle:

*P1n*. If, at $t$, of all actions subjectively open to $S$ at $t$ that (1) do not compete\* with $S$'s $A$-ing at $t$ (where $A$-ing is what $S$ is most strongly motivated to do at the time) and that (2) are independent of $S$'s $A$-ing at $t$, $S$ is most strongly motivated to $B$ then (all motivation at issue being buffer-free), $S$ $B$-s then, or at least tries to $B$ then, if, at $t$, in addition to intentionally $A$-ing or trying to $A$, $S$ performs an independent intentional action.

This conjunction of principles (*P1m* + *P1n*) can be similarly conjoined with companion principles to accommodate additional intentional actions of $S$ at $t$ that are independent of his $A$-ing, his $B$-ing, and their conjunction. Indeed, *P1m* itself is applicable to any number of independent intentional actions (including tryings) performed by $S$ at $t$, provided that in each successive application we do two things: (1) exclude from the relevant domain of subjectively open actions the actions identified in the consequents of the preceding applications and all actions with which they compete\* and (2) suitably augment, à la *P1n*, the proviso with which *P1m* concludes. I dub the conjunction of *P1m* and the observation just made *P1m\**.

I suggest that *P1m\** expresses a central plank in a common motivational perspective on the explanation of intentional action. I suggest, as well, that *P1m\** is centrally constitutive of that perspective and that it functions therein as a conceptual truth about intentional action in light of which, within that perspective, explanations of particular intentional actions are offered. Within the motivational perspective, as I understand it, one does not *explain* $S$'s intentionally $A$-ing at $t$ by remarking (for example) that $S$ was more strongly motivated at $t$ to $A$ then than to do anything else then (the relevant motivation being buffer-free: henceforth, all references to motivation should be understood as references to buffer-free motivation, unless otherwise indicated). Rather, within the motivational perspective, one offers so-called reasons-explanations against a theoretical backdrop that includes *P1m** (cf. Mele 1992a, ch. 4).

To say that *P1m** functions as a conceptual truth in a commonsense motivational perspective on the explanation of intentional action is not, of course, to say that *P1m** *is* a conceptual truth. In another conceptual framework, *P1m** might well be false. Consider a libertarian perspective on intentional human action—in particular, one that involves agent-internal indeterminism of such a kind that, although any agent's being most strongly motivated at *t* to *A* at *t,* together with his correctly taking himself to be able at the time to *A* then confers a probability on his trying at *t* to *A* then, it (sometimes) does not confer a probability of 1. Further, in this perspective, it is (sometimes) possible that an agent who satisfies the relevant conditions does something intentionally other than what he is most motivated to do—something other than *A*, say—without even trying to *A*. If this libertarian view is coherent, *P1m** is possibly false. This indicates that any motivational perspective in which *P1m** functions as a conceptual truth disallows such indeterminism.

This last observation points up one source of resistance to *P1m* and *P1m**. Libertarians of certain kinds would view these principles as precluding human freedom. If *P1m* is true, no one, when acting intentionally, acts against his strongest (buffer-free) motivation at the time of action; and some libertarians will view that consequence as incompatible with human freedom.[11] It may be replied that *P1m* leaves it open that what we are most motivated to do is, in some measure, up to us (or under our control), and that believers in human freedom can take comfort in that. Some libertarians may respond that, given *P1m*, this is not really up to *us* at all but, rather, is determined by what we are most strongly motivated to do about our motivation.

I will set libertarianism aside in this chapter and operate within a framework that assumes "internal" determinism.[12] My aim in so doing is not to close theoretical options, but to provide a tight focus for this chapter's central issue. A deterministic variant of the issue just raised will be examined shortly. Detailed discussion of libertarian perspectives on the explanation of intentional action is reserved for later chapters.

## 3.   Self-Control and Proximal Temptation

If a desire is not irresistible, it is up to us, at least in a compatibilist sense of "up to us," whether we act on it. I take this idea to be part of a common motivational perspective on intentional human action. Another element in that perspective is the idea that relatively few of our desires are irresistible. Of course, a proper appreciation of the latter idea would require a full-blown analysis of irresistible desire; but I have offered an analysis elsewhere, and I will not trouble the reader with the details here (Mele 1992a, ch. 5). These two ideas jointly suggest that, often, it is up to us (at least in a compatibilist sense) which of two or more competing desires we act on. (This is not to say, of course, that it is up to us whether our intentional actions accord with *P1m**.) Is this suggestion coherent within the motivational perspective that is taking shape here?

A successful answer to this question requires attention to the resources for understanding *self-control* available in the motivational perspective. In some cases, exercising self-control in support of one's acting as one judges it best to act is entirely unproblematic, as I have observed. A smoker who is now more strongly motivated to bring it about that he does not smoke tomorrow than not to bring this about might hit upon, and successfully execute, an appropriate strategy—for example, driving tonight to a remote cabin and leaving his cigarettes behind. But consider a smoker who is now more strongly motivated to smoke a cigarette *now* than not to smoke a cigarette now; and suppose that, nevertheless, he judges it better to refrain from smoking now. Can such a smoker exercise self-control in support of his refraining from smoking now? (The question is whether he can exercise it at all, *not* whether he can *successfully* exercise it.) More specifically, does *P1m\** permit this?

It might look as though it does not. One might argue that, given how the agent's smoking wants stack up, he also wants to smoke now more than he wants to exercise self-control in support of his refraining from smoking now, and consequently he will not engage in this exercise of self-control.[13] If that is right, intentional exercises of self-control in support of one's *A*-ing are precluded by what may be termed *preponderant proximal temptation*: wanting more to *B* now than to *A* now (or *A* later), one also wants more to *B* now than to exercise self-control now in support of one's *A*-ing and hence will not intentionally exercise self-control to that end. This suggests that we are helpless against preponderant *proximal* motivation that clashes with our better judgments, that such motivation is *irresistible*. If we are going to exercise self-control, we had better do it in advance.

Imagine that our smoker's proximal urge to smoke (i.e., his urge now to smoke now) is stronger than his proximal desire not to smoke. Let us take that to entail that if the urge and the desire were the only relevant motivational states in the case, the agent would proceed to smoke (if he either smokes or does not smoke intentionally: he might not smoke, but nonintentionally, owing to a sudden heart attack or the disappearance of his cigarettes). Imagine also that our smoker recently acquired a science-fiction device for eliminating urges to smoke: to eliminate his present urge he need only press a button.[14] Can we imagine, as well, that, judging it better to refrain from smoking now than to smoke now, the man intentionally exercises self-control by pressing the button?

Notice that someone who wants to *x* more than he wants to *y* may also want to *y and z* more than he wants to *x*. For example, a man with limited funds may want to see a certain expensive play tonight more than he wants to see a movie tonight, but want to see a movie and eat dinner at a restaurant tonight more than he wants to see the play. (He may realize that, given his financial situation, he cannot see the play and eat dinner at a restaurant.) Our smoker's situation may be importantly similar.

In addition to his urge to smoke now and his desire not to smoke now, our smoker may have the following desire: the desire not to smoke now while also not experiencing the discomfort of an unsatisfied urge to smoke. His proximal desire to smoke may be stronger than his proximal desire not to smoke but weaker than a more complex proximal desire of his—the conjunctive one just mentioned. In that event (other things being equal), there is no problem about his exercising self-control. By pressing the button, he brings about what he wants most: that he not smoke while also not experiencing the discomfort of an unsatisfied urge. In eliminating the urge, he precludes the discomfort.

The case is not as far-fetched as it seems. As I observed in *Irrationality*, many dieters use appetite suppressants for roughly the reason that our smoker uses his device—that is, not only to bring it about that their actions accord with their better judgments, but also to preclude their experiencing the discomfort of unsatisfied appetites, or at least to minimize the discomfort by minimizing the appetites (Mele 1987, p. 66). Employments of "substitution strategies" of self-control often are motivated along similar lines. Beer drinkers who believe that they should reduce their alcohol consumption sometimes turn to alcohol-free beer. Many of them do this not merely as a means of bringing it about that they consume less alcohol, but also to make doing so less unpleasant than it would otherwise be. They have a *pair* of motives for turning to alcohol-free beer: to promote reduction of alcohol consumption by making the reduction less unpleasant than it would otherwise be *and*, separately from this instrumental consideration, to make reduced alcohol consumption less unpleasant. Desires to reduce alcohol consumption while minimizing displeasure can have more clout than desires simply to reduce alcohol consumption.[15]

In cases of the sort at issue, an agent can want to $A$ more than he wants not to $A$, but want not to $A$ while also accomplishing $B$ more than he wants to $A$. Such an agent can unproblematically be more motivated to engage in an exercise of self-control, $E$, that serves the conjunctive want than he is not to engage in $E$.

There is, however, a difficult question in the offing. Consider the following case:

> Ian turned on the television about a half-hour ago when he started eating lunch. He decided to have a quick meal so that he would have time to finish painting his shed before his wife came home from work. (He wanted to surprise her.) Ian has just finished eating and he is thinking that he ought (all things considered) to get back to work now. However, he is enjoying the golf tournament on TV and he remains seated. He tells himself that he will watch the match until the next commercial break; but the commercial comes and goes and Ian is still in front of the set. Thinking that he had better drag himself away from the television now, Ian utters a self-command: "Get off your butt, Ian, and paint that shed!" Ian turns off the set, picks up his painter's cap, and walks into his backyard. (Mele 1987, p. 69)

Folk wisdom suggests that often it is up to us whether we allow temptation to retain the upper hand or, instead, successfully exercise self-control to terminate akratic behavior in which we are presently engaged. On this view, an agent need not wait for a desire on which he is acting to grow weaker, or a competing desire to grow stronger, before he can exercise self-control: an agent whose desire to continue $A$-ing is stronger than his desire to cease $A$-ing can exercise self-control in support of his putting a quick end to his $A$-ing. Is this right? And, to return to Ian, can we coherently suppose—from our motivational perspective, a perspective that includes *P1m\**—both that, when he utters the self-command, Ian desires more strongly to continue watching the golf game than to stop watching it and that what motivates his desire to utter the command does not extend beyond his desire to get back to work together with whatever motivates the latter desire? (The second conjunct in this supposition imposes a restriction absent in the science-fiction case of the smoker. The smoker has motivation to press the button that is not also motivation to refrain from smoking, namely, his desire not to experience the discomfort of an unsatisfied urge to smoke: he can satisfy that desire by smoking, as he knows.)

I have argued elsewhere that the supposition about Ian is coherent (Mele 1987, pp. 69–72). David Pugmire has argued, in turn, that my argument fails (1994). I will offer a brief summary of some of the background against which my argument was offered, along with some summary remarks on a related matter, and then take up Pugmire's objections. My aim is to defend an important point about the extent of our control over our desires, including desires that motivate behavior already in progress. Unless a desire is irresistible, it is subject to the agent's control. Again, folk wisdom takes irresistible desires to be relatively rare; and it would take a dim view of the claim that Ian, in the imagined circumstances, is possessed of an irresistible desire to continue watching television. My primary question about Ian, in effect, is this: How can resistance be open to him, given his supposed motivational condition? If a plausible answer is unattainable, a much more inclusive conception of irresistibility than that offered by folk wisdom is in order. My argument for the attainability of such an answer is an argument for a particular answer.

## 4.   Background for a Diagnosis of Coherence

B. F. Skinner once wrote: "In getting out of a bed on a cold morning, the simple repetition of the command 'Get up' may, surprisingly, lead to action. The verbal response is *easier* than getting up and easily takes precedence over it, but the reinforcing contingencies established by the verbal community may prevail" (1953, p. 236; emphasis mine). In *Irrationality*, I unknowingly followed Skinner. I suggested that once we grant (if only for the sake of argument) that what motivates Ian's desire to issue the self-command does not extend beyond his desire to get back to work and whatever motivates the latter desire, we are inclined to take the following position: "[I]t is easier for Ian to utter the self-command than to get back to work now and . . . this helps to explain . . . why he was sufficiently motivated to utter the self-command but not to get back to work (prior to uttering the command)" (Mele 1987, p. 70). I then proceeded to develop that position.

My discussion of Ian's case was set within the context of a tripartite distinction among what I termed the *positive, negative,* and *total motivational bases* of a desire (1987, pp. 67–69). I will not motivate the distinction in full here. The basic idea (simplifying a bit) is that the strength of most desires is partially determined by other desires possessed by the agent at the time, and that these other desires can make either a positive or a negative contribution to a desire's strength. For example, a woman's desire at $t$ to smoke a cigarette soon may contribute positively to the strength of her desire at $t$ to buy a pack of cigarettes soon, thus being in the "positive motivational base" of the purchasing desire; and her current competing desire to abide by her New Year's resolution against smoking may render her desire to buy a pack of cigarettes less strong than it would otherwise be, thus being in the "negative motivational base" of the purchasing desire. Desires are not like marbles, having weights that are unaffected by the weights of other marbles in one's collection. The "total motivational base" of a desire is constituted by the desire's positive and negative motivational bases. As I noted, there are also (positive and negative) contributors to desire strength that are not themselves (wholly or partly) desires and are not part of the *motivational* base of a desire: for example, the vividness of an agent's representation of a desired object or the mode of representation (1987, pp. 26, 68–69, 88–93).

In Ian's case, I supposed (to make matters difficult) that the total motivational base of his desire to utter the self-command extends no further than his desire to get back to work together with the latter desire's motivational base. I argued that, even so, he can make the attempt at self-control in which uttering the command consists while being more motivated to continue watching television then than to get back to work then. Ian's desire to get back to work then ($Dw$), I noted, competes *directly* with his desire to continue watching television ($Dtv$); that is, satisfying either is incompatible with satisfying the other. However, his desire to utter the self-command ($Dc$) competes only *indirectly* with $Dtv$: he can continue watching television *while* uttering the self-command (p. 70).

I sought to exploit this difference, offering two strategies for exploitation. The first involved the following hypothesis: "[B]ecause $Dtv$ is directly opposed to $Dw$, but not to $Dc$, it (i.e., $Dtv$) exerts a stronger negative influence upon the motivational force of $Dw$, with the result that $Dw$ is weaker than $Dc$" (p. 71). If Ian is more motivated to utter the self-command than he is to get back to work, then from the fact that $Dtv$ is stronger than $Dw$ it does not follow that $Dtv$ is stronger than $Dc$. The second strategy, which I developed at greater length, involved another hypothesis: "[O]ther things being equal, $Dc$ need only be stronger than its *direct* motivational competition to result in action (i.e., the self-command) and the direct competition [i.e., Ian's desire, if he has one, not to utter the self-command ($D{\sim}c$)] may be weaker than $Dtv$" (p. 71). I return to both hypotheses shortly.

Although my concern was with motivational issues and not with the mode of operation of self-control techniques in general nor self-commands in particular, I offered a suggestion about the latter issue. "Ian may be in the *habit* of obeying his self-commands," I observed; and his uttering the command consequently "may tap an additional source of motivation" (p. 72; cf. Skinner 1953, p. 236). Further, "his utterance may focus his attention in such a way as to enhance his motivation to get back to work (while, perhaps, diminishing his motivation to remain in front of the set)."

The operational issue is worth pursuing here, if only briefly. I designed Ian's case with a view to keeping the dynamics of his attempt at self-control simple, so as not to distract attention from the motivational matters under investigation. Here, I turn to a more complicated technique for self-control on which there is a significant body of empirical literature—cognitive transformations.

The stage may economically be set by means of a brief review of some earlier studies of delay of gratification in which cognitive transformations were not involved. In these studies, preschool children first state a preference for one available reward over another (e.g., pretzels over marshmallows). They are then told that they can have the preferred treat if they wait for the experimenter to return and that they can have the lower-ranked treat whenever they wish: in the latter case, they need only signal the experimenter to return.

Delay of gratification was tested under a variety of conditions. In an early study, the conditions included the visible presence of both rewards; the absence of both rewards; and the visible presence of only one of the rewards—the preferred treat in some cases and the lower-ranked treat in others (Mischel and Ebbesen 1970). Delay of gratification was greatest when both rewards were absent. The mean delay time under that condition was 11.29 minutes, as compared with 1.03 minutes when both rewards were present, 4.87 minutes when only the preferred treat was present, and 5.27 minutes when the lower-ranked treat was present instead. Evidently, *inattention* to the rewards promoted delay of gratification.

In a later study, with the rewards absent, children instructed to "think fun" during the waiting period had a mean delay time of 14.48 minutes, as compared with 0.78 for children told to think about the reward objects (Mischel, Ebbesen, and Zeiss 1972). "Thinking fun" promoted delay, apparently by diverting the children's thoughts from the (absent) treats, whereas the instruction to think about the rewards prompted cognitive behavior that inhibited delay.

These two studies jointly suggest the hypothesis that, among young children at any rate, inattention to edible reward objects is more conducive to delayed gratification than is attention to such objects (either visual or in thought). However, the hypothesis was disconfirmed in a subsequent study (Mischel and Moore 1973). Subjects presented with slides of the reward objects during the waiting period delayed gratification significantly longer than did subjects presented with slides of unavailable objects, subjects presented with an illuminated blank screen, and subjects presented with an unilluminated screen; and they delayed longer than the subjects in the earlier experiments who attended (visually or in thought) to the reward objects.[16] The experimenters offered a plausible explanatory hypothesis about this last difference. Distinguishing between a stimulus's "motivational (arousal) function" and its "cue (informative) function," they advanced the following conjunctive proposal: (1) In the 1970 and 1972 studies, subjects attending to the reward objects (visually or in thought) were focusing on their *motivational* or *arousing* properties, with the result that proximal motivation for a snack was increased, which in turn made waiting more aversive; (2) subjects viewing *slides* of the reward objects were instead attending primarily to *informational*, nonmotivational qualities of those objects; consequently, their attentional activities provided reminders of what was to be gained by waiting while not generating additional proximal motivation for a snack (p. 178).

The next stage in the experimental work featured cognitive transformations of reward objects and provided further evidence of the motivational significance of attentional modes or styles (e.g., Mischel and Baker 1975; Moore, Mischel, and Zeiss 1976; Mischel and Moore 1980). Children who "cognitively transformed" such edible rewards as pretzels and marshmallows into brown logs and white clouds delayed gratification much longer than did children instructed to focus their attention on arousing features of the rewards (e.g., their taste). Further, children who transformed *reward* objects in this way delayed significantly longer than did young subjects instructed to engage in cognitive transformation of *unavailable* objects during the waiting period. Both kinds of transformational act draw attention away from the arousing features of the available rewards; but only cognitive transformation of the *available* rewards tends to enhance attention to what is to be gained by waiting (Mischel and Baker 1975, p. 259; cf. Moore, Mischel, and Zeiss 1976, p. 423).[17]

*If* the motivational condition (at *t*) of a child who has learned the self-control technique of cognitive transformation may be such as to permit his employing the technique (at $t$) while he desires more strongly to call for the lower-ranked treat (then) than to wait for the higher-ranked one, we can understand how the attempt at self-control may succeed. By distracting the child's attention from motivationally arousing features of the treats, and perhaps also by enhancing his awareness of the value of waiting, employment of the technique can bring it about that he wants more to wait for the more highly valued treat than to ask for the more readily available alternative. The *effective operation* of the self-control technique is not problematic: Mischel and his colleagues have advanced a plausible explanation of the technique's influence on motivation. Our problem is, rather, with the possibility of agents' *employing* this technique—and *any* self-control technique—in support of their $A$-ing while desiring more strongly to $B$ than to $A$ (and believing $A$-ing and $B$-ing to be mutually exclusive). More specifically, the problem concerns this possibility in cases in which the total motivational base of one's desire to exercise self-control does not extend beyond one's desire to $A$ together with the total motivational base of the latter desire.

## 5.   Objections and Replies

Pugmire offers a collection of objections to my view on this matter. His first objection features the contention that "intending now to $A$ entails not intending now to take [a] measure that would bring about the intention not to $A$" (1994, p. 83). Applied to Ian's case, one implication is that Ian's "intending now to [watch TV] entails [his] not intending now to take [a] measure that would bring about the intention not to [watch TV]." Both the original contention and this implication are incomplete. Intentions, like desires, are doubly temporally indexed. We intend at, or during, or throughout $t$ to $A$ at, or during, or throughout $t^*$, where $t^*$ may or may not be identical with $t$. For example, Al intends at $t$, while strolling in the woods, to watch a certain television program later that day; Betty intends at $t$, while watching a television program, to continue watching it for at least several minutes; Connie, who is watching a television program at $t$, intends at $t$ to watch it then, but she is undecided about whether to continue watching it; and Don, who is watching at $t$ what he knows to be the conclusion of a program, intends at $t$ to do that while also intending at $t$ to switch off his set momentarily, as soon as the program ends.

That Ian intends at some time, $t$, to watch television then does not entail that he intends at $t$ to continue watching television beyond that time. Like Connie, he may be unsettled about whether to continue to watch it. Nor does it entail that he does not intend at $t$ to take measures then that are designed to terminate his television watching straightaway: intending at $t$ to watch TV then, but not being settled upon continuing to watch it beyond $t$, he may also intend at $t$ to make an effort then to bring it about that he stops watching it at once.

One might contend that even if Ian's present *intention* does not have the consequence at issue, his *motivational* condition in the case under consideration ensures both that he intends at $t$ to continue watching television and that he does not intend at $t$ to make an effort of the kind just mentioned. Now, by hypothesis, when Ian entertains the thought of uttering the self-command, his desire to continue watching TV is stronger than his desire to get back to work then. But it does not follow from this motivational point that he *intends* at the time to continue watching TV beyond that time.

Return to our smoker with the science-fiction device. Prior to pressing the button, his proximal desire to smoke ($Ds$) was stronger than his proximal desire not to smoke ($D\sim s$); but he did not proximally *intend* to smoke. At one point, while $Ds$ was stronger than $D\sim s$, he lacked both an intention to smoke and an intention not to smoke; his mind was as yet not made up about what he would do (or attempt). A moment later, while $Ds$ was stronger than $D\sim s$, he made up his mind, forming an intention to use the device as a means of bringing it about that he did not smoke while also not experiencing discomfort. (Even *starting* to smoke takes time, of course. In common circumstances, one must first take a cigarette from one's pack and light it. One starts smoking with one's first puff. Under such conditions, even an effective proximal desire to smoke does not *immediately* give rise to smoking: brief intermediate steps must be taken.)[18]

Ian's case is similar in some respects. While entertaining the thought of uttering the self-command, we may coherently suppose, Ian takes it to be up to him what he will do and is genuinely unsettled about whether to continue watching the program beyond that time. In that event, he neither intends to continue watching television beyond that time nor intends not to do so, even though he is more motivated at the time to continue watching it than to stop. At something approaching the speed of thought, he may move beyond merely entertaining this thought and form or acquire an intention to utter the command. (I will argue later that he can intentionally utter the self-command—and *intend* to utter it—even at a time at which his proximal desire to continue watching TV is stronger than his proximal desire to get back to work.)

The point that an agent's being more motivated to $A$ than not to $A$ is compatible with his lacking an intention to $A$ merits further consideration. Set aside the science-fiction case of the smoker and consider a real-world scenario. Sam, who has just run out of cigarettes, now desires more strongly to buy a pack later, on his way home from work, than to refrain from doing so. However, he has, from time to time, considered kicking the habit; and he thinks that this is as good a time as any to quit smoking. Sam believes—truly, I am supposing—that he currently is more motivated to continue smoking than to quit and that he currently is more motivated, as well, to buy a pack later that day than not to do so. Other things being equal, unless the balance of his present relevant desires changes, he will buy a pack later that day; and he may explicitly view things in just this way. But Sam takes it to be up to him what he will do about his smoking, and he is unsettled, at present (i.e., at $t$), about whether to buy a pack later that day. He decides that he will leave the issue open for now, so that he can concentrate on his work; he intends to make up his mind about it later, during his scheduled coffee break. Given that Sam is genuinely unsettled about the matter at $t$, he lacks an *intention* at $t$ to buy a pack of cigarettes later that day, even though he is more motivated at $t$ to buy one later that day than not to do so. (Compare Sam with the agoraphobe in sec. 1 of this chapter. The agoraphobe's motivational condition at $t$ is such that, unless it changes, he will intentionally stay home on his daughter's wedding day, other things being equal. Still, he does not intend at $t$ to stay home on her wedding day, as is indicated by his embarking at $t$ on a project of desensitization with a view to enabling himself to attend the wedding.)[19]

*Proximally* desiring to smoke more than one proximally desires to refrain from smoking also leaves open one's not proximally intending to smoke—even in some agents who lack science-fiction devices for eradicating desires. In the science-fiction case, a proximal desire not to smoke while also not experiencing the discomfort of an unsatisfied urge is stronger than a proximal desire to smoke, even though the latter desire is stronger than the agent's proximal desire not to smoke. Other cases not involving imaginary devices are structurally similar. Sally wants to smoke now more than she wants not to smoke now; but it has just occurred to her that this might be a good time to practice using a self-control technique prescribed by her doctor—a technique for delaying her smoking, so that she will reduce her cigarette consumption. Although her proximal desire to smoke ($Ds$) is stronger than her proximal desire not to smoke ($D\sim s$), $Ds$ may be weaker than her proximal desire to practice using the technique while also not smoking. (Given the nature of the technique, she cannot practice using it while smoking, at least if she realizes that she is smoking.) And rather than proximally intending to smoke, Sally may proximally intend to practice using the technique while not smoking.

Consider a related case. Everything remains the same except that this time it has just occurred to Sally to *consider* whether to practice using the technique on this occasion. Here, again, although $Ds$ is stronger than $D\sim s$, $Ds$ may be weaker than Sally's (conjunctive) proximal desire to consider the matter at issue while also not smoking. (Present conscious smoking would preclude her presently considering the matter, since, given the nature of the technique, she cannot—as she knows—practice using it while consciously smoking.) And Sally may proximally (conjunctively) *intend* to consider the matter while not smoking, even though $Ds$ is stronger than $D\sim s$. While she is considering the matter, Sally is unsettled about whether to practice using the technique. She is unsettled, as well, presumably, about whether to smoke instead of practicing the technique. In any event, even though $Ds$ is stronger than $D\sim s$, Sally does not proximally intend to smoke. Again, proximally desiring more strongly to $A$ than not to $A$ does not entail proximally intending to $A$.

In another case, although $Ds$ is stronger than $D\sim s$, it occurs to Sally to consider whether to smoke now or to postpone smoking (without the assistance of any special self-control technique). Here, too, $Ds$ may be stronger than $D\sim s$ but weaker than a pertinent desire—the desire to consider the matter while also not smoking. Once again, an agent may proximally desire more strongly to $A$ than not to $A$ while not proximally intending to $A$.

That Ian desires more strongly at $t$ to continue watching television than to stop watching it (at once) does not *itself* entail that at $t$ he proximally intends to continue watching it. Whether other features of Ian's case together with the feature just mentioned entail that he has this intention remains to be seen.

I turn now to Pugmire's second objection. It addresses my hypothesis that $Dc$ might be stronger than $Dw$ owing to $Dtv$'s directly competing only with $Dw$ and its exerting a stronger negative influence upon the motivational force of $Dw$ than upon that of $Dc$. Pugmire contends that since what motivates $Dc$ is $Dw$ together with whatever motivates the latter, the negative influence of $Dtv$ on $Dc$ can be no less than that of $Dtv$ on $Dw$ (p. 84). This amounts to a simple assertion that my hypothesis is false, a hypothesis formed in the context of my supposition that the total motivational base of *Dc* does not extend beyond *Dw* together with the latter desire's total motivational base. My suggestion was that *Dtv*'s negative contribution to the strength of *Dw* need not be matched by its negative contribution to the strength of *Dc*. Pugmire insists that it must be so matched. Can the disagreement be resolved?

Let us say that, at a time *t*, a desire *D1* is *subordinate* to a desire *D2* if and only if, at *t*, *D2* contributes positively to the strength of *D1* but *D1* does not contribute positively to the strength of *D2*. *Dc* is, in this sense, subordinate to *Dw* (or so we may suppose). Consider the following thesis: (*T*) Whenever a desire *D1* is subordinate to a desire *D2* and the total motivational base of *D1* (excluding *D2*) does not extend beyond the total motivational base of *D2*, then (1) *D1* is no stronger than *D2* and (2) any desire that makes a negative contribution to *D2*'s strength makes at least as great a negative contribution to *D1*'s strength.[20] Is this thesis true?

A college student, Ed, must submit a term paper next week if he is to pass the course, and he has not yet started writing it. Ed has a desire to write it (*Dw*). He also has a desire to *start* writing it (*Ds*), realizing that he will not write it unless he starts. The desires that motivate *Ds* do not extend beyond the collection constituted by *Dw* and the desires that motivate *Dw* (e.g., desires to pass the course and to please his parents). (Similarly, the desires that make a negative contribution to the strength of *Ds* do not extend beyond those that make a negative contribution to the strength of *Dw*, or so we may suppose.) However, the thought of writing the paper immobilizes Ed, whereas the thought of starting to write it does not have this effect on him.[21] Whenever Ed thinks about writing the paper, the task seems formidable; but the task of starting to write the paper strikes him as entirely feasible. Ed thinks that if he focuses his attention now on *starting* and sets aside all thoughts of *finishing*, there is a chance that he will have written a paper by the due date. The strategy works; he starts writing.

Can we reasonably hold that, at *t*, Ed's desire to start writing the paper (now) is stronger than his desire to write the paper (by the due date)? Well, we can reasonably hold that *Ds* stands a better chance of mobilizing Ed at *t* than does *Dw*, partly in virtue of its being true that, whereas the thought of *Ds*'s object (i.e., starting the paper) does not immobilize him, the thought of *Dw*'s object (i.e., writing the paper) does have this effect. The desire to start writing has more here-and-now motivational clout because, in part, reflection on that desire and its object does not have the undermining effect that reflection on his desire to write the paper and its object has. And present desire strength just is here-and-now motivational clout. If Ed were able to get himself to act on the matter without reflecting on his relevant desires and their objects, things would be different; but let us suppose that he cannot do so in this case.

If this is right, then part 1 of thesis *T* is false. Part 2 is false, as well; and Pugmire's objection to my first hypothesis appeals to the truth of that part. Ed's desire (*Dn*) not to devote the next several days to the seemingly formidable task of producing a term paper, one may reasonably suppose, makes a negative contribution both to the strength of his desire to write the paper and to the strength of his desire to start writing it. But it is not difficult to see how the contribution in the former case may be greater than that in the latter. Ed can, in good conscience, tell himself that, after he has started writing the paper and has spent an hour or two on it, he will reflect upon his chances of completing it and consider whether to devote the rest of the week to more pleasurable activities. He can explicitly view his satisfying $Dn$ as compatible with his starting the paper while also recognizing that $Dn$ speaks directly against his writing the paper. Under these conditions, it is not surprising that $Dn$ may dampen Ed's desire to write the paper more severely than it dampens his desire to start writing it. After all, it is clear to Ed both that his starting to write the paper does not commit him to devoting several days to a difficult project and that his writing the paper does. To be sure, Ed would not be at all motivated to start writing the paper if he were not motivated to write it. But it does not follow from this, as I have argued, that $Ds$ can be no stronger than $Dw$. Nor does it follow that $Dn$'s influence on the strength of $Dw$ is matched by its influence on $Ds$. Pugmire's objection derives from a crude model of the transmission of negative influence on the strength of superordinate desires to subordinate desires.

Just as Ed's desire to start writing the paper can have more immediate motivational clout than his desire to write it, Ian's desire to utter the self-command may have more immediate motivational clout than his desire to get back to work. For example, focused attention on the thought of getting back to work may have an immobilizing effect on Ian that focused attention on the thought of uttering the self-command does not have; and Ian may be unable to root himself out of his easy chair unless his attention is focused on one or the other of these thoughts. Attending to the thought of getting back to work may draw Ian's attention to the drudgery of his task, with a dampening effect on his motivation to work, whereas attending to the thought of uttering the self-command may instead call Ian's attention to his conception of himself as a self-controlled agent, for example, and enhance his motivation to exercise self-control.

I will develop this suggestion further, in connection with my second hypothesis. First, a predictable objection should be disarmed. One might insist that Ian's attention cannot be focused on the thought of uttering the self-command without also being focused on the thought of getting back to work, since, after all, his purpose in uttering the command is to get himself to go to work. However, this is to take a simplistic view of our attentional behavior and abilities. Children who have learned the self-control technique of cognitive transformation can, in principle, focus their attention on nonarousing cognitive transformations of relevant reward objects without simultaneously focusing on the thought of waiting for the higher-ranked treat, even if they attend to the imaginatively transformed objects as a means of facilitating their waiting.[22] (Indeed, focused attention on the thought of waiting would tend to distract attention from the cognitive transformation. Harking back to a suggestion by Mischel and Moore, the children's cognitive transformations may provide informative reminders of the value of waiting while focusing attention, not on the task of waiting, but rather on the cognitively transformed objects—the imaginary logs and clouds.) Ed can focus his attention on the thought of starting his paper without simultaneously focusing it on the thought of completing the paper, even though his starting the paper is a necessary means to his completing it. Similarly, Ian's attention can be focused on the thought of uttering the self-command without simultaneously being focused on the thought of getting back to work. Not all of our occurrent thoughts at a time are thoughts on which our attention is focused.

As I mentioned, if $Dc$ is stronger than $Dw$, then from $Dtv$'s being stronger than $Dw$ it does not follow that $Dtv$ is stronger than $Dc$. Indeed, for all that Pugmire has said in response to my first hypothesis, $Dc$ may be stronger than $Dtv$: the former may have more motivational potential to result in Ian's intentionally uttering the self-command than the latter has to result in his intentionally continuing to watch TV. However, Ian's intentionally uttering the self-command need not, in principle, depend upon $Dc$'s being stronger than $Dtv$, since the former course of action is not in direct competition with the latter: he can do both things simultaneously. From one's being proximally more motivated to write a letter than to drink coffee, it does not follow that one will not intentionally proceed to drink coffee, even if these are one's only relevant desires at the time: one may do both simultaneously. Supposing that $Dtv$ is stronger than $Dc$, does it follow that Ian will not intentionally proceed to utter the self-command?

This brings us to Pugmire's objection to my second hypothesis. The hypothesis, again, is that other things being equal, $Dc$ need only be stronger than its *direct* motivational competitor (i.e., $D{\sim}c$) to result in Ian's uttering the command and $D{\sim}c$ may be weaker than $Dtv$. Pugmire's objection runs as follows. Since Ian's "desire to continue his present enjoyment is his strongest desire at the time, his desire to prevent anything that he recognizes would terminate it must be more forceful than the desire to do something that he recognizes would terminate it" (p. 85). So Ian wants not to make the attempt at self-control more than he wants to make it; that is, $D{\sim}c$ is stronger than $Dc$, where Ian conceives of $c$ (uttering the self-command) as a means of getting himself back to work and recognizes that resuming his work entails the termination of his enjoyment. (In what follows, $c$ should be understood as so conceived by Ian.)[23]

My original suggestion was that because the effect of Ian's enjoyment on $Dtv$'s strength need not be matched by its effect on the strength of $D{\sim}c$, and because $Dc$ can have representational advantages that $D{\sim}c$ lacks, $Dc$ might be stronger than $D{\sim}c$. Pugmire insists that, given the circumstances, $D{\sim}c$ must be the stronger of the two. Which of us is right?

Imagine that just after it occurs to him that a self-command may be in order, Ian thinks of refusing to command himself to get back to work. He finds the thought and prospect of refusing distasteful, but the desires that help to explain that reaction (we may suppose) include only desires of Ian's that already motivate his desire to get back to work (e.g., a desire to see himself as a self-controlled person and a desire to view himself as someone who values pleasing his wife more than frivolously pleasing himself). The reaction might not immediately render $Dw$ stronger than $Dtv$ (by enhancing the former's strength, diminishing the latter's, or both); but it might nevertheless have the prompt result that Ian wants more to utter the self-command then than not to utter it then. Ian's very representation of the object of $D{\sim}c$ (not uttering the self-command) presents that object in a way that he finds distasteful. (Contrast his representation of the object of $Dtv$.) And that may be enough, in the circumstances, to give $Dc$ the motivational edge it needs to prompt a self-command. Relaxing in front of one's television set is one thing; refraining from making even a modest effort to control oneself is another. The former is not *inherently* distasteful to Ian, but the latter might well be (given other motivational attitudes of his). Consequently, the motivational clout of a desire with the former representational content may outstrip that of a desire with the latter content. Here, as in many cases, mode of representation is motivationally relevant. Intentionally conjuring up a vivid, unattractive representation of a motivationally attractive item—for example, a smoker's picturing cigarette smoke as exhaust from a bus—can attenuate desire strength (Ainslie 1992, p. 139). Representations that come to mind without our intentionally generating them can have similar effects.

My point, in part, is that motivational force is not conferred upon subordinate desires by superordinate desires (and the motivational bases of the latter) in a uniformly simple and straightforward way. It is perhaps *tempting* to suppose, as Pugmire does, that one's proximally wanting to continue one's present enjoyment more than one proximally wants to get back to work ensures that one will not proximally want to exercise self-control in support of one's getting back to work more than one proximally wants to refrain from doing this. But it is a *mistake* to suppose this. Desires have representational content; and their representational content can present options to agents in a light that interferes with the smooth bestowal of motivational strength from one desire to another.

One might object that since Ian wants to prolong his present enjoyment more than he wants not to, and since thoughts about uttering self-commands and the like would distract him from the television program and therefore reduce his enjoyment, his motivational condition precludes his having such thoughts at all (cf. Pugmire, p. 86). However, the thoughts one has at a time need not be thoughts one wants most to have. If all havings of thoughts were intentional actions, $P1m^*$ might be true of all our thoughts. But, of course, thoughts sometimes come to mind without our intentionally bringing it about that they do. And thoughts sometimes attract our attention and distract us from various activities without our *intentionally attending* to the thoughts. We sometimes even find our attention *focused* on a thought that we did not intentionally focus on.[24]

Does my second strategy cohere with $P1m^*$? According to that strategy, Ian can utter the self-command while being less strongly motivated to do that than to continue watching television. Suppose that Ian's strongest (buffer-free) motivation at the time urges his continuing to watch television, that he takes himself to be able to do so, and that, at $t$, he does something intentionally. The conjunction of these suppositions and $P1m^*$ implies that Ian continues watching television (or at least tries to do so). One who takes this consequence in turn to imply that Ian does not utter the self-command will take $P1m^*$ to contravene my second strategy. But, as I have argued, there is no such implication. Ian can utter the self-command *while* continuing to watch TV and while being most strongly motivated to watch it. One pronouncement of $P1m^*$ is, very roughly, that we always do, or at least try to do, what we are most strongly motivated to do at the time. The principle does *not* say, however, that that is *all* we intentionally do at any given time.

Return to the matter of what Ian can *intend* while proximally desiring more strongly to watch TV than to get back to work. If my arguments in the last several paragraphs are successful, there is no motivational bar to Ian's proximally intending to utter the self-command (with a view, of course, to getting himself to go to work). He may be more motivated at the time to issue the command than not to do so; and it is possible that he is more motivated, as well, to issue the command than to continue watching television. Further, even if *Dtv* is stronger than *Dc*—even if the former has a greater motivational potential to issue in continued TV viewing than the latter has to issue in a self-command—that does not preclude Ian's proximally intending to utter the self-command. For, again, the two courses of action are not in direct competition. Recognizing the relevance to self-control of indirect competition, Skinner remarked that commanding oneself to get out of bed on a cold morning can be *easier* than getting out of bed at the time. Understanding why that is so, we understand, as well, how it can be easier to form or acquire a proximal *intention* to utter such a command than to form or acquire a proximal intention to leave one's bed: other things being equal, it is easier to commit oneself to doing something that it is easier (by one's own lights) to do.[25] Proximally intending to *A* because (in part) one believes that one's *A*-ing will, or might, promote one's chances of getting out of bed in a timely fashion is one thing; proximally intending to get out of bed is another. And having the former intention does not require simultaneously having the latter. Indeed, executing the former intention—uttering the self-command, in Skinner's example—may *issue in* a proximal intention to get out of bed.[26]

One last observation about intention is in order. Suppose that at *t* Ian is more strongly motivated to continue watching television than he is to do *anything else*. Suppose, as well, that Ian will acquire an intention to issue the self-command only if he forms one, and assume that forming an intention is an intentional action. *P1m\** implies (assuming subjective openness) that Ian will intentionally continue watching television if he intentionally does anything at the time. Does it also imply that Ian will not (straightaway) form an intention to utter the self-command? No. Even in the supposed motivational condition, Ian may be more strongly motivated to form the intention than not to form it, for reasons that are by now familiar. And he can form the intention to issue the self-command concurrently with his television viewing.

## 6.   Preponderant Proximal Temptation and Strict Akratic Action

In cases of preponderant proximal temptation, an agent holds a decisive judgment that it is better to *A* now than to *B* now, wants more to *B* now, and recognizes that he cannot do both. If we could not exercise self-control in the face of preponderant proximal temptation, one apparent species of strict akratic action would not be a genuine possibility. Setting aside scenarios of a kind discussed in chapter 5, section 2 ("Frankfurt-style" scenarios), strict akratic actions are motivated by *resistible* desires; and if self-control cannot be exercised against preponderant proximal temptations, such temptations are *irresistible*. Although folk wisdom apparently suggests, for example, that (nicotine addicts aside) many agents who are preponderantly proximally tempted to smoke may either akratically succumb to temptation or successfully exercise self-control and refrain from smoking, this suggestion would have to be rejected. *Akrasia*, in such cases, would be directly exhibited at most in one's not having taken preventive measures at some earlier time.

One moral of the preceding discussion is that a proximal temptation's being "preponderant" does not render it irresistible—even from a motivational perspective on intentional action articulated in accordance with $Plm^*$. In many cases, agents who judge it better to $A$ now than to $B$ now but want more to do the latter (and recognize that they cannot do both) may also want to $A$ and $C$ now more than they want to $B$ now; and they may act in accordance with the compound wants. To return to the example of nonalcoholic beer substitutes, someone who judges it better to refrain from drinking beer now than to drink beer now, and whose proximal desire for beer is stronger than his proximal desire to refrain from drinking beer, may have an even stronger proximal desire to perform the compound action of refraining from drinking beer while also reducing the likely discomfort of an unsatisfied desire for beer by drinking a beer substitute. He thwarts temptation in acting on the compound want. Further, even in theoretically more challenging cases, like Ian's, a preponderant proximal temptation may permit a successful exercise of self-control in support of action prescribed by the agent's better judgment. Wanting more to continue watching the program than to get back to work, Ian may nevertheless have what it takes to make a successful attempt at self-control. Desires typically do not come equipped with immutable weights; and if all goes well for Ian, his attempt at self-control will have the result that he proximally desires more strongly to get back to work than to remain glued to his television. His uttering the self-command, as I suggested, might tap an additional source of motivation.[27]

Our capacity for control over our desires, I have argued, extends even to proximal desires, including (many) proximal desires to $A$ that compete with our decisive better judgments and are stronger than our proximal desires not to $A$. That is a comforting thought for anyone who would like to believe that a robust and extensive autonomy is open to us. Agents who lack a capacity for control over a desire that competes with their decisive better judgment are cut off from autonomy in that connection. In the sphere of temptation (other things being equal), the more expansive the territory occupied by *uncontrollable* motivation, the slimmer our prospects for autonomous conduct.

## 7.  Motivation and Agency

Critics may claim that, on the view developed here, even though agents may exert considerable control over their desires, whether they exercise self-control still depends, implausibly, on how strongly motivated they are to exercise it. It may be claimed that this dependence on motivational strength would preclude agents' having the control over their behavior that many agents in fact possess. The imagined critics may be libertarians (see p. 41), but they need not be. Since I have reserved discussion of libertarianism for subsequent chapters, I address nonlibertarian critics here. Like some libertarians, they may claim that such principles as $Plm$ and $Plm^*$—which apply no less to intentional exercises of self-control than to other intentional actions—wrongly place motivation, rather than *agents*, in the driver's seat.

I invite such critics to consider the following doxastic counterpart to *P1m*:

*P1b.* If, at *t*, an agent takes himself to be able to *A* then and firmly believes (without qualification) that it would be better to *A* then than to do anything else then that he takes himself to be able to do then, he intentionally *A*-s then, or at least tries to *A* then, provided that he acts intentionally at *t*.

Set aside the question of *P1b*'s truth. Another question is more to the point. Would *P1b*'s truth place *evaluative beliefs* of the sort at issue, rather than *agents*, in the driver's seat?

I conjecture that most nonlibertarians would not take *P1b*'s truth, even on a deterministic reading, to have the consequence that agents' firm evaluative beliefs, rather than agents themselves, are in charge of intentional action. In all cases falling under *P1b*, agents might do what they do "because" they believe it best to do so; but that is not to say that the beliefs have taken over. Rather, setting aside bizarre scenarios, the agents would act on the basis of their beliefs. *Agents* would be in the driver's seat, steering by the light of their firm evaluative beliefs.

If determination of behavior by firm evaluative beliefs need not thrust agents out of the driver's seat, why would determination of behavior by preponderant motivation do so? Is it being supposed that agents' evaluative beliefs, but not their desires, speak for the agents? Are desires, but not evaluative beliefs, alien forces? Are evaluative beliefs, but not desires, such that agents—agents in the driver's seat—can act on the basis of them? These hypotheses are extravagant at best.

Even setting their extravagance aside, it may be noted that *P1b* is compatible with *P1m*.[28] Suppose that a particular agent's motivation to exercise self-control in any given case is always aligned with his firm evaluative beliefs and that the alignment is explained, in large part, by the agent's having a certain powerful global desire—a desire to see to it that whenever he firmly believes it best to do something, he conducts himself accordingly. If the agent's evaluative beliefs do not usurp his potential agency, neither do his particular desires to exercise self-control or the global desire just mentioned. The former desires are informed by the beliefs, and the global desire, let us suppose, is one the agent firmly believes it best to have. In this agent, we find, in the sphere of self-control, a smoothly integrated intellectual-motivational system. The desires identified do not hinder agency; at least, they hinder it no more than the beliefs do.

The nonlibertarian worry under consideration here turns, I suggest, on a mistaken view of desires as essentially brute psychological forces. If, at a fundamental level in the etiology of action, what agents do is determined by brute psychological forces, then it would seem that, at bottom, agents lack a major say in what they do. But desires suitably informed by firm evaluative beliefs are no more brutish or unreasonable than those beliefs are—and they are no more destructive of full-blown agency. Principles *P1m* and *P1m\** do not contravene there being desires of this kind. Nor do they suggest that "reasonable" desires are uniformly weaker than their competitors, or that desires that motivate exercises of self-control are brute forces, untouched by reason. An agent who is more strongly motivated to exercise self-control in support of a certain judgment than not to do so may firmly believe that an exercise

of self-control would be best; and his so believing may figure importantly in the etiology of his so desiring.

Readers should not leave this chapter with the impression that, in my view, self-
intervention and indirect control are the *norm* in the etiology of intentional behavior. My extended treatment of indirect control—control by way of self-commands,
cognitive transformations, and the like—is explained by the central problem addressed
in the chapter. When motivation and intellect march in step, there is no need for self-
intervention. The same is often true even when the marching is not ideally coordi-
nated (see ch. 2, sec. 5). Fortunately, most of us, much of the time, have no need to
exercise self-control. When the need is present, however, one hopes that the ability
is present, as well.

## Notes

1. Various strategies for controlling the effects of anger on one's behavior and for controlling the state itself are discussed in Tice and Baumeister 1993 and Zillman 1993.

2. On skilled versus brute resistance of temptation, see Mele 1987, pp. 26–27, 58–59.

3. A decisive better judgment need not *favor* overt action to be "about" overt action.
For example, the judgment that it is better not to smoke now than to smoke now is "about"
overt action, even though not smoking (typically) is not an overt action. An agent's smoking,
after all, is an overt action, and the judgment is partly about smoking. Similarly, the judgment that it is *best* not to smoke now counts as being "about" overt action, given the nature of
smoking and given that "It is best not to *A*" obviously implies "It is better not to *A* than to *A*."

4. 'Later' may or may not pick out the same time in both of its occurrences. For example, at 10:00 A.M. one might judge it better to leave home at noon for a concert than to
leave at 12:15 P.M., or one might judge it better at 10:00 A.M. to start grading papers at noon
than to leave for a concert at noon. Also, the reference of 'later' might be quite indefinite, as
in "I'll buy a burial plot later."

5. If *S*'s fear of leaving his home were accompanied by an equally powerful fear of
seeking to attenuate the former fear, matters would be different. Fortunately for *S*, the former
fear is not so accompanied.

6. Depending upon one's view of act individuation and of the proper analysis of intentional action, acceptance of this thesis may or may not embody a commitment to the thesis
that every intentional action is a motivated action. Reflection on cases of double-effect makes
that clear. Suppose that a sniper fires a shot at an enemy soldier, knowing that his so doing
will alert others to his presence but without at all intending or wanting to alert the others.
Some will say that the sniper's *alerting the others* is an intentional action, even though he
was not at all motivated to do *that* (Harman 1976, p. 433). If they also hold that the sniper's
alerting the others is a distinct action from his shooting at the soldier (his pulling the trigger,
his firing the gun, etc.), they may claim to have found what they take to be an unmotivated
intentional action. Still, they can hold that every *case* of intentional action is a case of motivated action, since, after all, in this case, some intentional action that the agent performed
was motivated—e.g., the sniper's shooting the enemy. The claim, roughly, is that there is no
time at which one is acting intentionally while being utterly unmotivated to do anything that
one is then doing.

7. See Toates 1986, ch. 2, for discussion and references, and Mook 1987, pp. 104–5, for
a statement of the prevailing view.

8. See Mook 1987, pp. 305–11, and Toates 1986, chs. 2, 6, 7.

9. Plainly, this does not entail that the judgment *is* a want.

10. This paragraph is borrowed, with minor alterations, from Mele 1992a, p. 47.

11. Such libertarians may nevertheless accept a probabilistic variant of *P1m*.

12. On internal determinism and indeterminism, see chs. 11 and 12.

13. See Pugmire 1994, p. 82: "The very willingness to try self-persuasion [i.e., to make an attempt at self-control] should be precluded by the predominant reigning motivational force of the temptation. To straighten myself out, I have to be straightened out." Cf. McCann 1995.

14. This case parallels one in Mele 1987, pp. 65–66.

15. A pair of desires—for instance, a desire to reduce one's alcohol consumption and a desire to minimize the unpleasantness of the reduction, should one attempt it—can give rise to a conjunctive desire: for example, a desire to reduce one's alcohol consumption while minimizing the unpleasantness of the process. On conjunctive desires and desire agglomeration, see Mele 1992a, pp. 50–53, 64–67.

16. The presentational conditions were investigated under two different activity conditions, waiting and working, and the presentations were periodic for some children and continuous for others. For a table of mean delay times, see Mischel and Moore 1973, p. 176, or Mele 1987, p. 89.

17. For a more extensive discussion of the studies cited in the last few paragraphs, see Mele 1987, pp. 88–91.

18. Of course, one still proximally desires to smoke when one starts puffing (assuming that one is *intentionally* smoking then). Proximal desires typically are not *momentary* states.

19. The thesis that wanting most to *A* (even in conjunction with the belief that one probably will *A*) does not entail intending to *A* is defended in Mele 1992a, ch. 9.

20. I include the parenthetical exclusion because *D2* might not be in its *own* total motivational base. This qualification is sometimes left unexpressed to simplify exposition. On a desire's being in its own motivational base, see Mele 1987, p. 68.

21. These plainly are not the same thought. Nor is Ed's thought of writing the paper a *part* of his thought of starting to write it. Ed cognitively separates his starting to write the paper from his writing it, recognizing that starting to write the paper neither encompasses nor entails writing the paper.

22. Some children do discover such strategies. See Mischel 1981, pp. 263–67; Mischel and Mischel 1983; and Yates, Yates, and Beasley 1987.

23. Pugmire says that *Dc* might be stronger than *D~c*, if *c*—uttering the self-command— were conceived by Ian merely as a "gesture" (1994, p. 85).

24. The commonsensical points made in the last three sentences are among the themes developed in various essays in Uleman and Bargh 1989. Also see Bach n.d.

25. On the committing aspect of intending, see ch. 4, sec. 3.

26. Given the agent's purpose in uttering the self-command, must he at least intend at *t* to get out of bed soon while proximally intending to issue the self-command? No. He might *hope* that the command will help to get him going soon without yet *intending* to get going soon. On cases in which *S* intends to *A* with the goal of *B*-ing, but does not also intend to *B*, see Mele 1992a, ch. 8.

27. All this is compatible, of course, with its being true that some instances of apparent strict akratic action are actually instances of action motivated by irresistible desires.

28. Their compatibility is required for the coherence of the unified intellectual/motivational perspective on intentional behavior traditionally attributed to Socrates (see p. 16).

# 4

# Self-Control, *Akrasia*, and Second-Order Desires

Traditional conceptions of continent and incontinent action, and associated conceptions of self-control and *akrasia*, feature *evaluative judgments*. They are *judgment-involving* conceptions. Akratic action is standardly conceived as uncompelled, intentional action that conflicts with the agent's better judgment. Similarly, acting in accordance with a better judgment is traditionally required for acting continently.[1]

The traditional, judgment-involving conceptions are challenged by alleged instances in which an agent akratically does something that he decisively judges it best to do, or in which an action that is at odds with one's decisive best judgment manifests one's powers of self-control.[2] The challenge is a genuine one, as I argue in section 1 of this chapter. But I argue, as well, that it does not force wholesale abandonment of the tradition. In this chapter, I advance judgment-involving conceptions of akratic and continent action that accommodate "unorthodox" cases, and I defend an account of self-control that is suited to traditional and nontraditional cases alike. My primary aim is to foster a deeper appreciation of the nature of self-control.

One response to nontraditional or unorthodox instances of akratic and continent action is to substitute *higher-order desires* for evaluative judgment in the traditional conceptions of continent and incontinent action. This response is considered and rejected in sections 2 through 4. More is at stake than might initially meet the eye. Pristine belief/desire psychology has its limitations. Recognizing this, some theorists have attempted to fill various gaps by adding more of the same, but at higher levels. For example, second-order desires have been imported into a more streamlined view to explicate such important notions as freedom of the will, autonomy, personhood, and valuing.[3] For reasons that I have presented elsewhere, I believe that we need to branch *out* as well as up, augmenting a familiar "philosophical psychology" with psychological items that are irreducible to beliefs and desires (Mele 1987, 1992a).

My guiding question in sections 2 through 4 is whether an action's counting as continent or incontinent depends upon the agent's having at the time a pertinent higher-order desire. The answer that I will defend is, in a word, *no*. Although our chief interest in behavior of these kinds is explanatory rather than definitional, how one defines phenomena obviously can have a marked effect on one's preferred explanation. Further, a proper understanding of continent and incontinent action adds to the growing case against pure belief/desire models of behavior, including *autono-*

59

*mous* behavior—models according to which the intentional attitudes figuring in the etiology and explanation of intentional action are beliefs, desires, and items reducible to collections thereof. Continent and incontinent action, properly construed, also pose problems for any decision theory wedded to such models that aspires not merely to prescribe, but also to explain, behavior; or so I will argue. Higher-order desires fit neatly into belief/desire psychologies constructed only with first-order states in view; but the additional resources provided by incorporating the higher-order states into the older models fall significantly short of recent advertisements.

Readers primarily interested in autonomy should be forewarned that among the issues investigated in this chapter are some specialized ones about self-control and *akrasia*. However, the disarming of specialized threats to judgment-involving conceptions of continent and incontinent action will promote our understanding not only of these phenomena but also of autonomy-promoting self-control and the place of evaluative judgments in full-blown, deliberative, autonomous action.

## 1. Unorthodox Instances of Continent and Incontinent Action

Young Bruce has decided to join some wayward Cub Scouts in breaking into a neighbor's house, even though he decisively judges it best not to do so. Suppose that at the last minute Bruce refuses to enter the house and leaves the scene of the crime. His doing so because his decisive judgment has prevailed is one thing; his refusing to break in owing simply to a failure of nerve is another. In the latter event, Bruce arguably has exhibited weakness of will: he "chickened out," as children are wont to exclaim.

Suppose alternatively that, experiencing some trepidation about the housebreaking, Bruce tries to steel himself for the deed. Although he judges it best not to participate in the crime, he attempts, successfully, to master his fear, and he proceeds to pick the lock. Here, it seems, Bruce has exhibited strength of will; he has exercised self-control in conquering his fear. If that is right, he has done so even if—as we may suppose—he did not judge it best to master the fear that he experienced, nor judge it better to do so than not to do so. Some exercises of self-control apparently are not performed in the service of a better or best judgment.

Euripides' *Medea*, on one possible reading, presents a more dramatic case of what may be termed *errant* self-control—that is, an exercise of self-control in support of behavior that conflicts with a consciously held decisive better judgment. After an episode of vacillation, Medea proclaims:

> I know indeed what evil I intend to do,
> But stronger than all my afterthoughts is my fury,
> Fury that brings upon mortals the greatest evils. (1078–80)

The intended evil here is Medea's murder of her children. In executing her intention, Medea may provide a counterinstance to the well-known Socratic thesis that no one knowingly and willingly pursues the greater of two evils or the lesser of two goods.[4] Owing to the close association of the behavior whose existence Socrates denies with the trait *akrasia* (want of self-control, incontinence, weakness of will), the Socratic thesis is sometimes formulated more concisely as follows: no one acts *akratically*.

Ironically, Medea's akratic murder of her children, if such it is, rests upon a remarkable exercise of self-control. When the time for action draws terrifyingly near, Medea steels herself for the deed, fighting off tender thoughts of her children—thoughts that previously (1021–58) had led to indecision. She marshals her psychological resources in support of her performing the evil intended deed:

> Oh, arm yourself in steel, my heart! Do not hang back
> From doing this fearful and necessary wrong.
> Oh, come, my hand, poor wretched hand, and take the sword,
> Take it, step forward to this bitter starting point,
> And do not be a coward, do not think of them,
> How sweet they are, and how you are their mother. Just for
> This one short day be forgetful of your children,
> Afterward weep; for even though you will kill them,
> They were very dear—Oh, I am an unhappy woman! (1242–50)

A common tendency, exhibited by Plato and Aristotle, makes the suggestion that an agent may exercise self-control in the service of an akratic deed more puzzling than it ought to be. This is the tendency to view akratic behavior (whether or not one regards it as possible) as the result of "reason's" losing a battle with appetite or passion.[5] One who supposes that *akrasia*, the trait, is exhibited only in the *defeat* of reason will naturally suppose as well that *enkrateia* (self-control, continence, strength of will) is exhibited only in its *support*. Both suppositions are reinforced by a related tendency mentioned earlier (ch. 1, sec. 1)—Plato's and Aristotle's tendency to identify a human being with what others, Euripides included, may regard only as an intellectual *aspect* or *dimension* of the person.

If, as I suggested in chapter 1, we can exercise self-control in support of decisive better judgments that derive in part from our appetites, emotional commitments, and the like, continent and incontinent behavior are not properly viewed universally as outcomes of a contest between intellect and passion. Sometimes there is passion (and calculation) on both sides, as in Medea's case. Strong maternal feelings for her children support her (supposed) better judgment while vengeful feelings toward her husband incline her against it.[6]

Return to the possibility of exhibiting *akrasia* in behavior that *accords* with one's better judgment. Suppose that, while raising the knife over her children, Medea catches a glimpse of their innocent, pathetically confused eyes, eyes of which Euripides makes so much (1038ff.). She tells herself to go through with the killing, but stops the downward path of the knife as it approaches their tender bodies—*not* because she has reached a practical decision on the basis of her better judgment, but rather owing to the dissolution of her intention by (resistible) passion. If it is replied that this does not exhibit a weak will, but something approaching a normal one, less dramatic cases can be adduced—for example, a version of young Bruce's case. He decides, against his better judgment, to join his friends in breaking into a neighbor's house while she is away. When the time comes, he backs out—not because his better judgment has gained the upper hand, but rather because he is (controllably) afraid. His action fits his better judgment, but it issues from an avoidable failure of nerve.[7] Such failures are plausibly taken to manifest weakness of will (or at least an associated imperfection; see p. 5).

Surely, if Bruce can exhibit *akrasia* in refraining from breaking into the house, he can exercise self-control in joining in the crime—even though he judges it best not to participate. He can exercise self-control in mastering his fear. Similarly, Medea can exercise self-control by forcing from her mind thoughts about her children that threaten to undermine her intention to kill them—by mastering the opposition to her intention.

We should not conclude, however, that self-control is *simply* an ability to master motivation that opposes one's intentions or decisions: an agent can display self-control in abandoning an intention. Medea might have exercised self-control in abandoning her intention to kill her children—in refusing to allow her passion for revenge to govern what she intends, and opting for the course of action recommended by the desires and feelings that have for her a higher evaluative ranking. This exercise need not be aimed at mastering motivation that opposes some other intention. Rather, it may serve a better judgment alone.

This last point merits further comment. The normal smooth transition from better judgment to intention may be blocked in Medea's case, for example, by her passion for revenge.[8] Suppose that, at some point, she decides what it would be *best* to do while remaining undecided about *what to do*. She may exercise self-control in support of her forming a decision or intention that fits her better judgment. Perhaps the most promising way to promote the formation of the intention would be to open herself to her strong maternal feelings while dwelling on stirring images of her sweet children, their love for their mother, and their innocent trust in her. Medea can exercise self-control in support of her acting as she judges best by using passion against passion to promote the formation of a continent intention.

I have argued that an agent's failure to execute a decision that conflicts with his better judgment may be due to *akrasia*, and that one can exercise self-control in support of such a decision. Some might take the latter point to imply that not all uncompelled, intentional actions contrary to a decisive better judgment consciously held at the time are akratic actions. One might conclude, for example, that if Bruce had mastered his fear and had broken into his neighbor's house, his housebreaking would not have been an akratic deed, even though it would have been directly at odds with his consciously held decisive better judgment. If this conclusion is properly drawn, I have forced a radical revision in the traditional conception of akratic action. However, the revision at issue seems to me *too* radical. The matter requires scrutiny.

One possible source of confusion must be eliminated immediately. To say that *S* performed an akratic action is not to say that *S* is an akratic *person*. Just as a generally honest person can lie without properly being branded a liar, someone can act akratically without properly being termed an akratic person.[9] Thus, Bruce's housebreaking can be an akratic deed without its following that he is an akratic boy.

In virtue of what, however, would the housebreaking count as akratic, given the deficiency in *kratos* or strength that the term '*akrasia*' denotes? After all, Bruce may exhibit considerable strength of will in mastering the fear that opposes his decision. One answer—a plausible one—is that precisely in *deciding* upon a course of action that directly conflicts with his better judgment on the matter, Bruce exhibits *weak-*

*ness of character,* or at least an associated imperfection. A boy of (significantly) stronger character, we naturally say, would not decide against what he decisively judges best. Strength or *kratos,* in the pertinent sense, need not be restricted to the sphere of overt actions; it may enter into decision making, as well.

Does this move to character commit me to something that I said I was concerned to avoid (ch. 1, sec. 1)—identifying a person with his "reason" (whatever the latter might amount to)? Not at all. For, again, better judgments may be based on, and supported by, a broad range of considerations, including appetites, emotions, and the like (ch. 1, sec. 1). There is no need to suppose that better judgments speak exclusively for a narrow, overly intellectualized self.

To be sure, if we say that Bruce exercises self-control in bringing it about that he performs a deed properly counted as akratic, we are claiming that there is something akratic and something enkratic about what happens in this scenario. This is hardly self-contradictory or incoherent, however. Bruce exercises and exhibits self-control in mastering the fear that opposes his decision. Owing to the way in which an exercise of self-control figures in the etiology of his breaking into the house, that action itself, we may say, manifests some measure of self-control and thus is properly counted as a continent action. But this does not preclude its *also* properly being deemed an *incontinent* action. Given that Bruce's (uncompelled) decision to break into the house clashes with his better judgment on the matter, that *decision* exhibits *akrasia* (or, again, an associated imperfection). And, again taking etiology seriously, it is plausibly held that (uncompelled) executions of akratic decisions are akratic actions. Indeed, that should be uncontroversial. So we can have it both ways. The housebreaking is an indirect manifestation both of the powers of self-control that Bruce employed in resisting his fear and of the weakness that helps to account for his having decided to break into the house in the first place and, thus, for the housebreaking act in which the execution of his decision consists.

What my earlier remarks show, then, is not that the traditional conception of akratic action must be radically revised, but rather that the conception should be expanded to include cases such as that of the boy who, owing to a failure of nerve, refrains from housebreaking. Though he does what he judged it best to do, his doing so resulted from his failure to control a controllable fear, and, therefore, from something that is naturally counted as an instance of weakness.

My discussion in this section of the influence of *akrasia* upon an agent has revolved around action and such psychological antecedents as better judgments, decisions, and intentions. However, *akrasia* can influence even something as grand as an agent's conception of "the good life"—a conception that may occasionally figure explicitly in the formation of better judgments and intentions concerning specific courses of action. Someone who is strongly tempted to A but who regards his prospective A-ing as incongruous with his conception of the sort of life he deems best may resolve the dissonance by way of akratic reasoning. His temptation may prompt thought that results in his accepting, if only for a short while, a modified conception of the good life that permits his A-ing.[10] We may suppose that the thinking itself is at odds with principles of reasoning that the agent still accepts; that, in the absence of temptation, he would reject the modified conception; and that, some time after he *A*-s, he will recognize the modified conception for what it is, a product of self-deception. In some instances or series of instances, *akrasia* may issue in long-term or even permanent modifications of one's conception of the good life. Akratic reasoning can also influence one's better judgments more directly, without altering one's conception of the good life. By way of akratic reasoning one may deceive oneself into believing that one's (unaltered) conception of the good life supports one's taking a particular course of action and that that course of action would be best.

These possibilities open the door to something akin to errant self-control, as characterized above—namely, exercises of self-control in support of better judgments that are themselves akratic. If there can be akratic modifications in what I am calling an agent's conception of the good life, self-control can apparently be exercised on behalf of decisive better judgments that derive in part from an akratically acquired conception of the good life. Similarly, one can exercise self-control in support of better judgments that result more directly from akratic reasoning.

Under what conditions is it true, then, that someone has exercised or displayed self-control? Two preparatory observations are in order. First, an agent's exercising or displaying self-control does not depend upon his being a self-controlled person, if the latter involves being possessed of more than minimal powers of self-control. Even a minimally self-controlled person may exercise and display the powers of self-control that he has. Second, exercises of self-control oppose something in support of something else. In familiar instances, an agent exercises self-control in opposing motivation that threatens to generate conduct that is contrary to his better judgment; and he does so with a view to promoting conduct that accords with the judgment. However, as I have suggested, self-control may also be exercised in support of decisions and intentions that are not recommended by decisive better judgments, and that are, in fact, at odds with such judgments.

Though desires are not as tightly connected (causally and conceptually) as intentions to subsequent action, self-control can be exercised even in the service of a desire.[11] Suppose that at some point Medea desires to punish her husband by killing their children, but that she has reached neither a better judgment nor an intention on the matter. To increase the likelihood that the desire will issue in a corresponding intention, Medea shifts the focus of her thought away from her children and onto Jason and the wrong that he has done her. She exercises control over her conative condition by directing her thoughts. This is at least a borderline instance of exercising self-control. In a related case, Medea has judged it best not to kill the children; but, upset by the emotional weakness that the judgment seems to her to reveal (cf. 1051–52) and by the prospect of Jason going unpunished (1049–50), she decides to resist the maternal and prudential motivation that supports her better judgment and to fuel her desire for revenge. Again, she selects the focusing technique.

We are verging on an account of *exercising self-control* as purposive intervention into one's own motivational condition—quite independently of whether the purpose of the intervention is to support a better judgment. This account poses an apparent threat to the traditional, Aristotelian view that self-controlled individuals characteristically manifest the trait in behavior that accords with their better judgment. The threat is addressed in section 5.

## 2. Higher-Order Desires: Are They Essential to Continent and Incontinent Behavior?

A suggested replacement for the traditional view of continent and incontinent action features *higher-order desires.* Perhaps what is essential to action of these kinds is the presence of a second-order desire that either loses or wins against a first-order desire in the determination of action, independently of what (if anything) the agent judges it best to do (Bigelow, Dodds, and Pargetter 1990). Perhaps, other things being equal, an agent acts continently when, and only when, a higher-order desire is victorious against a lower-order one; similarly, assuming the absence of compulsion, an action is akratic if and only if its performance involves the defeat of a higher-order desire by a lower-order one. So, at least, some have maintained.[12] The claim, in part, is that the full range of continent and incontinent action can be captured only by viewing the possession of second- (or, more generally, higher-) order desires of a certain kind as *essential* to each.

Harry Frankfurt called attention to the notion of a second-order desire in his influential paper "Freedom of the Will and the Concept of a Person" (1971). (For a classical precedent, see Plato, *Republic* 440b). On Frankfurt's account, a person "has a desire of the second order either when he wants simply to have a certain desire or when he wants a certain desire to be his will" (1971, p. 10). We can say, more generally, that a higher-order desire is a desire whose representational content encompasses a representation of another actual or possible desire of the person whose desire it is. Thus, for example, my desire not to have a certain desire would be a higher-order desire, as would my desire that a certain desire of mine be stronger (or weaker) than it is, or stronger (or weaker) than some other desire of mine. Wanting a certain desire to be one's *will,* is, for Frankfurt, wanting that desire "to be the desire that moves [one] effectively to act" (p. 10). Such a second-order desire Frankfurt terms a "second-order volition." That there are second-order desires and volitions in Frankfurt's sense is indisputable; and I appealed to such desires on several occasions both in chapter 3 and in the preceding section.

The focal question of the present section is nicely introduced by a collection of claims advanced in Bigelow, Dodds, and Pargetter 1990. "Strength and weakness," they contend, "are determined by whether the governing desire is a second- or a first-order one, respectively. (Or more generally, it is determined by whether the governing desire is of a higher or a lower order than the others)" (p. 47). "To be tempted," they claim, "is to have a desire which you want *not* to be your strongest desire" (p. 44). And they view continent and incontinent action as responses to temptation. "When faced with temptation," they argue, people "who act in accord with their second-order desire . . . display strength of will," and those who "act in accord with their first-order desire . . . are weak willed" (p. 44).

Now for my question: When a person acts continently or incontinently, must he have a second-order desire that a certain desire not be his strongest desire? A commonsense understanding of 'desire,' like most philosophical construals of the term, permits an agent simultaneously to possess desires that he knows cannot be jointly satisfied.[13] For religious reasons, Sally has a desire to attend midnight mass.

For other reasons, she has a desire to see a midnight movie. Depending upon additional features of the case, Sally may be in a position to exhibit strength or weakness of will. Whether her attending the mass or her going to the movie is the continent (or incontinent) option hinges upon further details. If, in the absence of a second-order desire pertinent to $A$ or $B$, an agent can judge it better to do $B$ than to do $A$, traditional accounts of continent and incontinent action suggest that what it would be continent or incontinent for Sally to do might not depend at all upon her having a *higher-order* desire concerning one or the other of her competing desires. Is this suggestion preservable in the face of unorthodox instances of continent and incontinent action?

Like Bigelow et al., I view continent and incontinent action as importantly interrelated; and, like them, I think that the relationship will be revealed in proper analyses of those species of behavior. Now, a certain understandable intuition about continent action is not likely to be mirrored in standard intuitions about akratic behavior. Consider the notion of *resisting a desire*. If an agent intentionally resists a desire, then, setting aside various complications about intention and intentional behavior, she *wants* to resist the desire.[14] And, of course, a want or desire (I use the terms interchangeably) to resist a desire is a *higher-order* desire. So, perhaps, any agent who tries to resist a desire has at the time an operative higher-order desire. If continent action were to require intentionally resisting desires, then, it seems, continent action *would be* essentially tied to higher-order desires.

One may, to be sure, define a sense of 'continent action' in which the phenomenon essentially involves intentionally resisting desires. But then one will distance continent behavior considerably from its akratic counterpart. Akratic $A$-ing does not require the intentional doing of something in addition to $A$. It certainly does not require, for instance, that the agent intentionally refrain from resisting the desires with which his better judgment competes. An agent who, decisively judging it best not to $A$, is possessed of a desire to $A$, may self-indulgently act on that desire straightaway, without even considering resistance. In such a case (provided that the action was not compelled), readers with no axes to grind will harbor no reservations about counting the $A$-ing as akratic. Surely, only agents who fall significantly short of ideal self-control behave like that. And, in such a case, there is no evident need to suppose that the agent is possessed of a second-order desire that his desire to $A$ not be his strongest desire, or any comparable second-order desire.

Akratic action, traditionally conceived, seems often to be a first-order phenomenon. (I will reinforce the claim later, my present aim being stage setting.) On a natural counterpart conception of *continent* action, not all such behavior involves an attempt to resist, or otherwise manipulate, desires. Fred, who has just been offered another beer, feels an urge to accept. Knowing, however, that he will be driving soon, he judges it best to decline the offer; and he behaves accordingly. In turning down the beer, Fred is naturally said to have acted continently—even if he made no effort at all to resist his desire for the beer, or, more generally, to manipulate his motivational condition. We are, to be sure, more impressed by heroic efforts to resist temptation, especially when they meet with success. But we frequently are impressed, as well, by people who, in the absence of attempts at desire control, act as they judge best in the presence of competing desires. Weaker agents, we think, would not find continent behavior so easy.

Must second-order desires play a role in every more complicated instance of continent or incontinent behavior involving an *internal struggle,* as it were? Consider Albert, an eight-year-old who is sorely tempted to join his friends in a game of baseball now even though his mother has told him to finish his homework first. (He can see them playing in the park across the street.) Albert thinks that it would be best to finish his homework before going out, largely on the grounds that it would be wrong to disobey mom and that disobedience would be met with punishment. He believes, in light of these considerations, that although playing baseball now and leaving his homework for later would certainly be fun, it would be best to stay indoors with his nose to the grindstone. Albert remembers acting contrary to his better judgment in the past, and he recalls his father's advice. Focus your attention, Dad said, on your reasons for not doing what you know you shouldn't do; don't dwell on the thing that you would enjoy doing; and imagine the *consequences* of doing the wrong thing: imagine how bad you will feel when Mom and I find out, and picture how you will feel when you are grounded for a week and can't watch television (standard punishments in Albert's house). Dad, as you can see, tries to keep things simple. Albert follows his advice.

This little drama will remain incomplete for a time, leaving it open whether Albert's efforts were successful. Independently of the outcome, an important question may be asked and answered. When Albert, under the conditions described, performs attentional and imaginative activities of the sort recommended by his father with a view to bringing it about that he finishes his homework before going out to play, *must* he have a second-order desire that his desire to play ball now not be his strongest desire? Or, so as not to focus too narrowly on desire of the precise kind that Bigelow et al. present as being definitive of temptation (1990, p. 44), must Albert have any pertinent second-order desire at the time?

Albert's father, Ray, may have a relatively sophisticated theory about how the suggested techniques work. He may think that their employment attenuates motivation to perform the action that one is tempted to perform while enhancing motivation to engage in the alternative behavior judged better. Ray may regard the techniques as strategies for producing in oneself a certain motivational condition—a certain balance of wants—that will in turn result in the behavior judged best. But what about little Albert? Must he have a two-tiered theory of that sort, linking the strategies to motivation and motivation to action? Or might he have only a simpler theory according to which executing the techniques simply increases the likelihood that he will stay in and study rather than go out to play before he has completed his homework—a theory that does not postulate an intervening motivational variable?

Owing to a battery of first-order desires—desires not to upset his parents, to avoid punishment, to finish his homework before going out, and the like—and to beliefs of his to the effect that the recommended attentional and imaginative activities will enable him to do all this, Albert might engage in those activities. That is, he might direct his attention as his father advised and imagine the unpleasant consequences of disobedience simply as means to ends that are objects of *first*-order desires. If things go according to plan, Albert displays self-control and continently completes his homework before playing ball. None of this requires that he be possessed of a second-order desire that his desire to play ball now not be his strongest desire, or that he have some comparable second-order desire. Albert might not at all regard his situation as calling for him to control his *desires*. It is possible that, thinking strictly in terms of actions and consequences, Albert is motivated to employ his powers of attention and imagination as he does only by first-order desires.

Suppose, alternatively, that Albert *unsuccessfully* employs the strategies, and that, succumbing to temptation, he goes out to play before completing his schoolwork. Assuming that his desire to play then did not *compel* him so to act and that he did not change his mind about what it would be best to do, we have a straightforward instance of akratic action. And, once again, that assessment does not depend on Albert's having had a second-order desire concerning his desire to play ball (or concerning his desire to finish his work first).

What holds here of Albert is true, as well, of some adults in comparable situations. Return to Ian (ch. 3, sec. 3), Albert's uncle. After spending the morning painting a good bit of his tool shed in an attempt to surprise his wife, who is away at the office, Ian goes inside for some lunch and watches a telecast of a golf tournament while eating. Although Ian does not care much for golf, he is enjoying his respite. Thinking that he should resume his painting soon, he judges it best to start up again at the next commercial break. However, the commercial comes and goes and Ian has not budged. Feeling a bit perturbed with himself, Ian utters a self-command: "Get off your butt, Ian, and paint that shed!" Ian switches off his TV and gets back to work.

Here, too, it seems plain, an agent may exhibit a modicum of self-control and behave continently in the absence of any relevant second-order desire. Rather than desiring, for example, that his desire to relax not be his strongest desire, or that his desire to finish painting the shed be stronger than his competing desires, Ian, owing simply to a battery of first-order desires and beliefs, may bring it about that he gets back to work. Execution of the simple self-control technique—the self-command—need not derive from any second-order desire. Rather, thinking perhaps that an inner goad would help to get him back to work (but without considering that the self-command or goad might favorably affect his motivational condition), he utters the command with a view to getting himself up off the couch and into the yard.

Some readers might worry that I have been employing or presupposing an excessively restrictive criterion for the presence of higher-order desires. It might be claimed (1) that any agent possessed of the concept of desire who knowingly has competing desires at a time $t$ (a desire for $x$ and a desire for $y$) will at least tacitly believe, for example, that if he acts on his desire for $x$ he will not get $y$ and (2) that insofar as such an agent wants $y$ and tacitly believes that his getting $y$ requires his not acting on his desire for $x$, he wants (at least tacitly) not to act on his desire for $x$. And, of course, a desire not to act on a desire is a higher-order desire. One might contend accordingly that even if Ian, for example, does not explicitly regard issuing a self-command as a means of changing his motivational condition and has no occurrent belief to the effect that by uttering a suitable command he can affect his desires in a way favorable to his getting back to work, he at least tacitly believes something to that effect. Further, such a belief, conjoined with a desire to get back to work, commits Ian to wanting (at least tacitly) to affect his desires in the way indicated. Or so one may argue.

Notice, however, that such a route to the postulation of higher-order desires in a case like Ian's—I dub it the *simple route*—has the consequence that whenever an agent with the pertinent conceptual machinery knowingly is possessed of competing first-order desires, he has competing second-order desires, as well. An agent who has the tacit belief about $x$ and $y$ just identified presumably also believes—at least tacitly—that his getting $x$ requires his not acting on his desire for $y$. So, on the simple view, he wants (at least tacitly) not to act on his desire for $y$, given that he wants $x$— just as he wants not to act on his desire for $x$, given that he wants $y$. If second-order (tacit) desires are consistently paired off against each other in this manner, the difference between continent and incontinent action cannot hinge on them in the way proposed by the view under attack: action on either member of a pair of competing first-order desires will accord with at least one second-order desire and clash with at least one other second-order desire. Ian's getting back to work, for example, will accord with a desire to affect his desires in such a way as to bring it about that he gets back to work, and it will clash with a desire *not* to affect his desires in this way (after all, he is possessed of a desire to continue to relax and tacitly believes that his so doing depends on his not affecting his desires in such a way as to bring it about that he gets back to work).

Perhaps it will be replied that Ian will tacitly want it to be the case that his desire to get back to work be *stronger* than his desire to continue relaxing—that $Dw > Dr$— and that whether his behavior counts as continent or incontinent hinges on the relation of his conduct to *this* higher-order desire. But if Ian has the tacit beliefs already mentioned, surely he tacitly believes, as well, that if $Dw > Dr$ he probably will not continue relaxing, and that his continuing to relax probably will depend upon $Dr > Dw$—in which case, on the simple view, he tacitly wants it *not* to be the case that $Dw > Dr$ and tacitly wants it to be the case that $Dr > Dw$, given that he has a desire to continue relaxing. Again, second-order desires are paired off against each another.

I conclude that proponents of the view under attack about continent and incontinent action want to avoid taking the simple route to the postulation of higher-order desires. A better route would explicitly appeal to conceptual or explanatory needs (or both). If we could not adequately characterize continent and incontinent action, or explain their occurrence, independently of the postulation of pertinent higher-order desires *in each instance* of these phenomena, that would be another matter entirely.

I will return to the claims made in this section shortly. The grounds for them may be strengthened. That is best done in the course of developing characterizations of continent and incontinent action and assessing the merits of alternative views.

## 3. Continent and Incontinent Action

Cautious readers may wish to reserve judgment on my central contentions in the preceding section until a further question has been answered. If higher-order desires are not essential to continent and incontinent action, how should such behavior be characterized?

This question is profitably addressed in stages. One may ask first whether traditional characterizations of continent and incontinent action, which are phrased partly in terms of better judgments, provide sufficient conditions for the phenomena. If an affirmative answer is forthcoming, one may then ask how the traditional, judgment-involving characterizations might be modified to accommodate akratic action that accords with the agent's better judgment and continent action that is at odds with such a judgment.

Bigelow et al. argue that if a person who believes that his $A$-ing would be morally wrong nevertheless intentionally $A$-s, his $A$-ing is an incontinent action only if he has some pertinent second-order desire (1990, pp. 46–47). Here, they are criticizing the idea that acting against a *moral* better judgment (in the absence of compulsion, we may suppose) is sufficient for acting incontinently, and they are advancing an alternative account of akratic action featuring second-order desires. However, one might endorse the criticism while rejecting the alternative.

Owing partly to Davidson's "How Is Weakness of the Will Possible?" (1970), it is now widely accepted that akratic action is not a strictly moral matter, and that one may act akratically against a nonmoral better judgment. Further, even setting aside "unorthodox" cases, agents may continently act against what they judge morally best, as I have observed (p. 15). Consider someone who thinks that the moral considerations in favor of his doing $A$ are outweighed by nonmoral grounds for performing a competing action $B$, and who consequently judges that although, morally speaking, it would be best to $A$, it would be better, overall, to $B$. (Moral considerations are not always regarded as evaluatively overriding, even by agents who take morality seriously.)[15] Such a person, feeling that his considered better judgment is in danger of being thwarted by, say, an irrationally strong emotional attachment to morality, might exercise self-control to bring it about that he acts as he judges best on the whole.

Bigelow et al. have failed to undermine the thesis that the following is sufficient for having acted akratically: intentionally $A$-ing—in the absence of compulsion—even though one consciously holds the decisive judgment that it would be best not to $A$. At most, they have falsified a comparable claim concerning *moral* judgments.

The preceding discussion contains the seeds of a felicitous extension of traditional, judgment-involving characterizations of continent and incontinent action. Two further preparatory observations are in order.

1. Even within the boundaries of a traditional, judgment-involving conception of continent action, the phenomenon may be defined more or less broadly. On a broad, or inclusive, conception of continent action, every intentional action that accords with a decisive better judgment held by the agent at the time might be so counted. However, in the absence of temptation, action that accords with one's better judgment might not manifest even a modicum of continence. An agent who, in the absence of competing motivation, desires to do $A$, the action judged best, might intentionally $A$ even if he is wholly lacking in continence. There being no motivational obstacle to his $A$-ing, not even an approximation of the trait is required for his so acting. On a narrower conception, an action is a continent action only if it is performed in the presence of competing motivation. Following Bigelow et al., I will assume (for the sake of argument) that the motivational condition just identified is a necessary condition of continent action.[16] Even then, just as an action may be deemed incontinent although it exhibits, not *akrasia*, but only an associated imperfection, an agent may continently $A$, as he judges best, in the presence of only a modest temptation.

2. As I observed in chapter 1, *akrasia* and *enkrateia* (weakness and strength of will) can figure in the etiology of action at a variety of junctures. To keep things relatively tidy, I will limit the discussion to what may be termed *bottom-line* akratic action and its continent counterpart. In bottom-line instances of the former, on the traditional, judgment-involving view, the "akratic break" occurs between a concluding decisive better judgment and action. In bottom-line continent action, traditionally conceived, such a judgment wins out in the determination of action.

Now, to plant the seeds. Traditional conceptions of continent and incontinent action revolve around a certain species of *commitment* to action—the sort of commitment constituted by a decisive better or best judgment. An agent who decisively judges it best to *A* is thereby *rationally committed* to *A*-ing, in the sense that (as long as the judgment is retained) the uncompelled, intentional performance of any action that he believes to be incompatible with his *A*-ing would open him to the charge of irrationality. Such action would be at least *subjectively* irrational—irrational from the agent's own point of view. For, while explicitly holding the judgment, an agent cannot rationally take himself to have, from his own point of view, better (or equally good, 'best' being understood exclusively) grounds for not *A*-ing. Similarly, an agent who decisively judges it better to *A* than to *B* is rationally committed to doing-*A*-if-he-does-either-*A*-or-*B*.

In the young Bruce scenario, we find both a commitment of this kind and a commitment of another type. In deciding (or forming an intention) to *A*, one makes a commitment of sorts to *A*-ing: the basic point of decisions or intentions to *A* is to issue in the agent's *A*-ing (even if, occasionally, what we decide or intend to do is something that we would have done anyway).[17] Thus, Bruce has conflicting commitments. His decisive better judgment commits him to refraining from breaking into the house; his decision commits him to participating in the crime. The former, we may say, is an *evaluative* commitment, the latter an *executive* one, decisions and intentions being executive states (Mele 1992a, ch. 9). The genus may be termed *practical* commitment, commitment to engage in a course of *action*.

A salient shared feature of evaluative and executive commitment is that the acquisition of a commitment of either sort settles, for the agent, an important practical issue. *Evaluative* commitments settle questions of the form "What (from the perspective of my own desires, beliefs, etc.) would it be best to do?" or "Which of *A* and *B* (from the same perspective) would it be better to do?" Having decisively judged it best to *A*, reasoning about means to *A*-ing may be called for, but the question whether it would be best (in the pertinent sense) to *A* has been closed—at least temporarily. (The same holds for an analogous comparative question.) Things typically do not end there, of course. Often enough, we attempt to settle upon what *to do* by trying to ascertain what it would be *best* to do. And genuinely practical reasoning guided by a concern to identify what it would be best to do is guided, as well, by the practically more fundamental concern to identify what *to do*. When things go smoothly, a decisive best judgment in favor of *A*-ing prompts a decision or intention to *A* (ch. 2, sec. 5; Mele 1992a, ch. 12).

*Executive* commitments settle practical questions of the form "What shall I do?"[18] When an agent faced with a practical question of this form decides to *A*, or otherwise acquires an intention to *A*, that closes the question—at least for the time being. If the question is "What shall I do *now*?," where the *now* is narrow enough to preclude the question's being reopened, the question is closed permanently (which is not to say, of course, that the agent will succeed in doing what he intends). Settling and closing of the kinds that I have sketched are essential to what I am calling *practical commitment*. Whereas decisions and intentions straightforwardly settle a question of the form "What shall I do?," decisive best judgments in favor of *A*-ing settle a comparable evaluative practical question, thereby providing (in the sense identified) *rationally* sufficient grounds for a decision or intention to do or attempt *A*.

Do first-order desires (in a common sense of 'desire' that permits an agent's possessing desires that he knows cannot be jointly satisfied) constitute practical commitments? Plainly, first-order desires, as a class, are not *evaluative* commitments, since an agent who desires to *A* may nevertheless rationally (from his own point of view) intentionally refrain from *A*-ing: after all, he may justifiably want to do *B*, a competing action, more than he wants to do *A*. Nor do first-order desires constitute *executive* commitments, if, as I have argued elsewhere, such desires motivate intentional behavior only by contributing to the acquisition or formation of intentions.[19] First-order desires, in that case, rather than being executive states, dispose agents to enter corresponding executive states.

Concerning executive commitment, it should be noted that the connection between deciding (or intending) to *A* and *A*-ing is much tighter than that between desiring to *A* and *A*-ing. This is reflected in the obvious point that, other things being equal, the information that an agent has just decided to *A*, or intends to *A*, warrants greater confidence that he will *A* than does the information that he is possessed of a desire to *A*. We have fleeting desires, relatively weak desires, and even some very strong desires, to do any number of things that we do not do, largely because we decide or intend to do something else. Here, the commonsense notion of *settling* upon a course of action is useful. In deciding to *A*, one *settles*, we say, upon *A*-ing (at least tentatively), and one enters a state (often a revocable and revisable one) of being settled upon *A*-ing; but one may have a desire to *A* without being at all settled upon *A*-ing. Moreover, owing significantly to the settledness feature of decisions and intentions, agents who decide or intend to *A* are disposed to see the practical question, "Shall I *A*?," as closed, at least then; but we desire to do many things without being at all disposed to see the pertinent practical questions as closed (see Bratman 1987). It is for this reason that decisions and intentions for the nonimmediate future facilitate planning in a way that temporally comparable desires, as a class, do not (Bratman 1987). Having formed or acquired, during breakfast, an intention to take Bruce to dinner, I am better situated to coordinate the day's activities than I was when, merely *desiring* to take him to dinner, I still regarded the matter as open.[20]

On the supposition that *practical commitments*, in the sense articulated, are exhausted by evaluative and executive commitments, desires, as a class, do not constitute practical commitments. Even setting that supposition aside, however, it should be noted that desires, as a class, do not close questions of the forms "What would it be best (or better) to do?" or "What shall I do?"[21]

Do *second-order* desires constitute practical commitments to present action? Consider Sally, a smoker who, although she genuinely enjoys the activity, is convinced that she would be better off if she were to kick the habit. Suppose that Sally has a second-order desire that she not desire to smoke. Suppose also, however, that she has a competing second-order desire to continue desiring to smoke. Although Sally believes that if she were no longer to desire to smoke she would cease to find smoking pleasant, she thinks that, even in that case, she would miss the activity, and even the associated pleasures. (What, she wonders, will take the place of those pleasures? Will there be a hedonic gap in her daily routine?) Smoking has become a significant part of Sally's life. She smokes not only for the pleasure, but also to calm herself, to keep alert, and even, she believes, to help her think more clearly when writing her philosophical papers. Moreover, for years, Sally consciously has regarded her smoking habits as motivating her, advantageously, to put in long hours at her computer, having discovered, after deciding to cut down on cigarettes by smoking only at the office, that the practice considerably extended her workday.

Even at the level of second-order desires, then, Sally faces a conflict; and neither desire itself constitutes a practical commitment. Her second-order desires themselves do not determine what it is rational (by her own lights) for her to do and, therefore, do not constitute *evaluative* commitments. Nor do they constitute *executive* commitments. In deciding to A (thus forming an intention to A), or in otherwise acquiring an intention to A, one becomes *settled* upon a practical matter—thus acquiring an *executive* commitment. However, Sally's second-order desires do not at all settle in her mind what she will do (or attempt). They leave the matter unresolved. (A philosopher can try moving up another level, of course; but it is easy enough to find conflicts there as well.)

The points just made are worth emphasizing. First, second-order desires, as a class, are not *evaluative* commitments. Sally's desire to desire that she continue smoking, for example, does not rationally commit her to desiring to continue smoking. If it did so commit her in virtue simply of its being a second-order desire, she would be rationally committed, as well—given her competing second-order desire—to ceasing to desire to smoke. And any view requiring that whenever an agent's second-order desires compete she is rationally committed to x and simultaneously rationally committed to something incompatible with x is in serious trouble.

Second, second-order desires, for the reasons identified, are not *executive* commitments to present action either. Rather, like their first-order counterparts, they are best viewed as encompassing dispositions to make corresponding decisions and acquire corresponding intentions, which in turn have a more direct grip on intentional behavior. For example, a smoker's desire not to desire to smoke may motivate overt intentional action conducive to that end by motivating him to decide to do his best to bring it about that he no longer desires to smoke.

Finally, higher-order desires, as a class, do not settle for agents practical questions of the forms "What would it be best to do?," "Would it be better to A or to B?," "What shall I do?" Hence, they do not, as a class, constitute what I am calling practical commitments. In this fundamental respect, they differ significantly from decisive evaluative judgments, decisions, and intentions.

Promising modifications of the traditional, judgment-involving conceptions of "bottom-line" incontinent and continent action, I suggest, may be framed in terms of *practical commitments* quite independently of the notion of second- (or higher-) order desires. The suggestion may be tested first with respect to the following question:

What is common to akratic action against a decisive better judgment and akratic action that accords with such a judgment? A straightforward answer is readily available. In both cases, a practical commitment is thwarted by noncompelling competing motivation. In the former case (akratic action traditionally understood), the commitment is an evaluative one. In the latter case ("unorthodox" akratic action like Bruce's refraining from breaking into the house owing to a failure of nerve), it is an executive one. This is not to say, of course, that the thwarting of an executive commitment by noncompelling competing motivation is conceptually sufficient for the agent's having acted akratically. If, owing appropriately to his evaluative commitment and to associated desires of his, Bruce had abandoned his intention to break into the house and acted on the basis of his better judgment, he would not have acted akratically in refraining from breaking in. In unorthodox cases of bottom-line akratic action, the thwarting or overturning of an akratic decision or intention has *another* source—for example, controllable fear. The agent abandons his akratic intention and does the (subjectively) right thing, but not for the (subjectively) right reason.

What about continent action? What is common to the traditional and "unorthodox" species? One might look for an exact parallel to the preceding answer: in both cases, a practical commitment prevails against competing motivation in the determination of action. However, when the practical commitments are executive ones and the motivation against which they prevail is precisely the motivation that supports competing decisive better judgments, it would be absurd to count the actions in which the execution of those commitments consist as continent precisely in virtue of the commitments' having prevailed against *that* motivation. If these actions were so counted, all orthodox bottom-line incontinent actions would also be continent actions (for all orthodox bottom-line incontinent actions are performed in the presence of competing motivation associated with the agent's decisive better judgment). In mainstream cases of unorthodox bottom-line continent action, a practical commitment prevails against a potential undermining by competing motivation that overturns the commitment without contributing to the agent's intending on the basis of his better judgment. Bruce's executing his intention to break into the house is a case in point. His fear threatened to undermine his practical commitment via a route not involving his intending on the basis of his better judgment—or more fully, via a route other than one in which an intention based on his better judgment replaced his akratic intention to break into the house. In the case as described, if Bruce had abandoned his intention to break into the house in favor of an intention not to break in, he would not have acquired the latter intention on the basis of his better judgment, but would instead have been led to that intention by his fear. It would have been a case of "chickening out," *not* a case of doing the (subjectively) right thing and abandoning the (subjectively) wrong intention for the (subjectively) right reason.

Cases are imaginable in which motivational attitudes that provide support for one's decisive judgment that it would be best to A undermine a competing akratic intention (an intention not to A, say) and give rise to an intention to A, but without contributing to the agent's intending *on the basis of* his judgment. For example, someone who is afraid of heights may judge it best to decline an invitation to take a ride in a hot air balloon, largely on the grounds that he deems what is to be gained by taking the ride—making a favorable impression on friends, say—not to be worth the emotional toll that the flight would take on him, given his fear of heights. Neverthe-less, he akratically intends to take the flight. His fear enters into his grounds for the judgment; but it may undermine his akratic intention and issue in an intention, at the last minute, to decline the invitation that he has already accepted, without the latter intention's being formed or acquired on the basis of his better judgment. His fear may simply unnerve him. (Similarly, in a variant of the Medea case, her tender feel-ings for her children may simply unnerve her.) Here, his intention not to take the flight *accords with* his better judgment, but it is not *based on* that judgment. If, alter-natively, his akratic intention to take the flight had prevailed and the case had, thus, been one of unorthodox bottom-line continent action, the case would so count in virtue of the akratic intention's prevailing against a potential undermining via a route of the kind identified—a route involving "chickening out," as opposed to a reversal of intention based on the agent's better judgment.[22]

Consider an exceptional case. Fyodor decisively judges it best to do *A* but intends to do *B*, a competing action, because he has a perverse wish to prove to himself that he can resist the pull of his own decisive better judgments. If Fyodor does *B* (inten-tionally and without compulsion), this apparently is a case of unorthodox bottom-line continent action in which the action counts as continent precisely in virtue of the corresponding, effective intention's having prevailed against the motivational pull of the agent's decisive better judgment. If Fyodor struggled mightily to resist the pull of his better judgment and managed to bring it about that he retained and executed his intention to *B*, he apparently exhibited some powers of self-control. Cases of this kind, assuming that they are conceivable, are extreme cases of unorthodox, bottom-line continent action. However, counting them as such does not have the (unaccept-able) result that all executions of akratic intentions—or all orthodox akratic actions—are unorthodox continent actions; for the present case has a feature that sets it apart from mainstream cases of akratic action. In *this* case, the agent is concerned precisely to resist the pull of a decisive better judgment.

Suppose that, in the end, Fyodor had abandoned his intention to *B* and had done *A*, the action judged best. Would his *A*-ing have been an instance of unorthodox in-continent action? That depends upon whether his *A*-ing was due to weakness of will (or an associated imperfection). If Fyodor abandoned his intention to *B* because he rationally deemed his project to be unacceptably silly, then, other things being equal, he did not exhibit weakness (or an associated imperfection) in abandoning the inten-tion and doing *A* instead. However, if, for example, a (manageable) fear of being scorned by his peers for acting in a blatantly irrational way simply unnerved him, with the result that he abandoned his intention to do *B* and instead did *A*, his behavior was due to weakness of will or some approximation thereof. In that event, it is worth noting, he did not do the (subjectively) right thing for the (subjectively) right reason, as in cases of orthodox continent action, but did it owing partly to his having been unnerved by his fear of scorn. The case is one of unorthodox incontinent action.

Any proper conception of continent behavior will be bound up closely with a proper conception of continence. Now, continence is traditionally treated as a trait constituted by the capacity to restrain or contain desires that threaten to lead one in a direction that is at odds with what one judges best. However, there is also the commonsense notion of *self-control*, which leads a less tidy conceptual life. The expression 'self-control' is sometimes used as a synonym for 'continence' narrowly construed, but it also has a broader sense in which self-control may be exhibited even in behavior that goes against what the agent judges best.[23] One may try to locate, as well, for 'self-control' a third, narrower, sense according to which self-control is exhibited only in behavior motivated by a desire or intention to control (some aspect of) one's motivational condition and in appropriate behavioral products of such behavior. In this third sense, intentional behavior that exhibits self-control is motivated at least in part by higher-order motivational attitudes.

So, focusing on a narrow notion of *continence* for direction (and on self-control in *that* sense), one might restrict continent behavior to executions of best (or better) judgments. Alternatively, turning to self-control in the broader sense for guidance, one might push for a more inclusive conception of continent action. In either case, however, there is no need to hold that an action, $A$, is a continent action only if the $A$-ing is promoted by the agent's intentionally resisting or otherwise manipulating motivation of his. And that closes the most direct justificatory route to the claim that acting continently at $t$ requires the possession of a relevant *higher-order* desire at the time. The *third* notion of self-control does make higher-order motivation essential to the intentional behavioral phenomena. However, restricting the extension of 'continent action' to action served by self-control in this narrow sense would preclude there being a continent analogue of garden-variety akratic behavior that does not involve the defeat of a higher-order desire (in which case a concern for symmetry that I share with Bigelow et al. is thwarted).

A general moral is in the offing. Even if conceptions of continent and incontinent action were, in some manner, tightened up to include only behavior that depends upon the agent's possessing pertinent higher-order desires, that would not make the excluded behavior disappear—it would still require explanation. Relevant higher-order desires being absent in instances of such behavior, we would still be faced with explanatory problems of the sort that higher-order desires were imported to resolve. (More on this shortly.)

## 4.  Akrasia, Decision Theory, and Second-Order Preferences

In his intriguing paper "Preferences among Preferences" (1974), Richard Jeffrey introduces the notion of a second-order preference into the system that he developed earlier in *The Logic of Decision* (1965). His aim, in part, is to elucidate akratic behavior. (The protagonist of his central case, George M. Akrates, is an akratic smoker.)

To the extent to which a decision theory is normative, akratic action need not be a problem for it. But akratic behavior poses a *prima facie* difficulty where a decision theory purports not only to be normative, but to be descriptive and explanatory of behavior, as well. Suppose that preferences were to be equated with better judgments. Then, if akratic action is not a fiction, it sometimes would happen that, preferring $A$ to $B$, an agent intentionally $B$-s without also $A$-ing (or even trying to $A$). Given the present suppositions, a decision theory that tells us that we always do (or try to do) what we most prefer doing (preference being understood—nonstandardly—as evaluative judgment) speaks falsely. If, alternatively, preferring $x$ to $y$ (where $x$ and $y$

are options for the agent) is equated with being more motivated to make $x$ true than to make $y$ true[24] (or with "wanting more," in that sense), decision theory might avoid the empirical problem at the expense of normative unacceptability. A normatively satisfactory decision theory will not advise us to act as we most prefer when what is so preferred is at odds with our carefully considered decisive better judgments.

Jeffrey shows both that George can prefer smoking to not smoking while also preferring that he prefer not smoking to smoking and that second-order preferences can be smoothly integrated into the decision theory articulated in his book. On Jeffrey's view, if, at a time, the top spot in George's preference ranking is occupied by smoking then, George will smoke then (if he can: e.g., cigarettes are available, he is not paralyzed)—even if his second-order preference that he prefer not smoking to smoking comes in a close second. Understanding preference ranking, in the words of Bigelow et al. (1990, p. 42), as "the order in 'causally operative strength,'" the conditional claim about George's behavior is on solid ground. Of course, we do not want a decision theory that would *prescribe* George's smoking, given the situation; but we need not accept one that would. We may adopt a decision theory that has higher-order preferences prescriptively trumping competing lower-order ones, for example. (If there can be competing higher-order preferences at the highest level at which preferences are possessed at the time by the agent, this procedure will not do; but I will let that pass.)

Here, I want to examine two questions. *Question 1*: In order to make sense of akratic smoking, *must* we advert to second-order preferences? *Question 2*: Are the following conditions sufficient for $S$'s smoking at $t$ being a bottom-line akratic action? $S$ smokes intentionally at the time; at $t$, $S$ prefers his preferring not smoking then to his preferring smoking then; $S$ has, at the time, no preference about preferences (or desire about desires) that competes with the second-order preference just identified; and $S$'s smoking is not due to motivation that is irresistible by him at $t$.

I start with question 1. Since it parallels a question discussed earlier about second-order *desires*, I will be brief. Suppose that all preferences are intentional attitudes on a par with so-called occurrent desires and beliefs. Then, it seems, preferences will be fit to perform causal work of the sort often attributed to occurrent beliefs, desires, intentions, and related intentional attitudes—and work often attributed to preferences themselves, of course. (They will, at least, be *no less* fit to figure in the production of intentional behavior than are the other occurrent intentional attitudes.) Imagine that a particular smoker, Bruce, experiences an urge to smoke soon and that he prefers smoking soon to not smoking soon, preference being understood in the motivational sense identified. Imagine also that he decisively judges it best not to smoke soon, but, in the absence of compulsion, he self-indulgently decides to smoke and proceeds to execute that decision, realizing full well that this violates his judgment. That Bruce has no preferences at the time about his smoking preferences is, I should think, eminently conceivable. Yet, this is a garden-variety instance of self-indulgent, akratic action. What justifies classifying the behavior as akratic is its being intentional, uncompelled behavior that the agent recognizes to be at odds with a decisive better judgment that he explicitly holds at the time. Such a judgment, again, constitutes a practical commitment.

A pair of objections may be anticipated and rebutted. First, the decision that I quite naturally described as a decision *to smoke* need neither itself be, nor depend upon, Bruce's having a second-order attitude concerning smoking. What he decides to do need not, for example, be to *act on his desire to smoke*, or to act on his *preference* for smoking, or to act on his desire to smoke rather than on another desire. What we find here might be a state whose attitudinal mode is *decision* and whose representational content is as simple as "I smoke here and now." Second, it does not follow from the absence of second-order attitudes of the sort at issue in conjunction with the smoking desire's being stronger than its nonsmoking counterpart that Bruce's smoking is motivationally *compelled*, and therefore not akratic. Recall little Albert. In the absence of second-order attitudes of the relevant sort, he was capable of engaging in mental activity with a view to bringing it about that he finished his homework before joining his friends. Similarly, Bruce may try—and try *successfully*—to bring it about that he does not smoke, even though he lacks such second-order attitudes as a preference that his first-order preferences favor his not smoking. To be sure, if (during *t*) Bruce were intentionally to refrain from smoking, then, given popular assumptions about the connection between wanting and intentional action, he would (during *t*) want not to smoke then more than he wants to smoke then. But Bruce may cause it to be the case that his wants stack up in this way—or that he prefers not smoking then to smoking then—without having a (second-order) desire to do *that*. His resultant motivational condition might well be a *byproduct* of activity of his that is not motivated by any second-order desire or preference.

*Why* would Bruce try to bring it about that he does not smoke, given that he lacks at the time pertinent second-order preferences and desires? Well, he may think that one should try to do what one judges it best to do, and he may be possessed of a generic desire to do whatever he thinks he should do. The generic desire is not a *second-order* desire.[25] It is just what it purports to be, a desire "to do whatever he thinks he should do." There is, in the quoted expression, no mention of a desire. And even if thinking that one should do something were to entail desiring to do it, it would not follow that Bruce (who, we may suppose, is entirely ignorant of that entailment) is possessed of a generic desire whose representational content encompasses a representation of some other desire of his.

I turn now to question 2. Suppose that another smoker, Peter, satisfies on a particular occasion each of the conditions identified in the question. Our protagonist, a three-pack-a-day man and a militant advocate of smokers' rights, recently started dating a physician who deplores his smoking. During a party at her house, Peter feels an urge for a cigarette and immediately experiences a worry about offending his host. It occurs to him (he is a moderately reflective fellow) that if only he did not want to smoke (soon), or did not prefer smoking soon to not smoking soon, there would be no problem. On the heels of that thought comes a second-order preference: he prefers having a preference for not smoking soon to having a preference for smoking soon. However, being a militant smoker, Peter is upset with himself for even entertaining the above-mentioned counterfactual thought. Without acquiring a competing second- or higher-order preference about preferences (e.g., without preferring his preferring preferring smoking soon to his preferring preferring not smoking soon—a complicated intentional attitude, indeed), and without losing the identified second-order preference, Peter straightaway forms the decisive judgment that it would be best to start smoking at once. And he proceeds, accordingly, to light up. (Peter's judgment, incidentally, is based largely on his long-standing principle that smokers' rights always evaluatively trump considerations of politeness.)[26]

In this case, plainly, Peter's smoking is not akratic. And there is no need to appeal to the nonviolation of a decisive better judgment in accounting for our natural intuitive assessment of the case. What accounts for that assessment is our recognition that Peter has at the time no *practical commitment* to refrain from smoking. His second-order preference (or desire) does not constitute such a commitment. Nor does any other attitude of his.

Some might be tempted to suppose that Peter had a preference about preferences that outranked his preference to prefer not smoking then to smoking then. But I see no *need* to suppose that he is possessed of such a competing preference at the time. On principle, he judges it best to smoke; and being more motivated to smoke than to refrain from smoking, he smokes. Further, as the case makes sufficiently plain, there is no conceptual impossibility in someone's judging it best to *A* while preferring that he prefer not *A*-ing to *A*-ing (and possessing no competing occurrent preferences about preferences). For an agent may deem such a preference *irrational*—and deem it irrational independently of his having a competing occurrent preference about preferences. Peter need not, for example, occurrently prefer preferring supporting smokers' rights to preferring his preferring not smoking then to smoking then. And it need not be the case that, preferring having rational preferences to having irrational ones, Peter prefers his not preferring preferring not smoking just now to his having that second-order preference. Occurrent representations required for such occurrent preferences are, we may coherently suppose, absent at the time.

The correct answer to question 2, then, is *no* (given the assumption currently in operation, that preferences are occurrent intentional attitudes). The conditions identified in that question, featuring higher-order preferences, are not sufficient for an agent's having *akratically* smoked. And I can think of no *more* promising set of sufficient conditions in terms of occurrent second- or higher-order conative or orectic states—unless, of course, those conditions include, *in addition to* the agent's occupying such states, his possessing what I have termed a *practical commitment*. Once practical commitment is brought in, however, reference to higher-order preferences or desires in a statement of sufficient conditions of an action's being akratic would be otiose.

I have been operating in this section with a notion of preference that is on all fours with familiar notions of occurrent intentional attitudes generally. Given less restrictive conceptions of preference, we might begin to see higher-order preferences at every turn. Suppose one accepts a view of preference according to which, (1) with respect to any proposition *p* that an agent *S* is *capable* (at *t*) of entertaining (at *t*), *S* (at *t*) either prefers *p* to be true, or prefers *p* to be false, or is indifferent, and (2) not actually entertaining a proposition at a time is not sufficient for being indifferent about that proposition at that time. Then Peter, Sally, Albert, the Bruces, and others may have all sorts of higher-order preferences that I have not countenanced. Such a view, however, places preference at a marked remove from the intentional attitudes commonly accorded causal, explanatory roles with respect to our intentional behavior. Perhaps, armed with a view of this kind, one could provide, in terms of higher-order preferences and desires, analyses of continent and incontinent action that are immune to counterexamples. Perhaps, wherever we find a *practical commitment*, some corresponding (predominant) second- or higher-order preference of the sort at issue could also be located.

Then again, perhaps not. Criteria for the ascription of higher-order preferences on the view in question might generate problems of the sort identified toward the end of section 2. The criteria might be so generous that, in any given case of continent or incontinent action, an agent will count as having competing higher-order preferences at the same level. Further, if practical commitments were themselves used as bases for the attribution of nonoccurrent higher-order attitudes of the kind called for, the game would be lost. In any event, suppose that alternative satisfactory analyses of continent and incontinent action are available, analyses framed in terms of states and events of a sort that plausibly have a clear causal and explanatory bearing upon intentional behavior. Which would you prefer?

Decision theory is a marvelous achievement indeed. Still, a word of warning is in order. Recent years have seen mounting evidence for the thesis that intention—a state presumed by many to have a significant causal, explanatory bearing upon intentional behavior—is not reducible to complexes of beliefs and desires.[27] If the thesis and the presumption are correct, any decision theory bound by a commitment to a pure belief/desire psychology will be of limited use in explaining intentional behavior.[28] Higher-order preferences and desires have a neat, clean slot to fill in a psychology of that type. Intentions and decisions (that is, decisions *to act*), if they are irreducible to belief/desire complexes, do not. And if I am right, executive states of this kind, along with decisive better judgments, play a prominent role in instructive analyses and explanations of continent and incontinent behavior. Since I have addressed the explanatory and etiological issues at some length elsewhere (Mele 1987, 1992a), I judged it best to focus on analytical matters here.

## 5.   The Self-Controlled Person

Exercises of self-control can serve a very wide range of masters, some of which oppose better judgments. Given this truth, can we preserve the traditional view that to be a *self-controlled person* is, in part, to be such that one's exercises of self-control typically serve one's better judgment?

This query is related to the more general question whether being a self-controlled person entails being rational, in a certain sense. The kind of rationality at issue is what may be termed *internal practical rationality*, the coherence of one's intentional behavior with one's own principles and decisive better judgments. However, Donald Davidson has argued, plausibly, that the very activity of interpreting an agent involves the presumption that he is largely rational in this sense (1985b). What evidence could we have that an agent's uncompelled, intentional actions, as often as not, are at odds with his better judgments? If someone were to allege that a particular agent's behavior is only randomly correlated with his better judgments, our natural inclination would be to suppose that his better judgments, or his actions, have been misidentified. And if the very contents of an agent's judgments, desires, and the like are partly determined by the relations that these items bear to one another and to behavior in which they are manifested, this inclination has much to recommend it.[29] So, to keep various apparent possibilities open, let us ask instead whether, as traditional conceptions of self-control suggest, a self-controlled person—precisely because he is such a person—is more likely to act as he judges best than is an akratic counterpart (even if both are largely rational).

The crux of the puzzle is easy to locate. Given that self-control can be exercised in support of intentions, desires, and the like that incline us toward behavior that clashes with our better judgments, how can an agent's being a self-controlled person have any bearing upon the frequency with which he conducts himself as he judges best? It may seem that little weight can be placed on the greater-than-normal powers of self-control traditionally attributed to self-controlled agents, since power can be misused.

Here, appearances are misleading. If, as Davidson insists, any interpretable human agent is largely rational, in the sense that his beliefs, intentions, and the like generally cohere with one another and with his behavior, we should expect this rationality to be exhibited in his exercises of self-control—and, more specifically, in the purposes for which he exercises self-control. In this connection, the self-controlled individual's alleged edge in the power department is quite relevant. Even if the frequency with which self-controlled individuals attempt to exercise self-control in support of their better judgments were not to exceed that of akratic agents, the former agents, owing to their edge in power, would tend to succeed more often. To be sure, owing to their supposed greater power, self-controlled agents may also have a greater rate of success in *errant* exercises of self-control. But given the presumption that every interpretable agent is generally rational, interpretable agents who make attempts at self-control will tend to do so much more often in support of their better judgments than in opposition to them. Greater success in the more limited domain of errant self-control is insufficient to counterbalance the effects of greater power of self-control in the much broader domain. (Skeptical readers need only do a little multiplication and subtraction.)

Though it would be a mistake to let everything rest on power, the matter can fruitfully be pursued a bit further. Self-control can be exercised on a variety of fronts. We can resist the pull of unruly desires and emotions not only in acting as we judge best, but also in reasoning and forming beliefs and intentions in accordance with principles that we judge best. Just as *akrasia* can be exhibited in our actions, in our reasoning, and in our acquisition and retention of beliefs and intentions, so can self-control.[30] A thoroughly self-controlled individual will be possessed of self-control on all of these fronts. Consequently, presuming the general rationality of each interpretable agent, a self-controlled person's edge in power will increase the likelihood that his decisions and intentions conform to his better judgments, thus decreasing the likelihood of akratic decisions and intentions—items that can be served by errant exercises of self-control.

'Power' here can easily be understood too crudely. The bulk of the normal agent's powers of self-control are not mental analogues of brute physical strength. We learn to control our feelings, desires, and the like by promising ourselves rewards for doing so, by directing our attention to certain thoughts or images, by deliberating about the advantages of acting on a certain desire or emotion, and in countless other ways.[31] Our powers of self-control include a variety of skills—and considerable savvy about which skills to use in particular situations. (What I have elsewhere termed the power of *brute resistance*—roughly, the power displayed in an agent's successfully resisting temptation by sheer effort of will—*is* analogous to brute physical strength.)[32]

The self-control of the self-controlled person is not reducible, however, to his pertinent powers/skills. A person who has developed remarkable powers of self-control may, owing to a personal tragedy, lose all motivation to exercise them. A man who recently lost his wife and children in a fatal plane crash may no longer care how he conducts himself, even if, out of habit, he continues to make better judgments: he may suffer from acedia. As a partial consequence, he may cease, for a time, to make any effort at self-control, even when he recognizes that his preponderant motivation is at odds with his better judgments. He may simply act in accordance with whatever happens to be his strongest motivation at the moment, without being at all motivated to bring it about that he acts as he judges best, or to exert an influence over how his motivations stack up. If, as seems plain, we are unwilling to describe such an agent at the time in question as a self-controlled person, we must add to our characterization of the self-controlled agent a motivational element. A self-controlled person cares how he conducts himself—he is a practically concerned individual—and he is appropriately motivated to exercise self-control.

Exercise it in support of what? Notice that although normal (hence, largely rational) human agents do care how they conduct themselves, they do not care *equally* about all of their projects, nor the objects of all of their hopes and desires. Practical concern is not egalitarian in this way. What one cares most about, if one is largely rational, are the things that one deems most important. In a largely rational individual, this variegated system of concerns is reflected in the agent's decisive better judgments. An occasional better judgment may miss the mark; but, on the whole, what an agent judges best indicates what he cares most about. And if it is his lack of practical concern that leads us to withhold the epithet "self-controlled person" from our unfortunate man, we should expect that the presence of such concern in the same man would provide motivation to attempt to make things go as he judges they should go, and motivation to exercise his powers of self-control in support of his decisive better judgments when they are challenged by competing motivation. Given the discriminativeness of practical concern, the self-controlled individual's motivation to exercise self-control will typically be aimed at the support of his decisive better judgments. A largely rational person who does not care equally about the objects of all of his desires will not be uniformly motivated to exercise self-control in support of each of them. Because he is for the most part internally coherent, his motivation to exercise self-control will generally fall in line with his *better judgments*.

The self-controlled person's motivation to exercise self-control, as I am understanding it, is associated with his practical concern—that is, with his caring how he conducts himself, with his not being a victim of acedia. *Because* he cares how he conducts himself, and because practical concern is discriminative in the way explained, he is disposed to see to it that his behavior fits his better judgments. This disposition is a motivational one; and its manifestations include desires for specific exercises of self-control on particular occasions. Such a disposition, I should think, is present to some degree in all normal adult human agents.

A possible misimpression must be corrected. I do not wish to claim that a self-controlled individual *must* have greater powers or skills of self-control than all who lack the trait. Power/skill is one variable, but I have located another. Not everyone is equally motivated to exercise self-control. Someone who cares deeply about his projects, values, and so on (not all of which need be egoistic, of course), and who is, accordingly, strongly motivated to exercise self-control in support of his better judgments, may be possessed only of normal powers of self-control. Such a person may be more self-controlled than someone who has greater powers of self-control but significantly less practical concern.

In this chapter, I have attempted to preserve what seems to me correct in a traditional, Aristotelian conception of continent action, self-control, and the self-controlled person while accommodating the point that self-control can be exercised in support of a wide range of items, and independently of the relation of these items to a decisive better judgment of the agent. My aim in so doing has been to deepen our understanding of self-control, exercises thereof, and the self-controlled person. Exercises of self-control are exercises of capacities (skills or powers) that can be used in support of almost any proattitude. But sufficient conditions for something's being an exercise of self-control should not be confused with sufficient conditions for someone's being a self-controlled person. Further, as I have argued, a self-controlled person is not properly defined simply as someone who is well endowed with these capacities. There is also a motivational constraint. A self-controlled person must be a practically concerned person. This practical concern provides, among other things, motivation to exercise self-control in support of one's better judgments. I return to the self-controlled person in chapter 7, section 5. My concern in the interim is with several domains in which self-control can function.

## Notes

1. Again, for stylistic reasons, I will often use "better judgment" as shorthand for "best or better judgment."

2. See Bigelow, Dodds, and Pargetter 1990, p. 46; Hill 1986, p. 112; Jackson 1984, p. 14; and Mele 1987, pp. 7–8, 54.

3. See, e.g., Dworkin 1988; Frankfurt 1988, 1992; and Lewis 1989. Frankfurt 1988, ch. 2, and Lewis 1989 are instructively criticized in Harman 1993. Frankfurt 1988, ch. 12, includes a response to some criticisms of his earlier work.

4. See *Protagoras* 352b–358d, esp. 358a6–d4. For the suggestion that Euripides, in *Medea* and *Hippolytus*, is responding to Socrates' view, see Collinge 1949–50; Dodds 1951, pp. 196, 199–200; and Snell 1964, pp. 59–68. Irwin 1983 instructively responds to skepticism about this suggestion. For a novel reading of *Medea* according to which the title character sees herself as having equally good reason to kill her children and to spare them, see Rickert 1987.

5. Plato, *Protagoras* 352b–e, *Laws* 689a, b. Cf. Aristotle, *Nicomachean Ethics* 1145b12–13 (reporting common opinion), 1147a10–b5, 1151a20–28.

6. I will assume that Medea killed her children *against* her better judgment and that the murder was *uncompelled*, motivated by *resistible* desires. For my purposes in this chapter,

little hinges on this assumption. Even if the conjunctive assumption is false of Euripides' Medea, it is true of some hypothetical Medea. (For an analysis of irresistible desires, see Mele 1992a, ch. 5.)

7. On avoidability, see ch. 8, sec. 1.

8. On this transition, see ch. 2, sec. 5 and Mele 1992a, ch. 12.

9. Cf. Aristotle's remark that *enkrateia* and *akrasia* "are concerned with that which is in excess of the state characteristic of most men; for the continent man abides by his resolutions more and the incontinent man less than most men can" (*Nicomachean Ethics* 1152a24–27). Also see ch. 1, sec. 1.

10. An uncompelled, intentional action performed on the basis of a decisive better judgment produced by akratic reasoning is *derivatively* akratic, but it is not an instance of strict akratic action, as characterized in ch. 2, sec. 1. On derivatively akratic behavior, see Mele 1987, pp. 6, 17–18, 30.

11. For useful discussions of the respective bearings of desire and intention on intentional action, see Brand 1984, ch. 5, and Bratman 1987, pp. 18–20. See also see Mele 1992a.

12. This view is advanced in Bigelow, Dodds, and Pargetter 1990. For a similar position on akratic action in particular, see Schiffer 1976. See also Swanton 1992, ch. 10: Swanton contends that "in the context of weakness of will, the will should be identified with strong evaluation," where strong evaluation is a certain kind of "evaluative second-order desire" (p. 149).

13. For a defense of this way of viewing things, see Mele 1992a, ch. 3, sec.1.

14. On some relevant complications, see Mele 1992a, p. 85, n. 6, and pp. 113–15, 174–75.

15. This point is ably defended in Foot 1978, ch. 13.

16. On broader and narrower conceptions of continent action, see Mele 1987, pp. 99–101. As I have mentioned, one may push for an even narrower conception than the one just sketched. But the harder one pushes, the harder it is to see continent and incontinent behavior as two sides of the same coin.

17. For some complications, see Pink 1991 and Mele 1992c. For a response to Pink, see Mele 1992b.

18. This obviously is different from the question "What *will* I do?" The latter question calls for a prediction; the former calls for a decision or intention.

19. Mele 1992a, chs. 9, 10; cf. Brand 1984, p. 127, and Castañeda 1975, p. 284.

20. For a variety of alleged differences between desire and intention, see Brand 1984, pp. 121–27; Bratman 1987, pp. 15–20; Harman 1986, p. 83; and McCann 1986b, pp. 193–94. In Mele 1992a, ch. 9, I argue that wanting *most* to A is neither sufficient nor necessary for being settled upon A-ing. See also Bratman 1987, McCann 1986b.

21. Notice that an agent who has a preponderant desire to A—even an irresistible preponderant desire—need not be settled upon A-ing. Such an agent may believe that it would be best not to A, and he may be settled upon doing his best to bring it about that he refrains from A-ing.

22. In a variant of the case, the agent might have judged it best to chicken out. Even then, there is a difference between chickening out on the basis of one's better judgment and chickening out that is not so based.

23. 'Continence' may also be used in this sense.

24. Jeffrey remarks: "'*OX*' is best read, 'Making *X* true is an option', and that may be taken as the intent of my barbarous '*X* is an option'" (1974, p. 386).

25. Contrast Bigelow, Dodds, and Pargetter 1990, p. 46: "In normal cases, a person who believes an action is morally right will also want to do what is right. In wanting to do what is right, they will have a desire that their operative desire be aligned with what is right." No argument is offered for the second sentence in this passage.

26. Readers who find it implausible that the polite second-order preference is not extinguished once Peter becomes upset with himself should observe that Peter's feelings for his date may be out of line with his current feelings about smokers' rights. Readers who are unmoved by this should suppose that the polite second-order preference is sustained by an external force (e.g., a handy demon).

27. In addition to the work cited in n. 19, see Davidson 1980, ch. 5, and Searle 1983.

28. Bigelow et al. are explicitly concerned to defend just such a theory and to display its resources for characterizing and explaining continent and incontinent behavior (1990, p. 39).

29. See Davidson 1980, ch. 14; 1982; 1984, chs. 9–11; and 1985b. For Davidson, *actions* are mental events (1980, p. 211).

30. On akratic practical reasoning and intentions, see Audi 1979; Mele 1987, pp. 34–35, 52–54; and Rorty 1980b. On akratic belief, see Davidson 1985c; Heil 1984; Mele 1987, ch. 8; Pears 1984, ch. 4; and Rorty 1983.

31. For a discussion of various strategies of self-control, see Mele 1987, pp. 23–27, 50–61, 88–90. See also Ainslie 1992, Elster 1984, and Thoresen and Mahoney 1974.

32. For an account, see Mele 1987, p. 26.

# 5

# Self-Control and Belief

One of my aims in part I of this book is to characterize an ideally self-controlled person, thereby providing a partial framework for the discussion of personal autonomy in part II. If there is such a thing as *doxastic* self-control (from *doxa*: opinion, belief), an ideally self-controlled person will possess it. Again, exercises of self-control oppose something in support of something else. In "orthodox" cases, they support a better judgment against (actual or anticipated) opposing motivation. My primary concerns in this chapter are with motivated instances of believing that violate a better judgment held by the believer and with our prospects for avoiding such instances of believing by exercising self-control.

## 1.  Biased Beliefs

So-called biased or irrational beliefs are biased or irrational relative to some standards or other.[1] In the context of a discussion of doxastic self-control, the most relevant standards are the believer's own. Biased beliefs divide into two general kinds— unmotivated and motivated, or "cold" and "hot." The extent to which motivational factors are involved in the production and sustaining of biased beliefs continues to be a source of controversy in social psychology, but even influential proponents of the "colder" views admit that "many inferential errors . . . can be traced to motivational or emotional causes" (Nisbett and Ross 1980, p. 228).[2]

Psychologists have identified a number of sources of *unmotivated*, biased belief. Attention to the following four proved particularly useful in my attempt to resolve a certain problem about self-deception in *Irrationality* (Mele 1987, ch. 10).[3]

1. *Vividness of information.* The vividness of a datum for an individual is often a function of his interests, the concreteness of the datum, its "imagery-provoking" power, or its sensory, temporal, or spatial proximity (Nisbett and Ross 1980, p. 45). Vivid data are more likely to be recognized, attended to, and recalled than pallid data. As a result, vivid data tend to have a disproportional influence on the formation and retention of beliefs.[4]
2. *The availability heuristic.* When people make judgments about the frequency, likelihood, or causation of an event, "they often may be influenced by the relative availability of the objects or events, that is, their accessibility in the

processes of perception, memory, or construction from imagination" (Nisbett and Ross 1980, p. 18). Thus, for example, a subject may mistakenly believe that the number of English words beginning with '*r*' is significantly higher than the number having '*r*' in the third position, because he finds it much easier to produce words on the basis of a search for their first letter (see Tversky and Kahnemann 1973). Similarly, attempts to locate the cause(s) of an event are significantly influenced by manipulations that focus one's attention on a potential cause (Nisbett and Ross 1980, p. 22; Taylor and Fiske 1975, 1978). "[B]y altering actors' and observers' perspectives through video tape replays, mirrors, or other methods, one can correspondingly alter the actors' and observers' causal assessments" (Nisbett and Ross 1980, p. 22).

3. *The confirmation bias.* When testing a hypothesis people tend to search (in memory and the world) more often for confirming than for disconfirming instances and to recognize the former more readily (Nisbett and Ross 1980, pp. 181–82). This is true even when the hypothesis is only a tentative one (as opposed, e.g., to a belief of one's that one is testing). The implications of this tendency for the retention and formation of beliefs are obvious.

4. *Tendency to search for causal explanations.* People tend to search for causal explanations of events (Nisbett and Ross 1980, pp. 183–86). On a plausible view of the macroscopic workings of the world, this is as it should be. But given (1) and (2) above, the causal explanations upon which we so easily hit in ordinary life may often be ill founded; and, given (3), one is likely to endorse and retain one's first hypothesis much more often than one ought. Furthermore, ill-founded causal explanations can influence future inferences.

These sources of biased belief are capable of functioning independently of motivation, but they may also be primed, as it were, by motivation in the production of particular *motivated* biased beliefs.[5] For example, motivation can enhance the vividness or salience of certain data. Data that count in favor of (the truth of) a hypothesis that one would like to be true may be rendered more vivid or salient given one's recognition that they so count; and vivid or salient data, given that they are more likely to be recalled, tend to be more "available" than pallid counterparts. Similarly, motivation can influence which hypotheses occur to one (including causal hypotheses) and affect the salience of available hypotheses, thereby setting the stage for an operation of the confirmation bias.

A host of studies have produced results that are far from surprising, on the hypothesis that motivation sometimes biases beliefs. Thomas Gilovich reports, "A survey of one million high school seniors found that 70% thought they were above average in leadership ability, and only 2% thought they were below average. In terms of ability to get along with others, *all* students thought they were above average, 60% thought they were in the top 10%, and 25% thought they were in the top 1%! . . . A survey of university professors found that 94% thought they were better at their jobs than their average colleague" (1991, p. 77). Similarly, Jonathan Baron cites evidence that "most drivers believe that they are safer and more skillful than average, and . . . most people believe that they are more likely than average to live past

80" (1988, p. 271). Apparently, we have a tendency to believe propositions that we want to be true even when an impartial investigation of readily available data would indicate that they are probably false. A plausible hypothesis about that tendency is that our *wanting* something to be true sometimes exerts an influence on what we believe.

Ziva Kunda, in a recent review essay, marshals empirical support for the view that motivation can influence "the generation and evaluation of hypotheses, of inference rules, and of evidence" and that motivationally "biased memory search will result in the formation of additional biased beliefs and theories that are constructed so as to justify desired conclusions" (Kunda 1990, p. 483). In a particularly persuasive study, undergraduate subjects (seventy-five women and eighty-six men) read an article alleging that "women were endangered by caffeine and were strongly advised to avoid caffeine in any form"; that the major danger was fibrocystic disease, "associated in its advanced stages with breast cancer"; and that "caffeine induced the disease by increasing the concentration of a substance called cAMP in the breast" (Kunda 1987, p. 642). (Since the article did not personally threaten men, they were used as a control group.) Subjects were then asked to indicate, among other things, "how convinced they were of the connection between caffeine and fibrocystic disease and of the connection between caffeine and . . . cAMP on a 6-point scale" (pp. 643–44). In the female group, "heavy consumers" of caffeine were significantly less convinced of the connections than were "low consumers." The males were considerably more convinced than the female "heavy consumers"; and there was a much smaller difference in conviction between "heavy" and "low" male caffeine consumers (the heavy consumers were slightly *more* convinced of the connections).

Given that all subjects were exposed to the same information and assuming that only the female "heavy consumers" were personally threatened by it, a plausible hypothesis is that their lower level of conviction is due to "motivational processes designed to preserve optimism about their future health" (Kunda 1987, p. 644). Indeed, in another study, in which the reported hazards of caffeine use were relatively modest, "female heavy consumers were no less convinced by the evidence than were female low consumers" (p. 644). Along with the lesser threat, there is less motivation for skepticism about the evidence.

*How* do the female heavy consumers manage to be less convinced than the others? One possibility—a testable one—is that, because they find the "connections" at issue personally threatening, these women (or some of them) are motivated to take a hypercritical stance toward the article, looking much harder than other subjects for reasons to be skeptical about the merits of its contents (cf. Kunda 1990, p. 495). Another testable possibility is that, owing to the threatening nature of the article, they (or some of them) read it *less* carefully than the others do, thereby enabling themselves to be less impressed by it.[6]

At any rate, since motivation can bias our beliefs, there might be a place for doxastic self-control in our lives. That will depend on whether we are capable of exercising self-control in such a way as to moderate the effects of motivation on belief, an issue addressed in section 3. It depends, as well, on whether motivation can bias our beliefs relative to *our own* doxastic standards or principles.

## 2.  Characterizing Continent and Incontinent Belief

One way to approach the psychological possibility of doxastic self-control or doxastic *akrasia* is to ask what it would be like to believe continently or incontinently. If beliefs were actions, prior characterizations of continent and incontinent action would provide the answer. But, of course, they are not. Actions are events, beliefs are states of mind, and even though *acquiring* a belief is an event, it is not (at least characteristically) an action.

Akratic action manifests weakness of will, or at least an associated imperfection. Similarly, continent action, on all but very thin conceptions, manifests self-control. The same is true of incontinent and continent belief. *Akrasia* is, by definition, a deficient capacity to contain or restrain one's desires, broadly conceived; akratic episodes, whether actional or doxastic, manifest this deficiency or an associated imperfection. Similarly, continent belief, if there is such a thing, requires self-control.

The agent who performs a strict akratic action acts against a consciously held better judgment. What sorts of better judgment might be violated in cases of akratic belief, or served by an exercise of self-control in instances of continent belief?[7] Here are two possibilities: (*J1*) the judgment that it is best not to allow what one wants to be the case to determine what one believes *is* the case; (*J2*) the judgment, in a particular case, that it is best to believe that *p* (cf. Mele 1987, p. 56). Judgments of the second sort are particularly relevant to a doxastic analogue of *strict* akratic action—*strict akratic belief*. In *Irrationality*, I characterized that doxastic phenomenon and offered an explanation of its psychological possibility and its occurrence (Mele 1987, ch. 8); I set it aside here. Judgments of the first sort are expressive of a general *principle* that an agent might accept concerning proper belief formation, belief retention, and belief revision—a principle relevant to the possibility of *nonstrict* akratic belief.

In instances of *strict* akratic action, again, the agent *A*-s intentionally, is not compelled to *A*, and consciously holds at the time a decisive judgment that it would be best not to *A*. In *nonstrict*, "orthodox" cases, the judgment condition is not satisfied. Aristotle mentions an impetuous, akratic agent who is influenced by desire in such a way that he does not look before he leaps (*Nicomachean Ethics* 1150b19–28). In the grip of a desire to *A*, he *A*-s straightaway; but if he had paused to deliberate about the merits of *A*-ing, he would easily have seen that the action violates his principles, he would have judged it best not to *A*, and he would have resisted the temptation to *A*. Assuming that the agent was capable of deliberating at the time and that he accepts a principle urging deliberation in situations like the one at issue, we can say that his action was *indirectly* akratic. *Akrasia* is exhibited in his desire-influenced nondeliberation and, derivatively, in his *A*-ing. Similarly, owing to desire, even an agent who *does* deliberate about the merits of *A*-ing may fail to see that his *A*-ing would violate a principle of his. For example, an athlete who decisively judges it best never to engage in behavior likely to endanger his career, may, owing to a powerful desire to excel, seriously underestimate the risk involved in using steroids and consequently engage in career-threatening use of the drug. He does not decisively judge it best to refrain from using steroids. Still, if his assessment of the risk itself manifests *akrasia*, then given the supposed connection between that assessment and his use of steroids, his use of the drug is derivatively akratic.

For the purposes of a comparison with nonstrict akratic belief, the point to be emphasized is that the performance of a nonstrict, orthodox, akratic action *A* may violate a principle that the agent accepts—even though he does not make or hold a decisive judgment at the time that it would be best not to *A*. Similarly, a person may akratically believe that *p* while not holding a decisive judgment that it would be best not to believe that *p*. The belief may be akratic in virtue of its having been generated by an akratic assessment of evidence, for example; the believer might have (avoidably) assessed the evidence in a way that violates a doxastic principle that he accepts.

A word of warning is in order. Not all of an agent's doxastic principles need be aimed at tracking truth. H. H. Price writes that in Victorian novels, "[L]adies acknowledged a moral obligation to believe that their husbands and fiancés were impeccably virtuous," and that some have "held that there was a moral obligation to believe that all the members of one's family were persons of the highest excellence, or at least of great excellence" (1954, pp. 13–14). Someone may accept the seemingly more reasonable principle that it is best not to believe ill of members of one's family, unless and until one has overwhelming evidence of wrongdoing on their part. The same person may endorse a considerably less generous principle about believing ill of people to whom he has no special ties.

Although there is much to recommend the popular view that "belief aims at truth" (Williams 1973, p. 151), not all reasons for believing have truth as their target. There is a difference between what may be termed *alethic* (from '*aletheia*': truth) and *practical* reasons for belief. Our alethic reasons for believing that *p* are constituted by our evidence for the truth of *p*. Our practical reasons for believing that *p*, by contrast, are analogues of reasons for action. On the assumption that reasons for performing an action *A* typically are constituted by desires for *x* and beliefs to the effect that one's *A*-ing would (or might) be in some way conducive to one's securing *x*, practical reasons for believing that *p* typically are constituted by desires for *x* together with beliefs to the effect that one's *believing that p* would (or might) conduce to one's securing *x*.[8] Someone who is convinced, for example, that his continuing to believe that God exists is crucial for his own well-being may have a practical reason for continuing so to believe (on the assumption that he desires his well-being).[9]

Return to reasons for *action*. Even if an agent would satisfy one of his fondest desires by *A*-ing and knows that he would, it is not clear that he has a reason for *A*-ing independently of his being *able* to *A*, or independently of what he believes about his abilities. A trustworthy billionaire promises Sam a million dollars for swimming a mile tomorrow. Sam covets the money and believes that it will be his if he swims a mile tomorrow. But Sam knows that he swims like a rock; it is painfully evident to him that he is incapable of radically improving his swimming skills by tomorrow. Does Sam have a reason to swim a mile tomorrow—one constituted by the desire and belief mentioned? I have addressed this issue elsewhere (Mele 1992c, pp. 186–89) and will not do so again here. Readers inclined to hold that Sam does have a reason for swimming a mile tomorrow may be inclined to hold, as well, that having a practical reason to believe that *p* is open even to someone who knows that believing that *p* is not a genuine option for him. Readers disinclined to take this view about Sam may be similarly disinclined to take it about counterpart doxastic cases. I will leave both views about possessing practical reasons open.[10] A related point requires attention.

One can hold that we sometimes have practical reasons for belief and take an ability-sensitive position on such reasons without committing oneself to the view that we can *believe at will*. Return to Sam. He is unable, as he knows, to swim a mile tomorrow. But suppose that the billionaire promises him the money for swimming a mile a year from now. Even on an ability-sensitive position about the having of reasons, Sam might now have both an excellent reason to swim a mile at the appointed time and an excellent reason to start taking steps soon to bring it about that he will swim a mile then. Similarly, beings who cannot believe things at will may nevertheless be able to take steps to bring it about that they acquire certain beliefs. Perhaps they can also take measures to forestall motivationally biased believing in some cases—a matter taken up in section 3. At any rate, it is no part of the view to be proposed that people can believe at will, or that they have, accordingly, *direct* control over what they believe. Doxastic self-control does not require such control; nor does the possession of practical reasons for belief, even on an ability-sensitive conception of the having of reasons.

It might be said that a being who cannot believe at will cannot, strictly speaking, have practical reasons for believing that $p$; at most, he can have practical reasons for bringing it about that he believes that $p$, or for trying to bring this about. For my purposes, the expression "practical reason for believing that $p$" can be treated as shorthand for "practical reason for bringing it about that one believes that $p$, or for trying to do so." A principle urging one to try to bring about beliefs of a certain kind would count as a *doxastic* principle, and my reason for taking up "practical reasons for belief" is to elaborate a point about doxastic principles and their bearing on incontinent and continent belief. However, it is worth noting that we have reasons for performing actions that we cannot perform at will. For instance, a quarterback may now have an excellent reason to throw a touchdown pass on the next play: he needs to throw one if his team is to win. But he cannot throw a touchdown pass at will. His throwing one depends on a receiver catching the ball, for example. Given that some of the actions that we have reasons to perform are not actions that we can perform at will, why can't we have reasons to believe that $p$ while being unable to believe that $p$ at will?

Perhaps it will be said that anything that we have a reason to *do* is, at least, something that we can do *intentionally*, but we cannot believe that $p$ *intentionally* (although we may intentionally bring it about that we believe that $p$).[11] The first conjunct is disputable. Yesterday, I had a reason to sink a hole-in-one. If I had sunk it, I would have won the golf match; and the distance on the par-three hole was well within my range. But, at least on some popular conceptions of intentional action, I am not sufficiently in control of the accuracy of my drives for my sinking a hole-in-one (under normal conditions) to be intentional.[12]

It might be urged that actions are at least things of a *kind* that can be done intentionally whereas beliefs are not. If one takes that observation to inform one's conviction that we cannot, *strictly speaking*, have practical reasons for belief, so be it. We can still have practical reasons for bringing it about that we believe that $p$, and we can have, in that sense, practical reasons for belief, *loosely speaking*.[13]

Now, just as a person who cares about morality can judge that his *A*-ing would be morally better than his *B*-ing while also judging that, all things considered, his *B*-ing would be better than his *A*-ing, a person who cares about truth can judge that his believing that *p* would be alethically better than his believing that not-*p* while also judging that, all things considered, it would be better to believe that not-*p* than to believe that *p*. More simply, the latter person can judge that his evidence for *p* is stronger than his evidence for not-*p* while also judging that his believing that not-*p* would be better on the whole than his believing that *p*. A case in point might be a theist whose religious faith is shaken by his introductory course in the philosophy of religion. The person might come to judge that his evidence for the nonexistence of his god is considerably stronger than his evidence for the existence of that god, but judge, as well, that it would be better on the whole to retain his belief than to abandon it. (Whether he *can* retain—or abandon—the belief under these conditions is a distinct matter. But notice that, under the conditions described, the person might believe that his own evidence is quite limited by comparison with the evidence that might, in principle, be available.)[14]

The moral, for present purposes, is that not all motivationally biased belief need be akratic belief, even if the biasing is avoidable. Such biasing, in some cases, may accord with a doxastic principle, or a relevant judgment, that the believer (non-akratically) accepts. Nonstrict akratic believing may be characterized, tentatively, as motivated believing that violates a doxastic principle accepted by the believer and that was suitably avoidable by the believer by means of an employment of self-control. Nonstrict *continent* believing may similarly be construed (again tentatively) as believing that accords with a doxastic principle accepted by the believer and that was suitably promoted by the believer's exercising self-control.

What does "acceptance" of a doxastic principle amount to? Certainly, that one's relevant doxastic conduct regularly accords with doxastic principle *D* does not suffice for acceptance of *D*. Consider the "anchoring effect," the tendency of our estimates to be sensitive to—"anchored by"—estimates that we have been given, even when we know that the initial estimates are arbitrary (Tversky and Kahnemann 1973). *S*'s estimating behavior may consistently conform to the following anchoring principle: "Whenever other estimates have been offered to one, base one's own estimates partly on the offered estimates, whatever the source of the offered estimates might have been." But we should not infer from this that *S accepts* that principle. If *S* were asked whether the principle is a good one, he might immediately point to major flaws in it, and he might be surprised to discover that his own estimating behavior, and that of many others, accords with this principle. One might, in fact, *reject* a principle to which one's cognitive behavior conforms.

Is it a *necessary* condition of accepting a doxastic principle *D* that one's doxastic conduct regularly accords with *D*, or, at least, accords with *D* more often than it violates *D*? If it were to turn out that one can believe that a doxastic principle is correct even though one's relevant doxastic conduct rarely conforms to the principle and that a particular agent, *S*, is in this condition with respect to doxastic principle *D*, would this preclude its being true that *S accepts D*? Of course, one may choose to use the expression "*S* accepts a doxastic principle" in such a way that *S*'s so doing requires more than *S*'s believing the principle to be correct. Alternatively, one may identify accepting a doxastic principle with believing it to be correct but hold that the latter entails conformity of one's doxastic conduct to the principle. The second alternative is unpromising. *S* may believe to be correct a doxastic principle speaking against the anchoring of one's estimates by arbitrary estimates that one has been given, and yet regularly unwittingly fall prey to the anchoring bias. Believing a doxastic principle to be correct does not ensure appropriate, effective vigilance.

For my purposes in this chapter, explicitly believing a doxastic principle to be correct suffices for explicitly accepting it. That is how *I choose* to use the expression "*S* accepts a doxastic principle."[15] Whether one can explicitly accept a doxastic principle that one does not explicitly believe to be correct is a question that can safely go unanswered here. (Notice that a noncognitivist about acceptance of doxastic principles would be quite happy to countenance explicit acceptance of doxastic principles that one does not believe to be correct.)

More important, for my purposes, is the observation that someone who does not explicitly accept a doxastic principle may *implicitly* accept it. Consider a geographically knowledgeable New Yorker who explicitly accepts W. K. Clifford's principle that "it is always wrong, everywhere, and for anyone, to believe anything upon insufficient evidence" (1886, p. 346). Supposing that he has never entertained the principle that it is wrong for anyone *in Iowa* to believe anything upon insufficient evidence, he does not *explicitly* accept that principle; but, other things being equal, he *implicitly* accepts it. We can say that, other things being equal, one implicitly accepts all principles that satisfy the following two conditions: (1) they are obviously implied (where obviousness is relativized to the accepter) by principles that one explicitly accepts together with propositions that one knows to be true; (2) one does not *explicitly* accept them.

The *ceteris paribus* clause is an important one. Sometimes, one is led to reject a principle that one accepts by the realization that the principle (together with propositions that one knows or believes to be true) implies another principle that one deems unacceptable. Prior to recognizing the implication—an obvious one, let us suppose—does the person implicitly accept the implied principle? Well, in one sense he does: it is obviously implied by a principle that he accepts (together with background knowledge or beliefs). In another sense, he might not. If he is psychologically so constituted that upon entertaining the implied principle he would reject, on reasoned grounds, both it and the principle that implies it, we might be disinclined to view him as implicitly accepting the principle. If so, the latter sense of "implicit acceptance" might be sensitive to a conception of the phenomenon entailing that (other things being equal) one implicitly accepts only those principles that one would accept if one both entertained and understood them.

I have no wish to offer an *analysis* of "accepting a principle," implicitly or otherwise.[16] For my purposes in this chapter, it suffices to have an understanding of a central range of cases of accepting a doxastic principle.

In some circumstances, doxastic principles that an agent accepts may yield or support conflicting prescriptions.[17] It may even happen that a doxastic principle conflicts (in this sense) with a principle of another kind. For example, an agent who accepts the principle that he should always avoid courses of action that he deems likely to make him unhappy may also accept a doxastic principle that prescribes, in a certain scenario, a course of investigative action that he deems likely to make him unhappy. In cases of either kind, an agent may nonakratically judge that one principle takes precedence over the other. Other things being equal, his not abiding by the subjectively trumped principle does not manifest *akrasia*.

To simplify matters, I limit my discussion of akratic and continent belief to cases in which the relevant doxastic principle is not in competition with any other principle of the agent's. Given this limitation, and in light of my discussion of acceptance, I substitute the following characterizations of two *central ranges* of cases for my earlier, tentative characterizations of nonstrict akratic and continent believing. First, a central range of cases of *nonstrict akratic believing* is constituted by instances of motivated believing that (1) violate a doxastic principle that the believer, *S*, either explicitly believes to be correct or undeniably implicitly accepts, which principle is not in competition with any other principle of *S*'s and that (2) were suitably avoidable by *S* by means of an employment of self-control. Second, a central range of cases of *nonstrict continent believing* is constituted by instances of believing that (1) accord with a doxastic principle that the believer, *S*, either explicitly believes to be correct or undeniably implicitly accepts, which principle is not in competition with any other principle of *S*'s and that (2) were suitably promoted by *S*'s exercising self-control.

The first of these two characterizations requires further attention on grounds that are of general significance for akratic episodes in any sphere (belief, action, emotion, etc.). When characterizing strict akratic action, I observed that it is, by definition, *uncompelled*. However, even setting aside deterministic worries (see ch. 8, sec. 1), not all imaginable uncompelled actions are *avoidable* by the agent. Imagine that a weak-willed agent, Brian, owing to the influence of desires that do not have compelling force for him, eats an extra piece of pie, intentionally and against his decisive better judgment. As it happened, there was a very powerful demon on the scene, an infallible mind-reader, who would have given Brian an irresistibly strong desire to eat the pie, if he had seen that Brian was not about to eat an extra helping— a desire so strong that it would have been psychologically impossible for Brian to refrain from eating the pie. Since the demon did not actually interfere, things transpired exactly as they would have transpired (for all relevant purposes) if the demon had been absent. Thus, Brian's eating the pie is a manifestation of his weakness of will; it is an akratic action even though he could not have avoided eating the pie. Readers familiar with Harry Frankfurt's attack on the principle of alternative possibilities (e.g., Frankfurt 1988, ch. 1), will recognize the inspiration for the scenario just presented. I will call such cases *Frankfurt-style cases*.[18]

A strictly analogous case can be constructed for akratic belief. An agent, owing appropriately to *akrasia*, acquires a belief that *p*; but if he had not acquired it in this way, a demon would have caused him to believe that *p* and would have done so in such a way that the agent could not prevent this from happening. The agent akratically acquires a belief that *p* even though his acquiring a belief that *p* was not avoidable by him. The easy way to resolve the apparent problem for my characterization of "*a central range* of cases of nonstrict incontinent believing" is to note that that range includes no Frankfurt-style cases—that is, no cases in which, if the causal process that actually issued in the agent's believing that *p* had not done so, a causal process that did not actually occur would have occurred and would have "compelled" the agent to believe that $p$ (at the pertinent time). A much harder route would involve developing an analysis of *compelled belief*. With the analysis in hand, the "suitable avoidability" condition could be replaced with a noncompulsion condition. Fortunately, owing to the plain *truth* of the observation that Frankfurt-style cases are not among the central range of cases of nonstrict akratic belief, the harder road need not be traveled.

## 3.   Self-Control and Self-Deception

Are there genuine occurrences of continent and incontinent believing in these ranges? Discussion of this question may come into clearer focus if we ask whether garden-variety instances of self-deception are avoidable by means of an employment of self-control. (Having argued in *Irrationality*, chs. 9 and 10, that self-deception is a genuine phenomenon, I take that for granted here.)

For the most part, people who deceive themselves into believing that $p$ want it to be the case that $p$.[19] To take some stock examples, people who deceive themselves into believing that their spouses are not engaged in extramarital flings normally want it to be true that they are not so engaged, and parents who deceive themselves into believing that their children were erroneously convicted of a crime normally want it to be the case that they are innocent of that crime.

In *Irrationality*, I identified some common ways in which desire can lead to biased belief in cases of self-deception (Mele 1987, pp. 125–26).[20]

1. *Negative misinterpretation. S*'s desiring that $p$ may lead him to misinterpret as not counting against $p$ (or as not counting strongly against $p$) data that, in the absence of the desire that $p$, he would, if the occasion arose, easily recognize to count (or count strongly) against $p$. Imagine a scholar who has just been informed that an article of his was not accepted for publication. He hopes that it was *wrongly* rejected, and he reads through the comments offered. He decides that the referees misunderstood a certain crucial but complex point, that their objections consequently miss the mark, and that the paper should have been accepted. However, as it turns out, the referees' criticisms were entirely justified; a few weeks later, when he rereads his paper and the comments in a more impartial frame of mind, it is clear to him that this is so.

2. *Positive misinterpretation. S*'s desiring that $p$ may lead $S$ to interpret as supporting $p$ data which count against $p$, and which, in the absence of this desire, $S$ would easily recognize to count against $p$ (if he considered the data). Sid is very fond of Roz, a young woman with whom he often eats lunch. If he wants it to be the case that Roz loves him, he may interpret her refusing to go out on dates with him and her reminding him that she is very much in love with her steady boyfriend, Tim, as an effort on her part to "play hard to get" in order to encourage Sid to continue to pursue her.

3. *Selective focusing/attending. S*'s desiring that $p$ may lead him both to fail to focus his attention on evidence that counts against $p$ and to focus instead on

evidence suggestive of *p*. Attentional behavior may be either intentional or unintentional. *S* may tell himself that it is a waste of time to consider his evidence that his wife is having an affair, since she just is not the sort of person who would do such a thing; and he may intentionally act accordingly. Or, because of the unpleasantness of such thoughts, he may find his attention shifting whenever the issue suggests itself to him. Failure to focus on contrary evidence, like negative misinterpretation, may contribute negatively to *S*'s acquiring the belief that *p*; for, other things being equal, it may be the case that if *S* had focused his attention on his evidence for not-*p*, he would not have acquired the belief that *p*. Selective focusing on supporting evidence may contribute positively to *S*'s coming to believe that *p*.

4. *Selective evidence gathering.* *S*'s desiring that *p* may lead him both to overlook easily obtained evidence for not-*p* and to find evidence for *p* that is much less accessible. Consider the historian of philosophy who holds a certain philosophical position, wants it to be the case that her favorite philosopher did so too, and consequently scours the texts for evidence that he did while consulting commentaries that she thinks will provide support for the favored interpretation. Our historian may easily miss rather obvious evidence to the contrary, even though she succeeds in finding obscure evidence for her favored interpretation. Such one-sided evidence gathering may contribute both positively and negatively to the acquisition of the false belief that *p*. Consequently, one might wish to analyze selective evidence gathering as a combination of hypersensitivity to evidence (and sources of evidence) for the desired state of affairs and blindness—of which there are, of course, degrees—to contrary evidence (and sources thereof).

This list, the earlier list of some sources of unmotivated, biased belief, and the observation that the latter sources can be primed by motivation collectively provide a rich background against which the avoidability of self-deception by means of an employment of self-control can be investigated. If an agent were intentionally to deceive himself, without compulsion and against a decisive better judgment consciously held at the time, his so doing would be an instance of strict akratic *action*. (Intentionally deceiving someone is plainly an action.) I have argued in *Irrationality* that self-deception commonly is *not* intentional (1987, chs. 9, 10). Still, this does not preclude the involvement of *akrasia* in garden-variety (hence nonintentional) instances of self-deception. That a self-deceived person did not intentionally deceive himself leaves it open that he akratically conducted himself in ways that violated his doxastic principles. It is left open, for example, that someone who accepts a principle expressed by judgment *J1* may, owing to weakness, allow himself to be unduly influenced by what he wants to be the case in acquiring or retaining the belief that *p*.

I have already argued that motivation sometimes biases belief. If it is also true that it sometimes does so in ways that violate a doxastic principle that the believer accepts and that, in some such cases, it was within the believer's power successfully to resist motivationally biased believing, we have all we need for akratic belief— belief that manifests "weakness of will," or an associated imperfection. Of course, whether a motivationally biased belief violates the believer's doxastic principles depends on what the believer's principles *are*. Other things being equal, the less exacting one's doxastic standards, the less likely one is to violate them. But none of us is immune to the biasing influence of motivation on belief, and some of us accept doxastic principles that are violated by some of our motivated beliefs—for example, a principle expressed by *J1*. So we are left with the issue of resistibility.

One naturally hopes that discovery of sources and mechanisms of biased belief will itself promote unbiased believing. The hope is bluntly expressed by psychologist Jonathan Baron, in a book on rational thinking and associated obstacles: "If people *know* that their thinking is poor, they will not believe its results. One of the purposes of a book like this is to make recognition of poor thinking more widespread, so that it will no longer be such a handy means of self-deception" (1988, p. 39). There is a lively debate in social psychology about the extent to which sources of biased belief are subject to our control.[21] And there is evidence that some prominent sources of bias are to some degree controllable. For example, subjects instructed to conduct "symmetrical memory searches" are less likely than others to fall prey to the confirmation bias, and subjects' confidence in their responses to "knowledge questions" is reduced when they are invited to provide grounds for doubting the correctness of those responses (Kunda 1990, pp. 494–95). Presumably, people aware of the confirmation bias may reduce biased thinking in themselves by *giving themselves* the former instruction, and, fortunately, we do sometimes remind ourselves to consider both the pros *and* the cons before making up our minds about the truth of important propositions—even when we are tempted to do otherwise.

People have been aware of biased thinking for centuries, of course. Even Plato warned against self-deception: "there is nothing worse than self-deception—when the deceiver is at home and always with you" (*Cratylus* 428d). This awareness itself promotes our prospects for doxastic self-control. As I noted in *Irrationality*, "[O]ne might suppose that when mechanisms of 'cold' irrational belief work in conjunction with motivational elements, the doxastic agent is at the mercy of forces beyond his control" (1987, pp. 147–48). But, as I also pointed out, "[T]his is to take the image of combined forces too seriously. Indeed, I suspect that when motivation activates a cold mechanism, the ordinary agent is more likely to detect bias in his thinking than he would be if motivation were not involved; and detection facilitates control. The popular psychology of the industrialized Western world certainly owes a great deal more to Freud than to the attribution theorists; and for members of that world, a thought-biasing 'wish' is likely to be more salient than, for example, a 'cold' failure to attend to base-rate information." The *extent* of doxastic self-control is an empirical issue in need of further empirical investigation. That we do have some control over the influence of motivation on our beliefs is, however, indisputable.

Return to a stock example of self-deception:

> Sam has believed for many years that his wife, Sally, would never have an affair. In the past, his evidence for this belief was quite good. Sally obviously adored him; she never displayed a sexual interest in another man . . .; she condemned extramarital sexual activity; she was secure, and happy with her family life; and so on. However, things recently began to change significantly. Sally is now arriving home late from work on the average of two nights a week; she frequently finds excuses to leave the house alone after dinner; and Sam has been informed by a close friend that Sally has been seen in the company of a certain Mr. Jones at a theater and local lounge. Nevertheless, Sam continues to believe that Sally would never have an affair.

Unfortunately, he is wrong. Her relationship with Jones is by no means platonic. (Mele 1987, pp. 131–32)

In general, the stronger the evidence one has against a proposition that one believes (or "against the belief," for short), the harder it is to retain the belief. Perhaps in this case, Sam's evidence against his favored belief is, at once, not so strong as to render self-deception psychologically impossible and not so weak as to make a charge of self-deception implausible. Supposing that Sam is properly regarded as self-deceived, his retention of the belief at issue is not difficult to explain. The confirmation bias, primed by a desire that Sally not be having an affair, may be at work: Sam may look primarily for evidence that confirms his favored belief and attend more carefully to evidence supportive of this belief than to disconfirming evidence, without realizing that this is what he is doing. Sam may positively misinterpret the evidence. Reasoning that if Sally *were* having an affair, she would want to hide it and consequently would not allow herself to be seen in public with her lover, he may conclude that the reports of her association with Jones are evidence that Sally is *not* having an affair with him. Similarly, he may negatively misinterpret his evidence, and even recruit Sally to this end by suggesting for her approval acceptable hypotheses about her behavior or by asking her to "explain" her connection with Jones.

Supposing that Sam's self-deception is explicable along the lines just sketched, could he have avoided self-deception by exercising self-control? An affirmative answer is plausible. Recognizing that his desire that Sally not be having an affair may incline him to self-deception, he may set himself to be on his guard against motivated biasing. He may commit himself to assessing the evidence from a variety of perspectives, including one that treats the case as a purely hypothetical matter designed to test his skills as a detective. He may even actively seek further evidence of an affair. In some versions of the case, Sam is psychologically incapable of taking such measures; the thought that Sally is having an affair may be so threatening that he simply cannot assess the data with anything approaching objectivity. But there is no reason to think that all possible versions must be like this, and in some Sam will avoid self-deception. Further, in those cases in which his efforts at doxastic self-control are successful, he believes *continently* (or, at least, continently ceases to believe that Sally is not having an affair: depending on the circumstances, he might continently withhold belief on the matter until he has conclusive evidence).

Self-control, then, extends beyond action to belief. People possessed of imperfect doxastic self-control are sometimes influenced by motivational pressures in ways proscribed by their doxastic principles, but they are not always helpless victims of those pressures. *Ideally* self-controlled individuals are such that what they want to be true influences what they believe to be true only in ways permitted by their (nonakratically held) doxastic principles.

## 4.  Doxastic Self-Control and "Cold" Biases

Self-control, on the model at work in part I of this book, is intrinsically tied to motivation. However, some nonmotivational tendencies may be resisted by means of an exercise of self-control in an extended sense. There is, as I have observed, considerable evidence of "cold" or unmotivated cognitive biases. An individual's awareness of such biases can promote less biased belief. Consider the biasing effect of the *vividness* of information—this time, vividness not motivationally enhanced—upon belief formation. People aware of that effect may resolve to be vigilant against it in important matters, and they may occasionally issue relevant, salutary reminders to themselves at crucial junctures. Needing a new computer, and faced with the question how I can best satisfy my computing needs given my limited funds, I can resist the tendency to be unduly swayed by John's vivid tale about Ken's horrible experiences with his XYZ machine and Linda's glowing praise of her own ABC system. Reminding myself that these reports are about single members of very large samples, I can make myself treat them as such and study the more informative, if much more pallid, data in *Consumer Reports*. In so doing, I exercise self-control in an extended sense vis-à-vis the belief that I acquire about which computer it would be best for me to purchase.

In this case, my exercise of self-control accords with my doxastic principle speaking against allowing my beliefs about important matters to be biased by informational vividness. In the absence of such an exercise, I might violate that principle. However, this exercise of self-control need not oppose *motivation* that threatens fidelity to my principle; instead, it might oppose only a cold tendency. Given the conceptual connection between continence and motivation, we might decline to count this as a case of *continent* believing. If so, we are treating the extended notion of doxastic self-control at issue as outstripping doxastic continence. By the same token, if, in violation of the above-mentioned doxastic principle of mine, I had believed, largely on the basis of John's and Linda's reports and in the absence of *motivated* bias, that an ABC is best for me, I would not have believed *akratically*, assuming the conceptual connection between *akrasia* and motivation in traditional accounts.

I have concentrated in this chapter on the influence of motivation on belief and on the nature and possibility of doxastic self-control and exercises thereof. However, I had an ulterior motive—a concern to lay additional groundwork for a conception of an ideally self-controlled person. The sphere of self-control, as I have argued, extends beyond action to belief. The next two chapters show that it extends considerably further. Appreciation of the range of self-control promotes appreciation of the robustness of the self-control possessed and exercised by an ideally self-controlled person. It contributes, as well, to a proper understanding of the resources for control over their lives available, in principle, to autonomous agents.

## Notes

1. For a catalogue of doxastic biases, see the entry under 'biases' in Baron's index (1988, p. 514).

2. See Kunda 1990 for a review of recent literature on the controversy.

3. The following descriptions are taken from Mele 1987, pp. 144–45. I have eliminated the notes from the quoted material, all of which provide references to supporting empirical work.

4. Taylor and Thompson 1982 contend that research on the vividness effect has been flawed in various ways, but they observe that studies conducted in "situations that reflect the informational competition found in everyday life" might "show the existence of a strong vividness effect" (pp. 178–79).

5. This theme is developed in Mele 1987, ch. 10, in explaining the occurrence of self-deception. Kunda 1990 develops the same theme, paying particular attention to empirical evidence that motivation sometimes primes the confirmation bias.

6. For an interesting discussion of the effects of motivation on time spent reading threatening information, see Baumeister and Cairns 1992.

7. On akratic belief, see Davidson 1985c; Heil 1984; Mele 1987, ch. 8; Pears 1984, ch. 4; and Rorty 1983.

8. The conception of reasons for action mentioned here is a familiar Davidsonian one (Davidson 1980, ch. 1). I defend a modified version of this conception of reasons—or, alternatively, of psychological states of reason having—in Mele 1992a, ch. 6. As I explain there, those who view reasons as abstracta (e.g., propositions) should understand my claims about reasons as claims about psychological states of reason having. I have no wish (or need) to take a stand on whether reasons for action and belief are properly conceived as abstracta or as states of mind.

9. For a doxastic principle that is sensitive to both alethic and practical reasons for belief, see Nozick 1993, p. 89.

10. Notice how natural it is to hold that someone who has good evidence for the truth of *p* has an *alethic* reason to believe that *p*—even if we learn that, owing to machinations of a powerful demon, the person in question *cannot* believe that *p*. The demon will not permit a belief that *p* to be among the person's beliefs.

11. Someone offers me a thousand dollars for believing that I have been to a Lakers basketball game. I know that the easiest way to bring it about that I believe that is to attend next week's Lakers game in Charlotte.

12. For discussion, see Mele 1992e and Mele and Moser 1994.

13. A desire for *knowledge* may sometimes be a constituent of a practical reason for believing that *p*. Someone might believe both that his chances of acquiring knowledge in a certain sphere would be improved by his believing that *p* and that *p* has little evidential support. A philosopher desirous of knowing whether autonomy is open to human beings might believe that his believing that he has the philosophical skills required for ascertaining the truth of the matter would promote his chances of coming to know the truth while also believing that the evidence that he has these skills is weak. (He might also believe that, even given the evidence, there is some chance of his successfully talking himself into believing that he has the requisite skills.)

14. On evidence for theism that might in principle be available even though it is not available to us in our present state, see Hick 1960.

15. On some conceptions of belief and acceptance, this would be rejected. For example, L. Jonathan Cohen holds that one can believe that *p* without having or adopting a policy of "including [*p*] among one's premises for deciding what to do or think in a particular context" and that "to accept that *p*" is precisely to have or adopt such a policy (1992, pp. 4–5). Cohen also holds that one can accept that *p* without believing that *p* (p. 20). For Cohen, a belief that *p* is a disposition "normally to feel it true that *p* and false that *not-p*" (under certain circumstances), and one can have or adopt a policy of the sort described without being so disposed (p. 4). I do not accept Cohen's conception of belief, but that is another story. (For an alternative to Cohen's conception of the relationship between belief and acceptance, see Perry 1980.)

16. For skepticism about our prospects of producing an analysis of "accepting a norm," see Gibbard 1990, p. 55.

17. This does not entail, incidentally, that the principles constitute an inconsistent set: the source of the conflict may be the conjunction of the principles and the circumstances. For discussion of the general point about conflict and inconsistency, see Marcus 1980.

18. For a recent challenge to Frankfurt-style cases, see Lamb 1993. Lamb grants that if the demon were to interfere in such cases, the agent, $S$, would not be able to do otherwise. But he observes that it does not follow from this that when the demon does not interfere, $S$ is not able to do otherwise. Suppose that, at $t$, $S$ $A$-s under his own steam and that if he were not, at $t$, to $A$ on his own, the demon would compel him to $A$ at $t$. Then one might argue as follows: Provided that the demon does not interfere, $S$ has the ability to refrain from $A$-ing at $t$, and the demon does not interfere in this instance; so, in this instance, $S$ has the ability to refrain from $A$-ing at $t$. However, even if this argument is accepted, $S$'s $A$-ing at $t$ is not, as one may put it, "genuinely avoidable" by $S$ in the scenario at hand. Assuming that the demon is irresistible, infallible, and a resolute intender, and that these properties are to be held fixed in any instance of the general demon scenario under consideration (instances in which the demon does interfere and instances in which he does not), there is no instance of the scenario in which $S$ refrains from $A$-ing at $t$. That suffices, by stipulative definition of "genuinely avoidable," for $S$'s $A$-ing's not being genuinely avoidable by him in the scenario under consideration.

Consider the following reply. Provided that the demon does not interfere, $S$'s $A$-ing at $t$ is genuinely avoidable by $S$, and the demon does not interfere in this instance; so, in this instance, $S$'s $A$-ing at $t$ is genuinely avoidable by $S$. The problem with this reply is that, by definition, a necessary condition of an action $A$'s being genuinely avoidable by its agent in a scenario $C$ is that there be some admissible instance of that scenario in which the agent does not $A$. By hypothesis, the scenario at issue admits of no such instances. $S$'s possessing an "ability" to refrain from $A$-ing that is available to agents in demon scenarios of the sort at issue and contingent upon the demon's not interfering does not suffice for $S$'s $A$-ing's being genuinely avoidable by him. (For a related point about freedom to refrain from $A$-ing, see pp. 141–42; and for a detailed reply to Lamb's paper, see Fischer and Hoffman 1994.)

19. See Mele 1987, pp. 116–18 for an exception. We sometimes deceive ourselves into believing things that we want *not* to be true.

20. Cf. Bach 1981 on "rationalization" and "evasion," Baron 1988, pp. 258 and 275–76, on positive and negative misinterpretation and "selective exposure," and Greenwald 1988 on various kinds of "avoidance." For a useful review of literature on "selective exposure," see Frey 1986. Frey defends the reality of *motivated* selective evidence gathering, arguing that a host of data are best accommodated by a variant of Festinger's (1957, 1964) cognitive dissonance theory.

21. For a recent review, see Kunda 1990.

# 6

# Self-Control, *Akrasia*, and Emotion

Emotions undoubtedly play an important motivational role in our lives. To the extent to which we have control over our emotions and other feelings—not only over how we respond to them, but also over which emotions and feelings we have and lack—there might be prospects for some degree of autonomy regarding them. My reason for turning to the emotions here extends beyond this concern, however. Other things being equal, the broader the fruitful range of application of the account of self-control being developed in part I of this book, the more reason we have to accept it.

Several preliminary observations are in order. First, I will steer clear of the lively and important debate over what, exactly, emotions are.[1] Fortunately, that issue need not be settled for my purposes. Second, although I have already referred to emotions as feelings and will continue to do so, I do not mean to suggest that emotions are "purely affective" or that they lack cognitive and motivational constituents. Certainly, many *feelings* are not purely affective. A feeling of inadequacy, for example (which does not count as an emotion on some views), surely is partly cognitive. Third, since some relevant feelings—feelings of inadequacy or pleasure, for instance—are not emotions on certain conceptions, the ensuing discussion is framed more often in terms of feelings than emotions. Fourth, in the sphere of feelings, as elsewhere, ordinary linguistic practices often leave it open whether types or tokens are at issue; my concern here is with feeling-tokens (including emotion-tokens)—particular instances of fear, joy, sadness, anxiety, and the like. Unless I indicate otherwise, my use of relevant terms is intended to tag tokens. Finally, even among pertinent tokens, there is a difference between a long-standing condition of a given type and particular episodic feeling-states of the same type that are partially derivative from, or "activations of," the prolonged condition. Contrast, for example, someone's long-standing fear of heights with the episodic fear occasioned by his looking over the railing of a fortieth-story balcony at a particular time. Although I am concerned with both, I focus on shorter-term states.

## 1. Akratic Feelings

In his novel *Of Human Bondage*, W. Somerset Maugham presents a fascinatingly detailed account of a young man who despises himself for loving a shallow and unresponsive woman. Convinced that his love for Mildred is destructive of his well-being, Philip tries to eradicate the emotion. But his efforts fail. "He wanted passionately to get rid of the love that obsessed him; it was degrading and hateful." Unfortunately, "[H]e was helpless."

> He felt just as he had felt sometimes in the hands of a bigger boy at school. He had struggled against the superior strength till his own strength was gone, and he was rendered quite powerless—he remembered the peculiar languor he had felt in his limbs, almost as though he were paralysed—so that he could not help himself at all. He might have been dead. He felt just that same weakness now. . . . [H]e felt that he had been seized by some strange force that moved him against his will, contrary to his interests; and because he had a passion for freedom he hated the chains which bound him. (Maugham 1915, p. 286)

Maugham's explanation of Philip's failure to bring his feelings into line with his better judgment will remind R. M. Hare's readers of his much-discussed contention that ostensible akratic or incontinent action is really "a case of 'ought but can't'" (1963, p. 80): if an agent decisively judges it best to A and yet fails to do so, the explanation of his failure must be that he is physically or psychologically unable at the time to A.

My aim in this chapter is to defend and account for the possibility of feeling analogues of strict akratic action and (derivatively) of a corresponding species of continent action. If, as I have put it, *akrasia* and self-control are two sides of the same coin, the possibility of either in a given domain suffices for that of the other.[2]

Strict akratic action poses different philosophical problems for different theories. In general, however, the challenge is to explain how an agent can intentionally A even though he consciously holds a decisive best judgment against A-ing and is not compelled to A (ch. 2, sec. 1). Perhaps a natural response is that an agent need not be most motivated to do what he decisively judges it best to do (see, e.g., Watson 1977; Mele 1983, 1987). But if the balance of an agent's motivation may be at odds with his decisive best judgment, this too requires explanation. The explanation, if it is to support the possibility of strict akratic action, cannot apply only to uncontrollable motivation, or motivation with compelling force.

The hypothesis that akratic *feelings* are possible raises similar problems. What can account for an agent's avoidably acquiring or continuing to have a feeling that he judges it best not to have, or his avoidably lacking a feeling that he judges it best to have? Here, too, a natural response is at hand: our better judgments about feelings need not always be in line with the determinants of feeling-states (including states of *not* having certain feelings). But, as in the case of akratic action, we must ask how the disparity is possible; and our answer cannot entail that we have no control over what we do and do not feel, if it is to leave room for strict akratic feeling.

Just as akratic actions, traditionally conceived, are distinguished from *compelled* actions performed against the agent's better judgment, akratic feelings, conceived on the same model, are also uncompelled. We distinguish some heroin addicts from relatively normal thrill-seekers akratically using the drug for the first time, on the grounds that the former alone cannot help themselves. Though both sorts of agent may act against a better judgment, only the former are in the grip of an irresistible or compelling desire for heroin when they use the drug. (This is not to deny, of course, that some thrill-seekers may have irresistible desires for thrills; nor is it to assert that all, or even most, heroin addicts have irresistible desires for heroin.)[3] Setting aside Frankfurt-style cases (ch. 5, sec. 2), the desires that motivate akratic actions, and the resulting actions, are subject to the agent's control: though the agent *can* control the desires that issue in his akratic actions, he fails to do so. Similarly, akratic emotions and other feelings, if they are to be genuinely *akratic*, must be subject to appropriate control by the person whose feelings they are (again setting aside Frankfurt-style cases). The person must have at his disposal suitable means of preventing the feelings from occurring, or of eradicating the feelings (should they occur), or of bringing the intensity of the feelings into line with his better judgments.

One who holds that better judgments exert less influence over feelings than over intentional actions may regard the possibility of akratic feeling as more readily explicable. But the latitude that one claims to find in the connection at issue may be counterbalanced by greater limitations on control. If better judgments can have no relevant influence whatever on feeling-states, we may be entirely lacking in rational control over the latter. This would preclude the possibility of a close feeling-analogue of akratic action. It may be that the looser the connection between better judgment and feeling, the less rational control we have over what we do and do not feel.

## 2.   Strict Akratic Feeling Characterized

Strict akratic feelings must, like strict akratic actions, be at odds with the agent's decisive better judgment. To see what sorts of decisive judgment might be violated by a feeling, we must attend to the various perspectives from which emotions and other feelings can be assessed or evaluated. A brief return to belief will prove useful. When we say that a belief is warranted, we typically have in mind what may be termed *evidential warrant*. Again, on a popular view, belief aims at truth, and evidence is the best guide. However, even false and evidentially unwarranted beliefs may have practical advantages. This goes part of the way toward explaining the occurrence of self-deception. One's belief that one's spouse is faithful, or that one's troubled child is just experiencing growing pains, may enable one to function normally, even if the belief flies in the face of the evidence. It seems possible, at least in principle, that a belief that it is best *all things considered* for a person to hold sometimes lacks sufficient evidential warrant.

When we speak of a warranted *emotion* or *feeling*, we typically have in mind an emotion or feeling that is an appropriate response to the evoking stimuli.[4] Crudely put, this appropriateness is a function of normal standards relating emotion- or feeling-responses to stimuli. Fear may be an appropriate response in this sense to certain threats but not to others. However, more than this can be said for a particular instance of fear. One's fear may motivate one to take life-preserving measures, for example: it may have *prudential* value. Furthermore, we attribute *moral* value to many feelings. It is morally proper to feel sympathetic in some circumstances and outraged in others, or so we say.[5] Often, considerations of appropriateness, prudential value, and morality pull in the same direction. But things are not always so neat. Although anger and resentment may be appropriate responses to one's spouse's extramarital fling, they may also be imprudent ones. The man who hopes to save his marriage may find that his hostile feelings toward his wife make this impossible.

A decisive better judgment in the sphere of feeling, like a decisive better judgment in the sphere of action, may be formed on the basis of a variety of considerations. Fred judges that although it would be best, financially speaking, to accept a certain job offer, it would be better, all things considered, to keep his job at the quarry. Barney judges that although his anger at Betty is warranted by the evoking stimuli, his ceasing to be angry would be better, on the whole. $S$'s being or remaining in a feeling-state, $x$, is an instance of *strict* akratic feeling only if $S$ consciously holds a decisive better judgment against his being or remaining in $x$—a judgment to the effect that there is good and sufficient reason for his not being or remaining in $x$.

If emotions were actions, as Robert Solomon maintained at one time (1973), a successful account of akratic action might be straightforwardly applicable to emotions. However, as Solomon later recognized, emotion is not a species of action (1980, pp. 276–77). The fear that makes James balk at his teacher's invitation to read a paper to the class, whatever it may be, is not an action of his. Akratic feelings, like akratic beliefs (ch. 5), are not akratic actions; a proper conception of akratic feeling must accommodate the difference.

The preceding remarks suggest the following characterization of *strict akratic feeling*:

> $S$'s being or remaining in a feeling-state, $x$, during $t$ is an instance of strict akratic feeling if and only if $S$'s being or remaining in $x$ during $t$ is uncompelled and, during $t$, $S$ consciously holds a judgment to the effect that there is good and sufficient reason for his not being or remaining in $x$. (Again, feeling-states include states of *not* having certain feelings.)

## 3. Controlling What One Feels

That an individual's feeling-states can be at odds with his consciously held decisive better judgments should be uncontroversial. Many phobic persons realize both that certain of their episodic fears are inappropriate responses to the evoking stimuli and that they would be better off without them (cf. Beck 1976, pp. 158–65; Marks 1969, p. 3).[6] The question before us, then, is whether consciously held decisive better judgments about emotions and other feelings are violated only by *compelled* feeling-states, feeling-states over which the person lacks appropriate control.

James, a college student, suffers from a severe fear of public speaking. Whenever he considers making a comment in class, his heart beats rapidly and he becomes exceedingly agitated and anxious. James has given the problem some thought. He has judged that anxiety is an inappropriate response to the situation, that in the absence of the feeling he would enjoy participating in class discussion and would find student life more pleasant and rewarding, and that, all things considered, it would be best not to be anxious about speaking in class. Suppose now that during a class discussion James has an urge to make a comment and forms a conscious judgment to the effect that there is good and sufficient reason for his not feeling anxious. Unfortunately, he also experiences the customary anxiety. Is this an instance of strict akratic feeling?

James may be significantly responsible for his *disposition* to feel anxious when, in the course of a classroom discussion, he considers making a contribution. Perhaps inexpensive behavioral therapy was readily available to him, and it may be that if he had sought help and done his best to benefit from it, he would not now have the disposition in question. Perhaps James *akratically* failed to seek help. If so, one might treat the instance of anxiety at issue as *derivatively* akratic. But (assuming that this is not a Frankfurt-style case) we have here an instance of strict akratic feeling only if, at the time at which he considers making the comment, James has at his disposal suitable means of preventing himself from feeling anxious, or of dissolving the anxiety that attends the consideration (or of reducing its intensity to an appropriate level).

A gloss on the notion of suitable means is in order. If James were to kill himself immediately upon considering making a comment in class, or render himself unconscious with a sharp blow to the head, he would either prevent or eradicate the anxiety. But only a very peculiar person would be (psychologically) capable of taking these means to secure the end at issue, and James, we may suppose, is not such a person. The means of self-control that an agent has at his disposal at a particular time do not include everything that the agent is capable of doing under some circumstances or other. Rather, they are limited to measures that the agent is physically and psychologically capable of taking in the situation at issue and for the end in question.

Depending upon the details of the case, James may have been psychologically unable to prevent his urge to make a comment from resulting in anxiety, and he may have been incapable as well of dissolving or suitably attenuating the anxiety once it occurred (i.e., without deciding to refrain from commenting). If so, we do not have here an instance of strict akratic feeling.

Must *every* feeling-state that is at odds with an agent's consciously held decisive better judgment be beyond his control? That we have some control over what we feel and over the intensity of our emotions and other feelings is clear. We stem a discomforting flow of sympathy for a character in a film by reminding ourselves that he is *only* a character (cf. Koriat et al. 1972, pp. 613, 617). The woman who regards her anger at her child as destructive may dissolve or attenuate it by forcing herself to focus her attention on a cherished moment with the child. The timid employee who believes that he can muster the courage to demand a raise only if he becomes angry at his boss may deliberately make himself angry by vividly representing the injustices that he has suffered at the office (cf. Skinner 1953, p. 236; Tice and Baumeister 1993, pp. 401–2). These are instances of what I will call *internal* control.

Many emotions and feelings are subject to *external* control as well—control through one's overt behavior. Jill knows that if, for some reason, she wants to be angry, a phone call to her mother will turn the trick. Jack defeats mild depression by calling his sister.

These points do not directly address the question whether we have control over the feeling-states that violate our consciously held better judgments, however. Are *these* states subject to our control? Or are they rather feeling-analogues of compelled action? (Notice that in each of my illustrations of internal and external control, *means* are taken to alter one's feeling-state. In the case of feelings, as in the case of beliefs, control should not be confused with *direct* control, or the capacity to *x at will*.)

An argument of Gary Watson's for skepticism about the possibility of akratic action is worth considering in this connection (1977, pp. 336–38). Watson argues that an ostensible akratic agent's succumbing to a desire against his better judgment cannot be explained by his choosing not to resist, or by his making a culpably insufficient effort to resist. He concludes that we are left with one explanation only: he was *unable* to resist. The agent's choosing not to resist, Watson argues, cannot explain akratic action, for to make such a choice "would be to change [one's] judgment" of the best (p. 337). Similarly, an insufficient effort cannot be due to a judgment that the effort is not worth the trouble, since the judgment that it *is* worth the trouble is implicit in the violated better judgment (p. 338). Nor can the insufficient effort be explained by a misjudgment of "the amount of effort required", for misjudgment is "a different fault from weakness of will."[7]

A very similar argument may be constructed for skepticism about the possibility of strict akratic feeling. If an agent's being or remaining in a feeling-state against his better judgment cannot be explained by his choosing not to take appropriate preventive or ameliorative measures, nor by his making a culpably insufficient effort along these lines, we may be left with the hypothesis that he was *unable* to avoid entering and remaining in the state. And if Watson's claims about choice and misjudgment are true, they will apply to emotions and other feelings as well as to actions.

I start with the point about choice. For years, Tom has felt inferior to his friend and colleague, Betty, owing to her greater success as a scholar. Tom, who does not wish Betty ill, has just learned that a paper of Betty's recently received its fifth rejection, and he finds that he is pleased by the news. Tom judges that his pleasure is unwarranted by the evoking stimuli and that his no longer being pleased by Betty's failure would be best, all things considered. Moreover, he believes that he can eradicate the pleasure simply by absorbing himself in his work. Nevertheless, he chooses to savor the moment, to allow himself to enjoy the news—but without revising his decisive better judgment.

If decisive better judgments were choices, this story would be incoherent; for Tom would be choosing to allow his feeling-state to persist while also choosing not to do this. But judgments are one thing and choices another (ch. 2). Though it may often happen that our choices are in line with our better judgments, sometimes we choose or intend to do one thing while judging something else better.[8]

Notice also that insufficient effort need not be due either to a judgment that taking preventive or ameliorative measures is not worth the trouble or to a misjudgment about the amount (or kind) of effort required. Tom may correctly judge that his absorbing himself in his work would put an end to his feeling-state, and he may be able to do this. But if he is less than perfectly self-controlled, he may make a half-hearted, unsuccessful attempt.

Even if Tom were to misjudge "the amount of effort required" to absorb himself in his work, and to make an unsuccessful effort to eradicate his feeling-state as a consequence, we could not justifiably conclude that his continued pleasure at Betty's failure is not an instance of strict akratic feeling. Misjudgment and *akrasia* need not provide *competing* explanations of behavior or feeling. Perhaps, if Tom had not been weak-willed, his effort would have been successful (i.e., "the amount of effort" that Tom supposedly made might have been sufficient to turn the trick, if he had not been a weak-willed person). His continued pleasure may be a product both of misjudgment *and* of *akrasia*, the trait.

## 4.   Explaining Strict Akratic Feeling

If strict akratic feeling is possible, how is its occurrence to be explained? If someone decisively judges it best not to be or remain in a feeling-state, $X$, and his being or remaining in $X$ is subject to his control, what can explain his entering or remaining in the state? Unless we are able to provide at least a sketch of a plausible causal story, the phenomenon may seem unintelligible. Return to Tom's case. I have suggested that, even in the absence of compulsion, he may remain in a feeling-state against his decisive better judgment. He may choose not to make an effort to eradicate the state, or he may make a culpably insufficient effort. But why isn't the decisive better judgment itself sufficient to dissolve the state? What sustains the state in the face of a proscribing better judgment?

A brief look at the relationship between decisive better judgments and the determinants of action and belief will prove instructive in defending and understanding the possibility of strict akratic feeling. Often, our decisive better judgments about action rest significantly on our assessments or evaluations of the objects of our wants or desires. But, as I have noted, an agent's assessment of a wanted item need not be in line with the *motivational force* of the want.[9] For example, $S$'s careful weighing of the pros and cons (including, of course, the merits of the objects of pertinent desires) concerning his continuing to smoke may support his decisive judgment that it would be best to quit smoking, even though he is and continues to be more motivated to smoke. Similarly, the assessments that support decisive better judgments about matters of *belief* need neither fully determine nor precisely measure the causal power of belief-influencing items. A datum that is given a relatively low rating in respect of evidential merit may, owing, for example, to the vividness of one's representation of it, exert a disproportionately powerful influence upon what one comes or continues to believe (ch. 5).[10]

The etiology of many emotions and other feelings is quite complex. Our emotions, in many cases, are products of desires, habits of interpretation, learned patterns of emotional response, other emotions, our physiological condition, and so on. The psychological possibility of strict akratic feeling rests on the psychological possibility that the evaluations that ground some decisive better judgments about matters of feeling neither fully fix nor exactly gauge the causal power of feeling-influencing items. If there is a mismatch between the determinants of a feeling and the agent's decisive better judgment, and if, despite this disparity, what the agent feels or continues to feel is subject to his control, the door is open to akratic feeling.

In Tom's case, apparently, the attractiveness of continued enjoyment of the news is out of line with his assessment of the merits of continued enjoyment. But it is doubtful that all akratic feelings are pleasant. We occasionally have *unpleasant* emotions and other feelings against our better judgment—fear and guilt, feelings of helplessness and inadequacy, and so on. Some such cases may be instances of strict akratic feeling.

The possibility of strict akratic feeling does not depend upon a *hedonically motivated* defeat of a decisive better judgment. The determinants of a feeling can extend well beyond items considered in the agent's formation of a pertinent decisive better judgment; and those determinants may yield an unwanted and unpleasant feeling. Controllable habits of self-recrimination, for example, may prompt unpleasant feelings of guilt, fear, and inadequacy that are radically at odds with one's decisive better judgment.

Jane has discovered that her husband, John, has been lying to her about working late at the office these past few weeks: he has been having an affair. Jane believes that anger and resentment are appropriate and morally proper responses. She believes, as well, that these responses would promote her chances of saving her marriage, something that she wants very much to do. John, she thinks, will break off the affair only if she makes it plain to him that she will not tolerate its continuation, and she believes that she will be able to convince him of this only if she is genuinely angry and resentful. Jane judges that there is good and sufficient reason for her to have these emotions. But this only increases her puzzlement at her feeling-state. She has neither of these emotions. Instead, she feels inadequate. The feeling persists despite her belief that it is inappropriate and counterproductive, and despite her decisive judgment that her not feeling inadequate would be better.

To see how this can be, we may find it instructive to consider Jane's history. Jane's parents were divorced when she was nine, and she held herself responsible. If only she had been a better child, she thought, her parents would have stayed together. Jane felt inadequate. A few years later, she learned that her father had left her mother for another woman. She blamed her mother: if Mother had tried harder to be attractive and interesting, she thought, Father would not have left. Eventually, Jane came to believe that the responsibility for the divorce rested primarily with her father. But this belief did not dislodge deeper feelings of personal responsibility for the divorce, nor her attribution of responsibility to her mother.

John's fling, we may conjecture, opened old wounds in Jane, reactivated a pattern of self-recrimination, and perhaps prompted an association of herself with her mother. If the conjecture is correct, we have the makings of a partial explanation of Jane's current feeling-state. And central explanatory items might have received no attention whatever in the process of thought that issued in Jane's decisive better judgment. Thus, it is not difficult to understand how Jane's assessment of the considerations to which she attended in forming her decisive better judgment may neither fully fix nor exactly gauge the causal power of the determinants of her feeling-state. Here, as in the case of akratic action, evaluation can go one way while the preponderant causal force of pertinent items goes another.

Once again, however, this disparity need not render the agent a helpless victim. Jane may have at her disposal a variety of techniques for bringing her feeling-state into line with her better judgment. She may struggle against the sources of her feeling-state in roughly the way that an agent who experiences a strong desire to engage in behavior that he deems wrong or imprudent may struggle against the desire. Strategies include forcing herself to focus her attention on her own virtues and John's vices, seeking to understand the deeper sources of her feelings of inadequacy, attempting to boost her self-esteem by associating more frequently and intimately with support-ive friends, and so on. On the supposition that Jane has no desire to feel inadequate and is not disposed to derive pleasure from feelings of inadequacy, her failure to "correct" her feeling-state is not explained by a hedonic attractiveness of the sort identified in Tom's case. But we need not conclude that it can only be explained by her being *unable* to bring her feelings into line with her better judgment. Though her feeling-state is unpleasant, the sort of attention to the state that its dissolution would require may be even more painful for Jane; and, as a partial consequence, she may fail to take action, or *choose* not to take action, or make only a half-hearted effort to change her feeling-state.

Does the suggestion in the last sentence entail that Jane decisively judges it best to allow her feelings of inadequacy to persist, on the grounds, say, that the cost of uprooting the feelings is too great? Not at all. Jane may decisively judge it best to do whatever it takes to uproot the feeling, and she may akratically fail to carry through.

The preceding two paragraphs might convey the impression that strict akratic feeling, on my account, necessarily derives from strict akratic action—specifically, a strict akratic action associated with one's not bringing one's feelings into line with one's better judgment. Now, if an agent's being in a certain feeling-condition during *t* is an instance of strict akratic feeling, it is true that he has not brought his feeling-state into line with a pertinent better judgment. But it does not follow that his not doing this is, or issues from, a strict akratic action. A person who judges, for example, that it would be best if he were not angry at *S* need not judge as well that it would be best to (try to) eradicate the feeling. In the absence of a judgment of the latter sort, his failing to eradicate the feeling is not a strict akratic action: strict akratic actions violate *practical* better judgments, judgments about what it would be best to *do* (or re-frain from doing). Perhaps it simply does not occur to the person to take measures to correct his feeling-state. Although this does not preclude the state's being one of strict akratic feeling, it does preclude the performance of the pertinent strict akratic action.

## 5.   A Question of Frequency

I have argued that strict akratic feeling is possible and explicable without taking a stand on how common the phenomenon is. Three considerations are of central im-portance in this last connection: the degree to which our emotions and other feelings are subject to our control, the frequency with which we make decisive better judg-ments about our feelings, and the frequency with which our emotions and other feel-ings fail to fit such judgments. A growing body of empirical work indicates that we have considerable control over a broad range of emotions and feelings.[11] Perhaps decisive better judgments about our feeling-states are relatively uncommon; and misfits between feeling-states and such judgments will undoubtedly be less common: presumably, our emotions and other feelings sometimes accord with our better judg-ments. Notice, however, that the frequency with which strict akratic feelings occur in us is, in significant part, an artifact of the extent to which we regard our feelings in general, or feelings of particular types, as being subject to our control. The more influence we take ourselves to have over what we do and do not feel, the more likely we are to make better judgments about our feelings. Ironically, increased awareness of the control that we are capable of exerting over what we feel may increase the frequency of strict akratic feelings—but only because it will tend to promote the formation of the better judgments that are essential to the phenomenon. More important, in promoting the formation of better judgments, this awareness may also reasonably be expected to increase the frequency with which we take steps to improve the quality of our emotional life. Given the profound influence of emotions and other feelings on behavior, successful rational intervention into one's affective life will tend to enhance the quality of one's life generally.[12]

I have attempted to characterize a close feeling-analogue of strict akratic action, to establish its possibility, and to sketch an explanation of the occurrence of strict akratic feelings. Where strict akratic episodes are possible, so, typically, are continent counterparts. If agents can akratically enter or remain in feeling-states against their decisive better judgments, agents can exercise self-control in the service of feeling-states recommended by decisive better judgments.[13] No special argument is needed for the possibility of strict continent feelings. Further, the machinery for handling "nonstrict" cases is present in chapter 5's treatment of akratic belief and chapter 4's discussion of "unorthodox" instances of continent and incontinent behavior.

## Notes

1. Important recent books addressing this issue include Gibbard 1990, Gordon 1987, Greenspan 1988, Oakley 1992, and de Sousa 1987.

2. An exception must be made for domains defined by Frankfurt-style cases (pp. 94–95).

3. Again, for an analysis of irresistible desire, see Mele 1992a, ch. 5.

4. See, e.g., Greenspan 1980 and de Sousa 1979. For detailed discussion of the appropriateness of emotions, see Greenspan 1988. A precise, successful account of the appropriateness and inappropriateness of emotions will depend on what, exactly, emotions are. The more relevant dimensions an emotion has, the more ways it can be appropriate and inappropriate.

5. For a recent defense of the justifiability of moral assessments of individuals for their emotions, see Oakley 1992, ch. 5. In ch. 4, Oakley offers telling objections to various arguments designed to show that we cannot be morally responsible for our emotions.

6. 'Phobia' is standardly defined as "an irrational fear." Often, phobic individuals regard some of their own fears as irrational. Some, wanting not to be saddled with fears that they know to be irrational, seek treatment.

7. I criticize this argument in Mele 1987, pp. 24–29.

8. For a related point about *intentions* and judgments, see ch. 2 and Mele 1987, pp. 19–20, 43–44. On misalignment between motivation and evaluation generally, see Mele 1987, chs. 3, 6.

9. For a detailed defense, see Mele 1987, chs. 3, 6.

10. See Nisbett and Ross 1980, ch. 8; cf. Mele 1987, pp. 115–20, 144–49.

11. For useful, documented discussion of the literature, see Frijda 1986, ch. 8, and Klinger 1993. See also Gordon 1987, ch. 6. For some remarkable reports of feeling-control, see Terr 1991, pp. 16–17.

12. That emotions have important behavioral consequences is a commonplace, but for a fascinating view on the depth of the practical significance of emotions, see de Sousa 1987; cf. Klinger 1993.

13. Again, Frankfurt-style cases are an exception.

# 7

# The Upper Reaches of Self-Control and the Ideally Self-Controlled Person

It is a commonplace that effective critical reflection upon one's own principles and values—reflection issuing in appropriate revision, acceptance, or identification—promotes individual autonomy. In the absence of such reflection, one is apparently a mere passive receptor and locus of principles and values; autonomous people are more active in this domain. In the present chapter, I examine the place of self-control in effective critical reflection on one's principles and values, gather together various pieces of a sketch of the ideally self-controlled person from this chapter and preceding ones, and present a preliminary argument that even *perfect* self-control combined with frequent and thorough critical reflection is not sufficient for autonomy.

## 1.  Values and Valuing

Although an attempt to provide *analyses* of the relevant notions of principles and values would be more trouble than it is worth for my purposes, some sense must be offered of how these notions will be understood in the ensuing discussion. I take a person's principles to be rules or maxims that the person accepts.[1] Principles of interest in this chapter include doxastic principles, principles about decision making, moral and prudential principles, and principles about the revision of one's collection of principles and values.

Values are trickier. Compare the expressions 'S values X' and 'X is one of S's values.' An instance of the former may be true while a corresponding instance of the latter is false. Ann may value her heirloom watch, but the watch is not one of Ann's values (cf. Harman 1993, p. 153). Both expressions—and the corresponding notions—require discussion.

David Lewis has claimed that "valuing is just desiring to desire" and that "to be *valued* by us means to be that which we desire to desire" (1989, p. 116). These claims merit attention both in the present connection and in connection with my interest (expressed in ch. 4) in an *uninflated* conception of the importance of higher-order desires in our lives.

Here is a counterexample to the quoted claims. A trustworthy millionaire—whose fortune, Carl is convinced, is due to his mind-reading talents—promises to give Carl $10,000 for *desiring* to fly to Cleveland. Because Carl wants the money and believes

112

that he will get it if he desires to fly to Cleveland, he desires to desire to fly to Cleveland. (All he needs to do now is to work up the first-order desire.) But his second-order desire notwithstanding, Carl does not *value* flying to Cleveland. Indeed, he intensely dislikes going to Cleveland, and he realizes that he need not actually go there to receive the money—he need only work up a desire to go there. As Carl sees it, there is nothing at all to be said for his flying to Cleveland.

In a footnote, Lewis says that "presumably it is intrinsic, not instrumental, desiring that is relevant to what someone values" (p. 115, n. 4; cf. p. 131). Neither Carl's second-order desire nor the first-order desire that he desires to acquire is an intrinsic desire: to desire something intrinsically is to desire it "for its own sake," as Aristotle put it (i.e., to desire it as an *end*). So, if the claim just quoted were correct, the Cleveland counterexample would be undercut. But the claim is false. First, people value many things instrumentally—for example, money. Second, they desire at least some of those things *only* instrumentally. (My desiring money is like that; I do not desire money for its own sake.) Third, supposing that some such cases involve second-order desires, the latter characteristically are not intrinsic desires. An intrinsic desire to desire money, for example, would be a desire that treated as an end one's *desiring* money: an odd second-order desire indeed. Some people might desire to desire money, on the grounds that if they did not desire money they might not acquire (or retain) enough of it to support themselves and their families. But a second-order desire so grounded is an instrumental desire.

Suppose that Lewis's claim that "to be *valued* by us means to be that which we desire to desire" were treated as a claim about *intrinsic* valuing in particular—valuing something for its own sake, or as an end—and that, in accordance with the quotation from Lewis's note, the relevant desires were understood as intrinsic desires. Then we would have the following: "To be valued [intrinsically] by us means to be that which we [intrinsically] desire to desire [intrinsically]." This would make intrinsic valuing incredibly rare. For we rarely *intrinsically* desire to *desire* something: again, such a second-order desire would treat having the first-order desire as an *end*. Although I intrinsically value the welfare of my wife and children, I do not intrinsically desire to *desire* their welfare. When moved to reflect on my attitude toward that first-order desire (or to *form* an attitude about it), I view the desire's worth as instrumental. If I desire to have that desire, I do not desire it for the sake of the end of *having* it, but rather for the sake of what I hope my having the first-order desire will promote—namely, the welfare of my wife and children (Harman 1993, p. 151). I might also congratulate myself for having the first-order desire, taking my having it as a sign that I am a decent husband and father. Even then, I am not desiring to desire my family's welfare for the sake of an end constituted by my *desiring* their welfare, although I might desire to desire this as an indication of my being a decent husband and father (cf. Harman 1993, pp. 151–52).

Revising Lewis's claim so that intrinsic second-order desiring is not required for intrinsic valuing will avoid the preceding objection. We now have the following: "To be valued [intrinsically] by us means to be that which we desire to desire [intrinsically]." However, this claim falls prey to a variant of the Cleveland example. Imagine that the payoff this time is for *intrinsically* desiring to fly to Cleveland: Carl will receive the money if he can get himself to desire to fly to Cleveland simply for the sake of flying there, as an end in itself. Carl desires to have an intrinsic desire to fly to Cleveland, but he does not intrinsically *value* flying to Cleveland. As in the original case, he does not value flying there at all, much less *intrinsically* value doing so.

Relatively mundane cases pose a similar problem. Don, an assistant professor of philosophy, would like to have an intrinsic desire to write philosophical papers: he would like to desire that activity as an end. He realizes that he needs to write papers if he is to receive tenure; but, as he also realizes, his character is such that he finds it difficult to write papers for what he regards as crass motives. So, thinking that his problem would be solved if he were intrinsically to desire to write philosophical papers, he desires to desire such activity intrinsically. The revision of Lewis's claim under consideration has the result that Don intrinsically values writing philosophical papers. But that result is false. If Don intrinsically valued so doing, he would not be in the fix that he is in; for, in that case (given a little self-knowledge), he would not view himself as having only crass motives for writing philosophical papers.

Notice also that although it is plausible that someone who values $X$ intrinsically also desires it intrinsically, neither Lewis's quoted claims nor the objection-circumventing revisions that I have offered imply this. Since second-order desires need not be satisfied, one may (intrinsically) desire to desire intrinsically to $A$ and yet not desire to $A$—intrinsically or otherwise.

Lewis's suggested analysis of valuing fails. Let us start afresh. As I have noted, we can value things intrinsically or extrinsically. An agent *intrinsically* values $X$ if and only if he values $X$ for its own sake, or as an end. An agent *strictly* intrinsically values $X$ if and only if he values $X$ *only* intrinsically. (Some things are valued both as ends and as means: e.g., Ann values exercise both for its own sake and for its conduciveness to good health.) *Strict extrinsic* valuing may be defined, negatively, as wholly nonintrinsic valuing. Normally, extrinsically valuing something is a matter of valuing it for its conduciveness to something else: this may be termed *instrumental* valuing. For example, I may value exercise for its conduciveness to good health. There may be situations, however, in which a person values something, but neither intrinsically nor instrumentally values it (Harman 1993, p. 149).

A subject, $S$, in a psychological experiment is led to believe that the length of time he can leave his arm in a vat of ice-water without experiencing great pain is indicative of the health of his heart (the longer, the healthier), and $S$ values his leaving his arm in for a lengthy period.[2] Presumably, he does not intrinsically value his doing this. Nor does he regard his doing it as conducive to his having a healthy heart. One might suggest that $S$ values his leaving his arm in for a lengthy period as a means of reassuring himself that his heart is healthy. But suppose that $S$ is convinced that if he were to leave his arm in the vat for a long time *as a means* of reassuring himself about his health, he would recognize that that is what he is doing and, consequently, would not be reassured. Then $S$ may value his leaving his arm in the vat for a lengthy period, not for its conduciveness to any end, but rather simply because he believes that it would indicate that he has a healthy heart, something that he very much wants to be true. Such valuing is noninstrumental extrinsic valuing.

All this leaves it open, of course, what valuing is. Valuing $X$ is often viewed as encompassing a positive motivational attitude toward $X$. On this view (in a familiar, broad sense of 'desire'), one values $X$ only if one desires $X$; or desires to acquire, or to promote, or to protect, etc., $X$; or desires that others will do one or more of these things; and so on. For example, Ann values truth, justice, and the American way, and she desires to acquire true beliefs, to promote justice, and to protect the American way. I will accept this view for the purposes of this chapter, while also granting that there may be other uses of '$S$ values $X$' that do not require $S$ to have a positive motivational attitude toward $X$.[3]

Having a positive motivational attitude toward $X$ is not, however, *sufficient* for valuing $X$. Ann is now experiencing a fleeting desire to strike her crying baby, but she does not now value her striking the baby (cf. Watson 1975, p. 210). Indeed, she finds the presence of that desire very upsetting: as she sees it, the desire is disgusting and entirely at odds with her values. A familiar conception of valuing builds in not only desire but also "believing to be good." On this view, Ann's not believing that it would be good to strike her baby suffices for her not valuing striking her baby. I will accept this cognitive requirement, as well.

The sentence, '$S$ believes $X$ to be good,' is ambiguous. Does $S$ believe $X$ to be good only in some respect and not on balance? Does $S$ believe $X$ to be good on balance or on the whole? Does $S$ believe $X$ to be good without qualification? Believing to be good simply in some respect is too weak as a cognitive requirement on valuing. To be sure, we value certain things for some, but not all, of their properties: for example, one may value physical exercise only for the contribution that it is likely to make to one's health. But if someone who believes physical exercise to be good in this connection also believes it to be bad on the whole—because, say, he believes that everything that detracts from his work is bad on the whole and that physical exercise detracts from his work—we would not say that he values physical exercise, even on those occasions when he feels an urge to exercise. The cognitive requirement that I will accept on valuing is disjunctive: either $S$ believes $X$ to be good on balance or $S$ believes $X$ to be good without qualification. Henceforth, such expressions as 'the belief that $X$ is good' are to be understood as shorthand for this.

Is valuing $X$ simply the conjunction of a positive motivational attitude toward $X$ and the belief that $X$ is good? In at least a thin sense of 'valuing,' it might be. In this sense, someone with no special fondness for peanut butter sandwiches values (at $t$) eating a peanut butter sandwich (soon) provided only that he desires (at $t$) to eat one (soon) and believes that his so doing would be good. Similarly, one may value scratching an itch, even though one places no special importance on that activity.

If believing $X$ to be good were conceptually sufficient for having a positive motivational attitude toward $X$, this sketch of valuing could be simplified: valuing $X$ might be nothing more than believing $X$ to be good. However, in a familiar sense of 'believe,' there is no such sufficiency. Return to the man in chapter 4, section 5, who, owing to the loss of his family in a plane crash, now suffers from acedia. The man may continue to believe that certain things are good without, for a time, having any positive motivational attitude toward them.[4]

Michael Smith has suggested that if "valuing is a matter of desiring," it is difficult to understand how people may, owing to weakness of will, act in ways that their values speak against (1992, p. 331). Notice, however, that a conception of valuing as a combination of desiring and believing good does not have to require that the strength of the valuer's desire be in line with his belief—or, more precisely, with his evaluation of the valued item. An agent who values $X$ may give $X$ a higher rating than $Y$ on a "goodness" scale while also desiring $Y$ more strongly than $X$. In some such cases, the strength of the agent's desire for $X$ falls short of the strength that his assessment of $X$ calls for.

We can say that $S$ at least *thinly values $X$* at a time if and only if at that time $S$ both has a positive motivational attitude toward $X$ and believes $X$ to be good. Unfortunately, accepting this analysis does not settle what it is for something to be *among one's values*.

Ann values truth, justice, and the American way, and each of these is among Ann's values. But what is it for something that one values to be among one's values? In the thin sense of valuing just sketched, one can value things that one does not take to be particularly important. A person's values, however, are standardly viewed as having, individually and collectively, special importance for the person. A normal person who occasionally values the eating of a peanut butter sandwich is not deemed to have such activity among his values. One might try to flesh out the importance dimension of values in a variety of ways—in terms of how much importance a person believes an item to have, how good a person believes an item to be, how strong a person's motivational attitude is toward that item, or some combination thereof. Conceptual spadework on this front might prove instructive, but it is not required for my purposes.

Can we properly say that $X$ is among a person's values if $X$ is both valued by the person and of special importance to the person? No. Even if Betty's philosophical advice, which Ann values, is of special importance to Ann, Betty's philosophical advice is not one of Ann's values (at least, the claim that it is has a jarring ring). Similarly, Ann greatly values an antique lamp and an heirloom silver bowl that her grandmother gave her as wedding presents; these things are very important to Ann, but the lamp and the bowl are not values of Ann's.

Why do truth, justice, and the American way count as being among Ann's values, but not Betty's advice, the lamp, and the bowl? Relative personal importance is not the key. The lamp may be more important to Ann than the American way; or it may be more important to her than another of her values, for example, her retaining the right to bear arms. If forced to choose between giving up that right and giving up the lamp, she may rationally prefer to do the former. The observation that material particulars do not count as personal values would exclude the lamp and bowl from Ann's collection of values, but it would not exclude Betty's philosophical advice.

Fortunately, I have no need for a precise delimitation of the range of personal values. Since we have a grip on what it is to value something, the range of personal values under consideration can be limited to things that are *valued by* valuers and are clear cases of the valuers' values.

## 2.   Identification

As I noted at the outset of this chapter, agents' "identifications" are commonly included among the products of autonomy-promoting critical reflection. Given the frequency with which 'identification' and its cognates appear in recent discussions of autonomy, surprisingly little work has been done on the analysis of an agent's *identifying* with a value or desire. Although these terms have the greatest currency in discussions of so-called "real-self" or "inner-self" conceptions of autonomy or free agency, a theorist who finds such conceptions wanting may have a use for a notion of identification.[5] For that reason, and others, it would be a mistake to build a special, narrow conception of "the self" or "the person" into an *analysis* of identification.

Harry Frankfurt claims that "when someone identifies himself with one rather than with another of his own [conflicting] desires, the result is . . . to alter" the nature of the conflict (1988, p. 172). "The conflict between the *desires* is in this way transformed into a conflict between *one* of them and the *person* who has identified himself with its rival." Obviously, to say that someone "identified himself" with a certain desire is not to say (in part) that he took himself to be identical with that desire. Such taking would manifest radical confusion, and Frankfurt does not view identification as open only to the radically confused. Frankfurt's claim in the second sentence just quoted suggests that identification renders one of the conflicting desires *external* to "the person"; and one of the purposes of another essay of Frankfurt's is to clarify the sense in which a desire seemingly attributable to someone is external to the person (1988, ch. 5). We might say that, at *t*, John desires *x*, desires *y*, and recognizes that he cannot satisfy both desires. We might add that, a bit later, owing to John's having "identified himself" with the former desire, the latter desire conflicts with, and is external to, "the person." But who is this person, if not John? And if John is this person, who desires *y*? *Someone* desires it; no desires float free from desiring beings. But who? Perhaps we can say that the "real," or "deeper," or "inner" John desires *x* but not *y*, and that *y* is desired by some "part" of John that is not in this real, deeper, or inner core. However, theorists who have no use for such talk may still have a use for a notion of identification. Of course, the expression '*S* identifies *himself* with a desire' is not only awkward but misleading, suggesting, as it does, that *S* takes himself to *be* a desire. But drop 'himself' from the expression and something remains.

For my purposes, an agent's identifying with a desire *D*, or a value *V*, that he has may be understood as a combination of his having *D*, or his having *V*, and his valuing his having it. Or better, this may be treated as a *central case* of identifying with a desire or a value that one has, thus leaving open the possibility of other kinds of identification with one's desires and values. On this view, central cases of identification encompass higher-order attitudes, as they are standardly regarded as doing. If, as I have suggested, valuing something is, roughly, a matter of having a positive motivational attitude toward it and believing it to be good, *identifying* with a desire or a value that one has (at least in central cases of identification) is, roughly, a matter of one's having both a positive motivational attitude toward one's having that desire, or that value, and a belief to the effect that one's having that desire, or that value, is a good thing.[6] This (partial) account of identification is open both to "real self" theorists and to their opponents, for it does not take a stand on who "one" is—that is, on how persons or "selves" are to be conceived. Of course, separated from "real-self" conceptions of autonomy, identification may be ill equipped to do all the theoretical work that proponents of those conceptions would like it to do. But that is as it should be. Judgments about the merits of "real-self" conceptions of autonomy should rest on an examination of those conceptions themselves.

When an agent's critical reflection issues in his identifying with a value of his, at least in central cases, that identification will rest in part on the agent's assessment of relevant values of his. It is to value assessment that I now turn.

## 3.   Assessing One's Values

Just as we can distinguish between intrinsic and extrinsic valuing, we can distinguish between intrinsic and extrinsic values. $X$ is among a person $S$'s *intrinsic* values if and only if $X$ is among $S$'s values and $S$ intrinsically values $X$. For example, justice is among Ann's intrinsic values if and only if justice is among her values and she intrinsically values justice. Similarly, $X$ is among $S$'s *extrinsic* values if and only if $X$ is among $S$'s values and $S$ extrinsically values $X$. For example, physical fitness is a value of Ann's, and she values it as a means to happiness. As in this instance, most extrinsic values are *instrumental* values. And as in the case of *valuing*, the same personal value can be both intrinsic and extrinsic: Ann may value physical fitness both as a means to happiness and for its own sake.

An agent concerned to assess an instrumental value of his is faced with an obvious question: Does this value promote what I suppose it to promote? For example, does physical fitness promote happiness? Or does *my* being physically fit promote *my* happiness. One's strictly intrinsic values are assessable on other grounds. Limiting the range of personal values to things valued by the person, one's values include only things that one believes to be good. And one can have noninstrumental grounds for believing something good. Ann believes her family's happiness to be a good thing, not on the grounds that it promotes something else, but rather on the grounds that it is an instance of something intrinsically good, human happiness. On what grounds does Ann believe that human happiness is good—indeed, *intrinsically* good? Perhaps on theoretical grounds like the following. Ann may be convinced both that some things are good for human beings in general and that nothing would merit this description unless something were *intrinsically* good for human beings in general. She may also hold that only states of human beings can be intrinsically good for human beings. And on the basis of a thorough survey of what she takes to be plausible candidates for intrinsically good states of human beings—pleasure, contentment, health, knowledge, courage, and so on—she may conclude that, of all of them, happiness (on her inclusive conception of it) encompasses the richest range of viable candidates for relevant intrinsic goods. Ann may judge, partly on these grounds, that happiness is the best candidate for the greatest intrinsic good for human beings. She may conclude from this, in conjunction with the conviction reported first, that happiness probably is intrinsically good.

There are, to be sure, numerous gaps in the reported reasoning. However, the point here is that a person can have grounds—noninstrumental ones—for believing something to be intrinsically good. Given that point, it is in principle possible for people to assess intrinsic values of theirs.[7]

Principles that one might accept for the assessment of one's values include principles about how this should be done (*procedural* principles) and principles about the conditions under which such assessment is called for (*initiatory* principles).

Sample procedural principles are (1) when assessing one's values, one should consciously formulate and test one's grounds for believing valued items to be good, or intrinsically good; (2) when assessing one's values, one should take care that what one believes to be good for one is not determined simply by what one wishes to be good for one; (3) when assessing one's extrinsic values, one should try to ascertain whether they are likely to promote what one supposes them to promote. Possible initiatory principles include (4) if two or more of one's values are in apparent conflict with one another, those values should be assessed; (5) if one comes to believe that a value that one holds was acquired mindlessly, the value should be assessed; (6) if, valuing *X*, one comes to believe that someone has significantly challenged the worth of *X*, the value should be assessed.

People who judge it best to conduct themselves in accordance with one or more of these principles in a particular situation, may, for a variety of reasons, be tempted not to do so. Laziness is one source of temptation. Aversion to change is another. And a desire to protect one's self-image as someone who has always possessed only sound values may incline one against unbiased value assessment and even against assessing one's values at all. Where such temptation is possible, so, often, are manifestations of *akrasia* and self-control. We can incontinently violate our principles of value assessment or continently assess our values in accordance with them. Ideally self-controlled individuals will assess their values when they judge it best to do so; they will assess them in accordance with their relevant procedural principles; and they will revise or embrace their values in accordance with their assessments.

In addition to principles for the assessment of their current values, agents can possess principles for the acquisition of new values. Elton, a hard-working philosopher, is often chided by friends for lacking an appreciation of the "finer things" in life—music, pictorial art, sculpture, and the like. Elton's excuse has been that if he were to value appreciating such things, he would be faced with a conflict that he has happily been able to avoid. People appreciative of the fine arts spend time enjoying them, and Elton realizes that cultivating in himself a proper appreciation of such things—and then enjoying them—would take considerably more time than he is willing to set aside for this, given his commitment to a rigorous philosophical work routine. He admits that he would like to enjoy the "finer things" in life, but he believes that it would be better to put such enjoyment off until he has attained the philosophical goals that he has set for himself (solving the mind/body problem, say), or at least grown weary of the struggle. Elton, it seems, accepts a principle for the acquisition of new values that speaks against his acquiring various aesthetic values (at least for some time).

A sketch of (nonstrict) akratic and continent *valuing* can be modeled upon my sketch, in chapter 5, section 2, of such *believing*. A central range of cases of *nonstrict akratic valuing* is constituted by instances of valuing that (1) violate a principle of value revision or value acquisition that the valuer either explicitly believes to be correct or undeniably implicitly accepts and (2) were suitably avoidable by the valuer by means of an employment of self-control. Similarly, a central range of cases of *nonstrict continent valuing* is constituted by instances of valuing that (1) accord with a principle of value revision or value acquisition that the valuer either explicitly believes to be correct or undeniably implicitly accepts and (2) were suitably promoted by the valuer's exercising self-control.

The point that I wish to emphasize now is that the ideally self-controlled person will not value akratically. Hence, again limiting a person's values to items valued by the person, such a person's values include none that are akratically possessed. In section 5, I will ask whether such a person—even assuming that he is especially reflective about his values and has a robust and reasonable collection of principles for value revision—is assured of *autonomously* possessing the values that he possesses.

## 4.   Assessing One's Principles

My sketches of akratic and continent valuing make essential reference to an agent's *principles*—principles of value revision and value acquisition. Such principles are themselves subject to the agent's assessment, which can in turn appeal to values that the agent possesses.

To the extent to which valuing involves *believing* to be good and personal values are tied to personal valuing, an agent's doxastic principles are relevant to his assessment of his values. At least some doxastic principles that agents accept presumably are sensitive, in some measure, to the agents' relevant interests and values. W. K. Clifford and William James endorsed quite different doxastic principles. As James saw it, their doing so was at least partially explicable in terms of differences in their values:

> Believe truth! Shun error!—these, we see, are two materially different laws; and by choosing between them we may end by colouring differently our whole intellectual life. We may regard the chase for truth as paramount, and the avoidance of error as secondary; or we may, on the other hand, treat the avoidance of error as more imperative, and let truth take its chance. Clifford . . . exhorts us to the latter course. Believe nothing, he tells us, keep your mind in suspense forever, rather than by closing it on insufficient evidence incur the awful risk of believing lies. . . . I myself find it impossible to go with Clifford. We must remember that these feelings of our duty about either truth or error are in any case only expressions of our passional life. . . . [A]nd he who says, "Better go without belief forever than believe a lie!" merely shows his own preponderant private horror at becoming a dupe. . . . I have also a horror of being duped; but I can believe that worse things than being duped may happen to a man in this world: so Clifford's exhortation has to my ears a thoroughly fantastic sound. ([1897] 1979, pp. 24–25)

James values possessing true beliefs about certain important issues—notably, the existence of God and what is entailed by that—more than he values being free of false beliefs on these issues; and, as James sees it, Clifford values avoiding error (false belief) more than he values believing what is true. Further, James claims, this accounts—at least partially—for differences in the doxastic principles that the two theorists accept. Clifford contends that "it is wrong always, everywhere, and for anyone, to believe anything upon insufficient evidence" (1886, p. 346); and James denies it, contending that "a rule of thinking which would absolutely prevent me from acknowledging certain kinds of truth if those kinds of truth were really there, would be an irrational rule" ([1897] 1979, pp. 31–32).

The dispute between Clifford and James need not rest on an irresolvable difference in rock-bottom values. In support of his proscription against believing on insufficient evidence, Clifford advanced what may be termed a *pollution* view of such believing. "Every time we let ourselves believe for unworthy reasons, we weaken our powers of self-control, of doubting, of judicially and fairly weighing evidence"; and in so doing we weaken these powers in people around us (pp. 344–45). It is our duty, he urged, "to guard ourselves from such beliefs as from a pestilence, which may shortly master our own body and then spread to the rest of the town" (p. 344). If a critic were to show that people are adept at a relevant sort of partitioning—that, for example, relatively weak standards for belief about religious matters generally do not leak over into other domains—at least this source of support would be undercut. Alternatively, if James could be convinced that, given people as they actually are, the cost of religious beliefs (religious wars, persecution, etc.) outweighs the gains, he might find considerably more merit in Clifford's principle.

The point to be emphasized now is that influence between personal principles for value assessment and personal values goes both ways. People can revise or embrace their values on the basis of principled reflection, but the principles that inform reflection can themselves be shaped by their values. People possessed of ideal self-control will engage in critical reflection on their principles when they judge it best to do so; they will be guided in that reflection by reflective principles that they accept; and they will revise or embrace their principles in accordance with the results of their reflection.

## 5.  The Ideally Self-Controlled Person and Some Possible Shortcomings

The ideally self-controlled person *perfectly* manifests what I will call *perfect* self-control. The relevant perfection has four dimensions: range, object, frequency, and effectiveness.

1. *Range*. In chapter 1, I distinguished between local and global self-control. Perfect self-control is perfectly global. It is manifested in overt actions, mental actions, intentions, beliefs, and emotions, in practical reasoning and decisive better judgments, in the assessment, acceptance, and revision of values and principles, and so on. It has, we may say, *maximal categorial range*.[8]
2. *Object*. Exercises of self-control combat something in support of something else. The ideally self-controlled person never exercises self-control *errantly* (ch. 4), but only in support of "pure" items—*nonakratically held* decisive better judgments, values, principles, and the like. The objects of exercises of self-control in the ideally self-controlled person are, in this sense, *perfect*.
3. *Frequency*. The ideally self-controlled person exercises self-control whenever he reflectively deems it appropriate to do so.
4. *Effectiveness*. The ideally self-controlled person's exercises of self-control always succeed in supporting what they are aimed at supporting. They are perfectly effective. This is not a matter of luck or causal deviance. Rather,

the ideally self-controlled person consistently *intentionally* brings about the success of his exercises of self-control.

Obviously, the ideally self-controlled person is an imaginary being. My question now is whether this superperson—even assuming that he exercises self-control regularly in all areas of his life—has everything that personal autonomy requires.[9] Such a person, in being a self-conscious, self-reflective, self-assessing agent, is at a great remove from cats and dogs, say—animals that can act intentionally but are too "simple-minded" for autonomous action (on standard views). Our superperson is also possessed of qualities that we normal human beings only approximate. But are this agent's capacities and numerous flawless executions thereof sufficient for autonomous agency?

Those who hold incompatibilist views on autonomy will note that my ideally self-controlled person can inhabit a deterministic world. Since they take determinism to preclude autonomy, my superperson falls short of their requirements for autonomy. This issue is addressed in subsequent chapters. Here, I take up another.

Consider Gerald Dworkin's claim that "autonomy is a second-order capacity to reflect critically upon one's first-order preferences and desires, and the ability either to identify with these or to change them in light of higher-order preferences and values" (1988, p. 108). The ideally self-controlled person has this capacity and ability. However, even ideal self-control—no matter how frequently and successfully exercised—might not be sufficient for autonomy. If, as it seems, every process of critical reflection is regulated or guided by principles or values already in place, some principle or value will be presupposed or taken for granted in each process. If the principles or values taken for granted are products of brainwashing or other forms of "mind control," the process is tainted. To be sure, one can advert to a capacity for third-order reflection on second-order preferences; but the problem can be repeated at that level too. Nor is the problem solved by evoking the image of Neurath's boat and observing that an agent can criticize each of his values from the perspective of some other value(s) without ascending a level; for an agent's collection of values may be engineered in such a way as to dictate the results of such criticism.

Apparently, an agent who is ideally self-controlled in my sense might ultimately be controlled by his brainwasher. Although the agent rigorously and effectively exercises a hefty capacity to master motivation that runs counter to his decisive better judgments about action, belief formation, value revision, and the like, the foundation on which these judgments rest might be wholly due to a malicious "mind controller." Arguably, then, an autonomous agent must have some feature that even an ideally self-controlled person can lack. Among the questions to be addressed in part II of this book are whether an argument along the lines just sketched is cogent, and, if so, how self-control may be supplemented in arriving at autonomy.

A related issue merits attention. As I have observed, self-controlled individuals need by no means be stoic or rigid in their behavior. They may lead rich, rewarding lives that give expression to a wide range of emotions, passions, appetites, and the like. They need not be excessively calculating or particularly industrious. How they conduct themselves depends on their values, principles, decisive better judgments, and so on—psychological items that need in no way favor especially rigorous or rigid regimes. Still, some self-controlled individuals may have certain psychological characteristics associated with people suffering from obsessive-compulsive disorders; and that possibility provides a point of departure for an interesting question.[10]

A salient characteristic of compulsive people, on a familiar view, is extraordinary, sustained engagement in and attention to "producing or accomplishing" (Shapiro 1981, p. 83). Imagine that my hard-working philosopher, Elton, who does not value the "finer things" in life, is *extraordinarily* industrious and productive; indeed, he arranges his life around his work. Even so, he need not be compulsive (in the sense of the term that identifies a psychological disorder). Compulsive people, on an orthodox characterization, experience "at least a moderate degree of distress" and take themselves to be troubled individuals (Rachman and Hodgson 1980, p. 12). However, Elton may consistently tackle his work enthusiastically, and he may thoroughly enjoy his rigorous routine. Elton may regard himself, correctly, as uncommonly dedicated to philosophical work and as a relatively distress-free, untroubled person. Of course, another philosopher, Zed, who works just as hard and productively as Elton may be a troubled individual, indeed; and Zed's psychological problems may help to account for his hard work. Suppose that both philosophers consistently conduct themselves as they judge best and that their better judgments in no way themselves derive from akratically held values, beliefs, or the like. Setting aside external manipulation (e.g., brainwashing) and worries about determinism, might it turn out that Elton is autonomous and Zed is not, or, at least, that Zed is significantly *less* autonomous than Elton?

Compulsive people, as psychologist David Shapiro views them, "are extraordinarily conscious of some aim or purpose beyond" their activities (1981, p. 83). Their "purposeful" behavior is never "motivated simply by interest" (p. 84); moreover, "they value activity *only* by its result"—only extrinsically (p. 83; my italics). The compulsive person "does not recognize the possibility that worthwhile activity or achievement may come not only out of strong will but out of strong interest, as he does not recognize the possibility of self-respect based not on his achievement or productiveness but on his existence" (pp. 86–87). His conduct is "dutiful"; and "its tense and driven style and, to some extent, the general nature of its purposes—for example, the emphasis on productiveness—reflect this fact" (p. 84). "The self-imposed regime of dutiful work and purpose is oppressive but, inasmuch as the compulsive person identifies with that regime and identifies its purposes as his own, he feels entitled by his work and accomplishments to self-respect and a sense of personal authority" (p. 85). His "conditional self-respect," however, "is unreliable at best": "even succeeding at a rate that falls short of his expectations . . . may trigger depression and acute feelings of insufficiency." "The compulsive person's identification of himself with the regime of dutiful work and purpose transforms the subjective meaning of autonomy from being free to follow one's own wishes and live according to one's own lights to self-discipline, self-control, the subordination of one's wishes to one's will. Such a person lives, therefore, in a state of continuous tension between will and underlying inclination" (p. 86).

Suppose that although at least some of these insightful remarks fit Zed, they radically misdescribe Elton. Elton intrinsically values his philosophical work and is guided in that work, above all else, by a desire to know how the philosophical questions that interest him most are best answered. He is productive, but he enjoys his philosophical activity itself much more than the significant recognition it brings him. Elton pursues his own philosophical interests wherever they lead; he is utterly indifferent to what happens to be trendy, and his choices of research topics are in no way influenced by his impressions either of the amount of attention a topic is receiving or of the prestige enjoyed by the people working on it. Elton reads widely on his chosen topics. But he strives always to make up his own mind about where the truth lies (on the basis of careful examination of arguments in the literature and meticulous construction of his own arguments), he is disinclined to accept any philosophical claim on authority, and he has no qualms either about defending unfashionable views or about criticizing fashionable ones.

Zed is different. Even as a child, he had an extraordinary need for the respect of people he regarded as his superiors. In school, Zed strove for the highest grades but did not find his school work particularly interesting. This was true, as well, at college, where Zed was much impressed by an authoritarian philosophy professor. Zed felt relatively comfortable in an academic setting. He was a superior student, and by the time he graduated he viewed himself as best prepared for success as a philosopher. He excelled in graduate school also, but still without taking an intrinsic interest in matters philosophical.

Now well into middle-age, Zed has long craved recognition and respect as a philosopher. He regards that craving as an utterly respectable, justified desire for his just deserts. Zed decided years ago that the best way to gain respect and recognition was not only to work extraordinarily hard, but always to work where the action is while being careful to advance no views that "the most important people" reject. Zed continues to monitor what such people are doing, with a view to selecting topics for his own writing. Not only are his philosophical interests derivative, but so is his work. Realizing that he lacks the talent to develop interesting, defensible positions that he can honestly call his own, Zed is inclined in his own thinking to accept views that he takes to be popular among the philosophers he most respects. His philosophical writing, as a result, typically presents a currently popular party line, the view and arguments being pieced together from others' work; and it is sprinkled with invitations to compare Zed's ideas with those of like-minded theorists. Zed never finds enjoyment in his philosophical work itself; indeed, he frequently experiences his routine as oppressive. But he greatly enjoys the recognition that his writing brings him, and he takes enormous pleasure in seeing his books and articles in print and in finding citations of them in the writings of philosophers he respects. When Zed discovers that relevant work of his has been ignored by such a philosopher, he is depressed for weeks and he takes himself to have suffered a grave injustice; when he is cited by those he deems most important, he is elated. Zed is utterly dependent for his self-esteem on how his work is received. Often, during bouts of depression, he has an urge to relax, to take a break from his demanding routine. But in accordance with his (nonakratically held) values, he judges it best to haul himself to the office to resume his work. Zed also values his having these values, believing that his life would be empty without them.

Qua *philosopher*, Elton plainly is more autonomous than Zed. Elton charts his own philosophical course; Zed cautiously follows in others' footsteps. Elton works out views of his own on the basis of his own theoretical reasoning; Zed's philosophical efforts are limited to reflection required for understanding the views and arguments of others and packaging them as his own. (This judgment about relative autonomy can be accepted by libertarians and compatibilists alike, whether Elton's and Zed's respective approaches to philosophy are imagined to be causally determined or undetermined. A philosopher's autonomy qua philosopher is not a deeply metaphysical matter; it is rather a matter, to put it crudely, of engagement in independent thought about philosophical issues that one finds intrinsically interesting.) But some readers will be strongly inclined to see Elton as a significantly more autonomous *person* than Zed, even if neither ever conducts himself akratically.

Among such readers, some may be tempted to speak of Zed's "real self" and to treat Zed's keen desire for philosophical recognition and respect along with related values as external to that self. In this vein, Shapiro writes,

> For all the intensity of his values, the compulsive person does not seem wholehearted about them; they do not seem thoroughly his own. . . . These are . . . not simply values, standards, and purposes but—something quite different—duties and responsibilities, values that the compulsive individual imposes on himself, values whose authority he regards as superior to his own values, inclinations, and judgments. (1981, p. 80)

This view of Zed, as I have described him, is only partially accurate. Zed does value philosophical recognition, and he values—albeit wholly extrinsically—his hard philosophical work. It is Zed himself who values these things, not something alien to Zed. There is no indication in the case as described that Zed regards "the authority" of these values "as superior to his own values, inclinations, and judgments." These values *are* "his own," at least in the sense that they are *his*; indeed, not only does he possess the values, but he identifies with them, as well. Further, although, when he is depressed, Zed sometimes has *inclinations* that oppose the prompting of these values, I have not attributed to him any *values* or practical *judgments* that are allied with these inclinations. Perhaps Zed occasionally wonders whether his life has gone astray; but when he casts about for values of his that are not well-served by his life, he might find none at all—perhaps because he has no such values. His single-minded pursuit of success and recognition might have destroyed any potentially competing values that he once embraced and blocked the acquisition of new, potentially distracting values.

One can view Zed as significantly less autonomous than Elton, however, *without* postulating a "real self" for Zed that opposes the desires, values, and decisive better judgments that drive and guide his hard work. The person who commits suicide is not only his own killer but also his own victim: he kills *himself.* Similarly, we might see Zed as victimizing, and victimized by, himself; and we might hold that to the extent to which his conduct is a product of his self-victimization, it is not autonomous. How might this be unpacked?

Shapiro speaks of "values that the compulsive individual imposes on himself." He apparently understands the imposing as being done from some point external to the person's "own values" and to what may be termed (following a familiar tradition) the person's "real self." On the *competing* view just introduced, any values that Zed imposes on himself are *self*-imposed. Now, in light of Zed's history, there is no apparent need to suppose that his valuing *respect* and *recognition*, or his valuing these things as *strongly* as he does, is to be explained as a product of self-imposition. His *rigorous work routine* and the value that he places on it, however, are more plausibly regarded as self-imposed. No one else imposes the routine or value upon Zed; and, at least when he is depressed, he treats the routine as an imposition. Still, given both the self-acknowledged value that he places on recognition and his conviction that maintaining his routine is essential to maximizing his recognition, Zed judges it best to abide by the rigid rules that he has set for himself: fourteen hours in the office each day, unless some other work *must* be done!

When Zed is viewed in this way, not only do we see his life as exceptionally limited or narrow, we also see Zed himself as self-limiting. In imposing his rigid routines on himself, he seemingly cuts himself off from prospects for a significantly more satisfying, enjoyable, and even fulfilling life. Perhaps he *now* lacks interests that he would pursue and enjoy if he relaxed his rules; but, we may conjecture, if he were to relax them he would develop such interests. One might contend that Zed's counterpart, Elton, is no *less* limited and self-limiting; after all, his hours are just as long as Zed's and his nonphilosophical activities may be every bit as thin. However, this is to take an unduly narrow view of limitedness. Elton's prospects for personal satisfaction, enjoyment, and fulfillment far outstrip Zed's. For Elton thoroughly enjoys his work, the activity to which he devotes most of his time, and Zed, far from enjoying it, regards it as a burden (albeit an instrumentally valuable one). Not only is the range of Zed's activities severely limited, but so are his prospects for satisfaction and enjoyment. This contrast, I suggest, is at least part of what inclines those who give a significantly higher autonomy rating to Elton than to Zed to rate them in this way. To the extent to which Zed severely narrows the range of his satisfaction and enjoyment by imposing on himself, and then abiding by, demanding rules, one may see him as a victim—indeed, as self-victimized. And to that extent, one may view him as falling far short of Elton's autonomy. If this view of the situation is right, autonomy is not *just* self-rule or self-government; for certain *kinds* of self-rule or self-government, on this view, are self-limiting, self-oppressing, and self-victimizing in a way that is at odds with a robust autonomy.

I have no wish to insist at this point that Zed *is* less autonomous than Elton. Rather, I have offered a partial diagnosis of the judgment that he is, a judgment that many readers of this book are likely to have made. One of my major aims in part II of this book is to identify *sufficient* conditions for personal autonomy. Some readers may be strongly inclined to hold that Zed, or a more severely self-limited, but thoroughly self-controlled, counterpart is nonautonomous. With such readers in mind, I here include among the elements of a sufficient condition for the possession of personal autonomy that the agent's life be unsullied by self-oppression or self-victimization.[11] Continuous "mental health" serves nicely as a tag for a broader condition that includes this negatively formulated one. If, as one should think, being autonomous is compatible with the possession of continuous mental health, the latter serves as an appropriate element in a sufficient condition for personal autonomy.

## Notes

1. On *accepting* a principle, see ch. 5, sec. 2.

2. For discussion of this experiment (Quattrone and Tversky 1984), see Mele 1987, ch. 10, sec. 4.

3. For one such use, see Smith 1992.

4. Suppose that the man believes his being healthy would be good (or valuable) but that he is not the least bit desirous of being healthy. Would most ordinary speakers of English hold that such a person *values* his health? I think not. However, even if I am wrong about this, my aim in this section is to sketch serviceable notions of valuing and values, not to capture ordinary usage. Incidentally, Michael Smith takes cases like the present one to motivate the view that valuing $X$ does not require desiring $X$ (1992, pp. 326–27, 337).

5. For a brief critical overview with references to the literature, see Christman 1989, pp. 7–11.

6. This does not entail, incidentally, that one who identifies with a value $V$ believes that the combination of his having a positive motivational attitude toward $V$ and his believing $V$ to be good is a good thing. It is a mistake to infer '$S$ believes that $q$' from '$S$ believes that $p$' and 'By definition, $p$ implies $q$.' Three-year-old Anna believes that Shamu is a whale, and, as we know, 'is a mammal' enters into the analysis of 'is a whale'; but Anna does not believe that Shamu is a mammal. She has no idea that whales are mammals. One can believe that one's having value $V$ is a good thing without also believing all the major implications of the conjunction of 'I have value $V$' and a proper analysis of the having of values.

7. On the possibility of justifying and assessing one's intrinsic values, see Audi 1982.

8. More strictly, ideal self-control has maximal range relative to the psychological and physical life of a being. Immaterial beings incapable of overt action may be perfectly self-controlled; the same may be true of some hypothetical emotionless beings. But such beings are not my primary concern. By "maximal categorial range" in 1, I mean, roughly, the full range of self-control open to a being whose life is at least as robust and complex, physically and psychologically, as that of the average reader of this book.

9. The assumption is motivated by the possibility that some ideally self-controlled person rarely, if ever, needs to exercise his powers of self-control.

10. People suffering from obsessive-compulsive disorders fall short of ideal self-control, on an orthodox conception of the disorders. Standardly conceived, one of the defining features is that the person recognizes his problem as a problem and regards relevant distressing thoughts, urges, and feelings of his as unreasonable (Rachman and Hodgson 1980, pp. 12–21). An ideally self-controlled person would lack such mental states, or at least swiftly eradicate them should they arise.

11. Although some elements in a complex sufficient condition of personal autonomy may also be necessary conditions of moral responsibility, not all of the elements need be. The element just identified is an unlikely candidate for a necessary condition of moral responsibility. Even so, to the extent to which so-called workaholics are genuinely obsessive-compulsive about their work, one may reasonably be inclined to attribute a diminished moral responsibility to them for some of their shortcomings (e.g., an exceptionally low level of involvement in family or community matters).

# PART II

# 8

# Transition: From Self-Control
# to Autonomy

In the preceding chapter, I offered grounds for thinking that even an ideally self-controlled, mentally healthy person might not be autonomous. Suppose that this thought is true. Then we should like to know what a nonautonomous, ideally self-controlled, mentally healthy person might be lacking. What can we add to such a person to yield an autonomous person? Naturally, compatibilists and incompatibilists about personal autonomy will disagree about how this question is to be answered. The former deny that personal autonomy depends on indeterminism (i.e., the falsity of determinism), and the latter contend that it does.

One approach to take in working one's way from an account of self-control to an account of autonomy would require defending either compatibilism or incompatibilism about personal autonomy. I have decided against taking this route. For the most part, I think, theorists who are reflectively committed to one side or the other of this debate cannot be budged from their position. And so much has been written on the topic in the last several centuries—some of it very good—that I think it very unlikely that I am capable of discovering a novel argument for one or the other of the two sides that is sufficiently powerful to persuade even the majority of uncommitted theorists who peruse it.

My own route is latitudinarian. First, I develop a collection of jointly sufficient conditions for compatibilist autonomy (chs. 9, 10). Then I turn to incompatibilism. A major problem for incompatibilists who are committed to the thesis that some human beings are autonomous (or free, or morally responsible)—that is, for *liber-tarians*—is to explain in virtue of what such human beings are autonomous, and in virtue of what a choice, for example, counts as autonomously made or an action as autonomously performed (cf. Kane 1989; Strawson 1986, pp. 31–33; Thorp 1980, p. 2). Progress on this front lags far behind that made in the argumentation for incompatibilism itself. In chapter 11, I motivate a collection of problems for libertarians, and in chapter 12, partly in response to those problems, I advance a coherent set of jointly sufficient conditions for libertarian autonomy—a set whose satisfiability by actual human agents, I argue in chapter 13, is not precluded by anything we know about human beings or the world. The two collections of sufficient conditions overlap, differing only in accordance with the central point of contention between compatibilists and incompatibilists.

I shall, then, have something to offer compatibilists and libertarians alike—statements of sufficient conditions for personal autonomy that they can employ. Given my skepticism about my chances of settling the dispute between compatibilists and incompatibilists, this seems to me to be the best course.

Not all incompatibilists are libertarians, of course. Some are *nonautonomists*, maintaining that no human being is autonomous. They might hold that incompatibilism and determinism are both true or that human autonomy is incompatible both with determinism and with indeterminism. Grounds for nonautonomism are assessed in chapter 13 and found deficient.

## 1.   Compatibilism and *Akrasia*

In chapter 7, I noted that incompatibilists about autonomy will contend that even an ideally self-controlled individual, on my account, might not be autonomous, on the grounds that such a person might inhabit a deterministic world. It is safe to say, at any rate, that my accounts of self-control and of action exhibiting self-control have at least the appearance of being compatible with determinism. However, some readers might take my position on akratic behavior to be incompatible with determinism.

I said in chapter 6 that "setting aside Frankfurt-style cases . . . , the desires that motivate akratic actions, and the resulting actions, are subject to the agent's control: though the agent *can* control the desires that issue in his akratic actions, he fails to do so." I made similar claims in chapters 5 and 7 about nonstrict akratic believing and valuing, contending that in a central range of cases the akratic episodes are "suitably avoidable" by the believer or valuer "by means of an employment of self-control." Regarding akratic feelings, which I argued to be psychologically possible in chapter 6, I claimed (again setting aside Frankfurt-style cases) that "if they are to be genuinely *akratic*, [they] must be subject to appropriate control by the person whose feelings they are. The person must have at his disposal suitable means of preventing the feelings from occurring, or of eradicating the feelings (should they occur), or of bringing the intensity of the feelings into line with his better judgments." Such claims as these might be taken to imply that determinism is false, on the grounds that determinism "is the thesis that there is at any instant exactly one physically possible future" (van Inwagen 1983, p. 3) and it is not physically possible for agents who have only one physically possible future to act otherwise than as they do. Thus, it might be claimed, the truth of determinism is incompatible with an agent's having been able to control desires that he did not control or having been able to avoid akratic episodes that he did not avoid, for we are not able to do what it is not physically possible to do.

As G. E. M. Anscombe, who is no fan of compatibilism, has bluntly put it, "[S]oft determinists hold that in one sense (the free-will sense) one can act otherwise than one does, while in another sense (deterministic causal necessity) one can't" (1981, p. 164). So matters are not as clear-cut as the preceding line of thought suggests. Perhaps the notions of ability and avoidability relevant to akratic episodes are allied with the "free-will sense" of 'can' and not with the "deterministic causal necessity" sense of 'can't.' If that is so, and if the "free-will" sense of 'can' is a legitimate one, the claims of mine that I have quoted do not themselves commit me to rejecting determinism. Dropping this talk of "senses," it can be observed, more directly, that if compatibilism about the relevant notions of ability and avoidability is true, controllable desires are present at deterministic worlds and are distinguishable from uncontrollable counterparts. (I return to this point in ch. 9.) Put even more directly, only if such compatibilism is false does determinism entail that all desires are uncontrollable, and only if a counterpart incompatibilism is true is my position on akratic behavior incompatible with determinism.

## 2. Determinism, Compatibilism, and Incompatibilism: Setting the Stage

I take determinism, in its most common forms, to be (in principle) an empirically testable thesis. Worlds at which universal determinism is true are logically or conceptually possible, as are worlds at which it is false. As an empirical thesis, a full-blown or universal determinism is apparently in dire straits, as I noted in chapter 1. So why should one be the least bit interested in advancing an account of autonomy (or free will, or free action, or moral responsibility) that is compatible with determinism? Perhaps because a cousin of determinism, a thoroughly *causal* account of human conduct (including mental conduct), is the best account we can hope for. Many contemporary compatibilists do not endorse determinism. They are best seen as being opposed to certain incompatibilist ideas. For example, they reject the idea, advanced by some libertarians, that actions, or certain kinds of actions (e.g., willings), are uncaused, and they are skeptical either about "nonstandard" conceptions of causation advocated by some libertarians (e.g., agent causation) or about the possibility of those conceptions doing the work that their libertarian advocates want them to do.

These matters are taken up in subsequent chapters. Here some brief remarks on the evidential merit of *experiences* of acting and choosing autonomously will prove useful as a way of highlighting some salient differences between compatibilist and incompatibilist approaches to understanding personal autonomy.

John Searle writes,

> Reflect very carefully on the character of the experiences you have as you engage in normal, everyday ordinary human actions. You will sense the possibility of alternative courses of action built into these experiences. Raise your arm or walk across the room to take a drink of water, and you will see that at any point in the experience you have a sense of alternative courses of action open to you. . . . In normal behaviour, each thing we do carries the conviction, valid or invalid, that we could be doing something else right here and now, that is, all other conditions remaining the same. This, I submit, is the source of our own unshakable conviction of our own free will. (1984, p. 95)

The "conviction of freedom," Searle adds, "is built into every normal, conscious intentional action"; "this sense of freedom . . . is part of any action" (p. 97). He suggests, as well, that this sense or experience of freedom is explicable on evolutionary grounds: "[E]volution has given us a form of experience of voluntary action where the experience of freedom, that is to say, the experience of the sense of alternative possibilities, is built into the very structure of conscious, voluntary, intentional human behavior. For that reason, I believe, neither this discussion nor any other will ever convince us that our behaviour is unfree" (p. 98). Still, as the last quoted sentence suggests, Searle argues that our behavior is never free, in what he takes to be an important sense: "Our conception of physical reality simply does not allow for radical [i.e., libertarian] freedom." Compatibilism, he contends, does not offer "anything like the resolution of the conflict between freedom and determinism that our urge to radical libertarianism really demands."[1]

Spinoza, in a related vein, imagines a falling stone becoming conscious. "Such a stone," he writes, "being conscious merely of its own endeavour [to move along its path] and not at all indifferent, would believe itself to be completely free, and would think that it continued in motion solely because of its own wish. This is that human freedom, which all boast that they possess, and which consists solely in the fact, that men are conscious of their own desire, but are ignorant of the causes whereby that desire has been determined" (1955, p. 390). The "human freedom" to which Spinoza refers is underdescribed: someone conscious of his desire to $A$ and ignorant of its causes will not, other things being equal, take himself to be acting freely, unless he takes himself to be $A$-ing, or at least endeavoring to $A$ (as the stone supposedly did). But that leaves it open to Spinoza to claim that the "human freedom" at issue, the freedom "all boast that they possess," consists solely in consciousness of relatively proximate psychological springs of one's actions and of corresponding endeavors together with ignorance of the sources of those springs. This, one might say, is ersatz freedom, and one might contend that our experience of acting freely in no way supports the claim that human freedom extends beyond ersatz freedom.

It is worth considering in this connection the bearing of experiences of acting *intentionally* on the claim that some people act *intentionally*. That people sometimes act intentionally is difficult to doubt. This is so even though no attempted analysis of intentional action (or action, for that matter) has won general acceptance. All readers of this book have had an experience of acting intentionally. (Probably you are having one now.) And they can distinguish, in their own cases, between what appear to be clear instances of intentional action and clear instances of unintentional action—for example, reading this line versus typing 'tommorow' when one meant to type 'tomorrow.' The operative sense of "experience of $x$" here leaves room for nonveridical experiences of $x$. But what would it take to convince *you* (dear reader) to doubt in a serious—hence, not purely academic—way that you have ever acted intentionally, limiting the discussion now to what I have called *overt* action (action essentially involving peripheral bodily motion)? Or, to put the question in a directly experiential way, what would convince you that there is a significant chance that all of your experiences of acting intentionally (and overtly) are nonveridical? A persuasive argument that you are a brain in a vat (or otherwise unembodied) should suffice; or a convincing argument that you are only a dreamer, or that *you* do not exist; or a compelling argument for a strict eliminative materialism (assuming that you are convinced that only beings with a mental life act intentionally). At any rate, it seems that only drastic hypotheses such as these would turn the trick.[2]

So why is it that something that has seemed so plausible to so many, and certainly less *implausible* than the hypotheses just mentioned—namely, determinism, or the more modest idea that everything we do and all that happens to us is causally explicable—has been taken by so many to preclude free or autonomous action? Do incompatibilists tend to take our experiences of acting freely or autonomously to be somehow either less robust than our experience of acting intentionally or more theory-laden—so that one's experiences of acting autonomously, individually and collectively, have less evidential merit and are more susceptible to theoretical challenge? Certainly, if there are mental episodes that count as experiences of acting autonomously, the occurrence of those *experiences* (in the sense identified) is compatible with the truth of determinism. An agent can be causally determined to have such experiences. (An agent can be causally determined to have the experience of acting intentionally also, but that does not threaten the veridicality of that experience.) So the experience of acting autonomously does not preclude the truth of determinism. But neither does the experience of acting intentionally preclude (at least in any obvious way) the truth of the hypothesis that one is a brain in a vat; and this observation does not stand in the way of our reasonably taking such experiences to count strongly in favor of the hypothesis that we sometimes act intentionally.

One might say, correctly, that the experience of acting autonomously requires more for its veridicality than does the experience of acting intentionally.[3] The "more" that it requires, as some incompatibilists view matters, includes *freedom from deterministic causation* at some juncture or junctures. Incompatibilists (and others) who take all causation to be deterministic will view the italicized expression as redundant. But there are incompatibilists who seek to benefit from nondeterministic conceptions of causation. Peter van Inwagen, for example, writes that according to "the standard theory of causation . . . instances of causation simply are instances of universal, exceptionless laws, . . . the concept of the instantiation of an exceptionless law and the concept of causation are one and the same concept" (1983, p. 139), and he proceeds to attack "the standard theory" in an attempt to defend incompatibilism against certain criticisms.[4] (I take up van Inwagen's defense in ch. 11.)

Is freedom from (deterministic) causation something that can itself be experienced? Some say *yes*, alleging that we often have the experience of possessing genuine options—the experience of its being up to us what we do next, in the sense that, given the total state of ourselves and the world at the time along with the laws of nature, it is open to us to do one thing next and open to us to do another instead. (Recall Searle's remark, quoted earlier, that "in normal behaviour, each thing we do carries the conviction, valid or invalid, that we could be doing something else right here and now, that is, *all other conditions remaining the same*" [my italics].) Is that right? Or is our experience of openness better characterized in another way?

In addressing this question, one may be excused, I hope, for commenting on one's own experience. Here I am, sitting at my computer, composing this paragraph. I am also a bit thirsty. I now have the experience of entertaining two genuine options, two alternative courses of action open to me: one is to continue to sit here thinking and typing, for several minutes at least; the other is to walk down the hall to the drinking fountain in a few minutes. I consciously regard these options as things I can do and as things I may or may not do, as I please. At least in that sense, I have an experience of its being "up to me" which of these I do, or an experience describable in that way. However—and this is just a report on how things seem to me just now—I find in myself no experience that the total state of myself and the world now is causally compatible with my sitting here typing and thinking for several minutes and causally compatible, as well, with my instead going to the drinking fountain in a few minutes. Nor do I find in myself an experience of regarding things this way. Call these last two experiences—experiences that it seems to me I lack—*deep openness* experiences.

How can I have my "up-to-me" experience without having a deep openness experience? Well, perhaps I am not a very deep fellow along experiential lines. Perhaps my "up-to-me" experience amounts to nothing more than what I have already described. I need not also have, for example, the experience of its being causally undetermined what I am most inclined to do during the relevant span of time, or causally undetermined what I intend to do during that span, or causally undetermined what I do then. Nor need I have an experience of regarding things this way.

As it happened, I stayed here thinking and typing for more than several minutes before I got a drink. While I stayed here, it seemed to me that it was up to me what I was doing, as it also did when I finally walked down the hall for a drink: neither my desire to continue working nor my desire, a bit later, to walk down the hall for a drink was an irresistible desire, or so it seemed to me. If nothing more is required for an experience of acting autonomously, then I had an experience of acting autonomously. If I thought that acting autonomously required freedom from deterministic causation and that deterministic causation of my behavior is a much less remote possibility than, say, my being a brain in a vat, it would be easy to see how I might not take my experiences of acting autonomously to count for much, since my having those experiences is quite compatible with the truth of determinism. So incompatibilists whose experiences of acting autonomously run no deeper than mine and who take relevant deterministic hypotheses seriously, understandably deem those experiences not to count for much as grounds for the belief that they do act autonomously. In this, experiences of acting autonomously differ markedly from experiences of acting intentionally—on an incompatibilist view. For a normal agent's experiences of the latter sort, as a class, do much to ground his belief that he sometimes acts intentionally. Compatibilists, by contrast, are in a position to put greater stock in experience, as I explain in chapter 13.

Suppose, with Searle, that the experience of acting autonomously (or freely) is quite common in human beings (cf. Ginet 1990, pp. 90–91). Some people also occasionally have the experience of acting *nonautonomously* (or unfreely)—for instance, the experience of being psychologically compelled to do something—just as people occasionally (but more often) have the experience of doing something unintentionally.[5] Concerning intentional and unintentional action, we can seek insight into how they differ by attending to differences in the relevant *experiences*; the experience of offending someone intentionally, for example, might differ in theoretically instructive ways from the experience of offending someone unintentionally. Similarly, a theorist might hope to shed light on differences between *autonomous* and *nonautonomous* action by investigating experiential differences in that sphere. For example, the experience of being psychologically compelled to do something presumably is quite unlike the experience of acting autonomously; the experiential difference might point to a deeper one.

A familiar compatibilist distinction between *compulsion* and *causation* deserves mention in this connection.[6] Representative instances of compelled action, on this view, include a heroin addict's being moved to use the drug by an irresistible desire for heroin and a kleptomaniac's pocketing a trinket owing to an uncontrollable urge to steal. All actions, on the view at issue, are caused; but most actions are considerably less dramatic than the ones just adduced. They include, for example, my typing this sentence and your reading it. Some compatibilists have claimed that their opponents confuse caused with compelled action, and that if they were to see the light on this issue they would abandon their incompatibilism. However, incompatibilists can grant the distinction and claim that the compulsion of action and the (deterministic) causation of action are each incompatible with autonomous action—that noncompulsion does not go deep enough and that one acts autonomously only if it is up to one what one does in a sense of "up to one" that is incompatible not only with compulsion but also with determinism (cf. van Inwagen 1983, p. 17).[7]

Imagine that a theorist, Zed, starts with the assumption that there is nothing more to acting autonomously or nonautonomously than the experience of acting autonomously or nonautonomously, and eventually constructs an analysis of autonomous action that is faithful to that assumption. Most theorists would object to Zed's *starting* where he does, although some come to that point as a conclusion. They can ask, nevertheless, how much deeper one would have to delve to construct an analysis that would satisfy them. On this issue—depth, at least on one interpretation of the metaphor—libertarians and compatibilist believers in human autonomy are already in disagreement. The former require that a thesis of epic proportions—determinism—be false, whereas the latter can afford to be neutral on the truth of determinism. (Compatibilists can observe, for example, that there is no reason to think that quantum mechanical indeterminacy blocks human autonomy, and they can add that, in their opinion, it does nothing to promote autonomy either.) For some compatibilists, all that is required for an experience of acting autonomously to be veridical is that the agent acted intentionally and was not compelled so to act (in a standard sense of 'compelled'). Of course, some compatibilists demand more. But what leads compatibilists to the metaphysical depths, by and large, are the incompatibilists' objections. Except in replying to their incompatibilist opponents, compatibilist believers in human autonomy generally do not seek metaphysical *support* for their view. However, a serious libertarian bent on showing that some human beings are autonomous and on explaining in what human autonomy consists would be committed not only to showing that determinism is false but also to explaining how (some of) what falsifies it conduces to human autonomy.

Each of the issues raised in this section is a topic of investigation in subsequent chapters. My aim, as the section heading indicates, has simply been to set the stage for the remainder of part II. I return to the evidential merit of experience in chapter 13.

## 3. Autonomy and Pro-Attitudes

Personal autonomy, if it exists, is a property of persons. If all or many normal human beings are autonomous to some (varying) extent, then autonomy (often, at least) is a property of relatively complicated persons—people with values, principles, beliefs, desires, emotions, intentions, and plans; people capable of reasoning effectively both about, and on the basis of, such things; and people who can judge, plan, and act on the basis of their reasoning. In subsequent chapters I will be concerned, accordingly, with autonomy in a variety of mental and physical connections. The first topic on the agenda is what I call "psychological autonomy"—roughly, autonomy regarding various aspects of one's mental or psychological life, including one's *pro-attitudes* (e.g., one's values and desires). Three species of autonomy that agents may, in principle, enjoy with respect to their pro-attitudes are distinguishable. There are at least *prima facie* differences among an agent's autonomously *developing* a pro-attitude over a stretch of time, an agent's autonomously *possessing* a pro-attitude during a stretch of time, and an agent's being autonomous regarding the *influence* of a pro-attitude on his intentional behavior.[8]

I made this tripartite distinction elsewhere (Mele 1993) in criticizing a thesis advanced by John Christman (1991). Brief discussion of that thesis will prove useful both in developing the distinction and in setting part of the stage for chapter 9. Christman maintains that "an agent is autonomous vis-à-vis some desire if the influences and conditions that gave rise to the desire were factors that the agent approved of or did not resist, or would not have resisted had she attended to them, and that this judgment was or would have been made in a minimally rational, non-self-deceived manner" (1991, p. 22). This claim is undermined by the following case.[9]

Alice, a specialist on drug addiction, once decided after careful reflection to make herself a heroin addict so that she could directly experience certain phenomena (cf. Frankfurt 1988, p. 14). She strove, accordingly, to develop irresistible desires for heroin and she fully accepted the developmental process on the basis of self-reflection that was at least minimally rational and involved no self-deception. Alice was careful to reflect on the process only when clear-headed. In due time, Alice developed irresistible desires for heroin, desires that (by hypothesis) she *autonomously* developed. At present, while in the grip of an irresistible desire to use the drug, Alice rationally judges that it would be best to refrain from using it now; she explicitly and rationally judges, as well, that it would be best to eradicate her standing desire for heroin, beginning immediately. She is convinced that the experiment is more dangerous than she had realized and that it is time to start setting things right. However, Alice is incapable of resisting her present desire for heroin. Moreover, she is incapable of immediately eradicating her standing desire for heroin, and she is presently incapable of strategically eradicating it any time soon (during *t*, say).

Although, by hypothesis, Alice autonomously developed irresistible desires for heroin, she is not autonomous with respect to the influence of her present desire for heroin on her present behavior. A clear sign of her nonautonomy in that connection is her *inability* to refrain from acting on that desire even though she judges it best not to use the drug now. (Notice that part of Alice's aim in cultivating her irresistible desires might have been to enable herself to experience what it is like to be *non-autonomous* regarding the influence of a desire on one's behavior.) Further, Alice is not autonomous (or self-governing) vis-à-vis her current *possession* of her standing desire for heroin, nor her continued possession of it during *t*—even though she satisfies Christman's conditions for being "autonomous vis-à-vis [that] desire."[10] If she were self-governing with respect to her possession of that desire, she would rid herself of it, as she judges best. Instead, she is stuck with the standing desire and victimized by it, while rationally preferring its eradication.

The autonomous *development* of a pro-attitude $P$ that one possesses throughout $t$ is not sufficient for the autonomous *possession* of $P$ throughout $t$. Alice (by hypothesis) autonomously developed her standing desire for heroin; but there was a time during which she possessed it nonautonomously. Having autonomously developed a pro-attitude is not *necessary* for autonomously possessing it either, as I will argue in chapter 9, section 8. Further, Alice's present occurrent desire for heroin counts as autonomously developed on Christman's view; but her supposed developmental autonomy vis-à-vis the desire does not suffice for autonomy regarding the *influence* of that desire on her current behavior. It is also plain that developmental autonomy regarding a desire is not *required* for autonomy regarding the influence of that desire on one's behavior. Provided that a desire is not irresistible, one may be in an excellent position to govern its influence—or to prevent it from influencing one's overt behavior at all—even if the desire was not autonomously developed (cf. Double 1992, p. 67).

What, exactly, these three kinds of autonomy amount to is a difficult question. My purpose in this section has simply been to mark the distinction for future discussion and use. The autonomous possession of one's pro-attitudes is a central concern of the following chapter.

## 4. Autonomy and Moral Responsibility

In this book, my primary interest in personal autonomy is an *intrinsic* interest. I am interested in personal autonomy in its own right. In particular, I do not view philosophical interest in autonomy as necessarily derivative from a philosophical interest in moral responsibility. Suppose that the hypothetical Aristotelian gods I mentioned in chapter 1 are autonomous agents, but morally responsible for nothing. We are still faced with the question in what their autonomous agency consists. I take that to be a philosophically interesting question. It is, in part, the question how (actual or hypothetical) autonomous agents differ from nonautonomous ones: for example, from cats and dogs, from children who are just beginning to act intentionally, from pervasively delusional agents, and, of course, from various nonautonomous agents in philosophical thought experiments. A plausible answer to this question should, one hopes, prove useful in illuminating moral responsibility. That, however, is not my *goal* here. In a chapter entitled "Free Will," Robert Nozick remarks: "[M]y interest in the question of free will does not stem from wanting to be able legitimately to punish others, to hold them responsible, or even to be held responsible myself" (1981, p. 291). The same may be said of my interest in autonomy.

That said, I realize that some, and perhaps many, readers of this book are interested in philosophical work on autonomous agency primarily for the light that it may shed on moral responsibility. I will have occasion to comment on moral responsibility in subsequent chapters, with a view to illuminating personal autonomy. Here, I address a particular alleged connection between personal autonomy and moral responsibility. If the connection holds, there are grounds for belief that truths about moral responsibility will shed light on personal autonomy.

In the course of stating an argument to be discussed in chapter 13, section 4, Peter van Inwagen voices a popular thesis about moral responsibility: "[M]oral responsibility requires free will" (1983, p. 188). Readers who take the existence of free will to require the existence of "the will," and who are disinclined to hold that there is such a thing, may wish to endorse a comparable thesis (*T*): Moral responsibility requires autonomous agency. On a natural reading, *T* asserts that *S* is a morally responsible agent only if *S* is (at least in some measure) an autonomous agent. Thesis *T* is specifically about agents, not actions. It does not, for example, entail the further thesis that an agent is morally responsible for an action only if he performed that action autonomously. That is fortunate for *T*'s proponents, for the further thesis is false. A drunk driver, Spike, owing to his drunkenness, did not see a pedestrian in his path and unwittingly drove over him. Other things being equal, we view Spike as morally responsible for having driven over the pedestrian—and for the harm done— even though we do not view him as having autonomously (or freely) driven over the pedestrian. However, if Spike were not an autonomous agent—if he were an inebriated stunt dog, say—we would not hold him morally responsible.

A pilot, flying a small passenger plane, passes out at the control panel, owing to drunkenness. When the plane lurches, his head crashes into the window, and he immediately dies. Minutes later, the eight passengers are killed when the plane hits the ground. Other things being equal, the pilot is morally responsible for the passengers' deaths. But at the time of their deaths, the pilot is not an agent at all, much less an autonomous agent: "dead agents" are dead *erstwhile* agents. That moral responsibility requires autonomous agency does not entail that all events or states for which one is morally responsible occur or obtain at a time at which one is an autonomous agent. The thesis, rather, is that *S* is not morally responsible for anything unless, at some relevant time, *S* is an autonomous agent. The relevant time need not be one at which an agent is actively pursuing an end. It may be one at which an agent passively *omits* to do something; it may be the time of a "not-doing." An autonomous agent may be morally responsible for not making an effort to save a child he sees drowning, and for the child's death by drowning. Even a sleeping autonomous agent may be morally responsible for events that he does not initiate and that occur while he is asleep. A lifeguard who carelessly falls asleep at his post may be morally responsible for the drowning of a swimmer in his charge. If the lifeguard were not an autonomous agent— if he were a trained canine member of the life-saving crew, for instance—he would not be morally responsible for the drowning.

What features of personal autonomy are required for moral responsibility? What features do autonomous agents possess (qua autonomous) and nonautonomous agents lack in virtue of which the former, but not the latter, can be morally responsible for various things? A variety of such features are identified in subsequent chapters. Here, I take up an alleged feature of autonomy that does not merit our endorsement.

It is sometimes held that moral responsibility for an action requires the freedom to have done otherwise; and the same requirement has been placed on the autonomous performance of an action (or on having acted freely). However, even the weaker claim that being a morally responsible and autonomous agent requires the freedom to act otherwise than one acts on at least one occasion is false.[11] Consider an expanded Frankfurt-style scenario (see ch. 5, sec. 2). *Whenever* Brian acts, there is (unbeknown to Brian) an irresistible demon on the scene—a prescient but myopic one—who intends to compel Brian to perform an action of a specific type (and will compel him) unless he sees that Brian is going to perform an action of that type on his own. At no time is Brian free to act otherwise than as he does. But, as it happens, by extraordinary coincidence, Brian always does on his own what the demon was prepared to compel him to do. The demon never interferes: Brian acts, at all times, just as he would have acted if there had been no demon. The existence of this demon, then, with his particular powers and intentions, constitutes no bar to Brian's deserving moral blame or credit for his actions; it constitutes no bar to Brian's being a morally responsible agent. Further, given that the demon in no way intervenes in Brian's life, the existence of the demon, with his powers and intentions, cannot plausibly be regarded as a bar to Brian's being an autonomous or self-governing agent. Although the demon has the power to govern Brian's behavior, he never exercises that power.

To be sure, most of us would like it not to be true that there is, unbeknownst to us, a demon who possesses such power over us. That may be due partly to the worry that such a demon might exercise his powers and take charge of what we do. It may also be due to a desire of ours to have the freedom to do otherwise. There being a demon of the imagined kind would preclude our possessing this freedom, and the freedom to do otherwise might be something that we value, even *deeply* value. The absence of such freedom, for those who value it, may be a matter of deep personal importance. However, we should not confuse our valuing freedom of this kind with our valuing autonomy. The demon would be a *potential* bar to our acting autonomously, insofar as he would have the power to *compel* us to act; but a noninterfering demon compels no actions. Neither moral responsibility nor autonomous agency requires the freedom to do otherwise.

This is not to deny, incidentally, that the existence of an irresistible demon who is always prepared to compel us to do something may limit the *chance* that we will act autonomously on any given occasion. The greater the chance that the demon will interfere, the greater the chance that we will act nonautonomously. Those who value not only *actual* autonomous agency but also, *beyond that*, an excellent *chance* of consistently acting autonomously have reason to hope that they are not subject to the influence of interfering demons.

A potential reservation about my use of the Brian scenario requires brief attention. Suppose that Brian *A*-s at a time *t*. It may be asked how the demon can render Brian unfree to refrain from *A*-ing at *t*, given that the demon does not intervene (cf. Lamb 1993, p. 523). Assume that the demon is irresistible, infallible, and a resolute intender, and that his having these properties is an essential feature of the scenario under consideration (i.e., eliminating any of these properties would change the subject). Then at no possible world at which the scenario obtains and the demon has the relevant conditional intention does Brian refrain from *A*-ing at *t*. (At some of those worlds, Brian *A*-s on his own; at others, the demon compels him to *A*.) Assuming that if Brian were free to refrain in my scenario there would be some possible instance of the scenario in which the demon has the relevant conditional intention and Brian does refrain, he is not free to refrain from *A*-ing at *t* in this scenario. The demon renders

Brian unfree to refrain from *A*-ing at *t* by rendering that course of action unavailable to Brian (in virtue of the demon's relevant powers and his resolute intention).[12]

## 5.  Some Definitions

As an aid to readers unfamiliar with standard terminology in the literature on autonomy, I include definitions of some common terms.

> *Compatibilism*: The thesis that human autonomy (or freedom) is compatible with the truth of determinism. (Compatibilists may or may not hold that human beings are autonomous, or that determinism is true.)[13]
>
> *Incompatibilism*: The denial of compatibilism. (Incompatibilists may or may not hold that human beings are autonomous, or that determinism is true.)
>
> *Libertarianism*: The conjunction of incompatibilism and the thesis that human beings sometimes choose and act autonomously (or freely). (Unfortunately, there is no standard term for the conjunction of compatibilism and the thesis that human beings sometimes choose and act autonomously.)
>
> *Determinism*: "The thesis that there is at any instant exactly one physically possible future" (van Inwagen 1983, p. 3). (There are more detailed definitions of determinism in the literature; but this one will do for my purposes. Some readers will wish to insert 'after the Big Bang' between 'instant' and 'exactly.')
>
> *Indeterminism*: The thesis that determinism is false. (The occurrence of *any* causally undetermined event at a world suffices for the falsity of determinism at that world. Indeterminism is not the view that *everything* is causally undetermined.)

Again, an event *e*'s being *causally determined* does not depend on the truth of determinism. Suppose that *C* or some part of *C* is not itself determined. Still, if determinism is false, *C* might occur or obtain; and *C*, together with the state of the world at the time and the laws of nature, might ensure that any physically possible future includes *e*.

### Notes

1.  Searle uses 'libertarianism,' nonstandardly, as a label for the view that some people have "free will" (1984, p. 92). By "radical libertarianism" here, he simply means 'libertarianism,' as the term is ordinarily used. In its standard usage, 'libertarianism' tags the conjunction of incompatibilism and the thesis that some human beings have free will.

2.  I realize, of course, that some readers might not find eliminativism terribly implausible. Some grounds for skepticism about the view are offered in Mele 1992a, ch. 2, sec. 7.

3.  Correctly, because, for example, the person executing a posthypnotic suggestion to open the window opens the window intentionally but does not open it freely, and the kleptomaniac intentionally steals the stockings but (assuming a common view) does not freely steal them.

4.  It merits mention that what van Inwagen refers to as "the standard theory" is taken by others to be currently nonstandard. Michael Tooley, for example, writes: "It would appear . . . that most present-day philosophers think that . . . there can be causal relations in cases where the underlying laws are probabilistic" (1987, p. 290). Also see Lewis 1986, p. 175.

5. Searle writes: "If . . . I am instructed to walk across the room at gunpoint, still part of the experience is that I sense that it is literally open to me at any step to do something else. The experience of freedom is thus an essential component of any case of acting with an intention" (1984, p. 96). Supposing that his claim about acting at gunpoint is correct, such cases differ from those in which, say, heroin addicts experience themselves as being *compelled* to use the drug by their craving and as literally having open to them, in the circumstances, no alternative to using the drug. They act with the intention of using the drug in these cases, but they do not have "the experience of freedom," in Searle's sense. This is not to say, of course, that all heroin addicts are like this. Some might "sense," even in the grip of a craving and in the presence of heroin, that it is "literally open" to them to refrain from using the drug.

6. See, e.g., Audi 1993, chs. 7, 10; Ayer 1954; Grünbaum 1971; Mill [1865] 1979, ch. 26, esp. pp. 464–67; and Schlick 1962, ch. 7. Also see Hume's remarks on the liberty of spontaneity versus the liberty of indifference ([1739] 1975, bk. 2, pt. 3, sec. 2).

7. The compulsion of an action, as I am using the term 'compulsion,' is a matter of an agent's being *compelled* to perform a certain action, or an action of a certain type. 'Compulsion' is sometimes used in the philosophical and psychological literature to mean 'irresistible impulse.' If an agent can be compelled to *A* by something other than an irresistible impulse, and independently of having such an impulse, then the compulsion of actions need not always involve compulsions, in the latter sense.

8. This tripartite distinction is not intended to be exhaustive.

9. For further discussion of Christman 1991, see Mele 1993, where essentially this case appears.

10. This is not to deny that Alice is *responsible* (causally or morally) for her continued possession of the desire.

11. For a comparable claim, see Lamb 1993, p. 527.

12. *S*'s possessing an alleged "ability" to refrain from *A*-ing that is available to agents in demon scenarios of the sort at issue and contingent upon the demon's not interfering (see Lamb 1993 and ch. 5, n. 18) does not suffice for *S*'s being free to refrain from *A*-ing.

13. Some compatibilists do not endorse the thesis that determinism is compatible with the freedom to do otherwise. See Fischer 1987.

# 9

# Psychological Autonomy and Personal History

The capacities involved in personal autonomy are of at least two kinds, broadly conceived. Some are directed specifically at one's environment. Assuming some autonomy for Prometheus, he was considerably less autonomous bound than unbound; chained to the rock, he possessed only a severely limited capacity to affect his environment. Others have a pronounced inner-directedness, their outward manifestations notwithstanding. Capacities for decision making and for critical reflection on one's values, principles, preferences, and beliefs fall into the second group. Capacities of both kinds have at least a partly psychological basis. Although beings lacking a mental life may affect their environment, they cannot do so autonomously; and, of course, such beings are incapable of decision and reflection. Reserving the expression "psychological autonomy" for the kind of autonomy open even to a shackled Prometheus, we can ask what it requires.

The present chapter examines a question about the place of *agents' histories* in a proper understanding of psychological autonomy, a question raised by various thought experiments that incompatibilists have designed to undermine particular compatibilist analyses of free action and free will. I will develop some scenarios in that genre and argue both that they motivate a certain history-sensitive view of psychological autonomy and that such a view is compatible with compatibilism. I will assume for the sake of argument that autonomy is possible for human beings like us. That assumption is addressed in chapter 13.

Philosophical thought experiments typically are designed to elicit relatively stable "intuitions" that can then be used in testing various claims. On most of the issues central to the debate between compatibilists and incompatibilists, if the history of the dispute is any indication, one cannot expect to find cases that have the widespread intuitive clout that, for example, Edmund Gettier's cases have concerning the analysis of knowledge (1963). (That partially accounts for the length of this chapter: various theoretical impediments to seemingly natural intuitions need to be uncovered and, if they deserve it, dissolved, and the cases must be carefully developed to circumvent a variety of worries.) Still, I hope to show that compatibilists can be responsive to some cases of a kind often viewed as yielding an incompatibilist moral without abandoning their compatibilism. That is a point of significance for all parties in the debate about personal autonomy. On some important matters, as I will argue in chapter 13, compatibilist and incompatibilist believers in autonomy can join forces against nonbelievers. When it comes to this, the more the believers have in common, the better prepared they will be to meet the nonbelievers' challenges.

## 1.   A Tale of Two Agents (and Two Tendencies)

I begin with a tale of two agents. Ann is an autonomous agent and an exceptionally industrious philosopher. She puts in twelve solid hours a day, seven days a week; and she enjoys almost every minute of it. Beth, an equally talented colleague, values a great many things above philosophy, for reasons that she has refined and endorsed on the basis of careful critical reflection over many years. She identifies with and enjoys her own way of life—one which, she is confident, has a breadth, depth, and richness that long days in the office would destroy. Their dean (who will remain nameless) wants Beth to be like Ann. Normal modes of persuasion having failed, he decides to circumvent Beth's agency. Without the knowledge of either philosopher, he hires a team of psychologists to determine what makes Ann tick and a team of new-wave brainwashers to make Beth like Ann. The psychologists decide that Ann's peculiar hierarchy of values accounts for her productivity, and the brainwashers in-still the same hierarchy in Beth while eradicating all competing values—via new-wave brainwashing, of course. Beth is now, in the relevant respect, a "psychological twin" of Ann. She is an industrious philosopher who thoroughly enjoys and highly values her philosophical work. Indeed, it turns out—largely as a result of Beth's new hierarchy of values—that whatever upshot Ann's critical reflection about her own values and priorities would have, the same is true of critical reflection by Beth. Her critical reflection, like Ann's, fully supports her new style of life.

Naturally, Beth is surprised by the change in her. What, she wonders, accounts for her remarkable zest for philosophy? Why is her philosophical work now so much more enjoyable? Why are her social activities now so much less satisfying and re-warding than her work? Beth's hypothesis is that she simply has grown tired of her previous mode of life, that her life had become stale without her recognizing it, and that she finally has come fully to appreciate the value of philosophical work. When she carefully reflects on her preferences and values, Beth finds that they fully sup-port a life dedicated to philosophical work, and she wholeheartedly embraces such a life and the collection of values that supports it.

Ann, by hypothesis, is autonomous; but what about Beth? In important respects, she is a clone of Ann—and by design, not accident. Her own considered preferences and values were erased and replaced in the brainwashing process. Beth did not con-sent to the process. Nor was she even aware of it; she had no opportunity to resist. By instilling new values in Beth and eliminating old ones, the brainwashers gave her life a new direction, one that clashes with the considered principles and values she possessed prior to manipulation. Beth's autonomy was violated, we naturally say.[1] And it is difficult not to see her now, in light of all this, as heteronomous to a signifi-cant extent. If that perception is correct, then given the psychological similarities between the two agents, the difference in their current status regarding autonomy would seem to lie in how they *came* to have certain psychological features that they have, hence in something *external* to their here-and-now psychological constitutions. That is, the crucial difference is *historical*; autonomy is in some way history-bound.

The reaction just adumbrated is a natural one; but it may be challenged. Psychological autonomy is frequently and naturally construed as a complex psychological capacity, one encompassing capacities for decision making, self-reflection, and the like. It may also be conceived, in the same vein but more robustly, as a condition requiring the effective *exercise* of a complex capacity of this kind. The capacity seemingly is *internal* to agents who possess it, even if it is a product of history and nurtured by a supportive environment; the same is true of its exercise.

Gerald Dworkin gives voice to a popular view when he writes,

> Autonomy is a second-order capacity to reflect critically upon one's first-order preferences and desires, and the ability either to identify with these or to change them in light of higher-order preferences and values. By exercising such a capacity we define our nature, give meaning and coherence to our lives, and take responsibility for the kind of person we are. (1988, p. 108)

On this account, psychological autonomy seemingly is a wholly internal matter; it is possessed independently of facts about how the capacities and abilities came to be present in agents. Thus, beings who are "psychological twins" over an interval *t* are equal with respect to psychological autonomy during *t* (cf. Schoeman 1978). If this is right, there is a stretch of time—perhaps a long one—during which Ann and brainwashed Beth are equally autonomous or nonautonomous with respect to their work and its place in their lives. If Ann is autonomous in that domain during that stretch, Beth is too.[2]

## 2.  Psychological Autonomy: Externalism vs. Internalism

The two reactions that I have sketched provide us, respectively, with what I will call an *externalist* and an *internalist* conception of psychological autonomy (the kind of autonomy open even to Prometheus bound). On an externalist view, there is more to being psychologically autonomous over a stretch of time than what goes on inside a person during that time. The psychological autonomy of (some) individuals also depends, for example, upon how they came to possess values and desires that guide self-reflection, decision making, and the like: it depends (in a way that requires articulation) on agents' *causal histories*.[3] The internalist, by contrast, maintains that history is relevant only insofar as it yields functional capacities for such things as decision making, self-reflection, identification, and self-modification. Given that the capacities are in place and are exercised with appropriate care and suitable frequency, all else is irrelevant to psychological autonomy. Harry Frankfurt's bold endorsement of an internalist conception of free, or autonomous, action sheds light on the general shape of an internalist conception of psychological autonomy:

> [T]o the extent that a person identifies himself with the springs of his actions, he takes responsibility for those actions and acquires moral responsibility for them; moreover, the questions of how the actions and his identifications with their springs are caused are irrelevant to the questions of whether he performs the actions *freely* or is morally responsible for performing them. (1988, p. 54; my italics)

Purely historical properties are sometimes legitimately employed for classificatory purposes. Consider two very similar burns on the backs of a pair of twins. They look and feel just the same. But only one is a *sunburn*; the other was caused by a heat lamp. Or compare a U.S. dollar bill with a perfect counterfeit made with plates and paper stolen from the United States Treasury Department. They fall into importantly different legal categories simply on the basis of their historical properties. However, division of *psychological* conditions into kinds, it is sometimes argued, is wholly nonhistorical. Thus, Jerry Fodor contends that "psychological states are individuated *with respect to their causal powers*" (1987, p. 42). This, conjoined with his further claim that "causal powers supervene on local micro-structure" and "in the psychological case, . . . on local neural structure," would place psychological autonomy, construed as a psychological state, wholly under the skin and render it independent of how what is internal to an agent came to be there (1987, p. 44).

Fodor's position is controversial, but it provides a useful way of focusing discussion. Is an agent's psychological autonomy just a matter of pertinent (Fodorian) causal powers that he possesses, in conjunction with various exercises of those powers? Or is there more to it? To be sure, one might argue that Fodor's notion of causal powers is unduly narrow, that there is a sense in which an agent's causal powers might be individuated partly on the basis of environmental and historical considerations. I have addressed this issue elsewhere, in another connection (Mele 1992a, ch. 2). I set it aside here and concentrate on a variant of the question just posed.

I have adverted to the internalism/externalism debate in the philosophy of mind only by way of *analogy* with my present concern. Whatever position one takes on the individuation of psychological states generally, internalism and externalism about psychological autonomy are options. For example, an internalist about psychological states may view psychological autonomy as more than just a psychological state and as having a nonpsychological, historical component, and an externalist about psychological states might deem Ann and Beth equally psychologically autonomous regarding their work, in virtue of their shared psychological capacities and abilities and their matching exercises thereof. My question is whether internalism or externalism specifically about psychological autonomy is the better option.

Many of our principles, values, desires, and beliefs come to us unbidden. Undeniably, our characters and values are in the process of being shaped before we are in any position to chart the course of our lives, to set up for ourselves principles and values with reference to which we may steer. Partly for this reason, a common approach to understanding psychological autonomy is to ask what autonomy implies about one's attitudes toward and control over principles, values, desires, and the like, of which one is already possessed. It is in this connection that Gerald Dworkin claims, to repeat, that "autonomy is a second-order capacity to reflect critically upon one's first-order preferences and desires, and the ability either to identify with these or to change them in light of higher-order preferences and values."

Possession of a capacity for critical reflection is a plausible requirement for autonomy. But the problem of value engineering raised in chapter 7, section 5, and again in Beth's case, suggests that even a robust and effectively exercised capacity of this kind is not sufficient for psychological autonomy. Again, any process of critical reflection is conducted, at any given time, from some perspective or other. If the perspective from which an agent critically reflects upon his "first-order preferences and desires" at a time is dominated by values produced by brainwashing, and dominated in such a way as to dictate the results of his critical reflection, it is difficult to view the reflection as autonomously conducted and the results as autonomously produced. There is at least a worry here that requires attention.

A familiar reaction is that autonomy requires what Dworkin has termed "procedural independence."[4] The requirement, as Dworkin sometimes represents it, is externalist. He writes, "Second-order reflection cannot be the whole story of autonomy. For those reflections, the choice of the kind of person one wants to become, may be influenced by other persons or circumstances in such a fashion that we do not view those evaluations as being the person's own" (1988, p. 18). Thus, a person can have and exercise precisely the capacities and abilities that Dworkin identifies with autonomy, and yet not be autonomous, on his view. (This indicates that Dworkin's identification should be construed as a conditional one—that is, conditional upon the person's having "procedural independence.")

Although Dworkin offers no analysis of procedural independence, he does sketch a program:

> Spelling out the conditions of procedural independence involves distinguishing those ways of influencing people's reflective and critical faculties which subvert them from those which promote and improve them. It involves distinguishing those influences such as hypnotic suggestion, manipulation, coercive persuasion, subliminal influence, and so forth, and doing so in a non ad hoc fashion (1988, p. 18).

For some readers, this passage will have an internalist ring. If the proscribed influence amounts to the destruction or severe impairment—subversion in *that* sense—of agents' capacities for second-order reflection and the like, internalists can happily endorse the proscription. There is, however, a way of understanding the subversion of a person's reflective and critical faculties as at least sometimes an externalistic matter. By manipulating the perspective or orientation from which such faculties operate in another agent, one can subvert the faculties without dulling their edge. By controlling which principles or values an agent takes for granted, one can make another person's critical and reflective capacities serve one's own purposes—purposes perhaps violently opposed by the individual prior to manipulation. The nameless dean understood this well, and he took advantage of the strategy in changing Beth's life. Perhaps Dworkin means to count subversion of this kind, too, as precluded by procedural independence. If so, his position is externalist.

Unfortunately for the externalist who seeks a simple historical requirement for autonomy, even effective manipulation as severe and comprehensive as that found in Beth's case might not thwart autonomy. To the extent to which one can successfully counteract the influence of brainwashing, having been a victim of that form of "mind control" does not necessarily render one nonautonomous. The same is true of the items on Dworkin's list of subverters of reflective and critical faculties: "hypnotic suggestion, manipulation, coercive persuasion, subliminal influence." (Suppose that you know who hypnotized you; having it in your power to cause him to cancel the posthypnotic suggestion, you do so.) Whether an agent's having been subjected to a certain mode of manipulation deprives him of autonomy depends, among other things, upon the effects of the manipulation and whether those effects remain in force. Further, an agent may voluntarily arrange to be manipulated in various ways in order to *promote* his autonomy, and such manipulation can, in principle, be successful. Hypnosis, for example, might help one gain greater control over one's desires to smoke or over debilitating irrational fears. Perhaps there are similar possibilities for manipulation of one's values. Valuing an altered configuration of first-order values, an agent might hire a manipulator to produce the new configuration in him. The manipulation might promote, rather than block, psychological autonomy.

Value revision raises an additional problem for the externalist. If Ann can revise her values and take up, accordingly, a significantly different style of life, then so can her psychological twin. But if Beth has that latitude, how has her autonomy been diminished?

## 3.  Autonomy and Ability

I have provided thumbnail sketches of externalist and internalist conceptions of psychological autonomy and I have identified some of the issues that they must address. Eventually, we must choose between them. On what grounds can a proper choice be made?

Autonomy regarding the *possession* of a pro-attitude that one has (ch. 8, sec. 3)— what I will call *P-autonomy* (for 'possession')—seemingly is an integral part of psychological autonomy. An agent who lacks *P*-autonomy only regarding a few relatively inconsequential pro-attitudes of his may not be affected much by this. But the more numerous and more central to one's character one's nonautonomously possessed pro-attitudes are, the less autonomous one apparently is. This, too, may be challenged, as I will explain in section 4; but let us not get ahead of the story. My immediate aim is to ascertain what bearing certain kinds of ability might have on *P*-autonomy.

I will not offer an analysis of ability. The nature of ability is among the hotly contested issues in the dispute between compatibilists and incompatibilists. That dispute is not adjudicated here. However, there are a number of points about ability on which compatibilists and incompatibilists can agree. Brief identification of some of them will facilitate discussion in this section.[5]

First, the ability to do *A* intentionally has a *representational* dimension. In the case of action-types that are not "basic" for an agent, an agent incapable of *conceiving* of any means to *A*-ing is not able to *A* intentionally. Such an agent is representationally cut off from intentional *A*-ing. (*Unintentional A*-ing is another matter.) Agents for whom something *is* a basic action-type can perform tokens of that type "at will." In this domain, proximally intending to *A* (e.g., to raise one's right arm), under normal conditions, issues straightaway in one's *A*-ing; and an intention to *A* encompasses a *representation* of one's prospective *A*-ing (Mele 1992a, pp. 218–24). Further, one who merely *lacks* a suitable representation of *A*-ing, or of necessary means to *A*-ing, may nevertheless be able to *A* intentionally. Tom currently has no representation of a means of impressing his new neighbors; it has not even occurred to him to try to impress them. Even so, should he want to impress them, promising means would quickly come to mind (and nothing prevents Tom from wanting this). Lacking a representation of a certain sort must be distinguished from being incapable of having a representation of that sort.

Second, the ability to do *A* intentionally has a *motivational* dimension. Setting aside problems posed by "subsidiary" actions (i.e., relatively minute actional parts of intended actions) and by double effect (Mele 1992a, pp. 113–15), an agent who is incapable of being motivated to *A* is not able to *A* intentionally. If *S* has been conditioned in such a way that he is incapable of being motivated to pet a snake (even as a means to a strongly desired end), then he is unable intentionally to pet a snake. However, the mere *absence* of motivation to *A* (or of a desire to *A*, in a familiar, broad sense of 'desire') does not suffice for one's being unable to *A* intentionally. Tom now has no motivation to leave his office soon, because he is in the midst of a thoroughly enjoyable project. But if there is no bar to his acquiring such motivation, he is able intentionally to leave his office soon—other things being equal (e.g., he knows how to leave his office, he has no irresistible urge to remain inside, he is not paralyzed, he has not been locked in).

Third, the ability to do *A* intentionally has a distinct *executive* dimension. Even an agent who wants very much to *A* and who knows how to *A* may be rendered (temporarily or permanently) unable to *A* by a feature of his internal condition. For example, owing to illness, a weight-lifter who often has bench-pressed four hundred pounds may currently lack the strength to lift that much weight: owing to his diminished strength, he may temporarily be unable to execute an intention to bench-press four hundred pounds.

Fourth, the ability (during *t*) to *A* intentionally (during *t*) often is contingent upon environmental conditions. An agent who knows how to play tennis and who has the relevant motivational and executive properties may be unable (during *t*) to play tennis (during *t*). He may be stranded in a desert, miles from the nearest tennis equipment.

Return to Dworkin's claim that autonomy encompasses "the ability either to identify with ['one's first-order preferences and desires'] or to change them in light of higher-order preferences and values." (On identification, see ch. 7, sec. 2.) We must distinguish between what I will call *disjunctive* and *dual* ability in this connection—that is, between (1) "the ability either to identify with [*P*] or to change [*P*]" and (2) a pair of abilities constituted by the ability to identify with *P* and the ability to change *P*. On a *strict* reading, an agent has an ability of type 1 regarding *P* if and only if he has either of the following two abilities: (1a) the ability to identify with *P* and (1b) the ability to change *P*. (One way of having either is having both, of course.) Dual ability requires more, encompassing, as it does, *both* 1a *and* 1b.[6] Dworkin's claim, strictly interpreted, presents the ability mentioned there as *disjunctive* ability (or, at least, does not present it as dual ability).[7]

The distinction just drawn is a distinction with a difference. An agent can have either of 1a or 1b without having the other. To take an extreme case, imagine that there is a powerful demon on the scene who will allow Al to continue to identify with *P*, something that Al is able to do, but will not allow Al to change *P*: if Al were to attempt to change *P*, the demon would ensure that he fails. In a counterpart case, Al has the ability to change *P* while lacking the ability to identify with *P*.

Another kind of ability merits attention.[8] Let us say that, at *t*, *S* has "*X*-ability" regarding *P* if and only if *S* has the following two abilities at *t*: (2a) the ability to identify with $P$ (by some later time or other, $t^*$), should he judge it best at $t$ to do so and (2b) the ability to change $P$ (by $t^*$), should he judge it best at $t$ to do so. $X$-ability encompasses a pair of abilities. However, it falls short of what I have called "dual ability." Suppose that Bill has $X$-ability regarding $P$ at $t$. But suppose, as well, that he is incapable at $t$ of judging it best to change $P$. Then even though Bill has ability 2b, he might not be able at $t$ to change $P$ (by $t^*$). (Perhaps Bill is so constituted that he can change $P$ only if he can judge it best to change $P$.) And lacking the ability to change $P$, he would lack dual ability regarding $P$. Indeed, $X$-ability does not even suffice for disjunctive ability (in my sense). Just imagine that a certain agent's being able to identify with $P$ by $t^*$ depends upon his being able to make an evaluative judgment about $P$ by $t^*$, that the same is true of his being able to change $P$ by $t^*$, and that an irresistible demon will not allow him to make any evaluative judgment about $P$ during the relevant time. Then even if the agent has $X$-ability regarding $P$ at $t$, he is not able at $t$ to identify with $P$ by $t^*$ and he is not able at $t$ to change $P$ by $t^*$.

The significance of these observations for personal autonomy will emerge in what follows. But one point should be made here. Return to Bill, and suppose that, at $t$, he lacks a psychological basis for judging it best to change $P$ only because the $P$-challenging attitudes that he once had were erased by unsolicited new-wave brainwashing. Suppose, as well, that $P$ and a host of $P$-supporting pro-attitudes were implanted during the brainwashing. Then even though Bill has $X$-ability regarding $P$, it is difficult to view him, on that account, as autonomously possessing $P$.[9]

The possession of *dual* ability with respect to one's values, principles, preferences, and desires—one's *pro-attitudes*, for short—has an apparent implication that merits discussion. Suppose that $S$, who is possessed of a wealth of first- and higher-order pro-attitudes, has and exercises a potent capacity for critical reflection. Further, with respect to each of his pro-attitudes—of *any* order—he has dual ability. On a robust construal of 'ability,' according to which ability has considerably more bite than mere logical possibility, $S$'s history (whatever it may involve) seemingly constitutes no bar to his possessing psychological autonomy (at least, if compatibilism is true)—provided that his abilities are suitably employed. $S$ apparently would be the master of his values, principles, preferences, and desires: whether he identifies with them or changes them would be up to him. If dual ability with respect to one's pro-attitudes (paired with suitable employment of the ability) were not only sufficient for psychological autonomy but necessary as well, the internalists would carry the day.[10]

Is dual ability regarding a pro-attitude that one possesses a plausible requirement for one's autonomously possessing that attitude? Consider Cal, an ex-smoker who is glad that he quit smoking but occasionally experiences a desire to smoke. Suppose that during a stretch of time, $t$, Cal is unable to identify with these desires, in the following sense—his identification with other values, desires, and so on, of his precludes his identifying with his desires to smoke, and it is not within his power to modify those attitudes during $t$ in such a way as to enable himself to identify with his desires to smoke. Cal has no inclination at all to modify those attitudes. But even if he were so inclined, let us suppose, he could not accomplish the needed modifications during $t$: he would need more time. Suppose further that Cal is able to bring it about during $t$ that he never desires to smoke, but that he regards the time, effort, and money required for this as not worth the gain. He decides to live with his occasional desires to smoke even though he in no way identifies with them.

Other things being equal, Cal autonomously elects to continue to have such desires in preference to undertaking desire-eliminating procedures open to him. Even if the desires are not themselves *manifestations* of his autonomy, he is autonomous with respect to his continuing to have them. And this is true even though Cal is unable to identify with his desires to smoke (including his continuing to have them) during the period in question and hence lacks dual ability regarding those desires during that period.

Consider another case, this time an extreme one. Currently, Al desires his children's welfare and strongly identifies with that desire; he has been like this for a long time. Imagine that ten minutes from now a powerful spirit, Sal, decides that she will prevent Al from "changing" that desire and that Sal is so powerful that it is not within Al's power to change the desire. Imagine further that Sal believes herself to be prescient, that her decision was prompted by the belief that Al would eventually change his desire unless she intervened, and that in this case she misread the future. Sal never had to act on her decision. Al's desire remained intact for another forty years, when he died a peaceful death in the company of his loving family. Throughout that time, the desire was an integral, deeply rooted part of Al's character.

Although, owing to the presence and plans of the spirit, Al lacks dual ability regarding his desire for his children's welfare, it is difficult to view him, simply on that account, as heteronomously possessing that desire. He continues to identify with the desire for reasons of his own, as he has long done, and eliminating the spirit from the story of Al's life would have no relevant effect on what Al desires, values, prefers, and so on, nor on what attitudes he holds toward his desires, values, and the like.[11] For all practical purposes, the spirit makes no difference. A conception of psychological autonomy as requiring disjunctive ability (depending on what else is built into that conception) might allow Al autonomously to possess and identify with his desire for his children's welfare whereas a counterpart conception requiring dual ability does not, and that is a mark against the latter. (Notice that Al does not have $X$-ability regarding this desire: even if he were to judge it best to "change" the desire, the spirit would not allow him to do so.)

I have offered a pair of counterexamples to the thesis that dual ability regarding a pro-attitude that one possesses is required for autonomously possessing that attitude. The counterexamples leave the following claim open: setting aside cases in which what accounts for an agent's inability to "change" a pro-attitude $P$ has no causal influence on the agent, an agent autonomously possesses $P$ during $t$ only if he is able to "change" $P$ during $t$ "in light of higher-order preferences and values." (Since it is difficult to be excited by an externalism that hinges on the presence or absence of a noninterfering spirit like Sal, I have no objection to setting such cases aside.) If this claim can be substantiated, internalists about psychological autonomy have an avenue worth exploring in the Ann/Beth case. If the claim is correct and Ann and Beth are unable, during $t$, to change the collection, $C$, of values that accounts for their philosophical life-styles, then neither agent autonomously possesses $C$ during $t$; but if they *are* able during $t$ to change $C$, then, arguably, nothing stands in the way of Beth's autonomously possessing $C$ during $t$. Of course, the ability to change $C$ only in one direction—for example, to make *C* even more powerful—is not a promising mark of autonomy. The relevant ability, apparently, is the ability to uproot or attenuate some members of *C* in such a way as to promote some alternative or other to an intensely philosophical life. If autonomous pro-attitude possession—*P*-autonomy—turns on ability in the suggested way, and if Ann and Beth, being psychological twins, are equal regarding the relevant ability or inability, then the Ann/Beth scenario would not support an externalist view of *P*-autonomy, for we would not then have psychological twins such that one has—and the other lacks—*P*-autonomy regarding a shared pro-attitude.[12]

A thorough assessment of the internalist position just described would require an exploration of the notion of ability at work in it. Independently of this, one might try to motivate the suggestion that there is some respectable notion of ability according to which Ann and Beth are equally (un)able to "change" *C,* and yet one autonomously possesses *C* and the other does not. Motivating that suggestion would motivate externalism about *P*-autonomy, of course, given that Ann and Beth are psychological twins.

I will turn to that task shortly. First, since "the ability to *change*" a pro-attitude, for reasons just noted, is not a particularly apt expression, I need a replacement. I will replace 'change' with 'shed,' understanding the shedding of a pro-attitude disjunctively, as eradicating it or significantly attenuating it. (Readers who object to this use of 'shed' may substitute 'shed*' for the term.)

Is there a significant sense of 'able' in which someone who is not able to shed a pro-attitude *P* during *t* nevertheless autonomously possesses *P* then? Change the case of Al and the spirit by eliminating the spirit from the story. Imagine also that Al autonomously developed his parental values (ch. 8, sec. 3). In some robust sense of 'can,' it may be true that, given how deeply entrenched Al's parental values are, he can neither uproot nor attenuate them (during *t,* perhaps a two-week span): that is, Al's shedding those values (during *t*), given his psychological constitution at his world, is not a psychologically genuine option. Of course, there might be conditions beyond Al's control such that, were they to arise, he would shed these values. He might become hopelessly insane, for example. Or CIA agents might use Al's parental values as a lever to motivate him to uproot those very values: they might convince him that the CIA will ensure his children's flourishing if he uproots his parental values and that, otherwise, they will destroy his children's lives. Under these conditions (I will suppose), Al would take himself to have a decisive reason for shedding his parental values, and if he thought hard enough, he might find a way to shed them. (Once he sheds the values, he might not care at all how his children fare; but that is another matter.) However, if, in fact, conditions such as these do not arise for Al in the next two weeks, neither will he shed his parental values during that period. Insofar as the conditions that would empower Al to shed these values are "beyond his control"— that is, insofar as his psychological constitution precludes his voluntarily producing those conditions—and the obtaining of those conditions independently of Al's voluntarily producing them is not in the cards, he is apparently stuck with the values.

I will say that any agent who is stuck in this way with a value (during *t*) is *practically unable* to shed it (during *t*). Values that one is practically unable to shed may be termed *practically unsheddable.*

   The notion of ability at work here is similar to one implicit in commonsense conceptions of irresistible desires. We say that an agent in the grip of an irresistible desire to do *A* is, by definition, *unable* intentionally to refrain from *A*-ing: if he were able to do this, the desire would lack irresistible force. But, on the assumption that real people are sometimes possessed of irresistible desires, this is not to say that there are no imaginable conditions under which—holding the relevant desires fixed—the agents would intentionally refrain from *A*-ing. Such conditions are always imaginable, in the case of real agents, as many people who are willing to attribute irresistible desires to real agents grant.
   Consider the following case:

> Fred has agoraphobia and . . . his fear is so strong that he has not ventured out of his house in ten years, despite our many attempts to persuade him to do so. We decide finally that we just have not been presenting Fred with the right reasons and we threaten to burn his house to the ground if he does not open his door today. When it becomes evident that the threat will not work, we start throwing flaming brands through his windows. Fred, panic stricken, tears open his front door and runs screaming into the night, having finally been presented with what he takes to be a good and sufficient reason for leaving his home. (Mele 1992a, p. 87)

Treat this as a *counterfactual* scenario. At *t*, Fred would have intentionally left his house if his house had been burning down around him; but, in fact, his life was not threatened in his actual situation at *t*. Does it follow from the truth of this counterfactual proposition that Fred's desire to remain indoors at the time was not irresistible? *Yes*, on a strong reading of 'irresistible'; but on that reading it is unlikely that any real agent has ever had an irresistible desire. *No*, on a weaker reading that permits irresistible desires to be present in real agents.
   Consider the analogy of a woman who, "under ordinary circumstances, cannot even budge a three-hundred-pound weight, but who, upon finding her child pinned under a four-hundred-pound timber manages, due to a sudden burst of adrenalin, to raise the timber from his body" (Mele 1992a, p. 87). It would be misleading to say that the woman can lift four hundred pounds, if we leave it at that. A woman who can lift that much weight would excel on the women's professional weight-lifting tour! A more accurate claim is that in ordinary circumstances she cannot lift four hundred pounds—*no matter how hard she tries*—although in a certain kind of exceptional circumstance she can. By the same token, Fred might be unable, under ordinary circumstances, to leave his house intentionally, no matter how hard he tries to resist his desire to remain indoors, even though a towering inferno would drive him out.[13] There is a difference between irresistibility under ordinary circumstances and irresistibility under exceptional circumstances, just as there is a difference between the ability to lift four hundred pounds under normal circumstances and the ability to lift four hundred pounds when under the influence of an extraordinary burst of adrenalin. Similarly, there is a difference between the "practical ability" to shed a certain value and the ability to shed that value under certain counterfactual circumstances. Even if Al would shed his parental values under certain exceptional conditions, it does not follow that, during the two-week span, those values are practically sheddable by him.

Does Al's practical inability to shed his parental values render him nonautonomous regarding his continued valuing of his children's welfare over the next two weeks? It is partly because of the plausibility of the idea that values as deeply entrenched as Al's can be autonomously harbored that *identification* with one's values is featured in many accounts of autonomy. Recall Dworkin's requirement (strictly interpreted) that an agent who is autonomous regarding the possession of a pro-attitude be, in light of critical reflection, able to change that pro-attitude *or* able to identify with it. An agent who has *neither* ability with respect to a pro-attitude seemingly is victimized by the attitude's presence. But Al is implausibly deemed a victim of the deeply entrenched parental values with which he identifies.

The root notion of autonomy, again, is self-government or self-rule (ch. 1). Al's capacity to govern himself need in no way be hampered by his parental values. We may suppose that Al's commitment to his parental values is entirely rational by his own lights, that these values do not influence his practical reasoning and evaluative judgments in ways that violate deliberative principles of his, that they do not lead him to conduct himself (psychologically or overtly) in ways that clash with his decisive better judgments, and so on. Al is not victimized in any way by his parental values, and he wholeheartedly endorses them. If he had what he took to be decisive reasons to shed them, he would, but his psychological constitution is such that reasons of this kind can be found only in scenarios quite remote from his actual circumstances (at least during the period in question). Further, that Al reflectively judges it best to have the parental values that he has and deeply identifies with those values is a mark of his being self-governing regarding his current possession of them. He would have it no other way. If Al could lay it down as an inviolable law of his personal nature that he would have those values throughout his life, he would.

If Al's parental values had been instilled in him against his will—if he had once been among the most uncaring and abusive parents imaginable and had come by his deeply entrenched parental values as a direct result of new-wave brainwashing—our judgment about his autonomy might be different. (I address a closely related matter in sec. 5.) But in the case at hand, nothing stands in the way of our viewing Al as autonomously possessing his parental values, their practical unshedability notwithstanding.

Return to Ann and Beth. Suppose that Ann is no more able to shed her relevant values (over a certain two-week span) than Al is to shed his. The values are too deeply entrenched for that. Ann's commitment to the values that guide her intensely philosophical life is so deep that, given the constitution of her world, those values are practically unsheddable during that span. Suppose also that Ann is no less autonomous regarding her possession of those values during that span than Al is regarding his possession of his parental values. Brainwashed Beth, by hypothesis, is a psychological twin of Ann; and we may suppose that she is neither more nor less able than Ann to shed the values that they share. Does it follow that Ann and Beth are equally autonomous regarding their possession of those values?

The salient difference between Ann and Beth is that Ann's practically unsheddable values were acquired under her own steam, whereas Beth's were imposed upon her. Ann autonomously developed her values (we are entitled to suppose); Beth plainly did not. Except possibly for theorists in the firm grip of internalism about psychological autonomy, it is difficult to see this difference as irrelevant to the autonomous *possession* of these values. Given that they are psychological twins, Ann and Beth make equal use of the relevant, unsheddable values in "governing" their mental lives. But in Beth's case, one is inclined to view this as *ersatz* self-government. The dean and his cronies seized control of the direction that her life would take when they erased her former values and replaced them with the new, practically unsheddable ones. Behind the facade of self-government, external governors lurk—covert manipulators who engineered practically unsheddable values central to the psychological foundation on which Beth bases many of her identifications, evaluative judgments, decisions, and actions.

Some grounds for resisting this view of the case are assessed in the ensuing discussion, where a more disturbing scenario is featured. I return to the Beth/Ann scenario in section 8.

## 4. Autonomy, Authenticity, and Responsibility

For expository reasons, I organized earlier sections around a case of manipulation resulting in a way of life that many of us would find acceptable (if not for ourselves, at least for others). Other cases, though structurally very similar, seemingly present an intuitively more gripping challenge to internalism. Assume that an exceptionally evil person—for example, Adolf Hitler or Charles Manson—can be autonomous. (The plausibility of this assumption is addressed in sec. 5.) And suppose that Beth, via a process of the kind sketched earlier, is made a "psychological twin" (in my loose sense) of Hitler or Manson. To some, it may seem that not only would the manipulators violate Beth's autonomy in brainwashing her, but that the result would be a Beth who is largely nonautonomous with respect to her way of life—even if Hitler and Manson are largely autonomous with respect to theirs. If the appearances are on target—and I will argue later that, given further details, they are—what do they indicate?

They indicate, I will argue, that the autonomous possession of a pro-attitude requires *authenticity* regarding that pro-attitude, in a sense of the term to be spelled out in due course. Brief commentary on two conceptions of authenticity in the literature will prove useful. Gerald Dworkin, in an influential paper, understands authenticity as *identification* with one's motivations (1976, p. 25). Since the manipulated Beth identifies with her new motivations, authenticity in Dworkin's sense does not fit the bill. Joel Feinberg writes, in a similar vein:

> A person is authentic to the extent that . . . he can and does subject his opinions and tastes to rational scrutiny. He is authentic to the extent that he can and does alter his convictions for reasons of his own, and does this without guilt or anxiety. . . . [H]e will select his life style to match his temperament, and his political attitudes to fit his ideals and interests. (1986, p. 33)

But Beth can scrutinize her opinions and tastes, alter her convictions in accordance with her values, and select (or at least embrace) a lifestyle that fits her current temperament. Feinberg's expression, "reasons of his own," might leave open what we need, if reasons of one's own are not simply identical with one's reasons.[14] Perhaps one's reasons count as "reasons of [one's] own" only under certain history-sensitive conditions. On such a reading, Feinberg's conception of authenticity is closer to what we are after than is the more streamlined notion of authenticity as identification.

As most contributors to the literature on autonomy observe, including Dworkin and Feinberg, autonomy does not entail being a wholly self-made person. Any conception of authenticity that requires individuals who possess that property to be the sole source of their values, preferences, and the like would be poorly suited to our needs. External influences on our values are considerable; a view of autonomy that placed autonomous individuals above all that would exclude all of us. Still, apparently, some instances of effective external influence greatly reduce psychological autonomy, and attention to authenticity might help us see why.

Return to the difference between an authentic dollar bill and a perfect counterfeit. Both will get you a Coke from a vending machine or a pack of gum from the corner store. But only one of them can function in a *legal* purchase. Whether the two bills have the same causal powers is open to dispute. Some might claim that only one of them has the power to function—causally, of course—in your legally acquiring a Coke. Others might urge that because the distinction between the acquisition of a Coke and the *legal* acquisition of a Coke is a wholly conceptual matter, it has nothing whatever to do with causal powers. The bills have the same causal powers, but because only one of them is authentic, "purchasing" a Coke with the other does not *count as* a legal acquisition. This is a dispute that need not be entered for present purposes. It suffices to note that, given certain conventions (in this case, laws), the bills cannot function in precisely the same ways. (Both get you the Coke, but only one gets it for you legally.)

What are the conventions or principles with respect to which the sort of authenticity that I am pursuing would make a difference? One obvious answer is conventions or principles governing the attribution of *responsibility* to agents for their values, preferences, principles, and the like—or, more generally, for their *character*. To the extent to which we view psychologically autonomous agents, in virtue of their autonomy, as responsible (in some measure, at least) for their character, we are likely to view an authenticity that bears on responsibility for one's character to bear on personal autonomy, as well.[15] Now, even if we hold Manson responsible for his character, would we hold Beth, in the Beth/Manson scenario, responsible for her Mansonian character, given what we know about how she came to be a Manson "twin"? I doubt it, at least given further details (details that will emerge gradually).

My hypothesis that Beth might not be responsible for her Mansonian character even if Manson is responsible for his own evil character requires scrutiny. I start with an objection, an argument from determinism.[16]

Assume that determinism is true and assume as well that its truth is compatible with personal autonomy and responsibility. It might be argued that, with these assumptions in place, the notion of responsibility for one's *character* must be jettisoned and the best account we can give of autonomy regarding one's way of life is that such autonomy is precisely a matter of living in accordance with preferences and desires that one identifies with "in light of higher-order preferences and values." In the former connection, it may be claimed that character is *ultimately* a product of external causes present prior even to our own existence, and that, having no control

over such causes (events), we have no control over—hence no responsibility for—
our character.[17] In the latter, it may be argued that if autonomy in a given practical
domain suffices for an agent's being responsible for her intentional actions in that
domain, brainwashed Beth is responsible for her Manson-like behavior. She, like
Manson, conducts herself in accordance with higher-order preferences and values
with which she identifies, is capable of critical reflection, and so on.

So much the worse for determinism, some will respond. But I leave determinism open and take another tack. If a history-sensitive externalism about psychological autonomy is acceptable to a theorist who holds that determinism is compatible
with psychological autonomy, that is worth knowing. It has been claimed—wrongly,
I will argue—that "the internalistic view is implicit in compatibilism" and that "compatibilism has not a chance of plausibility without [internalism], since otherwise the
incompatibilist abhorrence of determinism will destroy it" (Double 1991, pp. 56–57).
The apparent problem is that once agents' histories are allowed to have a relevance
of the sort discussed here to their autonomy or freedom, their having *deterministic*
histories is relevant, as well, and relevant in a way that undermines compatibilism. It
may be thought that if instances of manipulation of the sort that I have been exploring block psychological autonomy, they do so only if they *causally determine* crucial psychological events or states, and that determinism consequently is in danger
of being identified as the real culprit.[18]

Assuming the truth of determinism, is it true that the internalist account of autonomy just sketched is the best possible? Well, determinists are in a position to distinguish among different causal routes to the collections of values (and the "characters") possessed by agents at a time. They are also in a position to provide principled
grounds for holding that distinct routes to two type-identical collections of values
may be such that one and only one of those routes blocks autonomy regarding a life
lived in accordance with those values. An analogue of the familiar compatibilist distinction between *caused* and *compelled* (or constrained) *behavior* may be employed
here (see ch. 8, sec. 2). Perhaps in engineering Beth's values we *compel* her to have
Mansonian pro-attitudes. Even so, a true and complete causal story about Manson's
having the values that he has might involve no compulsion. If Beth was compelled
to possess her Mansonian values while Manson was not, we have some apparent
grounds, at least, for taking the latter alone to be responsible for his character and for
value-guided vicious deeds of the sort at issue. And if these grounds are deemed irrelevant to responsibility, compatibilism is threatened. If the causal production and
sustaining of values and other pro-attitudes are indistinguishable from the compulsive production and sustaining of such things, then determinists would have to hold
that all of our pro-attitudes are effects of compulsion and none "merely" of causation—in which case, arguably, the causally determined behavioral consequences of
our pro-attitudes are themselves (indirectly) compelled, and no one is responsible
for any behavior at all that is driven by pro-attitudes.

I am not suggesting that compelling a person to acquire a collection of values,
as in the brainwashing scenarios, is *sufficient* for rendering a person nonautonomous.
Again, whether someone's having been subjected to effective manipulation deprives
him of autonomy depends upon whether those effects remain in force. A distinction
is in order, then, between being compelled to *acquire* a value at a time and being

compelled to *possess* a value over a stretch of time. I have been supposing that in the brainwashed Beth scenarios, she is no more likely to change her new values than are a mature Ann or Manson to change their deeply entrenched values. I want now to suppose, to keep things simple, that the prospects for such change in Manson are nil—at least for a significant span of time, *t*. More precisely, his evil values are "practically unsheddable" during *t*. They are so deeply entrenched and so strongly supported by Manson's psychological condition as a whole that any critical reflection upon these values is bound to lead only to a deeper identification with them. Again, any process of critical reflection is conducted from some perspective or other, and, I am supposing, the values at issue so dominate the perspective from which Beth and Manson would reflect upon corrupt values of theirs that further identification is ensured.

Aristotle once remarked, with characteristic good sense, that a corrupt individual who is unable to change his evil ways might nevertheless be responsible for having become that sort of person and, hence, for *being* a person of that kind (*Nicomachean Ethics* 1114a3–21). The underlying point about responsibility, if it is correct, applies also to agents whose "good" values are so deeply entrenched as not to admit of voluntary abandonment. Aristotle apparently thought that the point had greater *intuitive* appeal in the latter connection (1114b16–25); that might be true today, as well. For example, we are inclined to view Al, the dedicated parent in section 3, not only as autonomously possessing his deeply entrenched parental values but also as responsible for his continued possession of those values.

Suppose that what is true of "healthy" values in this regard can also be true of Mansonian values. Then, even if Manson is no more able to uproot his corrupt values than Al is to uproot his concern for his children's well-being, he might autonomously harbor those values, and he might be responsible for his continued possession of them. Imagine that, after some stage in his development, Manson is stuck with his corrupt values and with his identifying with those values (at least for a certain span of time), as Al is (happily) stuck with his parental values and with his identifying with them (at least for a couple of weeks). Imagine further that Manson autonomously possesses those values, as Al autonomously possesses his parental values. Still, even though Beth is a psychological twin of Manson (in salient respects), it does not follow that she autonomously possesses her Mansonian values. One indication of this is that, given the details of the case, we would not hold her *responsible* for her Mansonian character. Our reason for withholding attribution of responsibility (while supposing that Manson, her psychological twin, is responsible for his character) can only be that Beth was compelled to possess (throughout the relevant stretch of time) her corrupt, Mansonian values. And *that* is a *historical* point. Manson, on our suppositions, is not relevantly different internally, but he autonomously possesses his values.

The point here about responsibility admits of succinct formulation. Suppose that Manson is responsible for possessing corrupt values *V* during *t* and that Beth, who also possesses *V* during *t*, is not. By hypothesis, neither agent is practically able to shed *V* during *t*. So the explanation of the supposed difference regarding responsibility does not lie here. The only relevant difference between the agents is in how they *came to possess* the practically unsheddable values. That historical difference accounts for Manson's having, and Beth's lacking, responsibility for possessing $V$ during $t$, on the assumption that only one of them is responsible for this.

This assumption may be challenged. So may the supposition that my hypothetical Manson is no less autonomous regarding his possession of his evil values during a certain two-week span than Al is regarding his possession of his healthy parental values during a similar span. I take up a possible source of resistance to this supposition and then return to the assumption about responsibility.

Even though Manson identifies just as deeply with certain of his evil values ($E$) as Al does with his parental values ($P$), and even if they are, to the same extent, self-made with respect to these values, some may allege that they differ in a way that allows Al autonomously to possess $P$ but precludes Manson's autonomously possessing $E$. The alleged difference is that whereas there are *good* reasons (for some people) to identify with $P$, there are no good reasons (for anyone) to identify with $E$. Manson identifies with $E$ for reasons, it may be granted; but it is claimed that his reasons are not good reasons and that there are, in fact, no good reasons for this. Obviously, "good reasons" does not here mean reasons that are good from the perspective of the agent's own system of values, desires, beliefs, and the like. For our hypothetical Manson may have a consistent system of such things, and from that perspective he may have excellent reasons for identifying with $E$. Good reasons of the kind at issue are so-called external reasons (see Williams 1981). And the claim is that an agent's autonomously possessing a (practically unsheddable) value with which he identifies depends upon there being such reasons for identifying with that value.

One may opt for a notion of personal autonomy that incorporates a constraint of this kind. But in so doing (unless one embraces a certain theory of "the self"), one is departing significantly from the root notion of autonomy: self-government or self-rule (ch. 1). A self-governing state may be thoroughly corrupt and utterly insensitive to such truths as there may be about, say, the moral rights of noncitizens or the moral significance of pain and suffering in such people. The same is true of a self-governing person (substituting the person for the state and people other than oneself for noncitizens). On the conception under consideration, personal autonomy would be not merely self-government, nor even self-government without self-oppression (ch. 7, sec. 5), but rather self-government by agents whose identifications with any practically unsheddable values that may play a central role in guiding their behavior are in principle justifiable in an agent-external court—the court of external reasons.[19] This is not the notion of autonomy that I am after. In the same spirit in which I am leaving open the central point of contention between compatibilists and incompatibilists, I mean also to leave open the issue that divides external-reasons theorists (of the sort in question) from those who take all practical reasons (including reasons for identifying with a value that one has) to be states of mind. Manson may be self-governed, even if he does not govern himself in the light of an external "Good." He may govern himself by his own lights.

One might suggest that, even setting aside external reasons, Manson and Al differ in the following way: If Al were to have what he took to be decisive reasons for shedding his parental values, he would do so; but if Manson were to have what he took to be decisive reasons for shedding certain evil values of his, he still would not do so. But why suppose that this is true? Perhaps Manson would shed the relevant values under the imagined conditions.

Even if both agents would shed the values were they to take themselves to have a decisive reason to do so, it does not follow that they are able to shed these values. If, for example, they are (for a time) psychologically so constituted that they are incapable of taking anything to be a decisive reason for shedding the values, the truth of the pertinent subjunctive conditional would not suffice for their having this ability. This is easily seen. Suppose that the only conditions under which it would be psychologically possible for $S$ to shed $V$ during $t$ feature $S$'s taking himself at some point during $t$ to have a decisive reason for shedding $V$ and that it is psychologically impossible for $S$ to take himself to have such a reason during that time. Then it is not psychologically possible for $S$ to shed $V$ during $t$, in which case he is not *able* to shed $V$ during $t$—even if he would shed $V$ were he to take himself to have a decisive reason to do so.

One might doubt, of course, whether someone can be such that *nothing* would count for him as a decisive reason for shedding a certain value. The doubt merits consideration. Suppose that the authorities convince my hypothetical Manson that they will execute him unless he sheds evil value $V$. If Manson desires to live, he now has a reason to shed $V$. But he may deem life not worth living in the absence of this value and consequently regard this reason as far from decisive. Fates worse than death are imaginable; but so, I think, is a Manson who would not take avoidance of them to be a decisive reason for shedding $V$.

Suppose that there are counterfactual Manson-external conditions under which my Manson would take himself to have a decisive reason to shed $V$ and would, accordingly, shed $V$. Does it follow from this alone that my Manson, situated as he is at his world (where these conditions do not obtain), is *practically able* to shed $V$, in the sense glossed earlier? No, no more than it follows from its being true that Al would shed his parental values in the CIA scenario (sec. 3) that he is practically able to shed those values. This parallels the point about ability (sans 'practical') made two paragraphs earlier.

My Manson is an idealized one, of course, and I am by no means claiming psychological autonomy for all real-world criminals. It is an open question whether some of them (including the real Manson) were victims of circumstances that rendered them nonautonomous regarding central items in their collections of values and their ways of life. Independently of this, the idealized Beth/Manson scenario—if it is a coherent one—provides grounds for endorsing an externalist, history-sensitive conception of psychological autonomy. There, history evidently makes a genuine difference, if we are right in holding the idealized Manson responsible for his character and in viewing him as autonomously possessing certain practically unsheddable values that partially constitute his character while also refusing to hold Beth responsible for her Mansonian character and viewing her as nonautonomously possessing her equally unsheddable Mansonian values.

That Beth is not responsible for her Mansonian character—values, principles, and the like—is clear. She in no way contributed to the development of that character in herself, and she is not practically able to shed any of the values or principles that are central to it. She is simply stuck with her externally engineered character, at least for a time. I have offered some grounds for thinking that my idealized Manson can be responsible for possessing some of his (practically unsheddable) evil values, just as Al can be responsible for possessing his (practically unsheddable) parental values. Among the issues addressed in the next section are some putative grounds for resistance on this point.

## 5. Moral Responsibility: The "Reason View"

Susan Wolf has advanced a view of moral responsibility—the "Reason View"—according to which my idealized Manson (given further details, at least) lacks moral responsibility (1990). Wolf is led to the Reason View in part by her rejection of two other views of moral responsibility: the "Real Self View" and the "Autonomy View." The Real Self View is internalist. One's "real self" is the self with which one identifies, and "the attributability of an agent's behavior to her real self constitutes a necessary and sufficient condition of responsibility" (Wolf 1990, p. 34). This view is subject to the problem of value engineering: one's real self might ultimately be a product of brainwashing or mind control. The Autonomy View, by contrast, holds that an agent is morally responsible for her behavior only if she has "ultimate control": "her will must be determined by her self, and her self must not, in turn, be determined by anything external to itself" (p. 10). Wolf's chief objection to this view rests on a comparison of it with her own Reason View. The Autonomy View attributes to the morally responsible agent an ability that the Reason View does not; but this ability, Wolf argues, is not desirable. On "the Reason View, responsibility depends on the ability to act in accordance with the True and the Good" (p. 79). The Autonomy View requires, in addition, that the morally responsible agent be able to "make choices on no basis even when some basis is available," and, Wolf contends, this is "an ability no one could ever have reason to want to exercise" (p. 55).

Wolf summarizes her own view as follows:

> According to the Reason View, responsibility depends on the ability to act in accordance with the True and the Good. If one is psychologically determined to do the right thing for the right reasons, this is compatible with having the requisite ability. . . . But if one is psychologically determined to do the wrong thing, for whatever reason, this seems to constitute a denial of that ability. For if one *has* to do the wrong thing, then one *cannot* do the right, and so one lacks the ability to act in accordance with the True and the Good. The Reason View is thus committed to the curious claim that being psychologically determined to perform good actions is compatible with deserving praise for them, but that being psychologically determined to perform bad actions is not compatible with deserving blame. (1990, p. 79)[20]

Suppose that my idealized Manson, at some point in his life, is utterly insensitive to the Good and is psychologically unable to act in accordance with it. Suppose further that, owing to this fact about him, he is "psychologically determined" to perform an intentional evil act of a certain kind in a few minutes, and that he performs this act in order to cause pain and suffering. Then, on Wolf's view, Manson is not morally responsible for his action and is not deserving of blame for it. But imagine that Manson's insensitivity to the Good is due to a consciously adopted program of his to eliminate all such sensitivity in himself. At an earlier time in his life he was able "to act in accordance with . . . the Good," but he valued being the sort of person who cared not at all for the Good, and he intentionally set out to make himself such a person. One strand of his strategy was to perform cruel actions with great frequency in order to harden himself against feelings of guilt and eventually to extinguish the source of those feelings—namely, his sensitivity or responsiveness to the Good. Suppose, finally, that he was able to refrain—"for the right reasons"—from embarking on any heart-hardening project and that at any time prior to the success of his project he was able (again for the right reasons) to abandon the project.

"According to the Reason View," Wolf writes, "it is only the ability to do the right thing for the right reasons . . . that is required for responsibility" (p. 81). So in my last scenario, we can suppose that Manson was morally responsible, on Wolf's view, for undertaking to render himself insensitive to the Good and for rendering himself insensitive to it. However, once he succeeds, Wolf's view has the result that he is not morally responsible for any further evil deeds of his and is not deserving of blame for them. This result is implausible, to say the least. Manson's later behavior, we may suppose, has the same sources in his values and character as his earlier behavior. The salient difference is that now he is incapable of being guided by the Good whereas earlier he had this capacity. But since this is a capacity that he voluntarily and successfully sought to eliminate, it is difficult to see why its absence should absolve him of moral responsibility for his behavior and excuse him from blame.

An implausible consequence might have to be accepted, of course, if the theory that generates it is the best we can do. Whether we can do better than Wolf's Reason View remains to be seen. But it merits mention now that the externalist view that I have been sketching is distinct from the two views that Wolf uses as foils for her own position and from her Reason View, as well. The Real Self view is internalist (about moral responsibility); mine is not. The Autonomy View is incompatibilist; mine is not. Further, my externalist view rejects the requirement of dual ability regarding values and, in the same spirit, can reject the Autonomy View's requirement that morally responsible agents be able to choose and act "in accordance with the True and the Good" and able, as well, to choose and act "on no basis even when some basis is available." Finally, whereas Wolf's Reason View exempts my idealized, Good-insensitive Manson from moral responsibility for his evil deeds, mine does not. So it looks as though there is a possibility that Wolf has not addressed—one that avoids the problems that she identifies for her foils as well as the apparently problematic feature of her view that I have just identified.

It is worth noting that those who take my Good-insensitive Manson to be morally responsible for his evil deeds need not reject Wolf's objectivism about the Good.[21] On the externalist view under consideration, however the Good is to be understood, an agent's insensitivity to it does not *itself* preclude his being morally responsible for evil deeds of his. The issue of responsibility also turns on how he *came* to be insensitive. If a history-sensitive externalism about autonomy and responsibility is the proper view of things, both objectivists and subjectivists about the Good can and should endorse it.

Return to the matter of Manson's having moral responsibility specifically for possessing his evil character, or certain values partially constitutive of that character. An *analogue* of Wolf's position on moral responsibility for psychologically determined actions would assert that "it is only the ability to" possess the right values "for the right reasons" that is "required for responsibility" for the values that one possesses, and "being psychologically determined" to possess "bad" values at *t* is incompatible with being morally responsible for possessing those values at *t*. My Manson, once he makes himself insensitive to the Good, may be "psychologically determined" to possess his bad values for a time. Even so, it is implausible to hold, for *that* reason, that he is not morally responsible for possessing those values during that time. By hypothesis, this Manson was able to refrain from embarking upon his heart-hardening project. We may stipulate that he was able, as well, to shed his bad values prior to the completion of that project (at *t*) and to acquire good ones. However, he voluntarily sought to reinforce them, and he intentionally accomplished this reinforcement. No one and nothing *else* is responsible for this hypothetical Manson's having the bad values that he has after the completion of his intentional heart-hardening project. To be sure, he is stuck with these values, at least for a time. But he self-consciously and voluntarily *stuck himself* with them, while being able to do otherwise (at least on a compatibilist interpretation of that ability). If, given all that, and supposing that prior to *t* Manson was morally responsible for possessing his values, including values on the basis of which he elected to render himself insensitive to the Good, we would not hold him morally responsible for his present character, we are very tender-hearted indeed.

Wolf's Reason View is an internalist view about moral responsibility, and it merits further attention in that connection. Again, "it is only the ability to do the right thing for the right reasons . . . that is required for responsibility," or, as Wolf also puts it, "the ability to act in accordance with the True and the Good." Provided that an agent possesses this ability, it is irrelevant how he acquired it. Even setting aside worries about Wolf's objectivist conception of the Good, there are additional grounds for suspicion about her internalism.

Return to our latest Manson, and imagine that, via new-wave brainwashing and against his will, his evil values are eradicated and he is made to possess and to identify with a host of values generally deemed good. He now has "the ability to do the right thing for the right reasons," an ability that he exercises on a regular basis. Manson is now a model citizen, an upstanding member of the community. He gives generously to charities, performs valuable services for the Red Cross and the Boy Scouts, and starts a local Habitat for Humanity chapter. Does Manson deserve moral credit for his actions? I think not, for his actions flow from a collection of values, a "character," that was brainwashed in, against his will. People who knew nothing of Manson's history would undoubtedly confer moral praise upon him for his actions and his character alike. But knowing his history, those with no special philosophical axes to grind would be strongly disinclined to credit *him* for these things and to view him as morally praiseworthy for so acting.

Some may be disposed to resist this inclination, worrying that if we withhold credit from Manson we must do so for any agent who undergoes a radical change of character. However, here again history is relevant. It is the particular etiology of Manson's change that speaks against crediting him for his civic-minded behavior and against viewing him as praiseworthy for it. An agent who, in the absence of brainwashing and the like, sees the error of his ways and radically transforms himself might properly be credited for his own good behavior. At least, nothing that I have said closes this option.[22]

A view of agents as thin "time-slice" entities, bundles of nonhistorical properties, might speak in favor of crediting Manson for his good deeds. On this view, agential credit for deeds performed during $t$ should presumably be unaffected by anything prior to $t$. But this view of agents is radically at odds with our moral and legal practices and with our own view of ourselves. We often take our institutions or ourselves to be warranted in blaming and punishing, or praising and rewarding, an agent *now* for something done quite some time ago. Similarly, we feel remorse for certain deeds of ours long after the fact, and we take pride in temporally distant accomplishments of ours. These practices and attitudes presuppose a conception of agents as relatively thick, temporally extended beings.[23] If praise, blame, reward, or punishment is deserved by agents *now* for *past* deeds, it is partly in virtue of certain historical properties of agents that they deserve this. Similarly, justifiable regret, remorse, pride, and the like, often rest on an appreciation of our own historical properties. Further, many of our attitudes and practices in this connection are sensitive not merely to the deeds themselves but also to various historical facts about them— for example, whether they were done knowingly or unknowingly, intentionally or unintentionally, willingly or unwillingly.

Given our view of agents as temporally extended beings, why should one be reluctant to deem Manson's history relevant to whether *he* deserves moral credit for good deeds that are knowingly, intentionally, and willingly done? Perhaps because one worries that if his history blocks his justifiably being credited for his deeds, the same would be true of any agent at a deterministic world—any agent with a deterministic history. In defense of Manson, one might ask how he is to be distinguished from a virtuous agent at a deterministic world—someone whose history was such that, long before his birth, causally sufficient conditions for his virtuous character and virtuous actions were present. Or one might ask instead about a hypothetical woman whose upbringing was so good and whose environment was so pure as to ensure that she would be virtuous. This brings us back, of course, to a compatibilist distinction between compulsion and causation.

## 6. Complications and Compulsion

I return to a problem identified in section 2 for a simple externalist position on psychological autonomy. An agent might autonomously arrange for his own subjection to a mode of external manipulation viewed as autonomy-thwarting (or -diminishing) on some conceptions of procedural independence, and the manipulation might have autonomy-enhancing effects. Attention to this matter will help to flesh out the *authenticity* that an externalist might urge as a requirement on the autonomous possession of a pro-attitude.

Histories that block agents' autonomously possessing certain of their values, on the view generated thus far, do so by *compelling* agents to possess those values. The force of 'compel' is diminished, however, when we speak of an agent autonomously arranging to have himself *compelled* to do (or have, or be) something. If there is a sense in which Odysseus arranged for his crew to *compel* him to remain on board (by lashing him to the mast), it is a sense that does not carry the full weight of 'compel.' At any rate, we can distinguish in a principled way between some cases of effective compulsion voluntarily arranged for oneself and autonomy-thwarting compulsion. If pirates tie captured passengers to the mast in order to keep them aboard a sinking ship, the passengers are quite fully compelled to remain aboard (given certain natural assumptions, e.g., they wish to live).

The externalist notion of authenticity that I am after can now be partially articulated. It is a historical property of agents required for responsibility for the possession of a pro-attitude.[24] A necessary condition of an agent $S$'s *authentically* possessing a pro-attitude $P$ (e.g., a value or preference) that he has over an interval $t$ is that it be false that $S$'s having $P$ over that interval is, as I will say, *compelled\**—where compulsion\* is compulsion *not arranged by S.*

I will return to pro-attitude compulsion—or *P-compulsion*, for short—in sections 7 and 8, but some details can be provided now. I begin with a simple point. One agent may compel another to possess a value, say, throughout an interval without doing anything to the agent during that interval. In some cases, for example, by brainwashing someone at $t$ we may compel him to possess a certain value for a lengthy period beyond $t$ without any additional intervention. In other cases, a manipulator may compel $S$ to possess a value over an interval by compelling $S$ to acquire the value and subsequently compelling him to retain it, or by compelling $S$ to retain a value that was already in place (e.g., a juvenile valuing of sexual conquest).

An agent's being practically unable to abandon during $t$ a pro-attitude of which he is possessed throughout $t$ is a necessary—but not a sufficient—condition of his being compelled to possess that attitude (over that interval). If this inability were also a sufficient condition of $P$-compulsion, and Al (in sec. 3) is practically unable to shed his normal, healthy parental values in two weeks' time (values with which he strongly identifies), he would be compelled to possess them during that span—a thesis I have already attacked. The point just made might suggest that practical inability to shed a pro-attitude during $t$ conjoined with the agent's *not identifying* with that attitude during $t$ is both necessary and sufficient for $P$-compulsion of the pro-attitude during $t$. But this will not do either. For, as I have explained, a value with which an agent identifies may nevertheless be $P$-compelled; indeed, an agent's identification with a value may itself be a product of compulsion. Nonidentification with an attitude is not required for $P$-compulsion of the attitude.

In some cases of brainwashing, hypnosis, and the like, agents come to possess pro-attitudes in ways that *bypass* their (perhaps relatively modest) capacities for control over their mental lives.[25] In ideally self-controlled agents, these capacities are considerable. Such agents are capable of modifying the strengths of their desires in the service of their practical, evaluative judgments, of bringing their emotions into line with relevant judgments, and of mastering motivation that threatens (sometimes via the biasing of practical or theoretical reasoning) to produce or sustain beliefs in ways that would violate their principles for belief acquisition and retention. They are capable, moreover, of rationally assessing and revising their values and principles, of identifying with values of theirs on the basis of informed, critical reflection, and of intentionally fostering new values and pro-attitudes in themselves in accordance with their considered evaluative judgments. Presumably, most readers of this book have each of these capacities in some measure. All such capacities are bypassed in cases of pro-attitude engineering of the sort at issue. In such cases, new pro-attitudes are not generated via an exercise or an activation of agents' capacities for control over their mental lives; rather, they are generated despite the agents' capacities for this.

I offer two suggestions for consideration. First (as a first approximation), by-passing of this kind in conjunction with its issuing in a practical inability to shed a particular pro-attitude acquired in this way is sufficient for $P$-compulsion* with re-spect to that pro-attitude—provided that the bypassing was not itself arranged (or performed) by the manipulated person. Second (suppressing a qualification to be developed shortly), an agent who is practically unable (over a span of time) to shed a pro-attitude with which he strongly identifies for reasons whose possession is *not* explained by a bypassing of his capacities for control over his mental life is *not* com-pelled to possess that pro-attitude.

Is the latter suggestion falsified by some cases of manipulative indoctrination of the very young? Consider an extreme case. A religious fanatic initially conducts his child's religious instruction in the same matter-of-fact tone in which he teaches the child about mundane matters: there are birds, bees, bicycles, and buildings, and there is God, a devil, heaven, and hell. Then he teaches the child that there are a few ex-traordinarily evil people who "reject" God—the dreaded atheists—and that they will burn in hell forever, a prospect he graphically portrays. For good measure, he "in-forms" the child that people who even *entertain doubts* about his religious teachings also burn eternally. Suppose that the man does a thoroughly effective job, and the child—owing primarily to a deep-seated fear of eternal damnation—grows up with firmly held religious convictions and values that, even as an adult, he is practically unable to shed. Suppose further that very young children have no capacity for con-trolling what religious doctrines and values they accept, no capacity for making up their own minds about such matters. Then, it might be said, the father has compelled the child to have certain pro-attitudes without *bypassing* the child's capacities for control over his mental life: one cannot bypass nonexistent capacities.

This objection turns on an overly narrow construal of the relevant capacities. First, and most important, one's capacities at $t$ for control over one's mental life at $t$—one's capacities for *current* control—*are bypassed* by the inculcation of values that one is not, at $t$, equipped to assess then. The route by which the child's religious values are acquired bypasses his directly relevant (modest) capacity to believe and desire on the basis of an assessment of evidence. Even young children—five-year-olds, say—sometimes believe and desire on the basis of an assessment of evidence concerning matters that they comprehend (e.g., after attending their first concert, art exhibit, or circus, they may, on the basis of an assessment of their experience, be-lieve that they would enjoy going to another one and desire to do so). The capacity so to believe and desire is *inoperative* in the imagined inculcation: it is circumvented. (Such inculcation may be relatively common, but, again, bypassing is not itself suf-ficient for long-term nonautonomy regarding one's possession of the pro-attitudes produced. That depends on one's being practically unable to shed the pro-attitudes.) Second, even if the very young are not capable of making up their minds *then* about theological matters, they might then have the capacity to develop into individuals who would make up their minds about such things. For example, prior to his indoctrination, the child at issue might have had the capacity to become a person who would shape his own attitudes about theology later in life. If so, that capacity was bypassed— and, indeed, destroyed.

On the view just sketched, even pro-attitudes generally regarded as good may be compelled, of course. That is as it should be. Perhaps the father used the fear of God to cause his son to value the well-being of others (at least, of other like-minded folks), instilling the value in such a way that the son permanently lacked the practical ability to shed it. If that is the source of the son's value and practical inability, the son is not responsible for possessing the value, and he does not autonomously possess it.

I mentioned a suppressed qualification. It concerns some magically produced agents. Suppose that it is logically possible for a devil to create an agent with certain unsheddable pro-attitudes, "identifications," and reasons for identification already in place at the time of creation. In such a case, the devil did not "bypass" the agent's capacities for control over his mental life in producing these items, for the agent had no such capacities when the items were produced. Still, the agent is reasonably viewed as being possessed of some *compelled* pro-attitudes with which he identifies (for reasons); call them compelled *innate* pro-attitudes. A qualified version of the suggestion at issue, then, is this: barring compelled *innate* pro-attitudes, an agent who is practically unable (over a span of time) to shed a pro-attitude with which he strongly identifies for reasons whose possession is *not* explained by a bypassing of his capacities for control over his mental life is *not* compelled to possess that pro-attitude. This notion of "innate" pro-attitudes may be extended to apply to agents who, after coming into existence, but prior to having any (relevant) capacities for control over their mental lives, are subjected to pro-attitude engineering.

## 7.   Nonintentional Compulsion

My featured cases involve intentional manipulation. That, however, was a rhetorical device employed for the purpose of priming intuitions. We can imagine a variant of the Beth/Manson scenario, for example, in which, in the *absence* of intervention by an intentional agent, Beth's values are erased and new, Mansonian ones are implanted in her in such a way that she is practically unable to dislodge them. Suppose that a brain disorder has this result in Beth, although it does not deprive her of the capacity for critical reflection and identification—or that the change in Beth is a result of her passing through a strange, randomly occurring electromagnetic field at the center of the Bermuda Triangle. (As in the earlier cases, the change dictates the direction that her critical reflections and identifications will take.) Her capacities for control over her mental life are bypassed by the value-changing mechanism or process, but the bypassing is utterly nonintentional. If Beth lacks psychological autonomy in certain spheres of her life in the original Beth/Manson case, she does so here as well. Psychological nonautonomy does not entail *heteronomy*.[26] Histories incompatible with an agent's possessing authenticity, then, need not include intentional manipulation.

Here again deterministic worries might surface about an externalist conception of responsibility and autonomy. But, as I have argued, such worries should grip us only if we think that familiar compatibilist moves, and extensions thereof, are unacceptable. If one rejects those moves—for example, the idea that causation is distinguishable from compulsion (or constraint) in such a way that "mere" deterministic (event-) causation of an action, say, is compatible with that action's being freely performed—one has at least two options. One can be a "hard determinist" about autonomy and responsibility, holding that determinism is true and that it entails that we lack autonomy and responsibility. Or one can reject determinism (and compatibilism) and try to hold onto autonomy and responsibility. Another possible tack, of course, is to attempt to rescue compatibilism. These options are examined in subsequent chapters. The externalism that I have been developing is intended to be neutral on the truth of determinism, but that is not because I have a deterministic ax to grind (see ch. 1, sec. 2).

Some readers might be unwilling to hold that Beth is compelled to possess the implanted, unsheddable values in the brain disorder and Bermuda Triangle scenarios. One is compelled to *x*, they might insist, only if some *agent*, acting intentionally, does the compelling. I would like to avoid quarrels about ordinary usage. But it is worth noting that we do say such things as that the kleptomaniac was compelled to steal and the heroin addict compelled to seek the drug, by an irresistible urge; and, of course, irresistible urges do not act intentionally. As I will use the term 'compulsion,' the source of pro-attitude compulsion need not be an agent.

## 8.   Compulsion and Noncompulsion

Return to the Beth/Ann scenario. Imagine that a year later, Beth is informed about her brainwashing and is offered the opportunity to have the process reversed, returning her to her earlier condition. Suppose that, on the basis of careful reflection, Beth judges that she is considerably better off now and declines the offer accordingly.[27] Does this indicate that she has, for some time, been autonomous regarding her possession of the pertinent values?[28] Alternatively, in making the decision described, does Beth render herself autonomous in that connection?

Suppose that Beth well remembers her life prior to brainwashing, that she is in a position to compare the quality of her pre- and postbrainwashing lives, and that her judgment and decision are based, in significant part, on such a comparison. Of course, the comparison cannot be the sole source of her judgment and decision; Beth will compare the two lives from some evaluative perspective or other. Imagine that the perspective from which the comparative judgment is made encompasses, in a way central to the etiology of Beth's judgment and decision, the practically unsheddable collection of pro-attitudes that was brainwashed in (or a segment thereof). The highest psychological court, as it were, to which Beth can and does appeal in reaching a judgment on the issue is constituted by that collection of values. In that case, her judgment and decision themselves were, in effect, "engineered" by the brainwashers. So Beth is heteronomous with respect to the judgment and decision, and her making them neither *indicates* that she is autonomous regarding her possession of the values produced by brainwashing nor *renders* her autonomous regarding those values.

This is an externalist moral. Even though Beth now reflectively prefers a life expressive of her current collection of values to one expressive of her earlier values, that itself does not suffice for her being autonomous regarding her present way of life, or for her autonomously possessing those values. What blocks the inference from her reflective preference to autonomy in these spheres is the *etiology* of that preference, an etiology that renders a certain pivotal collection of pro-attitudes practically unsheddable.

Consider a counterpart scenario, in which the evaluative standard to which Beth appeals in making her comparative judgment is, by hypothesis, in no way influenced by her brainwashing. Her primary concern had always been to maximize her happiness, say. Prior to brainwashing, she reflectively believed that this concern was best served by the varied sort of life that she was living then, one rich in aesthetic enjoyment, in the pleasures of travel to far-flung places, in engaging conversation about world affairs, and so on. But having lived an intensely "philosophical" life for a full year, having thoroughly enjoyed doing so, and having found that life deeply satisfying and rewarding, Beth now regards living such a life as more conducive to her happiness. She realizes that if the brainwashing process were reversed and her new values and desires were replaced by her earlier ones, she would no longer find an intensely philosophical life so rewarding and would very much enjoy her regained varied life. She understands that part of what makes her present life so satisfying is her deeply, intrinsically valuing her philosophical work. But maximizing happiness is what Beth values—and has always valued—most, and it is from the perspective of the value that she places on happiness that she makes her judgment and her decision about the offer.[29]

The scenario just described leaves open an important issue. Suppose that the offer is not a genuine one, but only a test: Beth's manipulators want to ascertain where her current preferences lie, and they have no intention of reversing the brainwashing process, under any circumstances. Suppose, as well, that Beth's brainwashing rendered her practically incapable of shedding her present system of values in favor of her earlier system. Beth is able to identify with her present values, but she is not able to change them, at least in the specified direction. She lacks "dual ability" regarding those values.

I have argued that in some ordinary scenarios, one's being practically unable to shed a value with which one identifies is compatible with one's autonomously possessing that value. For example, I argued that Al may autonomously possess his parental values (over a span of time) even though he is practically unable to shed them (during that span). If that is right, lacking dual ability regarding a value that one possesses does not suffice for nonautonomy with respect to its possession. So might Beth be autonomous regarding the values at issue in the present (expanded) scenario?

Return to a pair of suggestions offered in section 6.

1. *A sufficient condition for its being false that someone who possesses a practically unsheddable pro-attitude,* P, *is compelled to possess* P. Barring compelled "innate" pro-attitudes, an agent who is practically unable (over a span of time) to shed a pro-attitude *P* with which he strongly identifies for reasons whose possession is *not* explained by a bypassing of his capacities for control over his mental life is *not* compelled to possess *P*.

2. *A first approximation of a sufficient condition for* P-*compulsion\**. If an agent *S* comes to possess a pro-attitude *P* in a way that bypasses *S*'s (perhaps relatively modest) capacities for control over his mental life, and the bypassing issues in *S*'s being practically unable to shed *P*, and the bypassing was not itself arranged (or performed) by *S*, then *S* is compelled\* to possess *P*.

Beth currently strongly identifies with values *V*—practically unsheddable values produced by brainwashing—for a reason *R*. If her possessing *R* is "not explained" by a bypassing of her capacities for control over her mental life, then suggestion 1 implies that she is *not* compelled to possess *V*. How is the antecedent of the preceding sentence to be interpreted? Currently, let us suppose, the reason for which Beth strongly identifies with *V*—reason *R*—is constituted by the value that she places on maximizing her happiness together with her belief that her possessing *V* is essential to such maximization. (Beth is convinced that if she were to lack *V*, her happiness would be diminished.) By hypothesis, Beth is not compelled by the brainwashing to value happiness. She has valued it for many years, and just as strongly as she does now. Suppose, as well, that the value that she places on happiness is *autonomously* placed on it. That brings us to the belief component of *R*, and that belief is a *product*, in part, of Beth's brainwashing. If she had not been brainwashed, she would not have led an intensely philosophical life and she would not have come to believe that living and valuing such a life is essential to maximizing her happiness (or so we may suppose). So, in that sense, her possessing *R* is "explained," in part, by the brainwashing—that is, by manipulation that bypassed her capacities for control over her mental life.

Those who view Beth as autonomously possessing *V* (partly in light of the reason for which she identifies with *V*) need have no quarrel with suggestion 1. Obviously, 1 does not imply that Beth *is* compelled to possess *V*. However, they will have a problem with 2, since it implies that Beth is compelled\* to possess *V*, and the compulsion\* of pro-attitudes is supposedly incompatible with the autonomous possession of those attitudes. Given that the value component of the reason, *R*, for which Beth strongly identifies with *V* is *autonomously* possessed and assuming that the belief component of *R* has solid epistemic credentials, I myself am inclined to hold that Beth (now) autonomously possesses *V*—even though she did not autonomously *acquire V* and the brainwashing procedure violated her autonomy.[30] (Discussion of the relevance of beliefs to personal autonomy is reserved for ch. 10.) If the value component of *R* included values contained in *V*, that would be another matter, as I have observed.

The following version of 2 leaves it open that Beth, in the present scenario, is not compelled\* to possess *V*.

2\*. If an agent *S* comes to possess a pro-attitude *P* in a way that bypasses *S*'s (perhaps relatively modest) capacities for control over his mental life; and the bypassing issues in *S*'s being practically unable to shed *P*; and the bypassing was not itself arranged (or performed) by *S*; and *S* neither presently possesses nor earlier possessed pro-attitudes that would support his identifying with *P*, with the exception of pro-attitudes that are themselves practically unsheddable products of unsolicited bypassing; then *S* is compelled\* to possess *P*.

This statement is too weak to cover all cases of *P*-compulsion\*. For instance, the possession of a relatively trivial untainted pro-attitude that would provide *S* only relatively trivial support for identifying with *P* presumably would not suffice for the noncompulsion of *S*'s possession of *P*. But 2\* will do for present purposes. If a person compelled\* to possess a pro-attitude does not autonomously possess it, then 2\* provides an externalist constraint on the autonomous possession of pro-attitudes. It implies, for example, that even someone who reflectively identifies wholeheartedly with *P* does not autonomously possess *P*, if he has a history of the relevant kind. His reflective, wholehearted identification may be a product of unsolicited brainwashing and find no support in any pro-attitudes of his that are not themselves practically unsheddable products of such manipulation.

## 9.  Ability and Authenticity Again

Part of what I have been arguing is that our ordinary notions of moral responsibility and of what I have called "psychological autonomy" latch on to a feature of agents that cannot be captured wholly internalistically.[31] "Psychological twins"—for instance, brainwashed Beth and the idealized Manson—may be such that only one of them is morally responsible for, and autonomous regarding, the current constitution of his or her "evil" character. The construction of a full-blown account of the "authenticity" to which I have adverted in this connection, and of the notion of an authenticity-blocking history, would require detailed attention to moral responsibility and to its historical presuppositions; but it is a good bet that scrutiny of various "normal" ways in which agents acquire, criticize, and modify their values would prove fruitful. (I return to these matters in subsequent chapters.)

I should emphasize that the historical, "authenticity" constraint that I have been urging on the autonomous possession of values and other pro-attitudes (i.e., on *P*-autonomy) is a *negative* one. My claim is not that *P*-autonomy regarding a pro-attitude, *P*, requires that the agent *have* a history of a certain kind, but rather that he *lack* a certain kind of history—a history yielding what I have called "compulsion\*" of *P*. Imagine, if you can, an agent who magically comes into existence with a wealth of beliefs, desires, and values in place. For some externalists about mental content, this is utterly impossible; given that it lacks a history, the being has no thoughts at all (Davidson 1987). But for present purposes we can set that worry aside. The point to be made is that, even assuming that such a being is possible, my proposed constraint does not entail that it lacks *P*-autonomy (or authenticity); for it does not entail that the being has any compelled pro-attitudes.

Suppose that this being, Athena, has and exercises a potent capacity for critical reflection. Suppose further that she has a robust ability to shed each of her pro-attitudes—an analogue of the ability that we have to refrain from acting on resistible desires (sec. 3). Other things being equal, there is no bar to Athena's autonomously possessing her pro-attitudes.

If all autonomous agents were like Athena regarding ability, a historical condition on psychological autonomy of the sort that I have been developing would be otiose. An agent possessed of Athena's ability would, *ipso facto*, have no compelled pro-attitudes. But, as I have argued, possession of an ability of that kind regarding a pro-attitude cannot plausibly be made a requirement for *P*-autonomy regarding it. And without such a requirement, there is no wholly internalistic way of distinguishing psychologically autonomous agents, as a class, from some victims of compulsion*. We must find a basis in external factors for certain needed distinctions: for example, a distinction that enables us to explain why Beth is nonautonomous and Ann (or Manson) is autonomous regarding the possession of values that are just as deeply resistant to change. Internalistic conceptions of psychological autonomy are untenable.

Hilary Putnam argued, famously, that "'meanings' just ain't in the *head*" (1973, p. 704). If I am right, psychological autonomy ain't in the head either; or, rather, it ain't *all* in the head. There is also a negative historical constraint on the autonomous possession of pro-attitudes: what I have called "authenticity." Agents possessed of a robust, global, "shedding" ability might satisfy an authenticity constraint—with respect to all of their attitudes—solely in virtue of what is in their heads: they have no compelled pro-attitudes. Where such ability is absent, a sufficient head-internal basis for authenticity is absent as well.[32]

That is one moral of the present chapter. Another merits emphasis. So-called mind control arguments are a favorite incompatibilist weapon. The primary intended challenge for the compatibilist who is sensitive to the force of certain mind control scenarios is to explain why, if mind-controlled agents are not autonomous (in certain spheres), agents who are causally determined to have the "minds" they have—the values, preferences, desires, beliefs, reflective capacities, and so on—may nevertheless be autonomous (in the same spheres). How is the control that manipulators exert over an agent in the brainwashing scenarios examined here, for example, relevantly different from the effect of the distant past on an agent at a deterministic world? Internalists about psychological autonomy naturally look for relevant internal differences between mind-controlled nonautonomous agents and autonomous causally determined counterparts.[33] I have argued that sometimes no significant internal difference is to be found. But if I am right, compatibilists need not despair; they can urge that certain historical differences are relevant without abandoning their compatibilism. A counterpart of the familiar compatibilist distinction between caused and compelled action can be employed at the level of "character." If compatibilists find the distinction between causation and compulsion useful in the former connection, they can help themselves to it in the latter, as well, provided that it can be given substance there. The present chapter has made a case for this application of the distinction, given the assumption of compatibilism. The following chapter provides additional support.

## Notes

1. This use of 'autonomy' is adequately captured by Joel Feinberg's gloss on it: "[T]he sovereign authority to govern oneself" (1986, p. 28).

2. Matters are not quite as simple as that, of course, since Ann and Beth are not complete psychological twins, but twins only in certain respects. However, their psychological differences may be ignored for present purposes.

3. On a nonhistorical externalism, see n. 19. The externalism explored in this chapter is a history-sensitive one.

4. See Benn 1988, Dworkin 1988, Haworth 1986, and Lindley 1986.

5. For a more detailed discussion of the first three points to be made, see Mele 1992a, pp. 91–97.

6. Obviously, "*S* is able to *A* and *S* is able to *B*" does not entail "*S* is able to *A and B*." One who is able to do each of two mutually exclusive things is not able to do both things (i.e., to do the conjunction).

7. This is not to say that Dworkin *intended* this interpretation.

8. Andrews Reath prompted me to explore this point.

9. A theorist may try to get greater mileage out of *X*-ability in an account of personal autonomy by conjoining it with a certain judgment ability; for example, an ability composed of the ability to judge it best to identify with *P* and the ability to judge it best to change *P*. *That* conjunction would yield dual ability with respect to *P*: an agent possessed of this conjunction of abilities would be able to identify with *P* and able to change *P*. Alternatively, the conjunction of *X*-ability and a certain disjunctive judgment ability—namely, an ability that one has if and only if one is able to judge it best to identify with *P* or able to judge it best to change *P*—would yield disjunctive ability.

10. Even from a compatibilist perspective, a proper assessment of an argument constructed along these lines would depend upon how "suitable employment" is to be understood.

11. This is not to deny that eliminating the spirit would affect various ways in which Al's attitudes might be described. For example, it would no longer be the case that Al's desire for his children's welfare is a desire whose continued presence is guaranteed by a spirit.

12. Actually, this oversimplifies matters, since not only are Ann and Beth only partial psychological twins, but their external circumstances may differ in a way relevant to value modification. In the latter connection, it might be the case, for example, that only one of them has the financial resources to hire an effective value modifier. These complications may be ignored for the sake of argument.

13. What if Fred's trying hard were to consist in his setting his house ablaze as a means of getting himself to go out? Would he drive himself out if he were to try *that* hard? Perhaps, but Fred may be unable (under ordinary circumstances and even many exceptional ones) to burn his house down for this purpose (Mele 1992a, p. 99). A person can try only as hard as he can, as Yogi Berra is said to have remarked.

14. For an attempted distinction along these lines, see Dworkin 1976, p. 25. See my remarks in ch. 7, sec. 5 on a putative distinction between 'his own' and 'his.'

15. The kinds of responsibility associated with autonomy may vary with the kind of agent at issue. If even the various actions and omissions of the morality-transcending Aristotelian gods mentioned in chapter 1 have no moral significance, *moral* responsibility does not apply to these beings. (Imagine that these gods are the sole sentient inhabitants of their universe.)

16. The determinism at work here need not be a perfectly universal one. It may be, instead, a deterministic theory specifically of human development and behavior. For a recent, detailed deterministic theory of the latter kind, see Honderich 1988.

17. See, e.g., Waller 1990. Waller argues that determinism is compatible with freedom

but not with moral responsibility. If there is a sense of 'freedom' in which this is true, most compatibilist believers in freedom are seeking something more robust.

18. Roughly this idea is a theme in various "mind control" arguments against compatibilism, as Blumenfeld 1988 observes. For a view of *moral responsibility* that is explicitly externalist *and* compatibilist, see Fischer 1987. (Fischer does not there endorse the compatibility of determinism with freedom to do *otherwise*; but compatibilists about determinism and free action need not be compatibilists about determinism and freedom to do otherwise.) Fischer's externalism (specifically, historicism) about moral responsibility is developed further in Fischer and Ravizza 1994.

19. Notice that this is a nonhistorical *externalist* notion of autonomy. On this view, an agent's psychological autonomy with respect to the possession of an unsheddable value with which he identifies depends on there being agent-*external* grounds or reasons for identifying with that value.

20. Among the theses expressed in this passage is Wolf's "asymmetry" thesis. I attack a particular application of it. For additional criticism, see Fischer and Ravizza 1991, pp. 258–60, and 1992a, pp. 375–89.

21. Wolf develops her pluralistic objectivism about the Good in 1990, ch. 6.

22. The "good" Manson case and others developed in this chapter might have prompted worries about personal identity. Is the transformed Manson the same person as the pretransformation Manson? Is Beth, after becoming a Manson "twin," the same person as the earlier Beth? This is not the place to advance a theory of personal identity. But, surely, the pre- and posttransformation agents have much in common? Manson just before his transformation (*t*-Manson) is much more similar, on the whole, to Manson just after it (*t*\*-Manson) than he is to neonate Manson or toddler Manson. Still, *t*-Manson is the same person as the neonate and toddler Mansons, in a familiar "personal identity" sense of "same person." So what is to prevent him from being the same person, in the same sense, as *t*\*-Manson? It is worth noting, further, that *t*-Manson and *t*\*-Manson may be strongly psychologically connected, in Parfit's sense (1984, p. 206). They may be such that the number of direct psychological connections between them "is *at least half* the number that hold, over every day, in the lives of nearly every actual person."

23. For an influential, insightful discussion of such practices and attitudes, see Strawson 1962.

24. Certain "negative" properties are historical properties; for example, my property of not having been born in the nineteenth century. A being who has just popped into existence at *t* in the twentieth century has this historical property too, even though, at *t*, the being has no personal history at all. In section 9, I discuss an imaginary being of this kind in connection with authenticity.

25. For a useful discussion of bypassing, see Blumenfeld 1988, pp. 222–23.

26. I understand heteronomy as rule or government by another *agent*.

27. For discussion of a similar case, see Blumenfeld 1988, pp. 224–25. For reasons to be developed in this section, his attribution of freedom to his manipulated agent is unwarranted.

28. Robert Audi and Lance Stell posed versions of this question in conversation.

29. Recall that one can value the same thing (e.g., one's philosophical work) both intrinsically and extrinsically (ch. 7, sec. 1).

30. Some of my students remarked that since an intensely philosophical life strikes them as considerably less pleasant and rewarding than the "varied" life that Beth previously led, they find it difficult not to see Beth as compelled\* with respect to her new values. Some readers may share this reaction. My diagnosis of my students' reaction is that they doubt that "the belief-component of *R*" can have "solid epistemic credentials," or that Beth can be warranted in believing, on the basis of her experience of the two types of life, that her present, intensely

philosophical life is better and more rewarding for her than her previous, "varied" life. Presumably, these students would not be impressed by Plato's argument, in book 9 of the *Republic* (580d–583), that his hypothetical philosopher, having experienced the various types of life and pleasures under review there, is a better judge of which kind of life and pleasure is "sweetest"—or, more to the point, sweetest for the hypothetical philosopher himself—than those who have not experienced a philosophical life. In any case, my claim in the sentence to which this note is appended is contingent on the assumption that Beth's judgment about which sort of life ranks higher in respect of happiness is an unbiased one based upon her extensive experience of both sorts of life and that the belief component of $R$ has solid epistemic credentials.

31. This leaves it open, of course, that for *some* agents (e.g., an imaginary being described shortly), possession of the feature is a wholly internal matter.

32. In being negative in the way explained, the externalism about psychological autonomy that I have defended is disanalogous to Putnam's "positive" externalism about "meanings."

33. Of course, it is also open to them to argue, sometimes correctly, that some mind-controlled agents are, at most, *apparently* nonautonomous.

# 10

## Compatibilist Autonomy and Autonomous Action

The argument in chapter 9 for externalism about psychological autonomy provides a partial answer to the focal question of part II of this book, the question what we can add to an ideally self-controlled, mentally healthy person to yield an autonomous person.[1] One worry is that values and other pro-attitudes on the basis of which a self-controlled person makes self-assessments, practical judgments, and the like might be attitudes that he is *compelled* to have. Bestowing what I have called "authenticity" on an agent helps with that problem: authentic agents have no "compelled*" pro-attitudes.[2] However, other problems remain. Those deriving specifically from incompatibilist worries are set aside in this chapter and taken up in the next.

In this chapter, as in chapter 9, I take no stand on the truth or falsity of determinism. Properly speaking, an account of autonomy that is presented as being neutral on this question is presented as being a compatibilist account. An account of autonomy that is correct *whether or not* determinism is true is correct *even if* determinism is true, and any such account is compatibilist. Here, again, I assume compatibilism while trying not to be heavy-handed about that assumption. I will examine a collection of obstacles to the autonomy of an ideally self-controlled person, with a view to locating sufficient conditions for compatibilist autonomy.

### 1. Autonomous Action and Deliberation

Full-blown, deliberative, intentional action, as I explained in chapter 1, involves some psychological basis for evaluative reasoning (e.g., values, desires, and beliefs); an evaluative judgment that is made on the basis of such reasoning and recommends a particular course of action; an intention formed or acquired on the basis of that judgment; and an action executing that intention. Starting at the bottom, we can see where the hard questions about autonomy lie.

Imagine that $S$'s proximal intention to $A$ issues smoothly in his intentionally $A$-ing. If the intention is autonomously possessed, the action is autonomously performed. For example, if Al autonomously intends to vote for the Democratic presidential candidate now and that intention unproblematically issues in his intentionally voting for that candidate now, then he autonomously votes for the Democratic candidate now.

Imagine next that $S$'s decisively judging it best to $A$ now issues directly in his proximally intending to $A$. If the judgment is autonomously made, the intention is autonomously formed or acquired. If Al autonomously judges it best to vote for the Democratic candidate now and that judgment issues directly in Al's proximally intending to vote for that candidate, then he autonomously intends to vote for that candidate.

In simple, straightforward cases of full-blown, deliberative, intentional action, then, the question whether an action was autonomously performed quickly brings us to the question whether a related evaluative judgment was autonomously made. Decisive better judgments, in cases of this kind, are made on the basis of deliberation. And it is plausible that autonomously conducted deliberation that unproblematically yields a decisive better judgment yields an autonomously made better judgment.

In what ways can agents fail to be autonomous with respect to their deliberative activities at a time? One way to approach this question—a particularly appropriate way, given my aim in part II of this book—is to ask how even an ideally self-controlled, mentally healthy individual might deliberate nonautonomously.

Obviously, the deliberation of ideally self-controlled agents is not tainted by *akrasia*. In my discussion of continent belief in chapter 5, I observed that the ideally self-controlled person is such that what he wants to be true influences what he believes to be true only in ways permitted by his principles. Since deliberation is partly a matter of belief formation, including the formation of evaluative beliefs about prospective courses of action, the observation applies straightforwardly to the deliberation of ideally self-controlled individuals. We can also note that such individuals will not akratically violate their specifically *deliberative* principles, principles about how they should conduct their deliberation. This is compatible, of course, with their being subject to unmotivated carelessness, to innocent mistakes about which procedures are best suited to particular deliberative issues, and the like. Ideally self-controlled deliberators need not be *perfect* deliberators.

Broadly speaking, the nonautonomy of an agent with respect to a deliberative process of his is explicable on either of two grounds: facts about the input to deliberation, and facts about what the agent does and is capable of doing with that input. Under *input* to a particular deliberative episode, I include all of the agent's propositional attitudes that enter into the deliberation, including not only such motivational attitudes as desires and values but also beliefs about proper deliberative procedures. For example, an agent's belief that his deliberation should never violate the dominance principle can serve as input to a deliberative process of his; the same is true of his belief that it would be rational to ignore his brother's advice in making financial decisions.

As I have explained, even an agent possessed of ideal self-control can have some compelled* pro-attitudes. Such pro-attitudes can function as input to deliberation, rendering the agent nonautonomous with respect to a particular deliberative episode. In the main Beth/Manson scenario of chapter 9, Beth may deliberate about how best to achieve her Mansonian goals, but when she deliberates about such things she does not deliberate autonomously. Even if the means to her Mansonian ends are not dictated by brainwashing, the ends are. In virtue of her being compelled* to have these ends or goals, Beth's deliberation with a view to their achievement is not autonomously conducted. An ideally self-controlled person can be cut off from autonomous deliberation in the same way. This bar to autonomous deliberation is handled by the attribution of authenticity to an agent.

In addition to pro-attitudes, human agents have more purely informational attitudes, and a variety of "executive qualities"—skills, capacities, and habits that play a role in the etiology of their conduct. Autonomous deliberation may be blocked not only on the first front but on the second and third, as well, as I explain in the following two sections.

The ensuing discussion is guided partly by a libertarian challenge to compatibilists. Robert Kane contends that "no existing compatibilist account of freedom . . . defines freedom" in such a way as "to ensure against the success of any potential covert non-constraining (CNC) control of the agent's will by another agent" (1985, p. 37). In cases of CNC control, as Kane understands it, the agent is not "constrained in the sense of being made to do things he does not want or desire to do." Rather, "the CNC controller" covertly arranges "circumstances beforehand so that the agent wants and desires, and hence chooses and tries, only what the controller intends." Kane's claim is that existing compatibilist accounts of freedom lack the resources for distinguishing cases in which $S$ is victimized by another agent's CNC control over him from cases in which $S$ conducts himself freely. His libertarian tack for blocking CNC control is to appeal to indeterminism. If it is causally undetermined what a particular agent will choose, "no potential controller could manipulate the situation in advance so that the choice necessarily comes out as the controller plans or intends" (p. 36). Thus, its being the case that $S$ is not causally determined to choose what he chooses at $t$ "thwarts[s] *any* potential CNC controller" intent upon controlling what $S$ chooses at $t$. The merits of this libertarian tack depend partly on the merits of libertarianism in general, a topic addressed in the next three chapters.

The brainwashed Beth scenarios in chapter 9 feature CNC control by another agent. There I offered compatibilist grounds for the judgment that Beth lacked autonomy in the relevant spheres. In the next two sections, I develop cases in which others exercise CNC control—on the informational and executive fronts—over an agent's deliberation and, thereby, over his evaluative judgments and corresponding intentions. In section 5, I offer compatibilist grounds for distinguishing these cases from cases of autonomous deliberation and action.

## 2.  Information and Autonomy

I start with a relatively simple case of covert, informational manipulation. Connie is deliberating about how best to invest her money. A respected investment firm has provided her with detailed information about a wide range of options. Connie has good reason to believe that the information is accurate and no reason to be suspicious of the firm. She deliberates on the basis of relevant values and desires of hers together with the information provided and rationally concludes that a certain investment policy would be best for her at this time. As it happens, however, Connie was systematically deceived by the firm. Their figures were contrived, assembled with the design of leading any rational agent with Connie's interests to decide on an investment policy that would maximize benefit to the firm at the investor's expense.

Connie's deliberation was manipulated by the firm; she was significantly heteronomous with respect to her deliberation and the judgment in which it issued.

Obviously, whether deception deprives an agent of autonomy with respect to a deliberative process depends on how important a role the contrived information plays in the agent's reasoning. At one extreme, the information plays no role at all, perhaps because it is simply irrelevant to the agent's deliberative question. In such cases, deception does not thwart autonomous deliberation. Near the other extreme are cases of the kind just sketched. Counting on the agent to reason rationally and knowing her interests, the manipulators provide her with false information that will yield the decision they want.

Deception on a grander scale can also be imagined. Imagine a futuristic king, George, whose only access to the state of his kingdom is through his staff of advisors. George's primary concern in life is to do what is best for his kingdom as a whole. The staff provide him with information, and he takes legislative and other measures on that basis. They also provide George with feedback about his measures, which information he takes into account in drafting further legislation and in modifying previous measures. They provide him, for example, with monthly figures on the gross national product, the distribution of wealth, the percentage of the population living below the poverty level, the king's popularity, and the popular reaction to his legislative acts. However the staff have their own agenda, namely, their own enrichment at the expense of the populace. Knowing the king's preferences, they systematically provide him with such false information as will lead him to make decisions that will further their aims. Of course, they are careful not to be so obvious about this as to call their loyalty into question. King George is naive, but he is not stupid.

George plainly is not ruling autonomously. Hence, he is not autonomous in the sphere of his life that is most important to him. The staff are in control of his activities in that sphere. They control George by controlling what information he receives. One can say, if one likes, that the staff *compel* George to have certain pro-attitudes: for example, a desire to enact a certain law. But the pro-attitudes that George is "compelled" to have are *instrumental* pro-attitudes, and thus differ from the values and desires featured in the Beth/Ann and Beth/Manson scenarios of chapter 9. George still intrinsically values the welfare of his kingdom as a whole, but he is systematically deceived about means to this end.

Suppose that good King George is an ideally self-controlled person, in the sense articulated in chapter 7, section 5. Then we have in George an ideally self-controlled agent who is heteronomous in a significant sphere of his life. What George lacks that an autonomous counterpart would possess is a body of information about the state of his kingdom and about how his measures affect the populace that would allow him to make informed decisions about how to pursue his political ends. Here we must be careful. Requiring that autonomous agents be *omniscient* would be extreme, to say the least, as would requiring that they have no practically relevant false beliefs.

George's problem, in part, is that as long as his unfortunate informational condition continues, the better he reasons about how to achieve his political ends, the less likely he is to achieve them. Indeed, given that his information combined with his values is such that rational practical reasoning is bound to thwart the achievement of those ends, George can reach them only coincidentally. If he is lucky enough to reason faultily in such a way as to cancel the predictable effects of his false beliefs, a policy of his might actually hit its mark. But, given his informational condition, George is unable intentionally to achieve his political ends. Owing to the nature of his information, George is in no position to learn from his failures; indeed, he has no way of knowing whether a policy has failed or not. Given his systematically misleading initial information and subsequent feedback, George is utterly lacking in control over the success of his political endeavors. Lacking such control for these reasons, he is, we may say, *informationally cut off* from ruling autonomously.

A distinction is in order between having control over whether one acts with the goal of *A*-ing and having control over whether, given that one acts with the goal of *A*-ing (i.e., given that one attempts to *A*), one succeeds in *A*-ing. Nothing in the case precludes George's having control of the former kind. He may have control over which goals he pursues. But George has no control over whether, given that he acts with the goal of improving the state of his kingdom, he succeeds in improving things. Again, he is informationally cut off from such control. We can say, more generally, that a sufficient condition of *S*'s being informationally cut off from autonomous action in a domain in which *S* has intrinsic pro-attitudes is that *S* has no control over the success of his efforts to achieve his ends in that domain, owing to his informational condition. (Notice that just as paralysis may be either temporary or permanent, an agent may be either temporarily or permanently informationally cut off from autonomy in a domain.)

Many efforts can fail for either of two general reasons—faulty execution or faulty planning. Someone's effort to rob a bank might fail because, although he formulated an excellent plan for robbing it, he failed to execute the plan properly (e.g., he forgot to turn off the alarm). Alternatively, his execution might have been fine but the plan seriously flawed (e.g., he neglected to include turning off the alarm in his plan). In the case of an effort that encompasses both the agent's own planning and an attempt at execution, control over its success extends not only to execution but to planning, as well. If *S* is unable to construct a plan for *A*-ing such that his flawlessly executing that plan would increase the likelihood that he will *A* above that provided by mere chance, and if *S*'s *A*-ing intentionally is contingent upon his constructing a plan for *A*-ing, then *S* has no control over the success of any attempt to *A* that he might make. Owing to a combination of faulty execution and luck—or owing to sheer luck—*S* might *A*, but his *A*-ing would not be intentional.

It is worth noting that George is in fact worse off regarding control than are gamblers who have control over whether they play certain games of chance but no control over whether, given that they play, they win. Relevant games involve chance alone, not a combination of chance and skill. Lydia, a lottery player, has control over whether she plays: she is not a compulsive gambler or otherwise compelled to buy lottery tickets. But owing to limited financial resources—she never has more than a dollar at any given time—and to the lack of special psychic powers, inside information, and the like, she has no control over whether her buyings of lottery tickets are buyings of winning tickets. Still, she has a fair chance to win.[3] George, however, owing to his informational condition, does not have a fair chance of improving his kingdom. Again, the more carefully and rationally he plans, the less likely he is to succeed.

A note on praiseworthiness and blameworthiness is in order. Although Lydia may deserve praise or blame for buying a lottery ticket, she obviously does not deserve praise or blame specifically for winning. For, beyond buying a ticket, she has no control over whether she wins. By the same token, although George may merit praise or blame for attempting to achieve a particular collection of political ends, he does not merit praise or blame for achieving those ends. For, again, given his informational condition, he has no control over the success of his attempts. If an attempt of George's does hit its mark, that will result from a combination of faulty reasoning and luck (or from sheer luck). Similarly, assuming that George is not responsible for his informational problem, he is not blameworthy for failing to achieve his political ends.

Is it plausible that although George is not autonomous in his efforts to improve his kingdom, he nevertheless is autonomous with respect to his deliberation about means of doing this? Not at all. Deliberation is informed by the deliberator's beliefs. By controlling what George believes in the ways described, his staff gain control over what deliberative conclusions George reaches. Again, George may be presumed to be autonomous with respect to his possession of his deliberative ends; but more is required for autonomous deliberation than that.

## 3. Executive Qualities and Autonomy

I turn now to "executive qualities"—skills, capacities, and habits. Here, too, autonomy-thwarting manipulation is possible. The leader of a religious cult has developed a sophisticated technique for producing certain deliberative habits in his followers. Disciples, typically recruited as teenagers, are required to deliberate aloud several times a day concerning such matters as how to spend their free time, what kind of diet to adopt, and what sort of literature to read. Deliberation appealing to theological premises endorsed by the cult is rewarded, whereas deliberation involving premises that one accepts on the authority of science is punished. Reward and punishment are subtly administered and members are never explicitly instructed that scientific authority is an illegitimate source of deliberative premises or that deliberation should be driven by theological premises. The leader operates on the hypothesis that habits not consciously possessed are more resistant to change than are explicitly held beliefs in dubious principles, and consequently he proceeds covertly. Some of his disciples develop the deliberative habits that he seeks to foster without also developing corresponding beliefs about the merits of deliberation involving the two kinds of premises. These disciples have no such beliefs to serve as input to deliberation. Still, by engendering in his disciples deliberative habits that suit his own aims, the leader exerts considerable control over some of their deliberative reasoning. Other things being equal, to the extent to which their deliberation is governed by the instilled habits, it is not autonomously conducted. (If a disciple were to become aware of his new deliberative habit and were to endorse it for reasons that are not themselves products of the described conditioning, matters might be different; but let us suppose that there is no such awareness or endorsement.)

In this case, as in the brainwashing scenarios discussed in chapter 9, agents' capacities for control over their own inner lives are bypassed by a process that significantly shapes their psychological make-up. If the leader had offered *arguments* for the utility of theologically guided deliberation and against that of deliberation guided by science, his disciples might have been able to exercise their capacities for control over their mental lives in assessing the reasoning offered and in coming to a conclusion about how best to deliberate. However, his method was designed to minimize the chance that their critical capacities would be brought to bear on the question of the relative merits of the two kinds of deliberation.

Consider another example. The leader of a commune, a man who has studied Plato, Skinner, and some recent work in attribution theory, arranges to have parents turn their children over to him at birth. They are raised in common by educators whom the leader has carefully trained. When the children reach the "age of reason," a certain kind of conditioning begins. Children are rewarded with praise and treats when, during their daily exercises in reasoning aloud about what to do, they take what they believe to be the leader's interests into account; otherwise praise and treats are withheld. The more time spent deliberating about the leader's interests during such exercises, the greater the reward. Children are never told that the leader's interests ought to be taken into account, and some of the successfully conditioned ones never come explicitly to believe this. The leader's object is to develop in the children a "leader's interest" bias that is analogous to some of the cognitive biases that he studied. He knows, for example, that when testing a hypothesis people tend to search more often for confirming than for disconfirming data even though most people lack a *belief* that this is how they should proceed, and he has learned similar things about the cognitive effects of the vividness of data and about the anchoring effect (see ch. 5, secs. 1–2). A "leader's interest" bias of this sort, he thinks, is more likely to persist as the children mature than is one resting on an education-engendered belief that the leader's interests ought always to have an important place in one's deliberation.

On the assumption that, at some point in their lives, the children had the capacity to develop into people who play a significantly greater role in shaping their own deliberative habits, this capacity was bypassed by their manipulators. Similarly, if the children once had the capacity to become people whose deliberative habits regarding the interests of others are shaped by their considered judgments about whose interests merit their deliberative attention, this capacity was bypassed.

In the cases presented, I am suggesting, to the extent to which certain "engineered" deliberative habits or dispositions are at work in deliberative processes, the agents are not deliberating autonomously. Is the same true of all imaginable engineered deliberative habits or dispositions, such engineering being understood, roughly, as the purposeful instilling of a habit or disposition in an agent in such a way that his relevant capacities for control over his mental life are bypassed in the process?[4]

Suppose that there were a device that, when installed in any person's head, would dispose the person to deliberate in ways that would reliably maximize his chances of locating efficient, effective means to his ends, whatever those ends might be. Imagine that neither the installation nor the operation of the device has any undesirable side-effects. One's capacity to reflect critically on one's ends is not diminished; one's collection of values, principles, desires, and the like is not altered in a way that by-passes the agent's capacities for control over his mental life; deliberation is not slowed down; and so on. Rather, one's capacity for deliberative excellence is enhanced. The installation and operation of such a device would not block autonomous delibera-tion—even though the very process of installation is one that bypasses the agent's capacities for control over his mental life.

Implicit in this little thought experiment is the assumption that, from some le-gitimate general standpoint, there may be better and worse ways of deliberating about means to ends. Certain deliberative practices might encompass unreliable cognitive procedures (e.g., procedures driven by the anchoring effect or the confirmation bias) whereas others might not. Other things being equal, the more reliable one's delib-erative processes, the better—from the point of view of *any* rational deliberator. After all, the basic point of means/end deliberation is to improve one's chances of achiev-ing one's ends. In principle, "engineering" that enhances one's deliberative prowess need not thwart autonomous deliberation.

I concede that in some special cases a rational agent may rationally cultivate in himself a deliberative disposition with the knowledge that the disposition promotes unreliable means/end reasoning. Someone who knows that in order to get a drug necessary for his family's continued existence he must humor a certain drug lord by cultivating in himself such a habit may have an excellent reason for attempting to do so: he may rationally judge that the benefits of so doing far outweigh the costs. And it requires little imagination to see how such an attempt might succeed; perhaps all he need do is take a certain disposition-altering drug. Similarly, a rational agent may have excellent reasons to bring it about that he deliberates about a certain issue in an unreliable way. Again, the lives of his loved ones might hang in the balance, the payoff being for unreliable deliberation itself.[5] But this is compatible with the truth of my claim about the basic point of means/end deliberation and with its being true that, in principle, the possession of "engineered" reliable deliberative dispositions need not block autonomous deliberation (in cases in which the dispositions are operative and causally efficacious).

In this respect, engineered deliberative dispositions differ from compelled* pro-attitudes. To the extent to which the latter drive deliberation, the deliberation is not autonomously conducted. But deliberation driven by engineered dispositions may or may not be autonomously conducted, depending partly on the nature of the dispo-sitions themselves.

An agent's using his engineered deliberative capacities in autonomous delibera-tion is compatible, incidentally, with his autonomy's having been violated by the in-stallation of the deliberation-enhancing device.[6] Imagine that the device is installed in an agent's head covertly, without his consent; further, if the agent had been informed about the device and the implantation procedure in advance, he would have refused to allow its installation. Under these conditions (perhaps with additional provisos), we naturally hold that the installers violated the agent's autonomy. But, supposing that we are right, it does not follow that whenever the device is at work in the agent he does not deliberate autonomously. Violating an agent's autonomy by changing his deliberative capacities against his will is one thing; cutting an agent off from autonomous deliberation (in instances of deliberation manifesting the change) is another. Again, the notion of autonomy at work in the judgment that someone's autonomy has been violated by a certain procedure is adequately captured by Feinberg's gloss: autonomy, in this sense, is "the sovereign authority to govern oneself" (1986, p. 28).

Consider an analogy. Physicians operate on a blind man's eyes against his will, enabling him to see. The man subsequently uses visually obtained information in making a variety of decisions. Other things being equal, the violation of his autonomy constituted by the surgery does not render those decisions nonautonomous. Further, even if the sighted man would prefer, on the whole, to have remained sightless, he may autonomously conduct deliberation that benefits from visually obtained information. Similarly, even if our agent, after the deliberation-enhancing operation, would prefer to possess only his earlier deliberative capacities, deliberative processes of his that manifest his new powers may be autonomously conducted. After all, when he is trying, for example, to find the best and most efficient means to his ends (in straightforward cases), he is assisted by these powers; they do not impede, but rather facilitate, his deliberative progress.

## 4.  Coercion

An armed trio of men stride into a bank, walk up to the bank manager, and demand that he open the vault, convincingly threatening to kill him and his patrons if he resists. The manager remains calm and quickly reviews his options as he speaks with the robbers and pretends to be searching for the key to the room that houses the vault (the key, as he knows, is in his pocket). He forms a decisive reasoned judgment that it would be best to follow the bank's policy concerning such cases—that is, to open the vault and to trigger a silent alarm, if that can be done without endangering the lives of innocent people. And he intends and acts on the basis of that judgment: he unlocks the vault (and triggers the alarm).

Did the manager autonomously or freely form the intention to unlock the vault? Some would say *yes*, others *no* (and some might claim that he formed it freely but not autonomously, or vice versa). Reasonable cases can be made for various alternative answers. The manager intended to do what he judged it best to do on the basis of utterly sane, informed deliberation: he did not intend or act out of panic. In a familiar sense of 'options,' he had options other than unlocking the vault; he calmly weighed them against compliance with the bank's policy and rationally decided not to pursue them. All this points to the conclusion that his intention was autonomously formed. Then again, but for the evident threat posed by the presence of the gunmen, he would not have handed over the money. They coerced him to unlock the vault. And, in cases of this kind, intentions and actions coerced by means of a convincing display of life-threatening force are regarded by many as nonautonomous (or unfree). The robbers *made* the manager open the vault, many are inclined to say; and given the etiology of his so acting, they can have done that only if they made him *intend* to open it.

Fortunately, for my purposes, it is not necessary to take a stand on whether the manager's intention was autonomously formed. My present concern is with sufficient conditions for psychological autonomy (and psychological episodes with respect to which the agent is autonomous), not with *necessary* and sufficient conditions. Those who view the manager's intention as not being autonomously formed will want a *noncoercion* constraint on autonomous intending. Of course, just what counts as coercion is a difficult and controversial issue, but compatibilists are not faced with any greater problems in this connection than are libertarians. Compatibilists who endorse a noncoercion constraint on autonomous intentions would be in serious trouble if that constraint had the result that all causally determined intentions, just in virtue of being causally determined, are coerced intentions. However, just as compatibilists can distinguish compulsion (i.e., an agent's being compelled to *x*, where *x* ranges not only over actions but also, for example, over the possession of pro-attitudes) from causal determination (ch. 9), they can, in principle, distinguish *coercion* from causal determination. The causal determination of an intention to open a bank vault by something that includes one's being at gunpoint differs markedly from the causal determination of such an intention under normal, utterly nonthreatening conditions. Plainly, a bank manager (in a normal scenario) who intentionally unlocks a vault as part of his normal weekly routine is not coerced into so intending, and this would be true at deterministic worlds.

Compatibilists inclined to place a noncoercion constraint on autonomous intending should be equally inclined to place the same constraint on autonomous judging and deliberating. To hold that the bank manager was not autonomous with respect to his intention to open the vault but was autonomous with respect to the decisive best judgment that issued in the intention and the deliberation that issued in the judgment is to advance an unstable position. The robbers influence what the manager intends precisely by influencing his deliberative process. If their influence on what he intends is a coercive influence, that is because their influence on what he judged best and on the deliberative process that issued in that judgment was coercive. This is not to say that they coerced him into deliberating. Rather, if this is a case of coercion, their convincing threat coercively produced in the manager motives to open the vault, motives in light of which the manager reached his deliberative conclusion. The robbers' most direct effect upon the manager was to produce in him these motives (e.g., a desire that the threat not be carried out). If there is coercion in this case, that is its basic locus.

## 5. Compatibilist Psychological Autonomy: Sufficient Conditions

There are, to sum up, three different fronts on which agents may be cut off from psychological autonomy in general and autonomous deliberation in particular, corresponding to three kinds of "equipment"—motivational attitudes, informational attitudes, and executive qualities—that agents bring with them to practical reflection, deliberation, and intentional action. Obviously, ideally self-controlled agents, if they are to be autonomous in a given domain, must not be motivationally (e.g., by compelled pro-attitudes), informationally, or executively cut off from autonomy in

that domain. Further, if there is a noncoercion constraint on autonomous deliberation, judgment, and intention, ideally self-controlled, autonomous agents will satisfy it, as well.

Assuming compatibilism about autonomy, what can we add to an ideally self-
controlled agent—and, more specifically, to a mentally healthy one (ch. 7, sec. 5)
who regularly exercises his powers of self-control in the various spheres in which
those powers can function—to yield a psychologically autonomous agent? The preceding discussion gives substance to the following suggestion. We have a psychologically autonomous agent if we add the following three conditions (the *compatibilist
trio*):

1. The agent has no compelled* motivational states, nor any coercively produced
   motivational states.[7]

2. The agent's beliefs are conducive to informed deliberation about all matters
   that concern him.

3. The agent is a reliable deliberator.

I am not claiming, of course, that this collection of conditions—including ideal self-
control—is *necessary* for psychological autonomy, but only that it is *sufficient* for
such autonomy, assuming the truth of compatibilism. One who accepts the suggestion may undertake the enormous task of whittling away at these conditions until one
locates what one takes to be an exhaustive statement of necessary and sufficient
conditions for compatibilist psychological autonomy. That is not a task that I will
attempt. However, the libertarian challenge identified at the end of section 1 should
be directly addressed. Is it true that compatibilists lack the resources to distinguish
cases of "covert non-constraining" (CNC) control by another agent from cases in
which an agent conducts himself autonomously?

I have sketched a number of examples of such control, both in this chapter and
in chapter 9. The cases of the deceived investor, King George, the disciples and children conditioned to have certain deliberative biases, and brainwashed Beth all feature CNC control by other agents. I have not offered a compatibilist *analysis* of freedom or autonomy; but I have advanced a compatibilist set of sufficient conditions
for psychological autonomy, a set that is easily supplemented to provide sufficient
conditions for autonomous action, as I explain in the following section. And those
conditions do exclude CNC control by another agent.[8]

A CNC controller can operate on three agential fronts: the victim's motivational
attitudes (as in the brainwashed Beth scenarios), the victim's informational attitudes
(as in the cases of the deceived investor and King George), and the victim's executive qualities (as in the examples of the covertly conditioned disciples and children
in sec. 3). The satisfaction of the "compatibilist trio" of conditions suffices for the
absence of CNC control by another agent on each of these fronts. Satisfaction of these
conditions also does *more* to protect an agent's autonomy from a "potential CNC
controller" than does Kane's condition of causally undetermined choice (see sec. 1).
The latter condition leaves it open that a prospective CNC controller can exert enough

control over an agent's choice to render the agent nonautonomous with respect to it (cf. Double 1991, pp. 214–15). A manipulative deceiver, for example, can severely limit the range of an agent's accessible options without reducing them to one. King George's advisors might be able to steer him in the direction of a handful of options—any of which would serve their purposes, and none of which conduces to George's aims—without being able to ensure that he selects their most preferred option. Exactly which choice George makes, we may suppose, is causally undetermined; but this is compatible with the advisors' having manipulated George in such a way as to ensure that, whatever choice he makes, he will not choose autonomously.

My point here is twofold. First, the CNC control problem can be handled by compatibilists. They can offer plausible compatibilist grounds for the judgment that agents manipulated by a CNC controller in representative cases do not conduct themselves autonomously. Second, the CNC control problem can be handled by them in a way that not only provides sufficient conditions for the absence of causally determining CNC control over a specific choice (or decisive better judgment, or intention) but also provides sufficient conditions for the absence of autonomy-blocking CNC control that leaves various relevant options open. In the latter connection, a compatibilist can go well beyond what is provided by Kane's condition of causally undetermined choice.

Libertarians may urge both that Kane's condition handles problems posed by counterparts of CNC control scenarios in which external intentional controllers are replaced by external blind forces and that compatibilists are in no position to explain how agents comparably affected in "blind forces" scenarios can fail to be autonomous in virtue of the effects of those forces. If relevant "blind forces" are construed so broadly as to include, in principle, any deterministic agent-external causal process that eventually issues in intentional behavior, committed compatibilists will not be impressed. But libertarians may, for dialectical purposes, agree to limit the counterpart cases to those in which *special* mindless forces do the work. The Bermuda Triangle scenario of chapter 9, section 7 is a case in point. If Beth's trip through the Triangle has the result that her making a certain choice is causally determined, that itself suffices for the choice's not having been autonomously made, on a view like Kane's. A libertarian may allege that compatibilists lack the resources to distinguish victims of blind forces in cases of this kind from autonomous agents.

As I have already explained, cases featuring *compelled* pro-attitudes are not limited to cases involving machinations by intentional agents (ch. 9, sec. 7). In my Bermuda Triangle scenario, Beth does acquire some compelled pro-attitudes and consequently does not satisfy condition 1 of the compatibilist trio. Similarly, someone whose beliefs are not conducive to informed deliberation about some matters that concern him, *whatever the source of his doxastic state*, falls short of satisfying condition 2; and an unreliable deliberator, *independently of the etiology of his unreliability*, fails to satisfy condition 3. To be sure, this compatibilist trio is too strong to constitute a *necessary* condition of autonomy, and an agent who falls short of satisfying the trio might act autonomously on a particular occasion. But I did explain why, in the Bermuda Triangle case, Beth lost her autonomy. And comparable explanations may be offered in cases in which a trip through the Triangle radically changes one's beliefs (rendering one's doxastic condition unconducive to informed deliberation) or renders one an unreliable deliberator by altering one's deliberative dispositions.

A compatibilist can offer necessary and sufficient conditions for what may be termed *strong* psychological autonomy—the conditions being ideal self-control, regular exercise of it in all domains, mental health, and satisfaction of the compatibilist trio. Those conditions distinguish agents possessed of strong psychological autonomy from agents in the grip of a CNC controller and from counterpart agents who, in the absence of such a controller, fall short of ideal self-control or mental health, or possess some compelled* (or coercively produced) pro-attitudes, or lack a collection of beliefs conducive to informed deliberation about matters of concern to them, or are not reliable deliberators. Moving from this to a compatibilist analysis of psychological autonomy *simpliciter* would be a challenging exercise, indeed; but if *strong* compatibilist autonomy is coherent, we need a special reason to think that a less demanding compatibilist autonomy cannot be. The crucial question, really, is this: If an agent who satisfies the compatibilist package of conditions just identified is psychologically autonomous even at a deterministic world, how far can an agent fall short of satisfying these conditions and still be psychologically autonomous at such a world? Presumably, if determinism leaves open *strong* psychological autonomy, on the characterization offered, it leaves open some approximations of this. In principle, compatibilists can loosen their constraints on strong psychological autonomy to arrive at a characterization of a weaker variety of psychological autonomy without thereby being committed to counting cases of autonomy-blocking CNC control as cases of psychological autonomy.

A putative counterexample to the proposed set of sufficient conditions for psychological autonomy merits attention. The alleged counterexample is designed to avoid the shortcomings of a trio of claims that may (naively) be thought to undermine the proposed set of conditions.

*Claim 1*: Suppose that *S*'s world is deterministic; then even if *S* satisfies the proposed set of conditions, *S* is not autonomous. *Reply*: The conditions are offered as conditions for *compatibilist* psychological autonomy. They cannot be undermined by the observation that they may be satisfied by an agent who does not satisfy an incompatibilist condition for incompatibilist autonomy.

*Claim 2*: By augmenting claim 1 with the supposition that there is a supremely intelligent being at *S*'s world (not *S*) who knows in advance everything that *S* will ever think, decide, intend, and so on, we secure claim 1's consequent. *Reply*: Its being causally necessary that an agent will engage in conduct *C* cannot itself be a bar to *compatibilist* autonomy, as I have just observed; and adding a being who knows that the agent will engage in *C* does not strengthen the necessity of the agent's so doing. The supposition that *X*'s knowing in advance what another being, *Y*, will do necessitates *Y*'s doing it rests on a modal fallacy. Necessarily, if *X* knows that *Y* will *A*, then *Y* will *A*; but this should not be confused with the distinct claim that if *X* knows that *Y* will *A*, then, necessarily, *Y* will *A*.

*Claim 3*: Augmenting claim 2 with the supposition that the supremely intelligent being is *S*'s creator yields claim 1's consequent. *Reply*: *X*'s creating an agent whose (entire) future *X* foreknows at the time of creation, including the agent's future decisions, does not suffice for $X$'s being in control of the agent's psychological life. The creator may foreknow that the agent he is about to create will enjoy compatibilist psychological autonomy.

I turn now to an apparently serious threat. Augment the scenario associated with claim 3 as follows. The creator creates a certain adult agent, Fred, precisely because the creator wants a certain event, $E$, to occur. Further, the creator gives Fred, at the time of creation, a particular collection of sheddable desires and values, knowing that, owing partly to Fred's having those initial desires and values, it is causally determined that a year later Fred will decide, on the basis of deliberation, that it is best to do $A$ and will, accordingly, do $A$, thereby bringing about $E$. Indeed, the creator knows that Fred will do $A$ only if he lives his life in a particular way during that year, and he knows just what collection of sheddable initial motivational states, together with the laws of nature and the state of Fred's world at the time of his creation, will result in his living his life in that way. Suppose that Fred satisfies the proposed set of conditions for compatibilist psychological autonomy: he is ideally self-controlled, he has no compelled* motivational states, his beliefs are conducive to informed deliberation about all matters that concern him, he is a reliable deliberator, and so on.[9] *Claim 4*: Fred lacks compatibilist psychological autonomy, even though he satisfies the proposed set of sufficient conditions. Hence, that set of conditions is inadequate.

The basic intuition at work is that Fred is an instrument of his creator and therefore lacks psychological autonomy. It should be noted, however, that Fred is not compelled, in any connection, by his creator. Fred has no compelled motivational attitudes, and his creator does not compel him to make certain deliberative judgments, to decide on particular options, or to perform particular actions. Fred can reflect intelligently on his values and desires, and he can (in a compatibilist sense of 'can') shed those values and desires and develop new ones. (He can, but he won't; and it is causally determined that he won't.) The view of Fred as an *instrument* undoubtedly is considerably more compelling to libertarians than to compatibilists. The former, viewing determinism as precluding autonomy, see the creator as exploiting his knowledge of the deterministic matrix into which Fred will be placed for the purposes of creating a human tool. But consider matters from the perspective of a compatibilist creator—a creator who embraces compatibilism. It may be important to such a creator that event $E$ be brought about *autonomously*; and he may create Fred with the particular set of sheddable motivational attitudes—together with a capacity for ideal self-control, for autonomous self-reflection and deliberation, and so on—in order to ensure that $E$ will be brought about (at Fred's deterministic world) by a psychologically autonomous agent's autonomously doing $A$.

Even compatibilists who embrace a history-sensitive externalism about psychological autonomy need not see the scenario associated with claim 4 as threatening. Such compatibilists hold that CNC control scenarios of various kinds detailed earlier preclude psychological autonomy. But, given Fred's qualities in the present scenario, they will not view Fred as *controlled* by his creator. Rather, they should see him as a self-governing individual whose path is causally determined partly by an intentionally instilled, but sheddable, collection of motivational attitudes. In one respect, Fred is like any autonomous agent at a deterministic world: his path is causally determined. He is *special* in having been endowed at the time of his creation with a collection of motivational attitudes for his creator's own purposes. But since these are sheddable attitudes, this detail of his creation does not render him non-autonomous, on the assumption that compatibilism is true.

## 6.   Autonomous Action

In chapter 9, I observed that the capacities required for autonomous overt action extend beyond those required for psychological autonomy. Imagine a hospitalized man who was seriously wounded in battle and now is totally paralyzed and incapable even of communicating. Imagine also that the man's cognitive faculties are in good working order, that he spends much of his time pondering philosophical and mathematical problems and developing solutions, and that he devotes some time to the question how he ought to lead his life. The man might possess psychological autonomy, but he is incapable of overt action. He cannot intentionally affect his external environment at all, much less do so autonomously.

As I have already remarked, depending upon one's position on what it is to act intentionally, it is open to one to hold that some actions that are not intentionally performed are nevertheless autonomously or freely performed (ch. 1, n. 11). However, for present purposes, attention can safely be focused on autonomous, intentional, overt action. Overt intentional actions, on a view that I defended in an earlier book, are partial causal products of acquisitions of corresponding intentions (Mele 1992a). I will spare the reader an account of the precise causal connection between acquisitions of *proximal* intentions (again, intentions for the specious present) and the intentional actions in which acquiring such intentions issues (see Mele 1992a, ch. 10). It suffices to note that when things proceed without a hitch on that front, whether the action is autonomously performed depends on whether the agent was autonomous with respect to his intention.

Consider relatively simple instances of full-blown, nonakratic, intentional action. Agents start with a practical question; reason carefully and rationally about what to do; rationally and decisively judge, on the basis of that reasoning, that it would be best to A straightaway; proximally intend, on the basis of that judgment, to A; and execute that intention. Intentions so acquired may fail to be autonomously acquired, for reasons that are by now familiar. For example, values, desires, or beliefs that figure importantly in the agent's reasoning might be products of unsolicited brainwashing and the like. However, assuming a psychologically autonomous agent, and, specifically, one whose autonomy pervades the psychological process that issues in the intention, that intention is autonomously acquired and the intentional action in which it issues is autonomously performed. In cases of the kind at issue, then, autonomous overt action requires nothing more than an autonomous psychological process (of the sort described), the ability to execute the intention in which it concludes, and an intentional action constituting the execution of that intention. Regarding these simple cases, all the hard questions about autonomy concern *psychological* autonomy.

Libertarians often claim, of course, that in order to act freely one must be able to act otherwise. But except for a libertarian who thinks that an indeterministic "break" between proximal intentions and intentional actions is required for free action, the "could have done otherwise" issue is best seen as an issue about what the agent could have *intended* (or chosen, or decided) to do.[10] And that takes us back to psychological autonomy.

The hard questions about autonomy have the same location in representative instances of "orthodox" continent action, including those in which an agent exercises self-control in the service of a proximal intention. If an agent is autonomous with respect to the internal, psychological process that nondeviantly produces a representative intentional action of this kind, the action is autonomously performed.[11]

Of course, there are tricky cases of intentional action, too. Are there scenarios in which, although an agent is fully autonomous with respect to the psychological process that nondeviantly issues in a decisive judgment that it would be best to A and in a corresponding proximal intention, the action, A, to which that intention nondeviantly leads is not autonomously performed? On the face of it, an agent would seem to be no less autonomous with respect to such an action than he is with respect to the psychological process that generates it. Is there a good reason to believe otherwise? It may be thought that some "willing addicts" provide such a reason.[12] The thought is that if, owing to their addiction, they have an irresistible desire to A, then even if they A on the basis of fully autonomous deliberation, they do not autonomously A.

In chapter 8, section 3, I considered an *unwilling* addict—an addiction specialist, Alice, who autonomously addicted herself to heroin and later judged that she would be better off without her addiction and the desires involved in it. Consider an earlier time at which Alice had not yet formed the negative judgment about her addiction. At this time, she asked herself whether it would be better to continue the experiment or, instead, to seek to put an end to her addiction, and on the basis of careful, clear-headed, unbiased, informed reflection upon the value of her experiment, the risks to her health, and the like, she judged that it would be best to continue the experiment. On the basis of that judgment and her recognition that her schedule called for another shot of heroin soon, Alice judged it best to make the necessary preparations and then to inject herself with the drug, which judgment issued nondeviantly in an effective proximal intention. At the time of the injection, Alice was possessed of an irresistible desire for the drug, but she was moved to use it by her considered reasons for continuing the experiment.

In this case, I submit, Alice autonomously used the drug. It is true, let us suppose, that if she had not been moved to use it by the pertinent reasons, she would have used it anyway, owing to the influence of an irresistible proximal desire for heroin. But this does not imply that she nonautonomously used the drug—any more than the fact that a mind-reading demon would have made us save a drowning child, if we had not saved her on our own, implies that we did not autonomously save her. If Alice's judgment had been clouded by her desire for heroin, or if, owing to the influence of that desire, she had *deceived herself* into believing that it would be best to continue the experiment, then she would *not* have been fully autonomous with respect to the process that issued in the relevant judgment and intention—in which case, the scenario would not pose even an apparent threat to the thesis under consideration. Assuming that she is fully autonomous in that regard (and assuming the truth of compatibilism), one is hard pressed to see how her using the drug can count as a nonautonomous deed. Alice is autonomous or self-governing with respect to her use of the drug at the time, even though her addiction would not have allowed her to refrain from using it.

Assuming that my suggested sufficient conditions of compatibilist psychological autonomy are correct, what would suffice for compatibilist autonomous overt action? A short answer is intentional, overt action, $A$, caused in part by the acquisition of a proximal intention to $A$, which acquisition event is a nondeviant causal product, in part, of the formation of a decisive evaluative judgment—specifically, a judgment that it would be best to $A$—on the basis of maximally autonomous deliberation, where the latter is understood as deliberation maximally manifesting the psychological autonomy of an ideally self-controlled agent. The deliberation in question is not driven by compelled*, coercively produced, or self-oppressively produced motivational states, it is informed deliberation, and it is reliable. Readers who do not share my assessment of the willing addict's case may wish to add a proviso: It is not the case that if $A$ had not been caused in the specified way, it would have been caused in some other way such that its being so caused would render $A$ a nonautonomous action. Since I am offering a sufficient condition for compatibilist autonomous action, and not a *necessary* condition, I have no objection to this addition.

Obviously, this short answer raises a lot of complicated questions, including the following. What is intentional action? What is action? What is an intention? How are events of intention acquisition caused? What is causation? I have addressed most of these questions elsewhere.[13] The point to emphasize now is that if a successful causal model for explaining *intentional* overt action is possible—and I have argued elsewhere for the possibility of this (Mele 1992a)—the compatibilist's main burden is to show how such a model in combination with determinism can accommodate *autonomous* overt action, and that will be accomplished by showing how determinism is compatible with *psychological* autonomy. If the latter can be demonstrated, compatibilists can rest their case; the possibility of autonomous overt action raises no special worries about determinism beyond those raised by the possibility of psychological autonomy itself.

My discussion of autonomous action has revolved around full-blown, deliberative action. That is not because I think that *only* such actions can be autonomously performed. However, wanting it to be true that we sometimes act autonomously, we want *most* that this be true in the sphere of full-blown, deliberative actions. An autonomy limited, for example, to relatively spontaneous actions performed in the absence of deliberation would not amount to much.

Again, it is not my purpose to establish the truth of compatibilism about autonomy. Rather, my aim regarding compatibilism has been to identify (nonvacuous) sufficient conditions for autonomous agency, given the assumption that compatibilism is true. The next major question on the agenda is whether the same can be done for autonomous agency given the assumption that compatibilism is *false*.

## Notes

1. On mental health, see p. 126.
2. Again, a *compelled** pro-attitude of an agent $S$ is a compelled pro-attitude, the compulsion of which was not arranged by $S$.

3. By this I mean only that the lottery is not rigged.

4. A more refined understanding would also cover cases in which a being creates an agent with certain deliberative dispositions already in place. Some such cases are comparable to the "devil" scenario at the end of ch. 9, sec. 6.

5. On the rationality of making oneself temporarily irrational in some cases, see Parfit 1984, pp. 12–13.

6. Robert Kane raised this issue in correspondence.

7. Those who accept the logical possibility of magically produced agents created with some unsheddable pro-attitudes already in place should augment condition 1 with the following: The agent has no compelled *innate* motivational states (see p. 168).

8. I am assuming that "CNC control" by another agent is to be understood as excluding "hired control": for example, cases in which one hires a covert controller to reshape—covertly, of course—one's values.

9. Randy Clarke suggested roughly this scenario in correspondence.

10. On where libertarians should want to place an indeterministic break, see ch. 12.

11. I have been silent on the question whether *akratic* actions can be autonomously performed, my aim regarding autonomous action being to locate *sufficient* conditions for it, not a collection of jointly *necessary* and sufficient conditions. The question raises the interesting issue whether an action might be freely, but not autonomously, performed (see Haji 1994). Akratic action is often understood as being, by definition, *free* action. However, someone who takes autonomous action to require an exercise of self-government may urge that akratic actions are not performed *autonomously*, on the grounds that the failure of self-control on which such actions depend is incompatible with the agent's being self-governing regarding those actions. This is a tantalizing issue; but it is also sufficiently complex that a proper treatment would require extensive discussion. I have decided to resist the temptation to address the issue in this already lengthy book and to reserve discussion of it for another occasion.

12. In personal correspondence, Ishtiyaque Haji suggested that this might be so.

13. On intentional action, action, intention, and intention acquisition, see Mele 1992a. For an analysis of intentional action see Mele and Moser 1994. Causation is addressed in ch. 11.

# 11

# Problems for Libertarians

The externalist position on autonomy developed in chapters 9 and 10 is officially neutral on the truth of determinism. It is a *compatibilist* position. The present chapter approaches autonomy from a libertarian perspective.

What bothers the libertarian about determinism is concisely expressed in the "consequence argument":

> If determinism is true, then our acts are the consequences of the laws of nature and events in the remote past. But it is not up to us what went on before we were born, and neither is it up to us what the laws of nature are. Therefore, the consequences of these things (including our present acts) are not up to us. (van Inwagen 1983, p. 16)

If determinism is true, then given the laws of nature and the state of the world at a time prior to my birth, there were present, at that time, causally sufficient conditions for everything that I would ever do. What is worrisome is that, seemingly, given that those conditions are not up to me, neither are any of their consequences. If my doing something freely requires that my doing it be up to me and determinism entails that nothing is up to me, then the truth of determinism is incompatible with my acting freely.

One requirement on a person's being autonomous (or free, or morally responsible), it is sometimes said, is that there not be a continuous deterministic causal sequence that begins prior to the person's birth and results in his actions: there must be one or more indeterministic "breaks" or "gaps." The libertarian who is concerned to provide an account of free choice and action—an account of what they are and of how free choices and actions come about—would do well to specify the sorts of indeterministic gaps that bear importantly on human freedom. The present chapter identifies and explores some problems that the libertarian faces in this and related connections. Chapter 12 takes up the burden of developing a libertarian response.

## 1. External Openness

In chapter 1, in connection with the deterministic thesis that "there is at any instant exactly one physically possible future," I mentioned the possibility of our building indeterministic triggers of personally significant events. Imagine that a century ago, extraterrestrial pranksters rigged such a trigger to a bomb that they placed in the ceiling of a certain college dormitory room. The bomb was set to explode on September 15,

1969, should a certain undetermined, physically possible, quantum-mechanical event occur on that day. Unbeknownst to them, the occupant of that room—namely, me— would be out of town that day. Even so, if the bomb had been triggered, it would have blown my room to bits, and my consternation would have been such as to result in my immediately leaving the college, never to return—or so let us suppose. In that case, it is likely that I would never have met my wife, Connie (I met her in the next term at that college). But then my life would have been very different: my children would never have been born, I would not have known Connie's family, and so on. So at a host of instants on and prior to September 15, 1969, I had more than one personally significant, physically possible future.

Does that gain me anything in the way of freedom or autonomy? Given that the bomb does not explode in the thought experiment, am I any more free in it than I would be if everything else were the same except that there was no such bomb in my room (and anything entailed by that)? More precisely, am I more free in the former scenario than in the latter just in virtue of the presence of the indeterministic bomb in my room in the former? Of course not. Suppose now, in the same thought experiment, that the only thing that ever provided me with more than one physically possible future was the presence of the bomb (rigged as I have described) in that dorm room. In that case, did my freedom or autonomy vanish once September 15 passed with no explosion? That seems preposterous too. How can my freedom hinge, in the case as described, on the physical "openness" of what happens to the bomb on September 15?

Compare a deterministic world *W1* with an indeterministic world (i.e., a world at which determinism is false) *W2* that is as much like *W1* as possible, given that *W2* has various indeterministic "land mines" in it—devices rigged to be triggered by undetermined quantum-mechanical events. Suppose that, as it happens, none of these land mines is ever triggered, since the requisite undetermined triggering events do not occur. Suppose, as well, that there is a counterpart of me at each of these worlds, and that some of the land mines are at my counterpart's spatiotemporal vicinity in *W2*. Given that the land mines never explode, their presence makes no difference to my counterpart's life in *W2*, at least in some versions of the story. And in some such versions of the story, I submit, my *W2* counterpart is no more free than my *W1* counterpart. One has physically possible futures that the other lacks, and only one has more than one physically possible future, but only because of the presence of certain indeterministic land mines—and those mines never explode. The actions, decisions, and lives of the two agents might proceed along exactly similar lines.

What libertarians want that they do not find in determinism is not merely that individual agents have, at some instants, more than one physically possible future, but that which future they come to have, among the ones physically possible for them, is in some sense and to some degree *up to the agents*. They want something that re- quires what may be termed *internal* indeterminism.

## 2.  Internal Openness

Return to the deterministic thesis that any agent has only "one physically possible future." It is not physically possible for an agent who has only one such future to do anything other than he does. If this *were* physically possible, the agent would have more than one physically possible future; it would be physically possible that he does *A* and not *B* at some future time *t\** and physically possible, as well, that he does *B* and not *A* at *t\**. The deterministic thesis seems dismayingly limiting. But is it? Is having only one "physically possible future," in the relevant sense of the quoted words, a dismayingly limiting thing?

I will approach this question in a somewhat roundabout way—by means of a discussion of Peter van Inwagen's criticism (1983) of a certain strand in what he calls "the *Mind* argument" (because it has appeared so often in the journal *Mind*). The *Mind* argument is an argument against any incompatibilist account of freedom, and van Inwagen has offered the most thorough defense of incompatibilism that I have seen.

The strand of the *Mind* argument at issue is a "slippery slope" argument. I will call it the "piano argument." Van Inwagen's presentation of an elaborate version starts with an invitation to imagine a scenario in which a demon has a piano keyboard that is connected by a "subtle wire" to a certain thief's brain: "by what he plays, he can 'direct' . . . the motions of the atoms in the thief's brain and can thereby direct the thief's inner life, including his deliberations" (p. 132). On a particular occasion, the demon did precisely this; the thief, consequently, "was merely the demon's instrument and *acted* only in the etiolated sense in which a fiddle acts in the hands of a violinist or a scalpel acts in the hands of a surgeon."

The next step is to imagine a modified case in which the demon's behavior at the keyboard "is undetermined by the demon's own inner states and by anything else." Again, the thief does not act. Nor does he act if we drop the demon from the story and imagine that the piano "is a sort of *player* piano: . . . the keyboard is worked by a mechanism internal to the piano," an indeterministic mechanism. Further, removing the piano from the story and supposing that "impulses simply *appear* in the subtle wire . . . undetermined by prior states of affairs" does not change the fact that the thief does not act. Again, he is not in control of what happens. Nor would this fact be changed, the argument proceeds, if the wire were shortened so that only the part in the thief's head were left: "[I]f impulses undetermined by past states of affairs appear in the wire and if these impulses determine the putative acts of the thief—determine what movements are made by his limbs and what thoughts pass through his mind—then these putative acts are not real acts, are not among the things he *does* or produces" (pp. 132–33).

The last step in the thought experiment is to replace the wire (actually, a wire surrogate by this point) with brain cells that are "a *natural part* of the thief's brain," a part "in which there arise impulses, undetermined by past states of affairs, which determine his every action" (p. 133). (It is preceded by a step in which the wire is replaced by a wire-shaped thing made of brain cells, which thing is not a "natural part" of the agent.) The argument proceeds from there as follows:

> In our original story, . . . the thief did not *act.* . . . None of our series of modifications introduced any "opportunity" for him to act. We must therefore conclude that in our *final* story the thief did not act. But our final story is just exactly the tale the incompatibilist tells when he is asked what goes on inside someone who acts freely. Therefore, the incompatibilist's story is incoherent. (pp. 133–34)[1]

I will take up van Inwagen's response to this argument shortly. I want to show first that there is a certain problem with the argument. The problem can be avoided by adjusting the conclusion, and the adjusted argument poses an important challenge for libertarians.

Again, the proponent of the piano argument contends that the agent does not *act* at any of the various stages in the example. However, the thought experiment gives us no good reason at all to believe this—at *any* of its stages! Imagine that among the aspects of the thief's "inner life" produced by the demon—even at the first step, say— are the thief's intentions. On a particular occasion, the demon causes the thief to intend to rob a poor box straightaway and the thief proceeds to execute that intention, independently of any further efforts on the demon's part. The thief's execution of his intention is itself in no way abnormal, we may suppose. What transpires once he acquires the intention to rob the poor box need in no way differ from what happens when normal agents—in the absence of demons, subtle wires, and the like—execute their proximal intentions. His acquiring a proximal intention to break into the poor box, let us suppose, issues smoothly in bodily motions suitable to the achievement of his intended goal, and those motions result in an open, and then empty, poor box, and in the money that had previously been in the box ending up in the thief's pockets—all in a way involving neither causal deviance nor exceptional luck. But then the thief plainly robbed the poor box; indeed, he *intentionally* robbed it, and his robbing it was an action.

So the piano argument fails miserably—as an argument for its stated conclusion. However, as an argument for the incoherence of "the incompatibilist's story" about *free* action, it merits consideration. It is easily reconstructed as such: just modify the verb 'act' with the adverb 'freely' at appropriate junctures in the preceding presentation.

Now, for van Inwagen's criticism. In his view, there is a crucial difference between the case involving the shortened wire (or one in which the wire is replaced by brain cells that are not a natural part of the agent) and the last case in the thought experiment, featuring a "natural part" of the brain. Van Inwagen attempts to show that "it is not clear that an apparent act of a human being that was the consequence of an undetermined change in a natural part of a human being *could not* be a real act" (p. 135). His tack is to sketch "two 'models' of human action according to which this *is* possible."

The first model is provided by agent (or "immanent") causation. Van Inwagen declines to say much about this model, "since so many philosophers are convinced of its incoherence" (p. 135), and perhaps also because he finds it "more puzzling than the problem it is supposed to be a solution to" (p. 151). My own discussion of it will be comparably brief. My gloss on agent causation in chapter 1, section 2 will serve as background.

Imagining that the thief refrained from stealing in "the actual world," van Inwagen writes,

> To say that it was not determined that [the thief] should refrain from stealing is to say this: there is a possible world that (a) is *exactly* like the actual world in every detail up to the moment at which the thief refrained from stealing, and (b) is gov-

erned by the same laws of nature as the actual world, and (c) is such that, in it, the thief robbed the poor-box. (p. 136)

Agent causation, van Inwagen observes, is consistent with there being such a possible world, since agent causation is the view that "the *agent himself* is sometimes (when he acts freely) the cause of his own acts, or, perhaps, the cause of the bodily or mental changes that manifest them" and an agent-caused act is not causally determined by any collection of events and states. The agent does not, for example, cause his act, *A*, by willing or deciding to *A* straightaway, which willing or deciding event (in conjunction with other events and states) then causally determines his *A*-ing. No event or "change in the agent causes" his *A*-ing; "rather the agent *causes* without himself changing in any way. (Save accidentally. The human agent . . . is *constantly* undergoing change . . .)."

As van Inwagen notes, his opponents are likely to reject agent causation as incoherent (p. 137). I must admit that I have never understood how agent causation is supposed to be causation and how it can help us understand what it is for agents to be in control of their behavior. The libertarian's *motivation* for introducing agent causation into the debate about human freedom is clear enough: it is to avoid a certain problem that the *Mind* argument is intended to highlight. This may be termed the *control problem*—a problem about how agents can have the control over their actions that acting freely requires, if these actions issue in part from causally undetermined internal events. In the absence of an account of how agent causation "works," one might as well just say that there is such a thing as agents' *control*—a mysterious thing that cannot be characterized in any detail and is not manifested in, as van Inwagen puts it, "'normal' causation, a relation that takes *events* or *states of affairs* or some such, and not *persons*, as its terms" (p. 138)—and assert that beings who have it can act and act freely. A genuine notion of agent causation should help to explain human behavior; it should be capable of playing a useful role in a theory of the production or explanation of human action.[2] But as van Inwagen admits, on his own way of rendering agent causation "less mysterious," it does no more than to mark the problem for which the libertarian seeks a solution (p. 152; cf. Nagel 1986, p. 115): the question how there can be action of a kind that satisfies the libertarian's constraints on free action simply *becomes* the question "'How can there be such a thing as immanent [i.e., agent] causation?'"

I turn now to van Inwagen's second model of action. It is composed of "a theory about the causes of human action" and "a theory about causation itself" (p. 138). The former "theory," set out in a single paragraph, is the familiar claim that agents' beliefs and desires are causes of their actions. The latter theory is central to van Inwagen's rebuttal of the piano argument.

At one point, van Inwagen writes that a certain case of his convinces him that it is "not part of the *concept* of causation that a cause—or even a cause plus the totality of its accompanying conditions—determines its effect" (p. 140). If this is right, then perhaps it is conceptually possible that the thief's refraining from breaking into the poor box is caused by *C* without *C* "plus the totality of its accompanying conditions" determining the refraining. And if a precise nondeterministic causal connection that may be imagined to obtain between *C* "plus the totality of its accompanying conditions" on the one hand and the refraining on the other would suffice for the agent's being in control of the refraining, then perhaps the control problem can be laid to rest. Perhaps under certain conditions, a bit of behavior can be caused in such a way that it counts as being under the agent's control and as a genuine action, even though the totality of causally relevant conditions do not determine the behavior. The "theory about causation" that forms a major part of the second "model of action" holds out the promise of shedding light on indeterministic control in a way that agent causation is apparently too murky to do.

Let us have a look at the case that produces the above-mentioned conviction in van Inwagen:

> Suppose someone throws a stone at a window and that the stone strikes the glass and the glass shatters in just the way we should expect. . . . God reveals to us that the glass did not *have* to shatter under these conditions, that there are possible worlds having exactly the same laws of nature as the actual world and having histories identical with that of the actual world in every detail up to the instant at which the stone came into contact with the glass, but in which the stone rebounded from the intact glass. . . . Does it follow . . . that the stone did not break the glass, or that the glass did not break *because* it was struck by the stone? . . . perhaps the only reason we could have for saying this is that we accept a corollary of the standard theory of causation: that instances of causation simply are instances of universal, exceptionless laws, that the concept of the instantiation of an exceptionless law and the concept of causation are one and the same concept. But this proposition is very doubtful. (p. 139)

Van Inwagen proceeds to imagine that we repeatedly view a slow-motion film of the event, displaying a moving stone, shattering glass, and the like. This engenders in us enormous confidence that "the stone . . . caused the glass to break," even though we grant, of course, that there are logically possible scenarios in which something else caused the breaking instead. God's revelation, van Inwagen contends, should not lead us to deny that the stone broke the window. Rather, it is "more reasonable" to hold that "while the stone did cause the window to break, it was not determined that it should; that it *in fact* caused the window to break, though, even if all conditions had been precisely the same, it might not have" (p. 140).[3]

When van Inwagen says "even if all conditions had been precisely the same," he evidently means, as he put it earlier, even if they had been the same "up to the instant at which the stone came into contact with the glass." Now (and here I depart from van Inwagen's presentation), imagine that the world, $W1$, at which the example is set has some indeterministic devices in it, and that one is rigged to the glass window. If a certain kind of undetermined event occurs in the vicinity of the device at $t$, the moment at which the stone comes into contact with the glass, the device will straightaway render the window unbreakable by a stone, so that a thrown stone will simply bounce off (perhaps after producing a small dent). We can then imagine another world, $W2$, that is exactly the same as $W1$ up to $t$, but at which the device is activated at $t$. At $W1$ the thrown stone crashes through the glass, breaking it to bits; at $W2$ it harmlessly bounces off. This is conceivable. What does it show?

Presumably, the window's breaking at $W1$ was not an uncaused event; that is, presumably, it was caused. If it was caused, it was caused by something. Picking out *the cause* of an event is a notoriously difficult matter; but we need not try to identify *the* cause of the window's breaking, and we can safely say that the stone's striking this window (a window having such and such properties) with a certain force played a significant causal role in the window's breaking. The main point to notice is that (other things being equal) prior to *t*—at both worlds—neither are causally sufficient conditions present for the window's breaking shortly after *t* nor are causally sufficient conditions present for the stone's harmlessly bouncing off the window then. Prior to *t*, at both worlds, what happens to the window—more precisely, whether it breaks or not—is causally open. Still, it is caused to break at *W1*. (Assuming that the locus for indeterminism that I have identified is the only relevant one in the scenario, then once *t* has passed, happenings involving the window proceed deterministically at both worlds.)

Does this help with agency? Does this observation provide any insight into how a libertarian might handle the control problem? Let us return to van Inwagen's thief, supposing that "his refraining from robbing the poor-box (*R*) was caused but not necessitated by his desire to keep the promise he made to his dying mother coupled with his belief that the best way to do this would be to refrain from robbing the poor-box (*DB*)" (pp. 140–41). Van Inwagen writes,

> *R* was caused by *DB* and *DB* did not *have* to cause *R*; it just *did*. We may suppose that God has thousands of times caused the world to revert to precisely its state at the moment just before the thief decided not to steal, and has each time allowed things to proceed without interference for a few minutes, and that *DB* caused *R* on about half these occasions. On the other occasions, we may suppose, *DB* did not cause *R*: instead the thief's desire for money, coupled with his belief that the best way for him to get money was to rob the poor-box, caused him to rob the poor-box. ... The thief's act—or what looks very much like his act—was *caused* by his desires and beliefs, after all. (pp. 140–41)

Van Inwagen certainly seems to be supposing that *DB* causes *R* by causing a *decision* to *R*, or that such a decision is a causal intermediary between *DB* and *R*. After all, in the thousands of re-runs God always makes the world "revert to precisely its state at the moment just before the thief *decided* not to steal," indicating that it is particularly important that we see the *decision* as not causally determined. Let us suppose that *DB* is intended to be understood as causing *R* via that route. Then we can ask whether it is indeed possible that on the thousands of reruns, *DB causes* a decision to *R* about half the time—even though, in each rerun, the world is returned to "precisely its state at the moment just before the thief *decided* not to steal." Some will say *no*, contending that *something* must be different at that moment in the two kinds of case, that a difference at that moment is required to explain why the thief decides to refrain from stealing in some reruns and decides to steal in others.

They have not absorbed the lesson of the augmented window example featuring a device triggerable by an undetermined event. Suppose that the thief has a little mechanical device in his head that works as follows.[4] His having a reason (*R1*) to refrain from stealing then while also having a reason (*R2*) to steal then—or his having such a pair of reasons together for a certain period of time (two minutes, say)—activates the device, which then goes into either state 1 or state 2. The device is indeterministic and is so constituted that it goes into state 1 on about half the occasions on which it is activated and into state 2 on the others. The immediate result of the device's going into state 1 is that *R1* is "enhanced" in such a way that *R1* (together with any other causally relevant factors) immediately causally determines a proximal decision to refrain from stealing; the device's going into state 2 has an exactly parallel result involving *R2*. If these little processes would take more than a "moment," let them take two moments, and let God's reruns start up two moments before the decision occurs. Given such a picture, we can understand, it seems, how it is possible for the reruns to divide as they do.

However the thief's decisions come about, if he unproblematically executes them he unproblematically acts. *Action* is not the problem. But does the thief *freely* decide in this scenario? Evidently not, for what determines *what* he decides, once the machine is activated, is what state the machine enters, and he is not in control of that.[5] Pursuing this observation in a certain direction will give us roughly the piano argument (about *free* action, or free will, or free decision) all over again. Just substitute for the mechanical device some "natural part" of the brain that works in essentially the same indeterministic way and argue that since the agent is no more in control of what state that part of the brain enters (once it is "activated") than he is, in the preceding case, of what transpires in the mechanical device, he is not in control of what he decides and therefore does not freely decide.

We can generate comparable scenarios that have less of an air of "randomness" about them. For example, we can imagine a device (and a corresponding natural part of an agent's brain) that blocks certain agent-internal causal transactions in a tiny fraction of cases. Imagine a device, rigged to be triggered by undetermined events of a certain kind, that will, when activated, prevent an agent's decisive better judgments from issuing in corresponding decisions or intentions. The frequency of the triggering events is such that if God were repeatedly to set things back to the point at which the judgment is made, the device would prevent the agent's reaching that judgment from resulting in a corresponding intention in only three percent of the reruns, and in those reruns it will produce an intention that clashes with the judgment. When the device is inoperative and judgment issues smoothly in intention, we have indeterministic causation in van Inwagen's sense. But although installing the device in an agent would render futures causally open that might otherwise be causally closed, it is difficult to see the installation as freedom-providing or freedom-enhancing. When the device operates, *it*, and not the agent, controls what the agent intends; and when the device does not operate, things proceed exactly as they would have done if the device had been absent. We get the same result when the randomly triggered mechanism is supposed to be a "natural part" of the agent's brain.

The problem here is a perfectly general one. Introducing indeterministic items of this kind—of either the mechanical or the "natural part" varieties—at any juncture in the etiology of human action seemingly would *weaken* agents' control over their behavior. Again, internal indeterminism apparently militates against agential control, and freedom requires such control. It can be replied, of course, that even if internal indeterministic "gaps" in the production of action diminish agential control at the time, they enhance control in the long run or on the whole. This response is considered in the following section. But it is worth noting now that augmentation of one's physically possible futures should not be confused with enhancement of one's control. Indeterministic devices of the imagined sort might provide physically possible futures for an agent that he otherwise would not have; but that does not imply that the agent is thereby given some control over which of his futures is realized.

Neither agent causation nor indeterministic "normal" causation of the sort that van Inwagen develops resolves the "control problem" that the libertarian faces.[6] Another libertarian response to the problem is considered in the following section. Let us return now to a question raised at the beginning of this section: Is the deterministic thesis that "there is at any instant exactly one physically possible future" a *dismayingly limiting* one?

Notice what this deterministic thesis amounts to, on van Inwagen's account, when applied specifically to the case of the thief who decides to refrain from breaking into the poor box and to the "instant" just prior to his so deciding. Regarding just the thief, it amounts to this:

> D. There is no "possible world that (a) is *exactly* like the actual world in every detail up to the moment at which the thief" decided to refrain from breaking into the poor box, "and (b) is governed by the same laws of nature as the actual world, and (c) is such that, in it, the thief" decided to rob the poor box (cf. van Inwagen 1983, p. 136).

I myself am willing to grant that *D* is false; again, I am not committed to determinism. The point to be emphasized now is that there being an indeterministic "gap" at the instant in question, assuming van Inwagen's second "model of action," in no way itself conduces to the thief's having freely or autonomously decided to refrain from stealing. Indeed, there being such a gap counts *against* the thief's having freely decided to refrain; for he has no control over what happens "in" that gap, and what the thief decides turns on what happens there. In light of this, perhaps we should be happy if a generalization of *D* were *true*; for, if anything, internal indeterministic gaps in processes leading to decision and action—depending on their location—seem incompatible with our being in control of what we judge, decide, intend, or overtly do.

A generalization of *D*, rather than appearing limiting, might well promote in agents who accept it a sense of personal control. If a generalization of *D* is true, there is no chance that random, undetermined, internal occurrences just prior to the moment of decision will interfere with agents' decision making: agents need not worry that such occurrences will prevent, for example, a smooth transition between their decisively judging it best to *A* and their deciding to *A*. People have enough to worry about in this connection: weakness of will, for example. The further worry that causally undetermined events might issue in decisions that fly in the face of their considered better judgments is, seemingly, an unwelcome one: a *justified* worry of this kind would point to serious *limitations* on agents' decision making powers. (Preemptive conditions of a default transition from a decisive best judgment to a corresponding intention [ch. 2, sec. 5] would, on the view under consideration, include not only the standard fare, but also the causally undetermined occurrence of transition thwarters.) The *indeterministic* thesis that causally undetermined internal events can prevent one's decisive better judgments from issuing in corresponding decisions would seem to be a limiting thing. The same is true of the indeterministic thesis that such internal events can prevent one from executing one's decisions and even from trying to execute them.

I conclude this section with a comment on probabilistic causation. There are various competing accounts, or partial accounts, of probabilistic causation in the literature; a detailed investigation of the topic is well beyond the scope of the present book.[7] If there are genuine instances of probabilistic causation, and if control is a causal phenomenon (ch. 1, sec. 2), there may be genuine instances of probabilistic agential control. For example, at an indeterministic world, $S$ might exert probabilistic control at $t$ over what he will straightaway attempt to do by forming a proximal intention to $A$.[8]

In expounding his own conception of probabilistic or "chancy" causation, David Lewis writes: "if distinct events $c$ and $e$ both occur, and if the actual chance of $e$ (at a time $t$ immediately after $c$) is sufficiently greater than the counterfactual chance of $e$ without $c$, that implies outright that $c$ is a cause of $e$" (1986, p. 180). Suppose that this is true, and suppose that the compound antecedent is satisfied in a case in which $c$ is $S$'s forming a proximal intention at $t^*$ to $A$ and $e$ is $S$'s attempting to $A$ ("at a time $t$ immediately after $c$"). Then $c$ is a cause of $e$, even if the occurrence of $e$ was not causally determined. Supposedly, even upon forming the proximal intention to $A$, $S$ was at the mercy of chance to some nonzero degree. There was a chance that, with the proximal intention to $A$ in place, and in the absence of paralysis, weakness of will, and so on, $S$ would not try to $A$. Apparently, the greater the chance, the less control intention formation at $t^*$ affords $S$ over what he will attempt at $t$. Here, too, indeterminism militates against control. This is not to say that indeterminism at a particular location in the psychological springs of an action *deprives* an agent of control at that location: the agent might have probabilistic control, if such control is possible. But probabilistic control at a particular location—whatever such control may be supposed to amount to—is "chancy." It is open to defeat not only by such things as sudden distraction and paralysis, but also by mere chance. Nonprobabilistic control is more dependable.

A libertarian who is prepared to shoulder the considerable burden of defending a detailed account of probabilistic causation may be able to do the same for probabilistic control. Equipped with a plausible account of such control, a libertarian may seek to show how any shortcomings in probabilistic control are outweighed, in understanding autonomous agency, by the "openness" that the indeterministic nature of such control provides. In the following chapter, I take an alternative tack, one that leaves open the conceptual possibility of probabilistic causation of the sort that Lewis seeks to illuminate but does not rely on that possibility. (As Lewis puts it, this is "causation in the single case: causation by one particular event of another event, not conduciveness of one kind of event to another kind" [1986, p. 177].) The tack is open both to proponents of genuinely probabilistic "single-case" causation and to those who insist that, necessarily, any genuinely *caused* event is a causally determined event. (Once again, the occurrence of causally determined events does not require the truth of determinism.)

## 3.   An Incompatibilist Theory of Freedom and Some Problems

Van Inwagen admits that he has "no theory of free action or choice that would explain . . . *how it could be* that, for example, our thief had a choice about whether to repent, given that his repenting was caused, but not determined, by his prior inner states, and given that no other prior state 'had anything to do with'—save negatively: in virtue of its non-interference with—his act" (1983, pp. 149–50). In short, he has no indeterministic theory of free action or free choice. Now, such a theory need not enter into a sound argument for incompatibilism; but, of course, to establish incompatibilism is not to show that we are free. Obviously, if determinism and incompatibilism are both true, then we are not free. More important for present purposes, the conjunction of the falsity of determinism and the truth of incompatibilism leaves it open that we are not free; freedom might be incompatible with indeterminism too (i.e., with the falsity of determinism). In this connection, people who are strongly inclined to believe that we are free and who take arguments for incompatibilism to have some force will want an incompatibilist theory of free choice or free action— or at least a sketch of such a theory. If the task of constructing an incompatibilist theory of freedom—a libertarian theory—seems doomed to failure, such people may be inclined to reassess the arguments for incompatibilism. In the absence of a *conclusive* argument for incompatibilism, a promising incompatibilist account of free choice or free action would certainly help the libertarian's case.

Robert Kane has advanced an incompatibilist theory of freedom (1985, 1989).[9] His view of free choice (and, derivatively, of free action) features an indeterministic gap between "prior character and motives" on the one hand and choices on the other. "Incompatibilist free choices," Kane writes, "arise at those critical junctures of human life when we are engaged in moral, prudential and practical struggle, where there is an inner conflict and the outcome is not obvious" (1989, p. 252). In cases of "moral" and "prudential" free choice, the agent, faced with conflicting motivation, makes an effort to resist temptation.[10] Kane claims that "the complex of past motives and character explains the *conflict* within the will from both sides; it explains why the agent makes the effort to resist temptation *and* why it is an *effort*" (p. 235). This effort to resist temptation is, more specifically, an effort to *choose* a particular option. What is undetermined is whether the effort will be successful or unsuccessful, whether it will issue in the choice at which it is targeted or fail to do so. Just as it is undetermined whether "an isolated particle moving toward a thin atomic barrier . . . will penetrate the barrier," it is undetermined whether an effort of the sort in question to choose $x$ will issue in a choice of $x$ (p. 236).[11]

Kane naturally wants free choices to be explicable choices. A theory of free choice that treats all such choices as inexplicable is not likely to impress his compatibilist opponents. On Kane's view, *efforts* to choose are explicable in terms of "motives and character," and even if the success of an effort is no more explicable than the particle's penetrating the barrier, the choice in which the effort issues—the choice that one was trying to make—is nevertheless explained well enough by the reasons that explain the effort. After all, the agent was trying or striving, *for those reasons*, to choose $C$. And when one succeeds in doing what one is attempting to do—when one's attempt to $x$ issues in an $x$-ing—the reasons for which one made the attempt typically shed explanatory light on the $x$-ing. Making a successful effort or attempt to $x$ is often a matter of $x$-ing *intentionally*, and we can intentionally make, or refrain from making, certain efforts. A certain thief's effort to choose to refrain from robbing a poor box might be an *intentional* effort in virtue of its having been made *for a reason*. This is a plausible line to take, one that derives support from the popular idea that intentional action is *identical with* action done for a reason.[12] Kane can reasonably hold, as well, that the thief's choice to refrain was an intentional choice, or a choice made for a reason, in virtue of its (nondeviantly) issuing from an intentional effort to choose to refrain.[13]

Imagine, however, that the thief's effort had failed and that, succumbing to temptation, he chose to rob the poor box. Might he still have chosen for a reason? Kane's answer is *yes*. Akratic choices, on Kane's view, rather than being "brought about by the effort," are "brought about *by the character and (self-interested or inclining) motives* which the effort *failed to resist*" (1989, p. 244). Kane writes,

> In the weak-willed case, the choice will be to make self interested reasons or present inclinations prevail over moral or prudential reasons then and there, which will be tantamount to accepting and acting on the conviction at that moment that they are, all things considered, the weightier reasons, more worth acting on by the agent *at that moment* than their alternatives. (p. 242)

The agent who akratically chooses to do *A* although he tried to resist the temptation to *A* comes to believe that his reasons for *A*-ing "are the better reasons" (p. 246). The akratic agent chooses (and then acts) as he judges best, but his *judgment* is akratically skewed. On this view, what I have called *strict* akratic action is illusory.

I turn now from choosing for reasons to choosing freely. Kane's view, as I understand it, is that a choice is free in virtue of being *undetermined, uncompelled*, and made for the reasons that the agent "believes at the time [to be] more worth acting upon than their alternatives" (1989, p. 232). What indeterminism can do for agents, on Kane's view, is enable them to "have *the power to make choices which can only and finally be explained in terms of their own wills* (i.e. character, motives and efforts of will)" (p. 254). He adds: "No one can have this power in a determined world. If we must give this power a name, let us call it 'free will'." Assuming the falsity of determinism, it is possible for agents to "have the *power to make choices for which they have ultimate responsibility*."

In a nutshell, Kane attempts to make room for "ultimate responsibility" regarding choices (and, derivatively, regarding actions in which choices issue) by rejecting the thesis that all choices are causally determined and to make causally undetermined choices respectable by explaining how they can be made for reasons.

One further feature of Kane's view merits mention before I turn to criticism. In the preceding section, I explained how various indeterministic gaps in the production of actions bring with them limitations on agential control. Kane grants this (1989, pp. 247–49, 254); but he holds that such limitations are required for ultimate responsibility and "ultimate control" (p. 248). Possessing "ultimate control" over a choice requires that the choice not be explicable by agent-external factors (e.g., the state of the world at some time prior to one's birth together with the laws of nature) and therefore requires indeterminism.

Grant, for the sake of argument, that an agent may choose for a reason even though his choosing as he does is not causally determined by anything. And suppose that when an intentional effort to make a choice *C* indeterministically (and nondeviantly) issues in $C$, and $C$ is not a compelled choice, the choice is free. How far does this get us? Not as far as many people would like, and not as far as Kane thinks either.

As I have noted, Kane explicitly limits free choices to choices made in the face of internal conflict. When there is no such conflict, and no effort to resist temptation, there is no free choice.[14] Others have held essentially this view (Campbell 1957, pp. 167–74; van Inwagen 1989).[15] But it is safe to say that only a prior theoretical commitment could move one to endorse it. Certainly, the commonsense view is that people often choose freely in the total absence of conflict. On this view, we can freely choose not to purchase the magazines, vacuum cleaners, and trinkets that we are invited to buy through the mail, over the phone, and in person—even though we are not tempted in the least to buy them. And we can freely choose to read a book, take a vacation, and chat with good friends even while not being at all tempted to eschew so doing. Of course, the commonsense view might be false, but we should not abandon it without a struggle.

A related point about the commonsense view merits mention. Believers in a very powerful, perfectly good God typically hold that God chooses and acts freely. Many such believers also hold that God never faces practical conflict and is not subject to weakness of will. God knows what is best and chooses it without any special effort. Limiting free choices to choices made in the face of internal conflict has the result that such a God does not freely choose. Here again Kane's position clashes with a common view of freedom. Notice also that an ideally virtuous agent, along Aristotelian lines, is devoid of motivation that competes with his better judgments.[16] This agent pursues what he takes to be best in the absence of internal conflict or struggle. Commonsense conceptions of freedom allow—indeed insist—that such an (imaginary) agent can act freely.

Kane's position on *akratic* choices is also problematic. As I noted, it entails that there are no strict akratic actions. I have argued for the reality of such actions in Mele 1987 and will not do so again here. For present purposes it should be noted that in Kane's explanation of how it is that agents choose *for reasons* in cases of akratic choice and action what carries the burden is not an effort to choose but rather a judgment or belief about what reasons are "the better reasons." If, as I have argued elsewhere, there are cases of akratic action in which an agent acts against a consciously held decisive better judgment, Kane has not explained how the corresponding choices are made for reasons; nor, consequently, has he explained how the choices can be free, given his own conception of what free choice requires. The range of free choice shrinks further.

Kane holds that the agent who akratically does $A$ came to "believe at the time" of choice that his reasons for $A$-ing "were all things considered the weightier reasons . . . because [he] brought this [belief] about by intentionally terminating the effort of will in this way and for these reasons" (p. 245). Further, the agent intentionally did the latter "because [he] came to believe at the time that [his reasons for $A$-ing] were all things considered the weightier reasons." Here, we apparently have something that might be on the explaining end of a choice, but we also have a tight circle: the agent "terminated" his effort to resist the temptation to $A$ with a choice to $A$ because he came to believe that it would be best to $A$, and he came to believe that it would be best to $A$ "because he brought this about by intentionally terminating the effort of will [with a choice to $A$] for these reasons."

Kane grants that there is a circle here, but he claims that the agent's intentionally terminating his effort to resist temptation with a choice to $A$ and his coming to believe that his reasons for $A$-ing are the better reasons are the same "act" under two different descriptions (1989, p. 246). This is multiply problematic. First, coming to believe that $p$ is not an action (or act) at all; so it cannot be the *same action* (or act) as anything. Second, events of choosing to $A$, in relevant cases, often plainly are not events of coming to believe that it would be best to $A$ (or coming to believe that one's reasons for $A$-ing are one's best reasons). In some simple instances of self-indulgence, for example, we choose to $A$ while continuing to believe that it would be best *not* to $A$ (Mele 1987, pp. 28–29). Indeed, we need a special reason to think that someone's choosing to $A$ is *ever* the same event as his coming to believe that it would be best to $A$.[17] Third, if we are properly to explain an agent's choosing to $A$ (or his terminating an effort to resist the temptation to $A$ with a choice to $A$) by observing that he came to believe that his reasons for $A$-ing were the better reasons, the change in belief will be a different event from the choice: it will be an event that somehow issues in the choice. Fourth, in that case, the making of the choice will not also explain (in this sense) why the change in belief occurred; it cannot happen, barring "backward issuing," that the choice issues in an event that issues in the choice.[18] (It is also worth noting that Kane needs to provide criteria for distinguishing between instances of akratically coming to believe that one's reasons for $A$-ing are one's best reasons and, e.g., instances in which one nonakratically changes one's mind about where one's best reasons lie.)

To sum up, not only does Kane limit free choice to cases of internal conflict, as he says, but his account of free choice is inapplicable to instances of conflict featuring strict akratic action (and corresponding choices). Further, his explanatory scheme for instances of akratic choice and action that involve akratic beliefs about where one's weightiest reasons lie is deeply problematic.

Now, for ultimate responsibility and ultimate control. Free agents, on Kane's view, "have *the power to make choices which can only and finally be explained in terms of their own wills* (i.e. character, motives and efforts of will)" (1989, p. 254). One who exercises that power successfully on a particular occasion has ultimate control over his choice and is ultimately responsible for it. Grant all this, for the sake of argument. It does not follow that an agent lacks ultimate responsibility for all causally determined choices of his. Imagine that a particular choice, $C$, is causally determined by the agent's effort to make that choice, which effort is causally determined by something, $x$, that includes agent-internal events that manifest stable features of the agent's character, features that developed out of some earlier, causally *undetermined* free choices of the agent. What stands in the way of the agent's being "ultimately responsible" for $C$? A backward tracing of $C$'s causal history would lead us to undetermined, free choices of the agent. So, barring causal overdetermination, $C$ would not *ultimately* be a causally determined product of factors beyond the agent's control.

If libertarians can consistently hold that choices like $C$ are free, they can draw the boundaries of free choice more broadly than Kane does, maintaining that even some causally determined choices are free.[19] Of course, being incompatibilists, they would claim that indeterminism must be *somewhere* in the background.

But *where*? At what locations would "indeterministic gaps" be consistent with agents' having the control over their (overt and mental) behavior required for free choice and free action while promoting their prospects of choosing and acting freely? And how is the occurrence of choices and actions that have such gaps in their etiology best explained? These are questions for chapter 12.

## Notes

1. Notice that the argument sketched in the last few paragraphs is not an argument for compatibilism; someone who wields it might consistently maintain that freedom is impossible and therefore cannot be found even at deterministic worlds. It is, rather, an argument against libertarianism.

2. Here, I have in mind agent causation of the sort proposed in Chisholm 1966 and Taylor 1963 (see ch. 1, sec. 2). For an alternative view of agent causation, see Clarke 1993.

3. The passage just quoted ends with a question mark but expresses van Inwagen's view.

4. For a similar thought experiment, see van Inwagen 1983, pp. 142–44.

5. If the thief were aware of the presence of the machine and its mode of operation, he could perhaps intentionally prevent it from operating by intentionally preventing the obtaining of its activation conditions. But I will avoid complicating matters unnecessarily.

6. Van Inwagen grants as much (1983, pp. 149–50); but recall that he is concerned with the piano argument as an argument for the incoherence of any indeterministic account of action itself, not free action in particular.

7. See Cartwright 1983, ch. 1; Eells 1991; Good 1983, ch. 21; Lewis 1986, pp. 175–84; Salmon 1984; Suppes 1970; and Tooley 1987, ch. 9.

8. On the possibility of a probabilistic "causal theory of action," see Bishop 1989, pp. 69–72.

9. Carl Ginet has developed an account of action explanation designed to cohere with libertarianism (1990, ch. 6). It is criticized in Mele 1992a, ch. 13, sec. 2.

10. Kane distinguishes "moral" and "prudential" free choice from "practical" free choice, on the grounds that choices of the third variety "do not ultimately involve . . . conflicts between perceived obligation and inclination" (1985, p. 110).

11. Kane intends this only as an analogy, of course. For an interesting discussion of what might be going on in the brain at the time, see Kane 1985, ch. 9.

12. See Anscombe 1963, p. 9, and Goldman 1970, p. 76. For approximations of this idea, see Audi 1986, pp. 544–45, and Davidson 1980, pp. 6, 264. Grounds for modifying the idea are offered in Mele 1992c, but the modifications need not concern us for present purposes.

13. Further, if the choice (nondeviantly) issues in a refraining, Kane can hold, on that basis, that the refraining was done for a reason and was intentional. Carl Ginet, another libertarian, advances a noncausal account of an action's having been done for a reason (1990, pp. 136–50). Ginet writes, e.g.: "The only thing required for the truth of a reasons explanation of [a certain] sort, besides the occurrence of the explained action, is that the action have been *accompanied* by an intention with the right sort of content" (p. 138). For criticism, see Mele 1992a, ch. 13, sec. 2. (The line sketched in this paragraph is not explicitly advanced by Kane.)

14. Two exegetical points are in order. First, strictly speaking, Kane explicitly limits "*incompatibilist* free choices" in this way (1989, p. 252; my italics). But Kane's incompatibilism precludes his allowing that there are "compatibilist" free choices—that is, that there

are free choices, the freedom of which is compatible with the truth of determinism. I assume in what follows that Kane takes "incompatibilist free choices" to be the only (genuinely) free choices. (Kane can grant, of course, that some choices that compatibilist believers in freedom standardly *count* as free are not made in the presence of internal conflict.) Second, in cases of what Kane terms "practical" free choice, 'temptation' (on some readings) is not an apt term, since "practical" conflicts do not essentially involve "perceived obligation" (1985, p. 100).

15. For an instructive response to van Inwagen 1989, see Fischer and Ravizza 1992b.

16. For Aristotle, such an agent possesses all the moral virtues (*Nicomachean Ethics* 6.13) and hence desires only as he ought to desire (*Nicomachean Ethics* 2.6).

17. Grounds for skepticism about the identity of an agent's judging it best to A with an agent's intending to A apply in the present connection, as well (see ch. 2 and relevant references provided there).

18. In personal correspondence, Kane indicated that his treating someone's "coming to believe that *p*" as an action was a "slip" on his part and that the relevant doxastic action is "bringing it about that one comes to believe that *p*." The modification avoids my first objection; but it is subject to a variation of my second one: in simple cases of akratic self-indulgence, agents choose to A without bringing it about that they come to believe that it would be best to A. Further, if an agent's akratically choosing to A is supposed now to be explained by his *bringing it about* that he came to believe that his reasons for A-ing were the better reasons, my remaining two objections may be modified accordingly with no loss of force.

19. Kane does hold, incidentally, that an agent can be *morally responsible* for a choice of this kind (1989, p. 252).

# 12

# Incompatibilist Autonomy and Autonomous Action

We now have a relatively firm sense of what libertarians want and of some of the important problems they face. Libertarians require that *free* choices, actions, and the like not *ultimately* be explicable by something external to the agent (e.g., the state of the world prior to the agent's birth together with the laws of nature). Their chief problem is to provide plausible accounts of what it is for a choice or an action to be free and of how free choices and actions come about. As I have said, I will not take a stand on whether compatibilism or incompatibilism is correct. Rather, in the present chapter I will do what I can to resolve the libertarians' problems.

## 1.  Introducing Modest Libertarianism

A distinction is in order between an agent's having *ultimate* control over $x$ and an agent's having what may be termed *proximal* control over $x$. When $x$ is an action of $S$'s—a particular, dated occurrence—$S$'s having ultimate control over $x$, I will say, requires that there not be any point in time at which minimally causally sufficient conditions satisfying the following condition are present for $S$'s $x$-ing at $t$: the condition is that the minimally causally sufficient conditions include no event or state internal to $S$. An agent's having proximal control over an action of his, however, is compatible with the truth of determinism—as is an agent's having proximal control over what he intends at $t$, what he judges best at $t$, and so on.

One approach to take in attempting to solve the problems that I have identified for libertarians is to ask just how far we would need to move from a very robust, deterministic proximal agential control to gain ultimate agential control. Perhaps we can secure libertarian ultimacy without sacrificing proximal control required for autonomy, and even without sacrificing very much—or anything at all—in the way of proximal control.

In chapter 1, I suggested that full-blown, deliberative, intentional action involves a particular collection of items. The list may be refined and expanded in light of subsequent discussion, as follows: (1) some psychological basis for practical evaluative reasoning, including not only such things as the agent's values, desires, and beliefs, but also the agent's deliberative skills, habits, and capacities; (2) an evaluative judgment that is made on the basis of such reasoning and recommends a particular course of action; (3) an intention formed or acquired on the basis of that judgment; (4) an action, $A$, executing that intention.[1] Starting at the bottom, one finds the following transitions: intention acquisition to action, evaluative judging to intention acquisition, and a process of reasoning to judgment as output. At the top, one finds what I have called input to deliberation along with various deliberative skills, habits, and capacities. Additional input can enter the picture during the deliberative process.

Consider a particular practical connection—that between forming a proximal intention to $A$ and making an attempt to $A$. Assume that at some point in time prior to intention formation it is causally determined that if at $t$ a certain agent $S1$ forms a proximal intention he will straightaway make a corresponding attempt, no matter what the intention is. Then all $S1$ need do to ensure that he will attempt at $t$ to $A$ is to form at $t$ a proximal intention to $A$. Assume now that, owing to indeterminism in the internal workings of another agent $S2$, there is some nonzero probability that no matter what proximal intention $S2$ forms (or otherwise acquires) at $t$ he does not make a corresponding attempt. Then $S2$ lacks the power to *ensure* that he will attempt to $A$, for any overt action $A$.[2] Imagine now that it is equally up to each of these two agents what he intends at $t$ and that the equal proximal control over this that the agents possess is nonzero control. Then, whereas $S1$'s proximal control over what he attempts at $t$ is limited only by whatever (if anything) limits his control over what intention he forms at $t$ (including whether he forms an intention at all), $S2$'s proximal control over what *he* attempts is limited additionally by the identified internal indeterminism.

An argument of roughly this form can be repeated at the next level up, the level at which evaluative judgments—for example, proximal decisive best judgments—are linked to proximal intentions. Imagine that it is equally up to each of two agents, $S3$ and $S4$, what they will (individually) judge it best to do in the situation in which they find themselves and that the equal proximal control over this that the agents possess is nonzero control. If it is causally determined that, whatever $S3$ decisively judges it best at $t$ to do at $t$, $S3$ will intend at $t$ in accordance with that judgment, then the limitations on $S3$'s control over what he intends at $t$ (assuming that it is causally determined that he will judge decisively) are exhausted by any limitations on his control over what he decisively judges best (and by any limitations imposed by its being causally determined that he will judge decisively). However, internal indeterminism at the relevant juncture brings with it limitations of its own. If it is causally open that whatever $S4$ decisively judges it best to do, he does not intend accordingly, then $S4$'s control over what he intends is limited in a way that $S3$'s control in this connection is not. $S3$ has the power to ensure what he will intend by making a better judgment, and $S4$ does not.

These observations indicate that it might be worth exploring the possibility of combining a compatibilist conception of the later parts of a process issuing in full-blown, deliberative, intentional action with an incompatibilist conception of the earlier parts. For example, it might be possible to gain "ultimate control" while preserving a considerable measure of nonultimate agential control by treating the process from proximal decisive better judgment through overt action in a compatibilist way and finding a theoretically useful place for indeterminacy in processes leading to proximal decisive better judgments.[3]

Recall that compatibilism does not include a commitment to determinism. The thesis is that determinism does not preclude autonomy. Treating the process from proximal decisive better judgment through overt action in a compatibilist way does not require treating it in a *determinist* way. Compatibilists may, in principle, be willing to accept an account of causation that accommodates both deterministic and probabilistic instances, and they are not committed to holding that probabilistic causation in the process just mentioned precludes the freedom of its product. In the same vein, advocates of autonomy who seek a "theoretically useful place" for indeterminism in the springs of action need not insist that indeterminism does not appear at other places, as well, in internal processes issuing in autonomous action. Their claim on that matter may merely be that indeterminism at these other junctures is of no use to them.

External indeterminism, as I have already explained, does not give libertarians what they want (ch. 11). That leaves internal indeterminism. Assume, for the sake of argument, that human beings sometimes act autonomously, that acting autonomously requires "ultimate control," and that the latter requires internal indeterminism. Then, with a view to combining ultimate control with robust nonultimate control, we can ask what location(s) for internal indeterminism would do us the most good.

It is important to be clear about the nature of the internal indeterminism required by the libertarian. Notice that it would not suffice for internal indeterminism of the requisite kind that causally undetermined *external* events have an effect upon the brain or other parts of the central nervous system (CNS). The resulting events in the CNS may, nevertheless, be causally determined by something that includes the causally undetermined external events, in which case a choice or action to which the CNS events contribute might *ultimately* be explained by something external to the agent: "ultimacy" would not be gained. That undetermined external events have effects upon the CNS is compatible with its being false that the CNS itself ever operates indeterministically. What the physicalistically minded libertarian needs is the truth of the thesis that some CNS events are causally undetermined. (The libertarian who is not physicalistically minded may prefer to speak of events in an immaterial soul or mind.)

On a modest libertarian view, *ultimate* agential control over a full-blown, deliberative, intentional action A may come to nothing more than (1) the satisfaction of my proposed sufficient conditions for compatibilist autonomous action (ch. 10), including robust proximal control at various junctures in the action-producing process, and (2) A's not being causally determined by agent-external items. On this view, roughly put, satisfaction of my compatibilist conditions for autonomous action, along with the proximal control that that involves, together with an internal indeterminism that is incompatible with the pertinent action's having been causally determined to occur by agent-external items, suffices for the agent's having ultimate control over that action. Ultimate control, then, rather than requiring the possession of any special "control power" beyond the powers required for the satisfaction of the conditions just identified, is something one has in virtue of satisfying the compatibilist conditions and being suitably internally indeterministic. This is the view to be explored here.

## 2.   Internal Indeterminism at Work

Jones has just started deliberating about how to spend his two-week summer vacation. Imagine that at this point in time it is causally undetermined what Jones will decisively judge it best to do and even whether Jones will make a decisive evaluative judgment at all. Imagine, as well, that this indeterminism is not an artifact of Jones's environment at the time but is instead a matter of how Jones's brain (or "mind") works. And suppose that Jones is an ideally self-controlled agent. He will not, then, reason akratically, akratically acquire or retain beliefs, and so on. If he does make a decisive better judgment, he will not make it akratically, and he will intend in accordance with that judgment. These points about Jones are compatible with the occurrence in him of causally undetermined events—provided that those events neither constitute nor give rise to akratic episodes in him.

Imagine that among Jonesian mental states and events only some *doxastic* states or events are causally undetermined. Imagine further that even in the doxastic sphere, all that is causally undetermined is which members of a shifting subset of Jones's relevant nonoccurrent beliefs will become occurrent and function in his deliberation. Some of these beliefs will "come to mind," as we might say, and play a role in deliberation; others will not. But it is not causally determined which of these beliefs will come to mind and which will stay on the sidelines.[4] Once a belief enters into the deliberative process, that "entering" event can play a role in the causal determination of subsequent mental events. Causally undetermined events can play a role in causally determining later events, as I have noted.[5]

Given this point about Jones's doxastic condition, when Jones starts deliberating it might be causally open what he will judge it best to do about his summer vacation, what he will intend to do, and what he will do. What Jones judges best, let us suppose, is contingent upon which beliefs in a particular subset of his nonoccurrent beliefs "come to mind." His better judgment, then, is not *ultimately* explained by external states and events; for what he judges best is contingent upon the occurrence of internal events that have no external explanation. That bar to "ultimate" control is absent in this scenario.

I grant, incidentally, that a belief that does not "come to mind" may nevertheless influence the outcome of one's deliberation. But we may suppose that the beliefs in the hypothesized subset will influence the outcome of Jones's deliberation only if they do come to mind. That may be treated as a *defining* condition on membership in the subset. Those who are not committed to an extreme holism according to which the outcome of every process of deliberation is influenced by *all* one's relevant beliefs should not find this supposition troublesome. And, of course, extreme holism of this sort is implausible. Sometimes, after deliberating and acting, we realize that if only we had thought of *p*—a proposition that we believed at the time—we would have decided differently. This is compatible with the belief's having had some influence on our deliberation, but there is no need to suppose that it did. And, at any rate, the belief did not have the influence that it supposedly would have had if it had come to mind.

The indeterminism in Jones's case presumably will not sustain the level of drama that we find in the case of van Inwagen's thief. It is not as though if certain of Jones's nonoccurrent beliefs come to mind, he will judge it best to spend his summer vacation robbing poor boxes whereas if others come to mind instead, he will judge it best to devote his summer to Red Cross relief efforts. What he will judge is conditioned by values, desires, and the like that may be presumed to limit the available drama to what is provided by the causal openness of various locations for Jones's vacation (including, perhaps, his home and his office), recreational activities, and the like. Still, when Jones starts deliberating, what he will judge best is open in a way that precludes the bar to ultimacy just identified.

Turning to nonultimate control, notice that if it is causally undetermined whether a certain belief will enter into Jones's deliberation, then Jones lacks deterministic proximal control over whether the belief enters his deliberation. But this need not be an impediment to Jones's proximal control over how he deliberates in light of the beliefs that *do* enter his deliberation. He may have considerable proximal control over how carefully he deliberates in light of these beliefs, over whether he deliberates in ways that violate his deliberative principles, and so on.

If, as the libertarian insists, autonomous agency requires internal indeterminism, the doxastic location that I have identified for the indeterminism leaves open the possibility of considerable proximal or nonultimate agential control, including self-control. Further, not only will deliberators, in indeterministic scenarios of the imagined sort, have open to them various causally undetermined options, but the better judgments and intentions that they form and the corresponding actions that they perform will influence their psychological make-up. Owing to doxastic indeterminism of the modest sort sketched, agents may shape their lives in ways that they are not, at some relevant point in time, causally determined to shape them. (I return to this point in sec. 4 and again in ch. 13.) Fortunately, none of this comes at the cost of a warranted fear, on the part of an imaginary agent who is aware of his doxastic indeterminism, that causally undetermined events may lead him to make better judgments and to perform, accordingly, intentional actions that are radically at odds with his "character." For character sets limits on the effects that the causally undetermined coming to mind (or not coming to mind) of a belief will have.

Can an agent who is a locus of doxastic indeterminism of the kind sketched be responsible for what he deliberatively judges best and for actions of his that accord with that judgment? This question is two-sided (at least). Does such indeterminism preclude responsibility? And does "ultimate" responsibility require a more extensive internal indeterminism? On the first count, notice that we are not always in (proximal) control of which of our beliefs come to mind anyway, even if determinism is true. Assuming determinism, everything that happens on this front is causally determined, but the causal story often does not place the agent in the driver's seat. So, other things being equal, if responsibility for one's judgments is compatible with determinism, it is compatible, as well, with a modest indeterminism of the sort at issue. Plainly, which of our nonoccurrent beliefs come to mind can influence the outcome of our deliberation. An internal indeterminism that, as it happens, does not render us any less in proximal control of what occurs in this sphere than we are if determinism is true does not bring with it any *direct* impediment to responsibility for one's judgments that is not to be found on the assumption that our world is deterministic.

This last point merits emphasis. One way to emphasize its significance is to make it a defining condition on the subset of one's beliefs that are subject at a time to indeterminism of the sort at issue that they are beliefs whose coming or not coming to mind is not something that one would control even if determinism were true. The agent who is subject to indeterminism in this sphere is not—*simply on that account*—worse off with respect to actual proximal control over his psychological and overt behavior than he would be at a deterministic world.

Suppose that a certain collection *C1* of beliefs came to mind during Jones's deliberation (where *C1* is a segment of a much larger collection of beliefs that came to mind), even though it was not causally determined at any point that any member of *C1* would come to mind. Suppose also that the coming to mind of these beliefs had some effect on what Jones judged best. Other nonoccurrent beliefs could have indeterministically come to mind instead, and if certain of them had come to mind, Jones would have reached a different judgment. Is it plausible to hold, in light of this, that Jones is not responsible for judging as he did, on the grounds that his judgment is contingent upon the occurrence of internal, psychological events for which he is not causally responsible?

Not at all. Jones need not be a pawn of these beliefs. He may assess the merits of his evidence for the believed propositions and abandon or retain the beliefs accordingly. He may decide how much weight the beliefs ought to be given in his deliberation and accord them the weights he deems most appropriate. And, of course, he may *use* these beliefs in an attempt to ascertain how he might best spend his summer vacation. Jones is not in control of whether these beliefs come to mind or not, but that does not imply that he is helpless with regard to the influence that they exert on him. He can treat these beliefs as he treats—and as *responsibly* as he treats—other doxastic input to deliberation.

This is not to say, of course, that Jones's control is such that what he judges best is *not*, after all, contingent upon which nonoccurrent beliefs come to mind. Jones may have a number of warranted relevant nonoccurrent beliefs, and he may reasonably regard various beliefs that indeterministically come to mind as suitable for use in his current deliberation. Which beliefs do come to mind can influence the outcome of his deliberation. My point is that this observation is compatible with Jones's having considerable proximal control over what he does with the beliefs that "come to mind" and over his deliberation.

Is the indeterminism at issue too skimpy for the purposes of ultimate responsibility? In being indeterministic, it certainly suffices to block the worry voiced in the consequence argument—the strongest argument for incompatibilism. It allows for an agent's having more than one physically possible future and for its being true, on some incompatibilist readings of 'could have done otherwise,' that an agent could have judged, intended, and acted otherwise than as he did. The modest indeterminism at issue seemingly does not promote sudden, radical character changes or the occurrence of decisive better judgments violently at odds with agents' characters; but such things would need to be promoted only on *extreme* libertarian conceptions of personal autonomy. Further, the doxastic indeterminism at issue is an agent-*internal* indeterminism: it provides for an agent's having more than one physically possible future in a way that turns, essentially, on what goes on in him.

I have imagined that, when Jones *starts* deliberating, it is causally undetermined what he will judge it best to do about his summer vacation. The relevant indeterminism also applies, of course, to which nonoccurrent beliefs, in a certain subset of such beliefs, do or do not come to mind while deliberation is *in progress*. And even when an agent is on the verge of reaching a decisive better judgment, the (undetermined) coming to mind of a belief might prompt reservations that lead to reconsideration. So, in a scenario of the imagined kind, what an agent decisively judges best can be causally open as long as deliberation continues. Further, as long as deliberation is in progress it can be causally open when that deliberation will end, for it can be causally open whether a belief will come to mind and prolong deliberation. Still, in my scenario, an agent can make a decisive better judgment—and it can happen that there is a proximate causal explanation, in terms of the agent's psychological condition, of his making the judgment he makes. He can make the judgment *for reasons*, and $x$-ing for a reason $R$, on a plausible view, requires that the psychological state of having $R$ figures in the etiology of the agent's $x$-ing. To be sure, if the decisive better judgment is made at $t$, then no deliberation-prolonging event occurred at $t$ (or "the moment just prior" to $t$), and there may be no causal explanation of the nonoccurrence of such an event. But that does not stand in the way of the agent's having judged as he did for reasons, on a causal conception of judging for reasons. A certain stone's striking a certain window can be a central part of what causes the window's shattering, in a scenario in which the occurrence of a certain causally undetermined event just prior to the breaking would have rendered the window unbreakable by the stone (ch. 11, sec. 2). Similarly, an agent's psychological condition (a combination of states and events) can be a central part of what causes his judging that it would be best to $A$, in a scenario in which the occurrence of a certain causally undetermined "coming-to-mind" event just prior to the judging would have resulted in a different deliberative outcome.

A certain objection to the line that I have been developing may be anticipated and disarmed.[6] What I have done, it may be said, is to attach a compatibilist species of control to a modest internal indeterminism, thereby opening up alternative physically possible futures in a way that preserves considerable agential control. But, it may be added, no libertarian can be satisfied with the agential control that is provided, for it is mere compatibilist control. On one interpretation, this objection can be advanced only by someone who confuses libertarianism with agent causalism. Not all libertarians accept agent causation, as I have observed (ch. 11); and some explicitly reject it (e.g., Ginet 1990, ch. 1; Kane 1989). Some libertarians want nothing to do with any incompatibilist "species of control" provided by agent causation (as an alternative to "event" causation). Setting this confusion aside, a more specific version of the objection may be addressed.

I said that the modest indeterminism that I have been sketching allows for its being true, on some incompatibilist readings of 'could have done otherwise,' that an agent could have judged, intended, and acted otherwise than as he did. That an agent could have done otherwise, in some sense or other, is often viewed as a requirement for his having had *control* over the relevant deed. Now, for some incompatibilists, that an agent who did something $x$ at $t$ (e.g., judged that it would be best to $A$, formed an intention to $A$, or $A$-ed) could have done otherwise at $t$ requires that at another possible world, given *exactly the same conditions* that obtained at the actual world *immediately prior to t* and *exactly the same laws*, the agent did otherwise at $t$. In chapter 11, section 2, I identified serious problems for the thesis that an agent did $x$ *freely* or *autonomously* at $t$ only if he could have done otherwise at $t$, in this sense. This requirement for autonomous $x$-ing (including making judgments and forming intentions) is no part of my modest libertarian picture. It may be thought that in the absence of the requirement, I have offered libertarians only a compatibilist species of control that they cannot accept.

Imagine that, at $t^*$, $S$ autonomously judges, decisively, that it would be best to $A$ and that his so judging immediately issues by default in an intention to $A$. Attributing to $S$, at $t^*$, a physically possible future in which he does not intend, at $t$, to $A$ gains $S$ nothing by way of autonomy regarding his intention to $A$. All it "gains" him is the possibility that he will not intend, at $t$, in accordance with his autonomously formed best judgment. And that is a *loss*—a diminution of his nonultimate control over what he intends at $t$. It may seem that $S$ does gain liberation from having only one physically possible future. However, that liberation is already provided by the modest indeterminism that I have described: prior to $t^*$, $S$'s physically possible futures included ones not involving the pertinent judgment and intention. It may be replied that on the supposition that once the judgment is made it is causally determined that $S$ will straightaway acquire an intention to $A$, $S$ lacks, *at that point*, the physical possibility of a future that does not include his intending at $t$ to $A$; and it may be claimed that his having, *at that point*, the physical possibility of such an alternative future is essential to his autonomously intending to $A$. The latter claim is mere dogmatism. It is a feature of some brands of libertarianism that libertarians would do well to reject.

Libertarians require that free or autonomous agents have both more than one physically possible future *and* appropriate control over what they do. My modest libertarian picture provides both. The thought that, necessarily, an autonomous agent (qua autonomous) could have intended otherwise (in the specified sense of 'could have'), *even at the last moment*, is motivated, often, by the mistaken idea that only if that is so is it "up to the agent," in an incompatibilist sense, what he intends. However, insofar as it is up to an agent, in an incompatibilist sense, what he decisively judges best, it is up to him, in the same sense, what he intends, provided that he intends on the basis of that judgment. And on the indeterministic view that I have sketched, it sometimes *is* up to agents, in an incompatibilist sense, what they decisively judge best: it is up to them what they judge best on an interpretation of "up to them" that requires that determinism (and internal determinism, in particular) be false. What libertarians need is an interpretation that not only incorporates this requirement but also attributes to autonomous agents significant *control* over what they judge best. Various features of the control available on my modest indeterminist suggestion have been noted already; I address other features shortly.

Perhaps it will be claimed that if at *any* point before $t$—even one "just prior" to $t$—causally sufficient conditions are present for an agent's judging it best at $t$ to $A$, he does not freely or autonomously *judge it best* to $A$. Imagine that $S$ has carefully weighed his reasons for various alternative courses of action, is on the verge of forming a decisive best judgment in favor of $A$ on the basis of his careful weighing, and no new consideration comes to mind. On the present hypothesis, if at that time ($t^*$) causally sufficient conditions are present for $S$'s immediately forming the judgment, he does not form it autonomously. Why? Surely, not *just* because he does not at $t^*$ have open to him a physically possible future that does not include his judging it best at $t$ to $A$? If an irresistible mind-reading demon were prepared immediately to cause $S$ to judge it best to $A$ should $S$ not be about to make that judgment on his own, then $S$ might autonomously judge it best to $A$, even if, given the demon's irresistibility, $S$ did not have at $t^*$ a physically possible future that does not include his making the judgment. The demon has no effect on what $S$ decides; he leaves $S$ to his own devices. Still, it may be claimed that because the *actual* causal transition from something just prior to $S$'s making the judgment to his making it was a deterministic one, it was out of $S$'s hands, at that point, what he would judge.

This claim is muddled. In his deliberation, $S$ took the matter of what he would judge into his own hands, where he carefully molded it until, finally, he settled the evaluative issue. And *while* he was deliberating it was causally undetermined how he would settle the matter, until the very last moment, "just prior" to his judging it best to $A$. Libertarians have no more need for decisive judgings that are *at no point in time* causally determined to occur than they do for intendings to $A$ that are not causally determined even when an agent decisively judges it best to $A$. (I return to this issue in sec. 5.)

Essentially the argument of the last four paragraphs may be run, necessary changes having been made, for intentional $A$-ings that are causally determined (in part) by acquisitions of intentions, where those intentions are deterministically produced (in part) by a decisive judging of the relevant kind. And, again, even some libertarians are happy to countenance a deterministic connection between choice or intention and action (see n. 3). It is time to move forward.

Robert Kane has claimed that "free will is the power . . . in persons or rational agents . . . to originate or bring into existence the *purposes* or *ends* that guide their deliberation" (1985, p. 2; italics mine). It is worth noting that the contingency of deliberative, decisive better judgments upon which nonoccurrent beliefs come to mind need not be a matter solely of the roles played by such beliefs in purely *instrumental* (means/end) deliberation. I have argued elsewhere, as have others, that we can deliberate about the *constitution* of particular ends of ours (Mele 1989a, pp. 430–31). The upshot of such deliberation can be influenced by the causally undetermined coming to mind of beliefs in one's deliberation.

The following case features what may be termed *constitutional* deliberation.

> Theresa, a young woman who is about to graduate from high school, has a burning desire to do something important with her life. She wants this, not as a means to a further goal, but simply as an end. However, because she has no clear idea exactly what would constitute her goal, Theresa's desire gives her little direction. Undaunted, she sets out to determine what it would be to live an important life. She starts by examining the sorts of life that, in her opinion, many people think to be important. Some of the life-types, she decides, are not all that they are cracked up to be. For example, any life dominated by a concern to make money is, she thinks, irrational, since money has no intrinsic value. On the basis of various items in her motiva-

tional set, she eliminates several other candidates: She will commit herself to no type of life that is incompatible with her being honest, bearing and raising at least one child, and so on. But she is still left with a number of candidates and with a crucial question: If these lives are important, what makes them so? She decides that she had wrongly been thinking that a necessary condition of doing something important with one's life is that one is thought by many to be an important person; and she gradually comes to believe that truly important lives have at least this in common: They are led by loving, unselfish, autonomous individuals who are dedicated to the achievement of a lofty goal or goals and possessed of strong moral character, and who, in pursuing their goals, make a significant contribution to the amelioration of the human condition. *This* is the kind of person she now wants to be; these are the traits that she wants to exhibit. And after further reflection she decides that, given her various talents, *she* can best live an "important life" in the political realm. (Mele 1989a, p. 430)

Theresa deliberates with a view to her doing something important with her life, an end of hers; but her deliberation is partly about *ingredients* or *constituents* of an important life. Her reasoned judgments about such matters can be contingent upon which beliefs happen to come to mind. For example, a memorial belief about a certain pronouncement of Aristotle's on the purely instrumental value of wealth (*Nicomachean Ethics* 1096a6–7) might happen to come to mind; and as a partial result, Theresa may be led to the idea that there are formal constraints on what can reasonably be desired as an end. Similarly, a vague recollection of a novel in which a heroic woman was deemed by all who knew her to be utterly pedestrian might happen to come to mind and suggest to Theresa the hypothesis that one's importance may be independent of how others regard one—a hypothesis that she then proceeds to examine. In short, the causally undetermined coming to mind of beliefs can influence "the purposes or ends that guide" instrumental deliberation.

Against this background, we can ask a libertarian variant of a compatibilist query posed in chapter 10, section 5: Assuming libertarianism this time, what can we add to an ideally self-controlled agent—and, more specifically, a mentally healthy one (ch. 7, sec. 5) who regularly exercises his powers of self-control in the various spheres in which those powers can function—to yield a psychologically autonomous agent? My compatibilist suggestion, again, is that it suffices to add (1) that the agent has no compelled* (or coercively produced) motivational states, (2) that his beliefs are conducive to informed deliberation about all matters that concern him, and (3) that he is a reliable deliberator. My libertarian suggestion is that it would be enough to add the following condition to these three: (4) doxastic indeterminism of the sort that I have described is a relatively regular feature of the agent. Since the suggestion under consideration here is that indeterminism in this sphere be combined with a *compatibilist* conception of that part of processes leading to full-blown, intentional, overt action that follows the making of proximal decisive better judgments, this latter part of these processes requires no further attention in the present connection.[7]

One naturally wonders whether and how indeterminism of the sort at issue is physically possible. Given my aims thus far, that is not a problem for me; for I have made no commitment to incompatibilism. The dialectical situation is straightforward. Having offered sufficient conditions for autonomous agency conceived along compatibilist lines, I realize that incompatibilists will find them too weak. Further, libertarians need *internal* indeterminism, for reasons that I have adduced. So I have added a condition to my list with a view to satisfying a libertarian demand for "ultimate control." I have no neurophysiological story to tell about internal indeterminism, and no physical story of any sort to tell about it.[8] But if internal indeterminism is a feature of human agents, the modest internal indeterminism that I have explored is no worse off in respect of physical realizability than any form of internal indeterminism that I have seen advocated by libertarians.[9] If it turns out that internal indeterminism is not a feature of any actual human agent, then libertarianism is false; for libertarians hold that at least some actual human agents are free, autonomous, morally responsible beings, and their view on the matter makes internal indeterminism a necessary condition of this. I return to this matter in chapter 13.

Early in this chapter, I asked how far we would need to move from a very robust, deterministic, proximal agential control to gain "ultimate" agential control and whether we can secure incompatibilist ultimacy without sacrificing very much—or anything at all—in the way of proximal control. The modest doxastic indeterminism that I have been discussing requires no great sacrifice: by hypothesis, the causally undetermined comings and not-comings to mind are events the agent (or a counterpart) would not control even at relatively nearby deterministic worlds. I developed the idea simply as a useful *illustration* of how the trick may be turned, of course. Other indeterministic scenarios may also be considered. For example, one may explore the benefits and costs of its being causally undetermined which of a shifting subset of *desires* come to mind at a time, or which of a changing segment of beliefs an agent actively *attends* to at a given time, or exactly *how* an agent attends to various beliefs or desires of his at certain times.[10] An examination of various combinations of indeterministic scenarios may also be undertaken. However, another matter is more pressing.

## 3. A Regress Charge and the Primacy of Free Agency

Galen Strawson has argued (in effect) that no form of indeterminism can give libertarians what they want, since libertarianism entails an impossible regress of choices. Consideration of the argument will promote a deeper appreciation of the place of indeterminism in a modest libertarianism.

Strawson's argument reads as follows:

1. Interested in free action, we are particularly interested in rational actions (i.e. actions performed for reasons . . .), and wish to show that such actions can be free.
2. How one acts when one acts rationally (i.e. for a reason) is, necessarily, a function of, or determined by, how one is, mentally speaking. (One . . . could add 'at the time of action' after 'mentally speaking'.)
3. If, therefore, one is to be truly responsible for how one acts, one must be truly responsible for how one is, mentally speaking—in certain respects.
4. But to be truly responsible for how one is, mentally speaking, in certain respects, one must have chosen to be the way one is, mentally speaking, in certain re-

spects. (It is not merely that one must have caused oneself to be the way one is, mentally speaking; that is not sufficient for true responsibility. One must have consciously and explicitly chosen to be the way one is, mentally speaking, in certain respects, at least, and one must have succeeded in bringing it about that one is that way.)

5. But one cannot really be said to choose, in a conscious, reasoned fashion, to be the way one is, mentally speaking, in any respect at all, unless one already exists, mentally speaking, already equipped with some principles of choice, '$P_1$'—with preferences, values, pro-attitudes, ideals, whatever—in the light of which one chooses how to be.

6. But then to be truly responsible on account of having chosen to be the way one is, mentally speaking, in certain respects, one must be truly responsible for one's having *these* principles of choice $P_1$.

7. But for this to be so one must have chosen them, in a reasoned, conscious fashion.

8. But for this, i.e. (7), to be so one must already have had some principles of choice, $P_2$, in light of which one chose $P_1$.

9. And so on. True self-determination is logically impossible because it requires the actual completion of an infinite regress of choices of principles of choice. (Strawson 1986, pp. 28–29)

If our acting freely is logically dependent upon our having made an infinite series of choices, we cannot act freely. But do libertarian conceptions of free action saddle libertarians with the regress described?

Suppose that Sid proximally intended to *A* and that, executing that intention, he intentionally *A*-ed. One might grant, in accordance with 3, that Sid is "truly responsible" for *A*-ing only if he is "truly responsible" for intending to *A*. Premise 4 *apparently* suggests the following: (4a) Sid is truly responsible for intending to *A* only if he *chose* to intend to *A*.[11] However, in light of 5 and 6, the intended thrust of 4 seemingly applies to the present case as follows: (4b) Sid is truly responsible for intending to *A* only if he chose some preference, or value, or pro-attitude, or the like—some *attitude*, for short—that is partially explanatory of his intending to *A*.[12] Imagine that Sid decisively judged it best to *A* and that his so judging issued directly, by default, in his intending to *A*.[13] Then we can read 4b as asserting that Sid is truly responsible for intending to *A* only if he chose some attitude that is partially explanatory of his *judging it best* to *A*. The basic idea will be the conjunctive one that when an agent intends to *A* on the basis of a corresponding decisive evaluative judgment, he is truly responsible for the intention only if he is truly responsible for the judgment *and* true responsibility for a judgment requires that one have *chosen* some attitude, $x$, on which the judgment is partially based. Having made it this far, 5 through 9 are easily brought to bear on Sid's case. Premise 5 implies that if Sid chose $x$, he did so at least partly on the basis of some other attitude, $y$, of his. Premise 6 implies that Sid is truly responsible (for intending to *A*) "on account of having chosen" $x$ only if he is truly responsible for "having" $y$. Premise 7 implies that true responsibility for having $y$ requires that Sid have chosen $y$. Premise 8 is another application of 5—this time to the implication yielded by 7. And so on.

I will not challenge the inference from 1 and 2 to 3. If the inference is valid, it is presented enthymematically. Suppose, for the sake of argument, that the following (comparatively specific) approximation of 3 is true: in cases of full-blown, deliberative, intentional action, one autonomously $A$-s only if one is autonomous with respect to a corresponding intention, and autonomy with respect to an intention formed on the basis of deliberation that yields a corresponding decisive better judgment depends on whether the judgment was autonomously formed, which depends in turn on the agent's having been autonomous with respect to his deliberation. Imagine that deliberating autonomously is sufficient for having "true responsibility" for one's deliberation. Then Strawson's argument suggests that having deliberated autonomously requires having chosen some attitude *from which* one deliberated. But if every true-responsibility-conferring choice is made on some grounds or other (see Strawson 1986, p. 28, n. 6 and premise 5), and a choice confers true responsibility only if some choice-grounding attitude is itself chosen in a way that confers true responsibility, we have an infinite regress.[14]

A straightforward way to block the regress, is to reject 4. Can libertarians reject this premise? The parenthetical part of 4 asserts that to be "truly responsible"—that is, to have freedom-level responsibility—for having an attitude $x$ that one has, it is not enough that one "have consciously and explicitly chosen" $x$; "one must have succeeded in bringing it about" that one has $x$. Is this plausible?

Consider another sort of responsibility—"responsibility sans 'true.'" Al agreed to care for the lawn of his rental house and to mow the grass periodically, never allowing it to grow higher than four inches. But he has chosen not to mow the lawn, and, in accordance with his choice, he intentionally refrained from mowing it. The lawn has grown well beyond four inches. Here, other things being equal, Al is responsible (at least sans 'truly') for the unsightly state of his lawn, even though he did not *bring it about* that his lawn is in that state: the lawn grew without any help from Al. And if responsibility of this kind for $c$ does not depend upon one's having brought about $c$, we need a special reason to think that *true* (i.e., freedom-level) responsibility for a mental state $m$ does depend upon one's having brought $m$ about. Strawson's argument provides no such reason. This criticism does not directly address the charge that libertarian free action "requires the actual completion of an infinite regress of choices of principles of choice," but it does address the related charge that libertarian free action requires the actual completion of an infinite regress of *bringings about*.

I turn to the former, more challenging regress charge. One result of applying 4 to the generic case of Sid is that, given the etiology of his $A$-ing, Sid is "truly responsible"—has freedom-level responsibility—for his $A$-ing only if he *chose* some attitude on which his $A$-favoring judgment was partially based. Is this plausible?

Consider relatively sophisticated intentional behavior of a kind open even to young children. Betty is six years old. For some time, she has been afraid to go into her basement by herself, especially when the lights are off. Betty does not understand why she is afraid, but she knows that nothing bad has ever happened to her there and that her seven-year-old sister apparently is not the least bit afraid of the basement. She comes to view her fear as a "babyish" one, and she decides to try to eliminate it. Betty's strategy is simple and direct: she will walk into the basement, and she will visit it periodically until the fear dissolves. If Betty succeeds in eliminating her fear in this way, this is an instance of intentional self-modification.[15]

Betty's choice or decision to try to eliminate her fear need not rest on any attitude that she *chooses* to have. Desires and beliefs of hers might ground her choice—

and her judgment that it would be best to try to eliminate the fear—without her having chosen to have any of those desires (or beliefs). Can she nevertheless be "truly
responsible" for her choice and her behavior? If it is claimed that *true responsibility*
for any choice, *by definition*, requires that the agent have chosen "in a conscious,
reasoned fashion" an attitude that grounds the choice, it is being claimed, in effect,
that the very definition of 'true responsibility' entails that possessing such responsibility for any choice requires having made an infinitely regressive series of choices.
But then libertarians should want to have nothing to do with *this* notion of responsibility, nor with any corresponding notion of free action.

Some notions of freedom-level responsibility and freedom are too weak for libertarians' purposes, of course—for example, any notion that permits agents at deterministic worlds to have freedom-level responsibility for their choices and actions and
to choose and act freely. It is worth noting in this connection that on familiar *compatibilist* conceptions of free action, Betty has acted freely in attempting to eliminate her fear. She made this attempt intentionally. She was not, we may suppose,
compelled to act (or choose, or reason) as she did, or manipulated in any relevant
way. And the psychological etiology of Betty's attempt is sufficiently rich and complex to distinguish it from intentional animal behavior that compatibilists and others
take not to be free. After all, the etiology involves Betty's engaging in self-conscious
thought, in relatively sophisticated self reflection, and in self-evaluation.

Compatibilists need not maintain that the freedom of Betty's attempt *derives from*
the freedom of her intention, which in turn derives from the freedom of her evaluative judgment, and so on. Indeed, this *top-down* way of viewing things arguably re-
verses the proper order of emphasis. The term 'free' may be viewed, for example, as
an appropriate *default* label for any uncompelled, uncoerced, intentional action of a
self-conscious, self-reflective, planning agent: it may be held that all such actions
are free *unless* there is some freedom-blocking property in their etiology. Analogous
default theses are available at the various main links in the action-producing chain.
One can hold that 'free' is an appropriate default label for any uncompelled intention—or decisive better judgment, or deliberative episode—of an uncoerced, self-
conscious, self-reflective, planning agent. Is this view justifiable?

Appeals to our ordinary practice and to commonsense views of freedom are
common on many sides of the debate about the nature and possibility of human freedom; and our ordinary practice features default attribution conditions along the lines
sketched. In ordinary practice (at least as a first approximation), when we are confident that self-reflective, planning agents have acted intentionally, we take them to
have acted freely *unless* we have contrary evidence—evidence of brainwashing,
compulsion, coercion, insanity, or relevant deception, for example.

In the same vein, we take Betty to have freely tried to eliminate her fear. Our
learning that she did not choose to have any of the attitudes on the basis of which she
chose or decided to make the attempt will not incline us to withdraw the attribution
of freedom, unless we are inclined to hold that free action derives from choices made
partly on the basis of chosen attitudes or, at least, that any action etiology that includes no such choice is a freedom-blocking etiology. Those who have this latter
inclination are, I suggest, in the grip of a crude picture of the freedom of an agent
with respect to an action (or "practical freedom," for short) as a *transmitted* prop-

erty—a property transmitted from above by earlier free behavior, including, of course, choice-making behavior. It is impossible for such a picture of practical freedom to capture the freedom that it is designed to represent, for reasons that Strawson makes clear: the picture requires an impossible psychological regress. And it ought to be rejected. Practical freedom, if it is a possible property of human beings, is, rather, an "emergent" property.[16] It must be, if some of us are free agents (i.e., agents who act freely, in a broad sense of 'act' that includes such mental actions as choosing) and none of us started out that way.

Still, it will be asked, how can someone have engaged in his *first* bit of free behavior *B* (mental behavior or otherwise), given that he has not freely done anything that accounts for the existence of those attitudes of his that help to explain the occurrence of *B*? And how can someone have freedom-level responsibility for *B*, if he lacks freedom-level responsibility for any of the attitudes that help to explain *B*'s occurrence? The answer, in part, is that practical freedom is a property of agents qua *agents*. Free agents are first, and most fundamentally, free with respect to what they *do*. A proper notion of freedom with respect to the possession of an attitude that one has— *attitudinal freedom*—is either a weaker notion than practical freedom or a derivative one. As a weaker notion, it does nothing more than give expression to the idea that actions with certain kinds of etiology are not free actions—for example, actions performed on the basis of compelled* attitudes, or on the basis of attitudes issuing from various kinds of manipulation, or from insanity. It is a notion of *negative* freedom— *freedom from* (i.e., the absence of) an etiology of one's action that precludes that action's being freely performed. As a notion of positive freedom—a notion, more specifically, of possessing an attitude that one freely brought about or freely reflectively endorsed—it is parasitic on a notion of free *agency*. On the weaker reading, attitudinal freedom *is* required for free agency, but an agent can have such (negative) freedom without ever having acted freely. On the stronger reading, attitudinal freedom is not a prerequisite of free action, but is, instead, a potential *product* of free action. So, at least, it may be argued.

Libertarians, like compatibilists, can reject the top-down view of practical freedom as a transmitted property. Unlike compatibilists, they view practical freedom as requiring, in Kane's words, "ultimate responsibility." But ultimate responsibility for one's action, *A*, need not be seen as requiring that some attitude on the basis of which one chose to *A* have been chosen itself. One does not find a requirement of this kind in Kane's work, for example, and Kane rightly presents his view as libertarian. For Kane, again, a free action issues from a free choice, and a choice is free if it is not a compelled choice and an intentional effort to make that choice indeterministically (and nondeviantly) issues in that choice.[17] Ultimate responsibility for the action, as Kane sees things, does not require that freedom be transmitted to the action by way of a choice that is made on the basis of a *chosen* attitude.

On Kane's view, free agents "have *the power to make choices which can only and finally be explained in terms of their own wills* (i.e. character, motives and efforts of will)" (1989, p. 254). Part of Strawson's claim, in effect, is (*a*) that agents who have libertarian freedom must also have the distinct power to have "wills" that can only and finally be explained by their choices, (*b*) that a "will" no part of which is chosen is not a "will" with respect to which one has libertarian freedom, and (*c*) that a choice that proceeds from a "will" no part of which is chosen is not a choice with respect to which one has libertarian freedom. However, libertarians can reject $c$ and maintain, roughly, that all that must be added to the compatibilists' grounds for holding that Betty acted and chose freely is that she "could have acted and chosen otherwise," on a libertarian reading of that expression.[18]

All practical reasoners are equipped with pro-attitudes, beliefs, and a capacity for reasoning. If Betty has no compelled pro-attitudes (nor any that were coercively or self-oppressively produced), is not cut off from autonomous reasoning by her doxastic condition, and forms a decisive better judgment on the basis of reliable reasoning, libertarians can hold that she has deliberated and judged autonomously—provided that indeterminism is involved in the process in a way acceptable to them. If the judgment issues unproblematically in a corresponding intention that issues smoothly in a corresponding intentional attempt to eliminate her fear, libertarians can hold that the attempt was freely made. To be sure, libertarians are more demanding than compatibilists, requiring that the etiology of free actions and choices not be (completely) deterministic. But they need not view the absence of an infinite series of choices in that etiology as a freedom-blocking property of the etiology. (Obviously, this latter view can be no part of a *coherent* libertarian package.) They can reject a top-down picture of practical freedom as a transmitted property in favor of a conception of practical freedom as an emergent property. And like compatibilists, they can view 'free' as a default label. The chief difference in their respective understandings of freedom by default is that libertarians endorse a preemptive condition that compatibilists reject: only the former require indeterminism.

In rebutting Strawson's argument, there is no need to attach special weight to his talk of *choosing to have an attitude*. Strawson offers a "slightly different" formulation of premise 4 for readers who take that premise to be unduly demanding: (4c) To be truly responsible for how one is, mentally speaking, in certain respects, "one must oneself have consciously and intentionally brought it about that one is the way one is, in certain respects, at least" (1986, p. 29). He adds: "But then the rest of the argument goes through as before, with only minor alterations."

On a proper reading of 4c, Strawson is right in seeing it as only modestly modifying the argument. Intentionally bringing it about that one is $x$ must be distinguished from the conjunction of intentionally doing $A$ and one's $A$-ing's having the result that one is $x$. For example, John might intentionally look into someone's desk drawer, and immediately and unexpectedly see there a delightful photograph, with the result that John experiences aesthetic pleasure. But John did not intentionally bring it about that he is pleased. Given a proper reading of 4c, premise 5 need only be adjusted to assert that one does not consciously and intentionally bring it about that one is $x$ unless one so acts on the basis of some "principles of choice." A suitably modified version of premise 6 will insist that to be "truly responsible on account of having" acted as one did, "one must be truly responsible for one's having *these* principles of choice"— which, according to a revised premise 7, will require that one have consciously and intentionally brought it about that one has the latter principles. And so on: there is an infinite regress of conscious and intentional bringings about of principles of choice.

The regress is impossible, but libertarians are not committed to it. They can consistently hold, for example, that Betty freely tries to eradicate her fear while also holding that she did not consciously and intentionally bring about any of the attitudes on the basis of which she chose to do so. If it is replied that Betty's cognitive behavior is too complex (or whatever) for an agent who did not consciously and intentionally bring about, at some time, an attitude that serves as a partial basis for the choice at issue, one who wishes to avoid quarreling over that point can adduce simpler cases. But insofar as agents consciously and intentionally produce or eradicate attitudes in themselves, they must produce or eradicate those attitudes *for reasons*; and that requires self-consciousness and self-reflection. The agents must have a proattitude toward having (or lacking) an attitude, they must be aware that they lack (or have) the attitude, and they must have some idea how to bring about the desired change. A corresponding intentional, self-shaping action may indisputably satisfy the noncompulsion requirement on free action and related requirements regarding deception, coercion, and the like (ch. 10). Further, actions of this kind have a psychological etiology that distinguishes them from stock cases of uncompelled, uncoerced, intentional animal behavior that does not count as free. And no new problems are raised about internal indeterminism.[19]

There is nothing incoherent—from some compatibilist and some libertarian perspectives—in the supposition that one may freely try to eliminate or foster an attitude in oneself even though the psychological basis of one's choice to try do this includes no attitude that one chose to have. So, in principle, not all libertarians need commit themselves to Strawson's premises 3 and 4. Libertarians who accept 3, on some reading of "truly responsible," may reject 4, on the same reading of the expression. A libertarian is not, simply in virtue of being a libertarian, committed to holding that we have freedom-level responsibility for an attitude only if we chose to have (or intentionally produced in ourselves) that attitude. Freedom-level responsibility for an attitude—construed as a requirement for the freedom of any action explained in part by our having the attitude—can be viewed by a libertarian as provided by the attitude's lacking a certain kind of history (along lines developed here and in chs. 9 and 10).

## 4. Becoming Free Agents

I have argued that Strawson's argument against libertarianism fails, but a certain challenge that it poses for libertarians merits attention. It brings into focus an important developmental matter. If people cannot become free agents by making infinite series of free choices, how *do* they become free agents? How does it happen that neonates who do not even act intentionally—much less freely—develop into free agents?

These questions do not pose any special threat to *compatibilism*. If there is a free, responsible (ordinary) human being at some deterministic world, he *developed* into such a being, and his so doing was the result of a deterministic process. Free agency, if some ordinary human being has it at a deterministic world, emerges in the being in a way explained by the laws of nature together with some earlier state of the world. Faced with an argument that free agency is not possessed by any human being at *any* possible world, on the grounds that the *emergence* of practical freedom is conceptually impossible, compatibilists might worry. But Strawson's argument does not provide them with grounds for fear on this score, for reasons developed in the preceding section. The emergence of practical freedom in an agent would be impossible if it required that the agent make an infinitely regressive series of free choices. But, again, this top-down picture can and should be rejected by believers in human freedom.[20] Only *naive* believers in human freedom would commit themselves to accepting it.

Libertarians may take comfort in these reflections, unless they believe their conception of practical freedom to be so unlike compatibilist conceptions that *nothing like* a compatibilist story can be told about the emergence of free agency in a human being. In their debates with compatibilist believers in freedom, they can (if ingenuity fails) ask for a compatibilist story about the emergence of free agency and then attempt to modify it in a way that is compatible with indeterminism. On both sides, it will be denied that the story must involve impossible regresses of choices.

In their debates with Strawson, however, the libertarians' situation is different. At a deterministic world, according to libertarians, neonates can develop in many ways, but they cannot develop into *free* beings. The consequence argument is supposed to establish this: libertarians allege both that, at a deterministic world, it is not "up to" one what one does and that agents act freely only if it *is* "up to" them what they do. In the present context, this raises interesting questions for libertarians. How is it that although, as neonates, it is not up to us what we do, later in life it *is* up to us what we do? How do we get from there to here? Or how *can* we get from there to here, barring divine intervention and the like? And if determinism is incompatible with an agent's ever becoming a being some of whose actions are up to him, how does indeterminism help in this regard?

A libertarian story about these matters may begin as compatibilist stories begin. As neonates mature, they develop some (proximal) control over their bodies and over their mental lives.[21] In the latter connection, they eventually gain at least a modest competence at identifying means to ends. Both accomplishments derive largely from practice. Our earliest limb movements are mere flailings, but the flailings themselves play a role in our gaining control over the motions of our limbs.[22] Our earliest sequences of practical thoughts might best be viewed as mental flailings, flailings that play a role in our becoming competent practical reasoners. Eventually, we are able to represent options, to select among them, and to take steps toward the selected goals. By that time, we are beyond mere bodily and mental flailing, and we are able to *choose*.

When we first engage in the business of choosing, it is often said, we are too simple-minded to act *freely*. In the relevant sense of 'choice,' it is frequently observed, even dogs can choose; but theorists are generally unwilling to hold that dogs act freely, and certainly not in a sense of 'freely' associated with moral responsibility.

An exercisable capacity for free action (as opposed to a capacity to become—eventually—a being who acts freely) is present, according to one version of the present story, once we are conscious of ourselves as agents, view ourselves as having options, and take it to be up to us which options we pursue. When our choices are informed by this self-conception and issue smoothly in a corresponding attempt, we are acting freely—*other things being equal*. (The "other things being equal" clause is an important one, of course, and I will return to it shortly.) On another version of the story, more is required: we must also see ourselves as beings whose actions affect others and as beings who are (sometimes) properly held accountable by others for what we do. It might also be insisted that we must explicitly see ourselves as *morally responsible* for our actions.

The story thus far, in its various versions, may be told by compatibilists; but libertarians need not *add* anything to the *developmental process* just sketched. The cognitive (and motor) developments that the story identifies obviously occur in many human beings, as libertarians agree. Determinism need not be viewed by them as a bar to the occurrence of the developmental *process* reported in the story. (The story does not assert that the process is a deterministic one.)[23] Rather, libertarians may see determinism primarily as a metaphysical bar to the *product* at issue, free agency. Simply put, libertarians need insist only that determinism is among the items covered by the "other things being equal" clause. Assuming that I am a free agent, a being at a deterministic world who is very much like me—who has a sense of himself as a morally responsible agent and so on—is not a free agent, precisely in virtue of his location. He views himself as free, but he is wrong; or so libertarians claim. He is wrong, on a libertarian view, because no matter how competent and sophisticated he is as a self-reflective, morally sensitive agent, determinism bars him from its being up to him what he does.

Strawson's fundamental thought is that the "ultimacy" (to quote Kane) that libertarians want, and that compatibilists urge is not required for free agency, can only be gained if lying behind every choice we make there is another choice: only then is it up to us what we do, on a libertarian reading of "up to us." But, as I have argued, some libertarians are given all the ultimacy they want by the addition of a suitable internal indeterminism to a compatibilist set of sufficient conditions for free agency. Such ultimacy is not precluded by the developmental story that I have sketched; libertarians can tell their own indeterministic version of it.

Earlier, in applying a portion of Strawson's argument to a remark of Kane's, I said that Strawson is claiming in part that agents who have libertarian freedom must have the power to have "wills"—that is, "character, motives and efforts of will" (Kane 1989, p. 254)—that can only and finally be explained by their choices. Libertarians do claim this power for free agents, but they need not do so in a way that commits them to an infinite regress of choices. The idea, rather, should be the familiar one that agents' free choices and actions have significant psychological consequences for them. By choosing and acting as we do, we affect our psychological constitution—sometimes, even, *intentionally* affect it, as young Betty did. Further, successes like Betty's may have important consequences for agents' psychological constitutions well beyond the immediate present. Betty's success in conquering her fear may, for example, enhance her self-esteem, expand her conception of the range of things she can control, and contribute to her deciding to try to conquer other fears of hers. Her successful effort at self-modification regarding her fear of her basement may lead to bigger and better things in the sphere of self-modification as a partial consequence of its relatively proximal effects on her psychological condition; and given that the effort was freely made, a *free* action of Betty's will have contributed to the psychological changes. Of course, the more proximal bigger and better things may lead to more remote ones that are bigger and better yet. Seemingly minor successes at self-modification may have, over time, a major impact on one's character.

That, too, is part of a familiar developmental story—a story about one's shaping of one's own character. The story rejects self-shaping *ex nihilo*; it grants the obvious point that self-shapers can work (at a time *t*) only with what they have (at *t*). And it avoids a commitment to an infinite regress of choices. One's earliest or most primitive free choices are not themselves made on the basis of freely chosen attitudes. It cannot be otherwise; the earliest free choices of an agent cannot themselves be made, even partly, on the basis of *other* free choices of the agent. But this does not preclude one's developing into a person like Betty: a self-conscious, self-reflective, self-assessing agent who can intentionally and freely undertake to eliminate or foster an attitude in herself—and succeed. Success in such endeavors can have consequences for the agent's developing character. The same is true of *failure*.

## 5.    More for Libertarians

Undoubtedly, some libertarians will take the modest libertarianism developed here to be *too* modest. Even if my criticisms of the reservations discussed in section 2 are persuasive, some libertarians will have additional qualms. In this section, I examine further libertarian worries on this score and then explain how my modest libertarian proposal can be rendered less modest without saddling libertarians with problems about control that my proposal was designed to handle. My strategy on that front was to find an epistemically open location for internal indeterminism that provides for the physical possibility of relevant alternative agential futures without depriving the agent of any actual control that he (or a counterpart) would have at nearby deterministic worlds. I concentrated on the coming to mind (and not coming to mind) of nonoccurrent beliefs, but I mentioned that something comparable may be done with desires, with attention, and with various combinations of belief, desire, and attention.

I have argued that libertarians do not benefit from the postulation of indeterministic transitions from proximal intentions to attempts or from evaluative judgments to intentions. Concentrating on deliberative settings, this leaves transitions from what precedes the occurrence of a deliberation-concluding judgment to the occurrence of that judgment, what happens earlier during deliberation, and the equipment that agents bring with them to the deliberative process.

Some libertarians might argue as follows. An agent judges *autonomously* only if he makes up his own mind about what it is best to do. If an agent is *causally determined* to judge that it would be best to *A*, his mind is made up for him by whatever causally determines the judgment. (For example, his mind might be made up for him, in part, by beliefs and desires that support his *A*-ing, or by the relative weights of his reasons, reasons being understood as states of mind.) So an agent *autonomously* judges that it would be best to *A* only if his judging that it would be best to *A* is not causally determined. Further, even if an agent judges partly on the basis of considerations that were not causally determined to occur to him, that itself cuts no ice. If at any time prior to *S*'s decisively judging it best to *A*, it is causally determined that *S* will judge it best to *A*, *S*'s mind is made up for him by the causal determinants of his judgment; he does not make up his own mind. So the argument runs.

A libertarian can *stipulate* a sense of 'makes up one's own mind' according to which it is true, by definition, that one makes up one's own mind that it would be best to *A* only if it is not causally determined *at any point* that one will judge that it would be best to *A*. But it certainly is not incumbent on a *critic* of the preceding argument to accept this stipulation. Earlier, I said that a decisive best judgment "settles in the agent's mind the question what (from the perspective of his own desires, beliefs, etc.) it is best . . . to do given his circumstances" (p. 15). A closely related claim is that, in making a decisive best judgment, an agent settles, in his own mind, the question what it is best to do given his circumstances. On natural readings of this use of 'settles' and of 'makes up his mind,' in settling a question of this sort an agent makes up his mind about what it would be best to do. His mind is not made up for him by something other than himself; *he* makes up his (own) mind.

In this sense of "makes up his (own) mind," an agent may make up his (own) mind *nonautonomously*. Various scenarios examined in chapters 9 and 10 illustrate this. For example, powerful manipulators may control deliberative input on the basis of which an agent decisively judges it best to *A*. But, again, there are salient differences between what goes on in these cases and what happens in ordinary cases of causally determined decisive better judgments. There is a difference between compulsion and (deterministic) causation, for instance. A libertarian who does not grant this difference will have to hold, among other things, that any attempt causally determined, in part, by the formation of a proximal intention is a compelled attempt. On the assumption that compelled attempts are not autonomously made, such a libertarian will have to plump for the view that there is an indeterministic connection between the formation of any proximal intention and any corresponding *autonomous* attempt. Such a view carries the cost of diminished proximal control over one's attempts, as I have argued. And some libertarians would be happy to avoid that cost, particularly those willing to countenance a compatibilist view about the connection between intention (or choice, or decision) and autonomous action.

Suppose it is granted that making up one's (own) mind is distinguishable from making up one's (own) mind *autonomously*—that the former is not conceptually sufficient for the latter. How should a libertarian draw the distinction? A libertarian may hold that an agent autonomously made up his mind that it was best to *A* only if it was *up to him* what he judged it best to do. A libertarian may maintain, further, that it was up to an agent what he judged best only if a condition identified earlier is satisfied (p. 211): namely, that there is no point in time at which minimally causally sufficient conditions that include no state or event internal to the agent are present for the agent's making the judgment he makes. If the condition is not satisfied, the agent lacks "ultimate" control over what he judges best; hence, what he judges best is not up to him in a libertarian sense. Rather, his judgment is ultimately the causally determined product of something external to the agent.

Deliberative judgments are made on the basis of a consideration of reasons. Libertarians do not deny this. Suppose that, on reflection, *S* takes the case for *A*-ing to be enormously strong. He has just disabused himself of his last reservation, and he confidently, decisively judges that it would be best to *A*. Imagine that, given background conditions, it is causally determined, once the last reservation is laid to rest, that $S$ will straightaway judge it best to $A$, on the basis of his deliberation. Must a libertarian hold that, at this point, it is not up to $S$ what he will judge best and that $S$ does not autonomously judge it best to $A$?

Some libertarians take this position. As I have observed, there are libertarians who maintain that agents conduct themselves freely or autonomously only in cases of "close calls"—only when competing considerations, or competing desires, are evenly matched (ch. 11, sec. 3). However, I also identified problems for this view, and I noted that libertarians need not seek a basis for the ultimacy they value in what goes on in present agential time slices. They may find it instead in the agent's *history*. An agent's present decisive best judgment—a judgment made on the basis of a consideration of reasons—may manifest a character that is, in significant part, a product of earlier autonomous judgments, intentions, and actions that were not ultimately causally determined by agent-external states and events. If there is a "close-call" requirement on autonomous conduct (e.g., judging, deciding, and overt action), the requirement need not be that such conduct occurs only in close-call cases. Relevant close calls might have occurred earlier in the agent's life, and his present "easy-call" decision may be autonomous partly in virtue of what happened in these earlier cases and of certain effects on his character of what happened then. A weaker, *historical*, close-call requirement would provide ultimacy without yielding the counterintuitive result that we cannot freely chat with good friends, or freely play a game of chess, when we have little or no reason to do anything else instead.

That one should need to work hard to convince libertarians to be properly sensitive to historical considerations would be ironic. After all, a standard libertarian charge against compatibilists is that *they* are insensitive to such considerations. This insensitivity supposedly is manifested in the ahistorical, internalist view of autonomy to which compatibilists allegedly are committed (see ch. 9). A libertarian who rejects a *time-slice* close-call requirement on autonomous conduct in favor of a historical close-call requirement can also reject the thesis that all causally determined decisive best judgments are nonautonomous judgments. A libertarian can maintain that a causally determined decisive best judgment made on the basis of an autonomous consideration of reasons may be *autonomously* made. On such a view, whether a causally determined deliberative judgment is autonomously made will depend on the agent's *history*.

We are back, then, to autonomous deliberation. Consider a realistic, complicated, close-call case of practical reasoning. When George and Martha married fifteen years ago, they discussed having children and decided to put this off until they were financially secure. They are now in their mid-forties. Their respective legal and medical careers flourished over the past decade, and money long ago ceased to be a problem. The problem became time: their demanding work load, they thought, would not permit them to raise a child in ways prescribed by their pertinent values. Now they are facing another problem with time: Martha's child-bearing years are nearly over. Realizing the apparent need to come to a decision on the matter relatively soon, the couple decide to spend their three-week vacation mulling the matter over. They cancel their trip to Jamaica and get down to business.

George and Martha have a lot to consider. Are they willing to scale back their work routines to raise a child in accordance with plans they formulated for this years ago? Are they willing to have a child without changing their work habits, or with only modest modifications in their daily schedules? In light of medical risks, should they consider adoption? How important is it to them to bear their own child, or to raise a child at all?

Considerations of another sort are also in order. To arrive at informed answers concerning some of their questions, George and Martha need a realistic conception of how raising a child is likely to affect their lives. How should the needed information be gathered, and how thorough should they be in their evidence gathering at this point? Certainly, it would be rash to base their conception of family life on vague memories of "Father Knows Best" episodes. But should they hire a family-planning consultant, discuss the matter with friends who have young children, or what?

Information of another kind is important, as well. What are the bases of their respective desires to have a child? If they were to become convinced that these desires rest upon unreflective acceptance of certain dated stereotypes, would the desires weaken, or even fade entirely away? Should they make a serious effort to discover the bases of these desires? Would it be wise, in this connection, to schedule some sessions with a psychologist?

Matters are complicated, indeed. In light of the daunting task, competing urges predictably arise. George and Martha at times feel inclined to procrastinate; at other moments, they are tempted to settle the matter one way or the other simply by flipping a coin. In both cases, they face a practical, evaluative question: Are these courses of action acceptable? Their serious attempts to arrive at an answer render salient for the couple principles of theirs about decision making. One result is that the principles themselves come under scrutiny. Is it really always best, they wonder, to make important decisions about the long-term course of one's life only after thorough evidence gathering and careful deliberation? Is it sometimes better, in such cases, to throw caution to the winds and to decide simply on the basis of whatever desires happen to be most intense at the time?

After three weeks of careful data gathering and detailed, honest discussion of the difficult questions identified, George and Martha decide that it is time to decide. They deem it unlikely that any crucial information remains to be gathered. The facts are in and have been hashed over at length. Their considerable efforts will have been wasted, they think, if they do not decide *today*, the last day of their vacation.

At this point, let us suppose, George and Martha are genuinely undecided on the issue. Neither has made a decision without reporting it to the other, and both regard the issue as a very close call. Earlier, they decided against adoption: they prefer to raise their own offspring, if they raise children at all. Each believes that there is much to be said both for having a child and for remaining childless, and they do not as yet believe that either set of considerations outweighs the other. Suppose that at this point it is causally undetermined what conclusion they will reach: strikingly different alternative futures are causally open to them.

After further discussion, George and Martha come to feel that the case for having a child has a slight edge over the case against. Each believes, as one may put it, that, on the basis of everything thus far considered, having a child is the preferable option, even though it is a close call; and each expresses this opinion to the other. George and Martha have not yet *decisively* judged it better to have a child than to remain childless, however, for they have not yet *settled*, in their own minds, the question what it is better to do. Nor do they view themselves as having settled this; and they proceed to consider whether they should deliberate further about whether to have a child or, instead, put an end to the matter and opt for parenthood. Should they decide such an important matter, they wonder, on the basis of a slight edge, or should they deliberate until they find a more compelling case for one option or the other? Suppose that at this point, too, it is causally undetermined how things will turn out.

Martha wisely observes that if a more compelling case were available for either option, they would probably have made it already. She voices an inclination to decide on the basis of the slight edge, reporting that this is only an inclination. George reports being similarly inclined, on the grounds that further deliberation would probably prove otiose. This is enough for both of them. They judge that a slight edge is good enough in the circumstances; they settle, in their own minds, the question what it is better to do; and they decide to pursue parenthood.

I have developed this case at length for a pair of reasons. One concerns the couple's deliberative capacities and the quality of their deliberation. An appreciation of the wide range of deep and challenging questions that emerge and are carefully addressed in the course of the couple's deliberation provides a sense of George and Martha as intellectually sophisticated, self-reflective, self-assessing agents who seriously and responsibly tackle their decision problem. Further, in light of the natural temptations identified and their resistance of them, we see George and Martha as manifesting self-control in the protracted deliberative process.

My other reason for detailed development was to highlight how little we understand about what actually goes on in complicated, real-life deliberative episodes. For example, we are in no position to explain why each thought—each question, reservation, and hypothesis, for instance—occurs just when it does, why each thought receives exactly the attention it does, why each thought has precisely the vividness (or pallidness) that it has, and so on. Further, we are ill-equipped to identify, in each case, the precise consequences of these things. Nor are we in a position to explain, in each case, why an agent pursues one question rather than another at a given time, or takes one consideration to be weightier than another, or juxtaposes a particular consideration with one rather than another of a pair of competing considerations—or what the overall effect would have been of a change in the order of questions pursued, or in the weighting of a particular pair of considerations, or in the juxtaposition of considerations. The details of the case also bring to light a variety of epistemically possible locations for significant, causally undetermined events in deliberative processes. At many points, for all we know, it may be causally undetermined what happens next. There may be at most a *probability* that a significant reservation will come to mind at a crucial juncture, or that a deliberator will muster the clarity of thought that would lead to a certain comparative assessment of a complicated collection of competing desires, or that a practical reasoner will articulate or represent a consideration to himself in a way that enables him to appreciate its full force, and so on.

Our recognition that we rarely, if ever, exert complete proximal control over the deliberative process naturally recommends deliberative reconsideration in many cases. This is recommended, as well, by the belief of some theorists that deliberative episodes are subject to genuine chance. We seek to compensate for our limitations as deliberators by searching for important considerations that we might have missed, by attempting to ascertain whether we *justifiably* arrived at certain (tentative) conclusions, by double-checking complicated calculations, and in many other ways. If we have neither perfect nor deterministic proximal control over every mental episode in our deliberative processes, at least we have resources for minimizing the potentially deleterious effects of our deliberative shortcomings. At various points, there may be at most a probability (less than 1) that $x$ will happen next. Even so, if, in the end, on the basis of careful, informed, rational, self-reflective, self-assessing, self-controlled, unmanipulated deliberation of the sort that we may suppose George's and Martha's to be, an agent with no compelled pro-attitudes decisively judges that it would be best to $A$, he may have autonomously so judged.

The primary constraint on a libertarian view that insists on a more extensive indeterminism than my modest libertarian proposal in section 2 provides is that the proposed indeterminism not deprive agents of autonomy-level, nonultimate control regarding the deliberative process. We have every reason to believe that real human beings sometimes exercise autonomy-level proximal control in their deliberative efforts, assuming a *compatibilist* view of autonomous deliberation. An indeterminism that does not render agents who meet robust compatibilist standards for autonomy any less in proximal control of deliberative events than they (or their counterparts) would be at the closest deterministic worlds does not run afoul of this constraint. Where compatibilists have no good reason to insist on determinism in the deliberative process as a requirement for autonomy, where internal indeterminism is, for all we know, a reality, and where such indeterminism would not diminish the nonultimate control that real agents exert over their deliberation even on the assumption that real agents are internally deterministic—that is, at the *intersection* of these three locations—libertarians may plump for ultimacy-promoting indeterminism.

Setting aside the matter of demonstrating that compatibilism is false, the hard problems for libertarians are the ones developed in the preceding chapter—problems about how actions can be both free (in a libertarian sense) and explicable, and related problems about how indeterminism can contribute to freedom (in a libertarian sense). In this chapter, I have developed resolutions to these problems—resolutions designed specifically to assist theorists committed to libertarianism and therefore to the thesis that free action requires internal indeterminism. I have fleshed out a modest libertarian view in constructing a libertarian response to Strawson's attempted reductio, and I have pointed the way to a less modest view. I also have offered a set of sufficient conditions for libertarian autonomy. It may be doubted whether that set is satisfiable by actual human beings. That doubt and others are addressed in chapter 13.

## Notes

1. The recommended course of action may be a refraining, of course.
2. I am assuming that making an attempt requires a relevant intention.
3. Kane remarks that libertarians "can accept a compatibilist account of the relation between choice and action, but not a compatibilist account of the relation between reasons and choice" (1985, p. 15).

4. On similar indeterministic gaps, see Dennett 1978, pp. 294–99, and Kane 1985, pp. 101–10. For an alternative libertarian suggestion, see Nozick 1981, pp. 294–316.

5. I am assuming the reality of "mental causation." In Mele 1992a, ch. 2, I provide an account of the causal bearing of mental events and states on the intentional behavior of physical agents.

6. This paragraph and the next five address a worry voiced by Roderick Long and Geoff Sayre-McCord in conversation.

7. I am not suggesting that all, or even most, intentional actions are preceded by proximal decisive better judgments.

8. Others do have such stories. See, e.g., Eccles 1953, 1970; Kane 1985, ch. 9; and Thorp 1980, pp. 67–71.

9. See, e.g., Kane 1985, 1989, and Thorp 1980, pp. 122–24, 128–31.

10. Roderick Long and Scott MacDonald suggested the attentional possibilities in conversation. On the practical significance of attention, see ch. 3; on its doxastic significance, see ch. 5.

11. Regarding 4a, it is worth noting that although cases of choosing to intend are imaginable, they are relatively rare. In choosing (or deciding) to $A$, one forms an intention to $A$ (Mele 1992a, p. 141); but such choosing should not be confused with choosing to *intend* to $A$. In choosing to intend to $A$, one forms an intention to intend to $A$; and second-order intentions are uncommon (Mele 1992a, ch. 11).

12. Thomas Nagel, another nonautonomist, demands even more by way of choice for freedom: "[T]o be really free we would have to act from a standpoint completely outside ourselves, choosing everything about ourselves, including all of our principles of choice— creating ourselves from nothing, so to speak" (1986, p. 118). My criticism of Strawson's argument in this section and the next undermines Nagel's argument, as well.

13. On intentions by default, see ch. 2, sec. 5 and Mele 1992a, ch. 12.

14. I am assuming that no choices are self-grounding.

15. We may safely suppose that her success is not causally deviant.

16. My use of 'emergent' here is an ordinary-language use, not a technical one, as the next sentence makes clear.

17. Notice that I here attribute to Kane a sufficient condition for a choice's being free, not a necessary condition. Kane, recall, holds that (some) akratic choices are free even though the agent made no effort to make those choices (see ch. 11, sec. 3).

18. I say "roughly," because Frankfurt-style cases need accommodating. Libertarians can offer a qualified account of "could have done (e.g., chosen, acted) otherwise" that accommodates these cases without going compatibilist. See p. 243 and Fischer 1982.

19. If intentional self-shaping actions are only possible in human beings who have managed to produce attitudes in themselves nonintentionally, so be it. That does not affect the argument. Perhaps, in this connection, as in others mentioned later, some early flailing is required.

20. Perhaps an agent who has no beginning in time (e.g., God, on some conceptions) can make an infinitely regressive series of choices. However, my present concern is human beings.

21. On the development of control in toddlers, see Lütkenhaus et al. 1987.

22. For an influential story about this, see James 1907, ch. 26.

23. For an interesting attempt to trace the development of autonomy from infancy through adolescence—one that does not manifest a commitment either to determinism or to indeterminism—see Shapiro 1981, ch. 2.

# 13

# Assessing the Denial of Autonomy

I have offered two overlapping sets of sufficient conditions for autonomous agency, one for compatibilist believers in autonomy and the other for libertarians. My tack, in essence, was to pursue the following question: Given a certain conception of an ideally self-controlled human being, and assuming that some human beings are autonomous, what can be added to ideal self-control to yield personal autonomy? The assumption has detractors, of course. The conditions specified in my compatibilist answer are satisfiable, but incompatibilists will urge that their satisfaction is insufficient for autonomy. All of those conditions are present, as well, in my libertarian answer. But the additional condition is satisfiable by actual human beings only if internal indeterminism is a feature of real people. This suggests a strategy for *nonautonomists* (theorists who hold that no human being is autonomous): first, argue against compatibilism; then argue that internal indeterminism, or internal indeterminism of any sort that would be of theoretical use to libertarians, is not a property of human beings. The present chapter assesses the case for nonautonomism and finds it deficient.

## 1.  The Dialectical Situation

It is important to understand the nonautonomists' dialectical situation. They cannot establish their thesis simply by showing that no human being is autonomous *on some conception or other of autonomy*. The targeted conception might be cooked up to suit their own purposes, and it might not be embraced by their putative opponents. One nonautonomist solution is to focus on a conception accepted by "most people."[1] But whether there is a single conception of autonomy that is accepted by most people (or most adults, or most adults in particular nations) is at best uncertain. Suppose, however, that most people were sincerely to assent to a putative definition of 'autonomy' that, as it turned out, was unsatisfiable by human beings, largely on conceptual grounds—for example, a definition that entailed that every autonomous being has made an infinite series of choices. Would that show that no human being is autonomous? What if a little noncoercive Socratic cross-examination would lead most people to form a conception of autonomy that did not suffer from this problem, or any comparably serious one? Why shouldn't this conception be taken more seriously than the assent of "most people" to the unsatisfiable definition?

Another strategy would be to canvass the conceptions of autonomy endorsed in the literature and to show that each is either unsatisfiable by actual human beings or falls short of capturing what an acceptable conception of autonomy must capture. Regarding the latter disjunct, it might be argued that the conceptions of autonomy that are satisfiable by human beings cannot do what any good conception of autonomy should do—for instance, help to specify that in virtue of which some people are morally responsible for (some of) their actions and thus are subject to merited moral praise or blame. But, of course, critics cannot properly rest content with showing that no conception of autonomy in the literature discharges the burden at issue with respect to *some conception or other of moral responsibility*. The critics' conception of moral responsibility might be cooked up to suit their own purposes, and it might not be accepted by their putative opponents. Here a nonautonomist would need some way of locating relevant conceptions of moral responsibility.

Consider compatibilism in this connection. Most experienced compatibilists about autonomy are not likely to be impressed by arguments designed to show that their conceptions of autonomy have no particular significance for moral responsibility, on some *incompatibilist* conception of the latter. For most experienced compatibilists about autonomy are compatibilists about moral responsibility, too, and about deserved moral praise and blame. Disagreements about autonomy between compatibilist believers in autonomy and nonautonomists are likely to be mirrored by disagreements about moral responsibility and deserved moral praise or blame.

A nonautonomist might attempt to circumvent the problem of locating relevant conceptions of autonomy by arguing that there is a single concept of autonomy (or free will, or moral responsibility), that it is incoherent, and that any coherent conception of autonomy (or free will, or moral responsibility) gains its coherence partly by omitting some plank in the concept. It might be argued that no conception of autonomy is acceptable unless it captures everything in the concept and that any conception that does this is unsatisfiable, in virtue of requiring that mutually exclusive conditions be satisfied by autonomous agents. It might be argued, as well, that the dispute between compatibilists and libertarians is to be explained by their latching onto different planks in the incoherent (i.e., internally inconsistent) concept.

This smacks of an extreme realism about concepts, but it does point to something that a nonautonomist might try to exploit. Apparently there are a number of relatively deep and widely shared intuitions about autonomy, free will, and moral responsibility, and some of those intuitions seemingly conflict with others. Richard Double puts these apparent data to work in an argument for the "non-reality of free will" that I examine in section 3.

## 2. Compatibilism, Incompatibilism, and Agnosticism

Peter van Inwagen imagines a debate between himself and a compatibilist before an audience of "agnostics about the compatibility of free will and determinism" (1992, p. 58). The object of the disputants, he says, is to persuade their audience, not each other. Nothing that I have said in this book keeps me out of the audience; I have not committed myself to one side or the other of the debate. It is possible for some who hear and understand the most thorough debate ever staged on compatibilism and incompatibilism to remain agnostic. They might not bring to the debate any beliefs whose propositional contents can be included among the premises of a knock-down argument for one or the other of the two theses at issue. Their agnosticism might run deep—so deep that nothing they accept can be used by either of the disputants in an argument that will convince them to go one way or the other.

Can agnostics of this sort consistently believe that there are autonomous human beings? They cannot consistently with their agnosticism about the compatibility of determinism with autonomy accept any set of conditions as sufficient for autonomy whose satisfaction they believe to be compatible with determinism. Such acceptance would encompass acceptance of compatibilism. However, they can accept an incompatibilist set of conditions as sufficient for autonomy—and hold that the conditions are satisfiable by actual human beings—without committing themselves to incompatibilism. They can be agnostic about whether the incompatibilist element in the set, and any alternative incompatibilist element, is *required* for autonomy. Such agnostics, if they are to be believers in human autonomy, will have some commitments, of course. They will believe that some incompatibilist collection or other of conditions is both sufficient for autonomy and satisfied by some human beings. If they are convinced, as I am, that any incompatibilist collection of conditions sufficient for autonomy includes internal indeterminism, they are also committed to believing that some human beings are internally indeterministic, and in a way theoretically useful to libertarians.

A weaker combination of agnosticism about compatibilism and belief in human autonomy is available. An agnostic (about compatibilism) believer in human autonomy may hold that there is some incompatibilist set of conditions the satisfaction of which would be sufficient for autonomy; may be agnostic about whether the internal indeterminism encompassed in those conditions is a feature of any actual human beings; and may hold that, if an internal indeterminism of theoretical use to libertarians is not a feature of any actual human beings, then compatibilism is true. Speculation about possible grounds for acceptance of a doubly agnostic view of this kind might prove interesting. On what grounds could someone who is agnostic about this much believe that some human beings are autonomous? What grounds can support the autonomist thesis while leaving open agnosticism both about compatibilism and about the satisfiability (by actual human beings) of any specifically incompatibilist (alleged) requirement for autonomy? Is a doubly agnostic believer in human autonomy stuck with nothing better than an appeal to faith? I return to these questions later.

## 3. Denying Autonomy

Add a nonautonomist to the slate of debaters. The new disputant readily identifies ground on which to attack the stronger combination of agnosticism about compatibilism and belief in human autonomy—namely, its commitment to the thesis that at least some human beings are internally indeterministic in a way useful to libertarians. A debater who can show that this thesis is false can convince such agnostic believers in human autonomy that they have only two theoretical options: embracing compatibilism, or abandoning their belief in autonomy.

A nonautonomist attempting to win points in this way will not have an easy time of it. Several theorists have proposed ways of making sense of, and exploiting for libertarian purposes, agent-internal physical indeterminism designed to be compatible with what is known (or was then known) about neurophysiology; and, for all anyone now knows, internal indeterminism is open.[2] A libertarian counterpart to a once-popular antilibertarian challenge may also be leveled. At one time, libertarians were challenged to produce convincing grounds for thinking that human beings fall beyond the boundaries of orthodox, deterministic physics. Libertarians may challenge their nonautonomist opponents to produce convincing grounds for thinking that the internal workings of human beings fall beyond the boundaries of orthodox, indeterministic physics. Further, even if our neurophysiological evidence is consistent with internal determinism, it is doubtful that our knowledge of neurophysiology is sufficiently advanced to warrant confidence that internal determinism is probably true (cf. van Inwagen 1983, p. 198). It might be argued, setting such empirical matters aside, that compatibilism is false and that internal indeterminism would deprive us of (nonultimate) control over—hence, freedom regarding—the very actions whose freedom is supposed to be rendered possible by such indeterminism. But I take myself to have undermined the second conjunct in chapter 12.

Other avenues are open to nonautonomists. Richard Double identifies six conditions that he thinks "any acceptable account of free will should meet" and he argues that "no account meets them" (1991, p. 217). Three of the conditions apply to the explication of "any philosophically interesting concept," and three apply specifically to free will (p. 218):

1. "Any attempt to explicate a concept . . . needs to be understandable."
2. A "philosophical account of the denotation of a term" is acceptable only if the satisfaction of the conditions in that account fits "harmoniously into the rest of what we *think* that we know about the world."
3. "If the explication is one of analysis, then the *analysans* must match the *analysandum* in extension, with only a little room for slippage. The greater the slippage, the more likely it is that we are revising the concept. . . . The same principle holds for explications that purport to be rough characterizations or to offer exemplars."
4. Any acceptable explication of free will "must entail that free persons could have chosen otherwise."[3]
5. Any acceptable explication of free will must explicate the "control" that free will requires.
6. Any acceptable explication of free will must explicate the "sensibleness" or "rationality" that free will involves. (pp. 218–21)

I have little to say about the generic requirements (i.e., 1 through 3). Condition 2 is excessive: it plainly is false, for example, that an analysis of 'miracle,' or 'traveling faster than the speed of light,' or 'backward time travel' is acceptable only if the satisfaction of the conditions offered fits "harmoniously into the rest of what we think that we know about the world." Some concepts are such that their satisfaction is quite improbable or even physically impossible, given what we think we know about the world.[4] Further, it is unclear what the harmony that Double mentions amounts to. Suppose we think, as van Inwagen does, that "the human organism and human behaviour are such terribly complex things, and so little is known about the details of that terrible complexity (in comparison with what there is to be known), that it is hard to see why anyone should think that what we do know renders a belief that human behaviour is determined reasonable" (1983, p. 198). And suppose we think the same about a belief that human behavior is *not* determined? Would *neither* a deterministic nor an indeterministic analysis of free will satisfy the harmony constraint, under these conditions? Or would determinism and indeterminism each count as harmonious enough with the what we think "we know about the world," in virtue of our thinking that we know too little to have good empirical grounds for rejecting either hypothesis?

I turn to the "content-specific" conditions (i.e., 4 through 6). Whatever one thinks about the merits of condition 4, Double's attempt to employ it in arguing for the "non-reality of free will" is interesting. He implies that any adequate explication of free will must include an explication of '*S* could have chosen otherwise.' And he writes,

> If the main theme of this book is correct, then the attempt by both sides [incompatibilists and compatibilists] to give a single correct analysis of the notion of choosing otherwise is fruitless, since there is no single *analysandum* to be captured. . . . My conclusion is that although any account of free will must hold that free persons 'could have chosen otherwise', that notion may be understood either categorically, as the incompatibilists do, or hypothetically, as most compatibilists do, and that there is no way to adjudicate the dispute about who is right. (pp. 219–20)

Suppose that the consequent of the first sentence in this passage, and the conclusion stated in the second one, are both true. Would it follow that there is no such thing as free will? Consider an analogy. There is an ongoing dispute about what actions are and how 'action' is to be analyzed. The range of acceptable options has been narrowed down (in my opinion) to a few; but (again, in my opinion) no one has offered conclusive grounds for accepting one of the options in preference to the others. Suppose that "there is no way to adjudicate the dispute about who is right" and that there is no fact of the matter about whether any of the live options is (exclusively) the best option. Would it follow—in light of the fact that having performed an intentional action requires having performed an action—that there is no such thing as intentional action, that no one ever acts intentionally?

Of course not. We can have excellent evidence that people sometimes act intentionally, even if "although any account of" intentional action must hold that people who perform intentional actions perform actions, 'action' may be understood in way *x* or in way *y* or in way *z*, and "there is no way to adjudicate the dispute about who is right" about 'action' and no fact of the matter about who is right. Similarly, making the parallel supposition about free will and 'could have chosen otherwise' does not itself commit one to holding that no one has free will. Perhaps we can have free will even if there is no fact of the matter about whether 'could have chosen otherwise' is to be understood along compatibilist or libertarian lines, just as we may perform intentional actions even if there is no fact of the matter about whether 'action' is to be understood in way *x* or in way *y* or in way *z*. Further, an agnostic (like me) concerning some disputes about the identity and individuation of actions, can consistently believe that there are intentional actions; and an agnostic about compatibilism can consistently be agnostic concerning some disputes about the meaning of 'could have chosen otherwise' while retaining his belief in free will. For example, an agnostic about compatibilism might be agnostic about whether compatibilists or libertarians are right about 'could have chosen otherwise' while also consistently believing that some libertarian account of 'could have chosen otherwise' is satisfiable by actual human beings. Such an agnostic might believe both that some libertarian set of conditions is sufficient for autonomy and that the set is satisfiable by actual human beings. (Alternatively, an agnostic about compatibilism and 'could have done otherwise' who believes that some human beings are free might accept the disjunctive thesis that either some human beings satisfy a libertarian set of conditions of the kind specified or compatibilism is true.)

Double's argument about condition 5—"the control condition"—parallels the argument just assessed. Compatibilists and incompatibilists disagree about the control encompassed in free will. And "again, there is no way to adjudicate the dispute over whether one-way or dual control matches *the* prephilosophical view, because there is no such view" (p. 220). Well, there is no prephilosophical view, I am convinced, of intentional action—or of action—that includes special allegiance to some one of the various live options on the identity and individuation of actions.[5] But it does not follow that there are no intentional actions, or that there are no actions at all.

Double takes a compound stand on condition 6. He reminds the reader of his earlier arguments that "any specification" of the "degree of sensibleness in one's choices" that is required by freedom "is bound to produce counterexamples that show it to be too stringent or too liberal" (pp. 220–21). And he suggests that a debate "over one way vs. dual rationality" would have theoretical consequences like those he sought to establish in his discussion of 4 and 5. My response to the latter suggestion is by now predictable, so I turn to the former one. Surely, it is no objection to the explication of *some* concepts that the explication leaves open certain matters of degree? Consider 'being exceptionally agile for a tall professional basketball player in the United States in the early 1990s.' Is there a precise cut-off point on the tallness condition—say 82.27 inches? The demand for such precision seems absurd. But it would not follow from the unavailability of such (nonstipulative) precision that there were not in the early 1990s any NBA players to whom the quoted description applies. David Robinson clearly was one such player, and Bill Laimbeer clearly was not. To return to the comparison with intentional action, it is generally agreed that complex intentional actions must accord significantly with the agent's action plan; but it would be foolhardy to specify a precise degree of accordance, such that that degree is sufficient for significance and anything less falls short (Mele and Moser 1994). Some concepts are vague on some questions of degree. If there is a widely shared concept of intentional action, it is one such concept, and those who seek to analyze intentional action should allow for vagueness. Similarly, we can allow for vagueness in a "rationality condition" on free will.

Many of us are justifiably confident that people sometimes act intentionally even though there is no widely accepted analysis of intentional action. So it is not universally true that the absence of a widely accepted analysis of $x$ precludes justifiable confidence that some things are $x$-s (and some other things are not). Nor, as I have suggested, is it a universal truth that the likelihood that some disputes about the analysis of $x$ will prove to be interminable warrants the belief that there are no $x$-s.

It might be said that the ongoing debate between compatibilist believers in autonomy and libertarians indicates that there are, in fact, at least *two* concepts of autonomy (or free will)—a compatibilist and an incompatibilist one—and that there is no "prephilosophical concept" of autonomy (or free will) so constituted that a proper appeal to it can settle the debate. This suggestion is by no means incredible. Some have taken Frankfurt-style cases (ch. 5, sec. 2) to show that libertarians were mistaken about the "could have done otherwise" requirement on free action, and *therefore* about the indeterminism requirement. They view libertarians as confused about what their conception of freedom requires; and they might hold that precisely this confusion accounts for the dispute between incompatibilists and compatibilists. On this view, both sides have the same conception of freedom, but one side is confused about what that conception entails. However, the view is simplistic. Libertarians who thought that the problem with determinism was simply that it entails that no one could ever have done otherwise than as he did (on some preferred reading of 'could have done otherwise') might have misidentified what actually bothered them about determinism. What bothered them might have been the entailment at issue in conjunction with the entailment that the causal sequence that actually issues in the agent's $A$-ing (as opposed to an unrealized, Frankfurt-style sequence) is such that he could not have done otherwise (cf. Fischer 1982).[6] If so, perhaps some incompatibilists and compatibilists do employ distinct (but overlapping) conceptions of freedom—one of which has as a rock-bottom, nonnegotiable constituent a kind of "openness" that the other one lacks.[7]

Even then, a compatibilist believer in autonomy can consistently maintain that some libertarian set of conditions is both sufficient for autonomy and satisfiable, for all we know, by actual human beings. Some compatibilists can, in principle, set aside their quarrels with libertarians and join forces with them in meeting nonautonomist challenges. Some theorists who argue under the banner of agnosticism about compatibilism might even be compatibilists in disguise.

## 4.  A Strong Argument for Autonomy?

Even if every argument for nonautonomism can be refuted, that leaves open the possibility of a stalemate. Are there any powerful arguments for the thesis that some human beings are autonomous and sometimes act autonomously? Are there stronger grounds for this thesis than for its denial?

Peter van Inwagen has said that the following (enthymematic) argument is "the strongest argument for the existence of free will" and, indeed, "the *only* strong argument for the existence of free will": "moral responsibility requires free will and we *are* responsible for at least some of the things we have brought about" (1983, p. 188). The first half of the argument is usually granted. Having been granted that premise, the trick is to show that we are morally responsible for some things. Nonautonomists who agree that "moral responsibility requires free will" argue that no human being is morally responsible for anything. Is it any easier to convince them that some human beings are morally responsible agents than to convince them that some human beings have free will?[8]

Van Inwagen's argument for the reality of moral responsibility is relatively straightforward. He claims that normal reactive attitudes and reactive behavior—including verbal behavior—of ours "demonstrate . . . that we believe in moral responsibility" (p. 207). For example, we blame people for having done certain "despicable" things and take ourselves to be justified in so doing, realizing that we are justified in this only if these people are morally responsible agents. And he suggests that

> if we examine our convictions honestly and seriously and carefully, we shall discover that we cannot believe that this assent [to the thesis that "responsibility exists"] is merely something forced upon us by our nature and the nature of human social life. . . . [W]e shall discover that we cannot but view our belief in moral responsibility as a justified belief, a belief that is simply not open to reasonable doubt. I myself would go further: in my view, the proposition that often we are morally responsible for what we have done is something that we all know to be true. (p. 209)

That is the argument, in a nutshell. (Van Inwagen also suggests that "the philosopher who denies moral responsibility speaks *words* that contradict his theories, words like 'That was a shoddy thing to do'" [p. 297]. But such a philosopher might be able to explain his words away as manifesting bad habits that he acquired prior to seeing the light about moral responsibility. And even if the philosopher does not believe his thesis about moral responsibility, that certainly does not establish that the thesis is false.)

Van Inwagen's argument has a curious structure. Suppose that an enormous number of "us" were to "discover" (1) that our reactive attitudes and behavior "demonstrate . . . that we believe in moral responsibility," (2) that "we cannot believe" that our belief in the reality of moral responsibility "is merely something forced upon us by our nature and the nature of human social life," and (3) that "we cannot but view our belief in moral responsibility as a justified belief, a belief that is simply not open to reasonable doubt." If that is *all* we discovered—if we did not also discover, for example, *why* we could not view our belief as anything but a justified belief, nor *why* it is not open to reasonable doubt—we would not have discovered why we are justified in believing in moral responsibility, *unless* our conjunctive discovery were itself to count as a justification for our belief (and we were to realize that it does so count). So unless our conjunctive discovery would itself count as a justification for our belief in moral responsibility, van Inwagen has not shown that the belief is justified and has not even identified a proposition to do the justifying work.

Would the conjunctive discovery count as a justification, assuming that "we" were to make this discovery about "ourselves." A predictable nonautonomist response is that "our" discovery simply reveals facts about certain beliefs of ours without also revealing that some people are, in fact, morally responsible for what they do. To be sure, we are supposed to have discovered that "we cannot believe" that our belief in the reality of moral responsibility "is merely something forced upon us by our nature and the nature of human social life." But even if we cannot have this second-order belief, it certainly does not follow that the first-order belief is *not* forced upon us in this way—a way supposedly having nothing to do with *justification* for the belief. And in the absence of an identification of what does justify us in believing in moral responsibility, we are in no position to claim confidently that we *are* justified in believing that some people are morally responsible for what they do.

I have no wish to contend that it is impossible for *S* to *be justified* in believing something if *S* has no idea what justifies him in believing it. But someone who has no idea what justifies him or anyone else in believing that *p* is in no position to produce a convincing argument for *p*. And given the argument that van Inwagen has produced, nonautonomists are well within their rights to claim that, *at best*, he is in *S*'s shoes. Nonautonomists want to be told why we *are* justified in believing in moral responsibility (if we are), not that we cannot help believing in it, cannot help believing that our belief in it is a justified belief, and so on.

The strangeness of van Inwagen's argumentative strategy may be brought out by means of an analogy. Imagine a time slice of a possible world during which every human being over the age of two believes in the existence of God. Imagine that they discover (1) that their behavior demonstrates their belief in God, (2) that they cannot believe that their belief in God was forced upon them in a nonjustificatory way, and (3) that they cannot but view their belief in God as a justified belief, "a belief that is simply not open to reasonable doubt." Imagine that at a later time an atheist or agnostic emerges among them. He grants their tripartite discovery, and he asks whether discoveries 1, 2, and 3 constitute the entire argument that they would offer him for the existence of God, were they to offer an argument for that thesis. They say *yes*. And he walks away, convinced that they have offered him only facts about themselves and no evidence for the existence of God. Van Inwagen has not offered the nonautonomist any more than the theists have offered the atheist or agnostic—with the exception of his claim that the behavior (including verbal behavior) of nonautonomists speaks against their view, and that claim is not likely to impress a committed nonautonomist.

Nonautonomists need not rest their case against van Inwagen's argument with the charge just made. They might also argue that certain commitments of many believers in moral responsibility, in conjunction with other points, show that their belief in moral responsibility *is* "open to reasonable doubt." For example, incompatibilist believers in moral responsibility (like van Inwagen) believe that it requires internal indeterminism; and the nonautonomist can argue that the truth of internal indeterminism is subject to reasonable doubt.

Of course, the believer in moral responsibility can get out of that bind by going compatibilist. Van Inwagen himself says that that is what he would do *if* science were to "present us with compelling reasons for believing in determinism"; for he takes his arguments for incompatibilism to be weaker than his argument for the reality of moral responsibility (p. 223). Fortunately for him, he is wrong about the relative merits of his arguments.

That the reality of moral responsibility is more evident or better grounded than that of free will is itself a surprising thesis in some ways. To be sure, in casting about for an argument for the reality of free will one is naturally inclined to look for something more evident that can be used to justify the thesis that some human beings are possessed of free will. But if, as van Inwagen says, and as is usually thought, moral responsibility requires free will (or freedom of choice and action), can it be more evident that some people are morally responsible for (some of) what they do than that some people freely do (some of) what they do? Any acceptable notion of moral responsibility that builds in free will as a necessary condition will be at least as complex as a corresponding notion of free will. And unless one holds that free will comes into play only in situations having moral significance, one's notion of moral responsibility will be *more* complex than one's notion of free will.[9] For one's notion of moral responsibility will encompass not only one's notion of free will, but also some notion of moral significance and hence some notion of what morality is. If moral responsibility is not better understood than free will (or autonomy, or free action)— and how can it be, on the assumption that moral responsibility requires free will?— then it is hard to see how the reality of moral responsibility can be easier to establish than that of free will (or autonomy, or free action).

## 5. A Stronger Argument for Autonomy

Consider the following claims:

1. I sometimes act freely. (Here and in claims 2 through 4, 'I' designates you, dear reader.)

2. Other people sometimes act freely.

3. I am morally responsible for some of what I do.

4. Some agents are morally responsible for some of what they do, and I am not the only such agent.

Most readers of this book accept all four claims. But on what grounds? A natural suggestion is that the grounds are at least partly experiential. We have a rich collection of experiences of our own agency, agency that sometimes involves self-reflection, self-assessment, careful deliberation, successful attempts at self-modification, and so on. We also have at least a dim understanding of what we and others mean by 'free action' and 'moral responsibility,' and we take some of our experiences of our own agency to be experiences of the sort that free, morally responsible agents would have. In addition, we hold ourselves morally responsible for some of our actions, and, accordingly, we blame ourselves for some of our deeds and congratulate ourselves for others. We do this to other people, as well, on the assumption that they are a lot like us; we hold them morally responsible for some of what they do, and dish out moral praise and blame.

It must be granted that our experience of our own agency *might* be radically misleading. It is logically possible, for example, that we are merely dreamers who have only dreamed that we were deliberating and acting, and what we dream (the contents of our dreams) might be engineered by a powerful deceiver. Such possibilities—the possible truth of propositions for which we have no evidence—are grist for another mill. For present purposes, we would do well to look for evidence that our experience of our own agency is radically misleading, or, more precisely, that it misleads us into believing that we are free, morally responsible agents. Evidence of internal determinism would count as such evidence, on the assumption that incompatibilism is true. And, again, the truth of internal determinism is compatible with our having the experience of our own agency that we have.

This is one reason—a practical reason—for going compatibilist. If compatibilism is true, there is little to block our rationally believing that we are free and morally responsible on the (partial) basis of our experience of our own agency. We grant that our having that experience does not *entail* that we are free, morally responsible beings. But, as compatibilists, we would notice that the hypotheses whose truth would entail that we lack free agency and moral responsibility are either unsupported by evidence or, at best, supported only by very weak evidence; and being reasonable people, we do not think that unsupported hypotheses and hypotheses enjoying little support should be allowed to stand in the way of our believing on the basis of our experience.[10]

It is also a reason for being agnostic about incompatibilism. For then, if we ever were to discover that there is overwhelming evidence for internal determinism, we would still have compatibilism to fall back on.

What might an experience of acting *freely* encompass in a particular case? Return to young Betty. I argued in chapter 12 that the following conditions are sufficient for Betty's having freely tried to eliminate her fear of her basement, in a *compatibilist* sense of 'freely': (1) She was not compelled to have any of the pro-attitudes that grounded her judgment that it would be best to try to eliminate her fear, nor were any of those attitudes coercively or self-oppressively produced; (2) she was not cut off from autonomous reasoning by her doxastic condition; (3) the reasoning that led to her decisive better judgment was reliable reasoning; and (4) the judgment issued unproblematically in a corresponding intention that issued smoothly in a corresponding intentional attempt to eliminate her fear.[11] And I implied that sufficient conditions for Betty's having acted freely, in a *libertarian* sense of 'freely,' are obtained by adding another condition to this list: (5) Owing partly to Betty's being internally indeterministic, prior to her deliberation it was not causally determined that Betty would judge it best to try to eliminate her fear, nor intend to eliminate her fear, nor try to eliminate her fear.

How far can experience extend with respect to these conditions? Well, Betty may experience the relevant pro-attitudes as states of mind that were not forced upon her. Her experience of having them may, in that respect, be quite unlike her experience of being fearful of her basement: she may experience her fear as something forced on her (in ways that she does not understand). Betty may experience her reasoning as a process that she is in charge of, and as a process that she directs in an uncoerced, careful, reliable way. She may experience her judgment as issuing from her reasoning, her intention as issuing from her judgment, and her action as issuing from all of this. Finally, Betty may experience her deliberation as aimed at settling which among two *open options*—trying to eliminate her fear, and allowing the fear to persist—she will select. Betty's having the collection of experiences just described would amount to her having an experience of acting freely (an experience that might not be veridical). A collection of experiences of that kind is by no means unusual. We often have similar experiences in cases of full-blown, deliberative action.[12]

Regarding the evidential merit of Betty's experience of acting freely, and of comparable experiences of other agents, one is faced with a pair of questions. First, what is the evidential merit, on the assumption that compatibilism is true? Second, what is the evidential merit, on the assumption that compatibilism is false? I address each question in turn.

Even on the assumption that compatibilism is true, Betty's experience of acting freely may be misleading. There are the remote possibilities already mentioned—Betty might just be a dreamer or a brain in a vat, for instance. There are also less remote possibilities: for example, a judgment-grounding pro-attitude of hers might be one that she is compelled to have. Still, Betty's experience does provide her with some grounds (however weak they may be) for believing that she is acting freely. It is not as though *nothing* can be said in support of the truth of her belief; nor does her experience count for nothing in that regard. Further, the assumption of compatibilism still being in place, her reporting her experience to us gives us some grounds for believing that she acted freely; it is not as though her report counts for nothing, unless we are warranted in believing her to be dishonest about such things. So suppose that a careful survey of Betty's history and psychological profile reveals to us that she has no relevant compelled or coercively produced attitudes and that she is not possessed of a collection of beliefs that deprives her of autonomy with respect to her reasoning; that we have evidence that she did reason reliably and no evidence to the contrary; and that we have no reason to think that Betty's decisive better judgments did not issue from her deliberation, or that the transitions from better judgment to intention, and intention to a corresponding attempt, were anything but normal default transitions. Then we have grounds for the judgment that Betty acted freely (on a compatibilist conception of free action) and no grounds for believing that she did not so act. Our belief that she acted freely is a warranted belief, and Betty's experience enters into the grounds for that belief.

Things are not so easy for libertarians. The line of reasoning just sketched applies to the first four conditions in the libertarian set of sufficient conditions for free or autonomous action, since they are just the compatibilist conditions. Condition 5—the distinctly libertarian contribution to the set—raises a special problem. I observed that Betty may experience her deliberation as aimed at settling which of two *open options* she will select, an experience seemingly relevant to her satisfying the indeterministic condition at issue. But the openness here would seem to be *doxastic* openness.[13] When she starts deliberating, Betty does not know whether she will try to eliminate her fear or, instead, make no such attempt; nor does she even *believe*, of either of these options, that she will select it (or so we may suppose). More positively, she may believe that both alternatives are open to her and experience them as open. However, an experience of doxastic openness does not amount to an experience of internal indeterminism, or of the absence of causally sufficient conditions, when deliberation begins, for the practical outcome of one's deliberation. If the best explanation of Betty's experience of openness were that she is internally indeterministic, her having that experience would provide grounds for the judgment that she is internally indeterministic. But no one has produced an impressive argument for the general explanatory thesis at issue; and on the face of it, the occurrence of experiences of doxastic openness are no more likely on the assumption that internal indeterminism is a feature of agents than on the assumption that determinism is true. Indeed, there is no reason to think that internal determinism or indeterminism would reveal themselves to us in our experience of our own agency.

In short, although agential experience carries some weight regarding the compatibilist conditions on the libertarians' list, it does not point any more strongly to internal indeterminism than to a doxastic openness that is compatible with determinism. Are matters hopeless, then, for libertarians?

Not really. Van Inwagen is right in suggesting that we know too little about the human organism to be warranted in insisting that internal indeterminism is not a live option (1983, p. 198). We do not know enough to be confident, for example, that it is always causally determined which of our beliefs enter into our deliberation and which do not. The truth of libertarianism does depend, as I have argued, on the truth of internal indeterminism. But a few causally undetermined internal events in the right places will do the trick. In the absence of a powerful argument for internal determinism, libertarianism is an open option.

Is it *less likely*, however, that we have libertarian freedom than that we lack it? A reasonable libertarian answer is that, given the state of our knowledge (and our ignorance) about our internal workings, we have no way of making a confident probabilistic judgment about the reality of the internal indeterminism on which the matter hinges. If that is so, the best nonautonomists can do against libertarianism is to achieve a stalemate. Their other objections—that libertarianism cuts agents off from nonultimate control required for freedom, that libertarianism requires an infinite regress of choices, and the like—have already been disarmed in this book.

Against agnostic (about compatibilism) believers in autonomy, nonautonomists cannot even achieve a stalemate—unless they can establish incompatibilism, thus forcing committed believers in autonomy to embrace libertarianism. The strongest argument for incompatibilism is some version of the consequence argument (p. 195). But it is open to compatibilists to argue that the notion at work there of something's being "up to" an agent (and any variant of that notion that fills its role in the argument) demands more than is required for free action. Thus, for example, a compatibilist can contend that the freedom of Betty's attempt to eradicate her fear does not require her having any more control over what she does—or its being up to her what she does in any deeper way—than what is provided by the truth of conditions 1 through 4 on p. 247. This is by no means an *ad hoc* response. The laws of nature and events that occurred prior to our birth allegedly are "not up to us" precisely in the sense that we have *no control over them*. But it does not follow from (*A1*) the supposition that these things are not up to us in this sense and (*A2*) the supposition that our actions "are the consequences of" these things, that (*A3*) our actions are "not up to us" in the *same* sense. Many of our actions are under our proximal control, and their being so is compatible with the truth of *A1* and *A2* (cf. Slote 1982). The incompatibilist can push for a reading of 'up to us' that is allied with "ultimate control" (in Kane's sense); however, that kind of control is viewed by the compatibilist as at best an excessive requirement for free action.

Some readers undoubtedly would like to have a knock-down refutation of nonautonomism. Such a refutation would require either a knock-down argument for compatibilism or an equally powerful argument for the reality of an internal indeterminism that gives libertarians what they want. Some day, perhaps, people will be in a position to address the latter matter in something approaching an authoritative way. Even today, some people can be bowled over by arguments for the former thesis. But it is hard to respond to familiar arguments for compatibilism with absolute, unconditional acceptance, once one understands that a modest libertarianism is coherent. (Indeed, the initially most gripping arguments for compatibilism are those encompassing a subargument that appears to show that libertarianism is *incoherent*.) For what some libertarians want, and what they require for autonomy, *is* attractive—if it is something that we can have with little or no sacrifice in proximal control. The attractive item includes our having, in van Inwagen's words (and in his sense), more than one "physically possible future"—more than one future that is compatible with the laws of nature together with, say, the state of the world prior to our birth. This is naturally viewed as part of a *metaphysically robust* autonomy. Agnostic believers in autonomy will settle for a metaphysically thinner autonomy, if they are convinced that that is the most they can have; but nothing shows that a more robust autonomy is unavailable.

An agnostic (about compatibilism) believer in autonomy—an *agnostic autonomist*, for short—can have much to offer. If I am right, there is, for all we know, a kind of internal indeterminism that is not an obstacle to compatibilist autonomy and promotes a libertarian autonomy. Agnostic autonomists can get off the fence and offer the following combination: the hope of a robust, libertarian autonomy and, should such autonomy prove to be unavailable to us, the reality of a less robust, compatibilist autonomy that is allied with moral responsibility and merited moral praise and blame. Such an autonomist can plausibly maintain, for example, that both *T1* and *T2* are true:

> *T1*. The satisfaction of conditions 1 through 5 (p. 247) is sufficient for Betty's having acted autonomously, in a robust sense of 'autonomously'; and for all we know, the libertarian condition (condition 5) is satisfiable by actual human beings (including Betty).

> *T2*. The satisfaction of conditions 1 through 4—conditions that are plainly satisfiable—is sufficient for Betty's having acted autonomously in a metaphysically less robust sense of 'autonomously,' but a sense allied with moral responsibility and deserved moral praise and blame.

Autonomists of this stripe are agnostic about the reality of libertarian autonomy, owing to an appreciation of how "little is known about the details of [the] terrible complexity" of the human organism (van Inwagen 1983, p. 198)—too little to warrant a confidently held belief in internal indeterminism, on the one hand, or internal determinism, on the other. However, they are not agnostic about the reality of a metaphysically less robust, compatibilist autonomy, one that offers less than libertarian autonomy, but enough to sustain moral responsibility.

Suppose it were established beyond a reasonable doubt that the human central nervous system (CNS) never operates indeterministically and that we, being reasonable people, fully accept this conclusion. As I have observed, that the CNS itself never operates indeterministically leaves it open that undetermined external events have effects upon the CNS: the present supposition is that there are no causally undetermined events in the CNS. We already have seen that external indeterminism does not give libertarians what they want. And assuming a modest physicalism, internal indeterminism is now, by hypothesis, out of the picture. One could advert to substance dualism and imagine that undetermined psychic events "in" an immaterial substance ("you" or "your mind") produce CNS events involved in deciding and acting; but that would open a can of worms better left for another occasion. Other options are compatibilist belief in autonomy and nonautonomism.

In the absence of a convincing argument for incompatibilism, nonautonomism has not achieved even a stalemate against compatibilist belief in autonomy. I have argued, in effect, that if compatibilism is true, then it is likely that human autonomy is a reality. Compatibilists advocate only a conceptual *possibility*—the possibility of the conjunction of the existence of human autonomy and the truth of determinism. If that conjunction is conceptually possible, then probably there are autonomous human beings. To block this probability, nonautonomists must advocate, not a mere conceptual possibility, but rather a conceptual *necessity*—namely, the conceptual *impossibility* of the conjunction at issue, the necessity of the conjunction's being false. They bear a heavier burden than compatibilists and than compatibilist believers in human autonomy.

## 6. Being Pragmatic and Keeping Score

It is, perhaps, tempting to say that a stalemate between libertarians and nonautonomists is compatible with its being rational of the former to believe that libertarian autonomy is a reality, on grounds familiar to William James's readers. Not all reasons for belief are *alethic* reasons (ch. 5, sec. 2). When alethic reasons weigh no more heavily one way than the other, when one is convinced that this is so regarding *p*, and when one is confident that more would be gained than lost as a consequence of the perseverance of one's cherished belief that *p*, it is rational of one to continue to believe that *p*. So, at least, it may be argued. Be that as it may, my concern regarding autonomy has been with the truth or falsity of the thesis that some human beings are autonomous agents, and, of course, with the interpretation of that thesis. Still, I did have a pragmatic reason for taking the approach I took.

Interminable disputes between libertarians and compatibilist believers in autonomy can give nonautonomists a rhetorical advantage. Nonautonomists can benefit from arguments on both sides, alleging that libertarians decisively reveal the ordinary person's notion of free will (or autonomy, or free action, or moral responsibility) and that compatibilist critics of libertarianism show the notion to be unsatisfiable. My own tack was to avoid, as far as possible, engaging in the in-house debate among believers in autonomy and to ascertain what would suffice for autonomy, first on a compatibilist conception and then on a libertarian conception. The compatibilist conditions that I have offered (ch. 10, sec. 5) are neither thin nor unsatisfiable. They feature, on the positive side, a rich and complex agency, involving mental health, a doxastic basis for informed deliberation, reliable practical reasoning, self-reflection, self-assessment, a capacity for self-modification, and enormous "nonultimate" control, and, on the negative, the absence of an agential history encompassing certain kinds of manipulation and compulsion. My libertarian conditions (ch. 12, sec. 2) are just the compatibilist conditions conjoined with an indeterministic one that, for all we know (or are warranted in believing), is satisfied by actual human beings. Libertarian autonomy is epistemically open; neither the compatibilist nor anyone else has closed that door. Nonautonomists cannot successfully ride piggyback on selected arguments offered by compatibilists and libertarians against one another. If they are to defeat their opponents, they must produce telling arguments for the nonreality of autonomy; and the nonautonomist arguments examined in this book were shown to be wanting.

I conclude with a summary of the major advantages and disadvantages of the four positions highlighted here, as I have developed them, and a parting comment.

## A.   Compatibilist Belief in Autonomy

*Advantages.* Proponents have available the robust, satisfiable set of conditions for autonomy just summarized. The conditions provide a basis for successful answers to incompatibilist challenges that do not hinge on the incompatibilist requirement of internal indeterminism—challenges involving hypothetical covert manipulators, autonomy-thwarting blind external forces, and the like. We arc warranted in believing that compatibilist autonomous action is a reality.

*Disadvantages.* From a compatibilist perspective there are no disadvantages, in principle. From an incompatibilist perspective, the disadvantage is that compatibilist autonomy cannot accommodate a certain necessary condition of autonomy, one that is not satisfied at any deterministic world. Compatibilism leaves it open that, in the case of any autonomous agent, the following is true: ($F$) each agent-internal state or event, and each action, is the product of some deterministic causal chain. Necessarily, agents of whom $F$ is true lack autonomy, according to incompatibilists. From an agnostic autonomist perspective, the disadvantage of compatibilism is that it commits itself to a thesis that agnostics regard as not known to be true—namely, that autonomy is compatible with determinism. (*Compatibilist* autonomy is compatible with determinism; agnostic autonomists are agnostic about whether compatibilist autonomy is autonomy.)

## B.   Incompatibilist Belief in Autonomy: Libertarianism

*Advantages.* A major advantage of the libertarian view developed here is that it solves the "control problem" supposedly posed by "internal indeterminism." The crucial "indeterministic gap" in this libertarian view is located in occurrences and nonoccurrences that an agent does not control even if internal *determinism* is true of him. Libertarianism is coherent and epistemically open to us, and the libertarian view developed here offers us no less *actual* proximal control than compatibilism does. Another advantage, this time from libertarian and agnostic autonomist perspectives in particular, is that the coherent libertarian package includes openness of a kind precluded by $F$ (under $A$).

*Disadvantages.* The major disadvantage of libertarianism in general is that, for all we know, we are internally deterministic, or internally indeterministic only in ways of no theoretical use to libertarians.

## C. Agnostic (about Compatibilism) Belief in Autonomy: Agnostic Autonomism

*Advantages.* This position can draw upon the resources both of compatibilism and of libertarianism. It can offer both a robust, satisfiable set of sufficient conditions for compatibilist autonomy and a coherent set of conditions for incompatibilist autonomy that, for all we know, is satisfied by real human beings. It has the resources to resolve alleged, determinism-neutral problems for compatibilist accounts of autonomy, to conquer the "control problem" that libertarianism traditionally faces, and to show that *if* compatibilism is true, belief in the existence of human autonomy is warranted. Further, agnostics have the advantage of not having the disadvantages identified under *A* and *B*. Agnostics do not insist that autonomy is compatible with determinism; nor need they insist that we are internally indeterministic, or more specifically, internally indeterministic in a way of use to libertarians.

*Disadvantages.* *Qua* agnostic, one is in no position to advance a knock-down argument for the reality of autonomy. The doubly agnostic autonomism that I have described officially leaves it epistemically open (1) that no set of sufficient conditions for *compatibilist* autonomy is sufficient for *autonomy* and (2) that human beings are not internally indeterministic in a way theoretically useful to incompatibilist believers in autonomy.[14] In leaving this open, agnostic autonomism leaves it epistemically open that no human being is autonomous, on the assumptions that incompatibilist autonomy requires internal indeterminism and that compatibilism and incompatibilism are jointly exhaustive. However, intellectual history teaches modesty. No one has yet produced a knock-down argument to close either of these options (i.e., 1 and 2). Agnostic autonomists do not take themselves to be in a better position to succeed in this than all those who have tried and failed.

## D. Nonautonomism

*Advantages.* The position apparently is epistemically open to us. If we do not know whether compatibilism is true and whether human beings are internally indeterministic in a way required for incompatibilist autonomy, then we do not know whether any human beings are autonomous.

*Disadvantages.* Significant grounds for nonautonomism are limited to grounds for rejecting compatibilism and libertarianism. A convincing case for nonautonomism must accomplish two things. It must provide a convincing argument for incompatibilism and convincing grounds for the thesis that human beings are not internally indeterministic in a way required for incompatibilist autonomy. Compatibilist and agnostic believers in human autonomy take comfort in the absence of any convincing argument of the first sort. Indeed, they take pleasure in this, since incompatibilists take on the burden of advancing a putative *necessary* truth, a burden that compatibilist and agnostic believers are pleased to be without. Further, libertarians and agnostic autonomists rightly observe that, given our present knowledge and ignorance about the workings of the human organism, we lack grounds for confidence that internal indeterminism of a sort required by a coherent, physicalistically minded libertarianism is not a feature of actual human beings.

On my scorecard, agnostic autonomism wins. First, it has the combined advantages of the compatibilist and libertarian positions developed here (*A* and *B*), without the reported disadvantages. (Its own disadvantages may even be seen as manifesting epistemic virtues by some.) Second, nonautonomism is on no firmer footing than either of these two positions (and it has a heavier burden than compatibilist belief in human autonomy). Agnostic autonomism is more likely to be true than each of *A* and *B* (after all, it is the disjunction of these two options: agnostic autonomism asserts "*A or B*" while being agnostic about which of the disjuncts is true). Nonautonomism (at best) fares no better than either of *A* and *B*. So agnostic autonomism emerges victorious. If compatibilism is true, then, as I have argued, a strong case—grounded significantly in human experience—can be made for the existence of autonomous human agents. Even if compatibilism is false, the nonautonomist is no better off than the libertarian. And in the absence of a knock-down argument for incompatibilism, the agnostic autonomist has a significant edge over the nonautonomist.

There is a great deal of truth in the old adage that winning is less important than how one plays the game. My game plan for the first twelve chapters was to develop an account of the nature and functions of self-control and of an ideally self-controlled person; to show that even such a person may fall short of autonomy; to ask what can be added to ideal self-control to yield personal autonomy, on the assumption that some human beings are autonomous; and to develop a pair of answers, one for compatibilist believers in human autonomy, and one for libertarians. The assumption mentioned is challenged by nonautonomists, and in philosophically interesting ways; a response was in order. So, in the present chapter, I set out to ascertain whether, equipped with my pair of answers, agnostic autonomists can hold their own against nonautonomists. They can, as I have argued. However, I take greater satisfaction in having executed the game plan.

My primary goal in this book was twofold. My aim was to improve our understanding of self-control and to illuminate autonomous agency—a kind of agency open to real human beings (for all we know, at least)—from a perspective that does justice both to compatibilist belief in human autonomy and to a coherent, nonmysterious libertarianism, the perspective of an agnostic autonomist. If your understanding of self-control and autonomous agency has been enriched by this book, I have hit my mark.

## Notes

1. Galen Strawson speaks of the "sense of the word 'free' . . . that matters most to most people—at least in so far as questions of morality are concerned" (1986, p. v). Thomas Nagel refers to "our ordinary conception of autonomy" and contends that "the intuitive idea of autonomy includes conflicting elements" (1986, pp. 114–15). Again, Nagel demands more for autonomy than Strawson does (see ch. 12, n. 12).

2. See Eccles 1953, 1970; Kane 1985, ch. 9; and Thorp 1980, ch. 4.

3. Double's precise claim is that certain facts about the debate between compatibilists and incompatibilists show that both sides "are committed to the view that any acceptable sense of 'free will' must entail that free persons could have chosen otherwise" (p. 219).

4. Perhaps Double had only *referring* terms in mind in 2; but 'miracle' and 'backward time travel' *might* be referring terms.

5. "The prephilosophical view" of action, if there is one, may leave it open, for example, whether actions are to be individuated coarsely (Anscombe 1963; Davidson 1980), or finely (Goldman 1970), or in a third way that finds a larger action having smaller actions among its parts where the coarse-grained individuators locate the same action under various descriptions and their fine-grained counterparts locate a collection of distinct actions "generationally" related to one another. For a useful recent discussion of competing views on act individuation, see Ginet 1990, ch. 3.

6. For critical exploration of the idea that actual-sequence determination precludes moral responsibility, see Berofsky 1987. For a critical discussion of Frankfurt-style cases and an argument that, in these cases, the agent could have done otherwise, see Lamb 1993. On Lamb's paper, see above ch. 5, n. 18, and pp. 141–42.

7. See Honderich 1988, ch. 8. For an interesting suggestion about a semantic divide between compatibilists and incompatibilists on this issue, see Unger 1984, pp. 54–58.

8. It merits mention that Waller 1990 accepts human freedom but denies that we are morally responsible beings.

9. For discussion of some ways in which moral responsibility is conceptually more complex than free will, see Clarke 1992.

10. I place various relevant Freudian hypotheses in that category. For a penetrating critique of the thesis that there is significant clinical confirmation of various fundamental Freudian claims, see Grünbaum 1984. Grünbaum also criticizes alleged extraclinical support for several Freudian claims (pp. 188–89, 202–05, 217–19, 270). For further discussion, including replies to critics, see Grünbaum 1993.

11. If every attempt to $A$ is an intentional attempt to $A$, as I believe, the expression "intentional attempt" in condition 4 is redundant. I include 'intentional' for emphasis.

12. Cf. Searle 1984, pp. 95–98; discussed earlier (ch. 8, sec. 2). Searle's concern is with a kind of experience associated with intentional action generally, both deliberative and non-deliberative.

13. On such openness, see Dennett 1984; Kapitan 1989; and Velleman 1989, ch. 5.

14. Henceforth, "agnostic autonomism" should be understood as naming an explicitly doubly agnostic view.

# References

Ainslie, George. 1992. *Picoeconomics*. Cambridge: Cambridge University Press.
———. 1982. "A Behavioral Economic Approach to the Defense Mechanisms: Freud's Energy Theory Revisited." *Social Science Information* 21: 735–80.
———. 1975. "Specious Reward: A Behavioral Theory of Impulsiveness and Impulse Control." *Psychological Bulletin* 82: 463–96.
Anscombe, G. E. M. 1981. *The Collected Philosophical Papers of G. E. M. Anscombe*, vol. 2. Minneapolis: University of Minnesota Press.
———. 1963. *Intention*. 2nd ed. Ithaca, N.Y.: Cornell University Press.
Aristotle. *De Motu Animalium*. Vol. 5 of William Ross, ed., *The Works of Aristotle*. London: Oxford University Press, 1915.
———. *Nicomachean Ethics*. Vol. 9 of William Ross, ed., *The Works of Aristotle*. London: Oxford University Press, 1915.
Atkinson, John. 1957. "Motivational Determinants of Risk-Taking Behavior." *Psychological Review* 64: 359–72.
Audi, Robert. 1993. Action, Intention, and Reason. Ithaca, N.Y.: Cornell University Press.
———. 1991. "Autonomy, Reason, and Desire." *Pacific Philosophical Quarterly* 11: 1–14.
———. 1986. "Acting for Reasons." *Philosophical Review* 95: 511–46.
———. 1982. "Axiological Foundationalism." *Canadian Journal of Philosophy* 12: 163–83.
———. 1979. "Weakness of Will and Practical Judgment." *Noûs* 13: 173–96.
Ayer, Alfred J. 1954. "Freedom and Necessity." In Alfred J. Ayer, *Philosophical Essays*. London: Macmillan.
Bach, Kent. n.d. "Emotional Disorders and Attention." In George Graham and L. Stephens, eds., *Philosophical Psychopathology*. Cambridge, Mass.: MIT Press. Forthcoming.
———. 1981. "An Analysis of Self-Deception." *Philosophy and Phenomenological Research* 41: 351–370.
Baron, Jonathan. 1988. *Thinking and Deciding*. Cambridge: Cambridge University Press.
Baumeister, Roy, and K. Cairns. 1992. "Repression and Self-Presentation: When Audiences Interfere with Self-Deceptive Strategies." *Journal of Personality and Social Psychology* 62: 851–62.
Beck, Aaron. 1976. *Cognitive Therapy and the Emotional Disorders*. New York: International Universities Press.
Benn, Stanley. 1988. *A Theory of Freedom*. Cambridge: Cambridge University Press.
Bergmann, Frithjof. 1977. *On Being Free*. Notre Dame, Ind.: University of Notre Dame Press.
Berlin, Isaiah. 1969. *Four Essays on Liberty*. Oxford: Oxford University Press.
Berofsky, Bernard. 1987. *Freedom from Necessity*. New York: Routledge and Kegan Paul.
Bigelow, John, S. Dodds, and R. Pargetter. 1990. "Temptation and the Will." *American Philosophical Quarterly* 27: 39–49.

Bishop, John. 1989. *Natural Agency*. Cambridge: Cambridge University Press.
———. 1983. "Agent Causation." *Mind* 92: 61–79.
Blumenfeld, David. 1988. "Freedom and Mind Control." *American Philosophical Quarterly* 25: 215–27.
Brand, Myles. 1984. *Intending and Acting*. Cambridge, Mass.: MIT Press.
Bratman, Michael. 1987. *Intention, Plans, and Practical Reason*. Cambridge, Mass.: Harvard University Press.
———. 1985. "Davidson's Theory of Intention." In Ernest LePore and B. McLaughlin, eds., *Actions and Events*. Oxford: Basil Blackwell.
———. 1979. "Practical Reasoning and Weakness of the Will." *Noûs* 13: 153–71.
Campbell, Charles. 1957. *On Selfhood and Godhood*. London: Allen and Unwin.
Cartwright, Nancy. 1983. *How the Laws of Physics Lie*. Oxford: Clarendon Press.
Castañeda, Hector-Neri. 1975. *Thinking and Doing*. Dordrecht: Reidel.
Charlton, William. 1988. *Weakness of Will*. Oxford: Basil Blackwell.
Christman, John. 1991. "Autonomy and Personal History." *Canadian Journal of Philosophy* 21: 1–24.
———. 1989. "Introduction." In John Christman, ed., *The Inner Citadel*. New York: Oxford University Press.
Chisholm, Roderick. 1966. "Freedom and Action." In Keith Lehrer, ed., *Freedom and Determinism*. New York: Random House.
Clarke, Randolph. 1993. "Toward a Credible Agent-Causal Account of Free-Will." *Noûs* 27: 191 203.
———. 1992. "Free Will and the Conditions of Moral Responsibility." *Philosophical Studies* 66: 53–72.
Clifford, William. 1886. *Lectures and Essays*. London: Macmillan.
Cohen, L. Jonathan. 1992. *An Essay on Belief and Acceptance*. Oxford: Clarendon Press.
Collinge, Neville. 1949–50. "Medea vs. Socrates." *Durham University Journal* 11: 41–67.
Davidson, Donald. 1987. "Knowing One's Own Mind." *Proceedings and Addresses of the American Philosophical Association* 60: 441–58.
———. 1985a. "Replies to Essays I–IX." In Bruce Vermazen and M. Hintikka, eds., *Essays on Davidson*. Oxford: Clarendon Press.
———. 1985b. "Incoherence and Irrationality." *Dialectica* 39: 345–54.
———. 1985c. "Deception and Division." In Ernest LePore and B. McLaughlin, eds., *Actions and Events*. Oxford: Basil Blackwell.
———. 1984. *Inquiries into Truth and Interpretation*. Oxford: Clarendon Press.
———. 1982. "Paradoxes of Irrationality." In Richard Wollheim and J. Hopkins, eds., *Philosophical Essays on Freud*. Cambridge: Cambridge University Press.
———. 1980. *Essays on Actions and Events*. Oxford: Clarendon Press.
———. 1970. "How is Weakness of the Will Possible?" In Joel Feinberg, ed., *Moral Concepts*. Oxford: Clarendon Press. Reprinted in Davidson 1980.
———. 1963. "Actions, Reasons, and Causes." *Journal of Philosophy* 60: 685–700. Reprinted in Davidson 1980.
Dennett, Daniel. 1984. *Elbow Room*. Cambridge, Mass.: MIT Press.
———. 1978. *Brainstorms*. Montgomery, VT.: Bradford Books.
de Sousa, Ronald. 1987. *The Rationality of Emotion*. Cambridge, Mass.: MIT Press.
———. 1979. "The Rationality of Emotions." *Dialogue* 18:41–63.
Dodds, Eric. 1951. *The Greeks and the Irrational*. Berkeley: University of California Press.
Double, Richard. 1992. "Two Types of Autonomy Accounts." *Canadian Journal of Philosophy* 22: 65–80.
———. 1991. *The Non-Reality of Free Will*. New York: Oxford University Press.

Dunn, Robert. 1987. *The Possibility of Weakness of Will*. Indianapolis, Ind.: Hackett.

Dworkin, Gerald. 1988. *The Theory and Practice of Autonomy*. Cambridge: Cambridge University Press.

———. 1976. "Autonomy and Behavior Control." *Hastings Center Report* 6: 23–28.

Eccles, John. 1970. *Facing Reality*. London: English University Press.

———. 1953. *The Neurophysiological Basis of Mind*. Oxford: Oxford University Press.

Eells, Ellery. 1991. *Probabilistic Causality*. Cambridge: Cambridge University Press.

Elster, Jon. 1984. *Ulysses and the Sirens*. Cambridge: Cambridge University Press.

Euripides. *Hippolytus*. In David Grene and R. Lattimore, eds., *The Complete Greek Tragedies*. Chicago: University of Chicago Press, 1959.

———. *Medea*. In David Grene and R. Lattimore, eds., *The Complete Greek Tragedies*. Chicago: University of Chicago Press, 1959.

Feinberg, Joel. 1986. *Harm to Self*. New York: Oxford University Press.

Festinger, Leon. 1964. *Conflict, Decision, and Dissonance*. Stanford, Calif.: Stanford University Press.

———. 1957. *A Theory of Cognitive Dissonance*. Stanford, Calif.: Stanford University Press.

Fischer, John. 1987. "Responsiveness and Moral Responsibility." In Ferdinand Schoeman, ed., *Responsibility, Character, and the Emotions*. Cambridge: Cambridge University Press.

———. 1982. "Responsibility and Control." *Journal of Philosophy* 79: 24–40.

Fischer, John, and P. Hoffman. 1994. "Alternative Possibilities: A Reply to Lamb." *Journal of Philosophy* 91: 321–26.

Fischer, John, and M. Ravizza. 1994. "Responsibility and History." *Midwest Studies in Philosophy* 19: 430–51.

———. 1992a. "Responsibility, Freedom and Reason." *Ethics* 102: 368–89.

———. 1992b. "When the Will is Free." *Philosophical Perspectives* 6: 423–51.

———. 1991. "Responsibility and Inevitability." *Ethics* 101: 258–78.

Fodor, Jerry. 1987. *Psychosemantics*. Cambridge, Mass.: MIT Press.

Foot, Philippa. 1978. *Virtues and Vices*. Berkeley: University of California Press.

Frankfurt, Harry. 1992. "The Faintest Passion." *Proceedings and Addresses of the American Philosophical Association* 66: 5–16.

———. 1988. *The Importance of What We Care About*. Cambridge: Cambridge University Press.

———. 1971. "Freedom of the Will and the Concept of a Person." *Journal of Philosophy* 68: 5–20. Reprinted in Frankfurt 1988.

Frey, Dieter. 1986. "Recent Research on Selective Exposure to Information." In Leonard Berkowitz, ed., *Advances in Experimental Social Psychology*, vol. 19. New York: Academic Press.

Frijda, Nico. 1986. *The Emotions*. Cambridge: Cambridge University Press.

Geach, Peter. 1977. *The Virtues*. Cambridge: Cambridge University Press.

Gettier, Edmund. 1963. "Is Justified True Belief Knowledge?" *Analysis* 23: 121–23.

Gibbard, Allan. 1990. *Wise Choices, Apt Feelings*. Cambridge, Mass.: Harvard University Press.

Gilovich, Thomas. 1991. *How We Know What Isn't So*. New York: Macmillan.

Ginet, Carl. 1990. *On Action*. Cambridge: Cambridge University Press.

Goldman, Alvin. 1970. *A Theory of Human Action*. Englewood Cliffs, N.J.: Prentice-Hall.

Good, Irving. 1983. *Good Thinking*. Minneapolis: University of Minnesota Press.

Gordon, Robert. 1987. *The Structure of Emotions*. Cambridge: Cambridge University Press.

Greenspan, Patricia. 1988. *Emotions and Reasons*. New York: Routledge.

———. 1980. "A Case of Mixed Feelings: Ambivalence and the Logic of Emotion." In Amelie Rorty, ed., *Explaining Emotions*. Berkeley: University of California Press.

Greenwald, Anthony. 1988. "Self-Knowledge and Self-Deception." In Joan Lockard and D. Paulhus, eds., *Self-Deception: An Adaptive Mechanism?* Englewood Cliffs, N.J.: Prentice-Hall.

Grünbaum, Adolf. 1993. *Validation in the Clinical Theory of Psychoanalysis*. Madison, Conn.: International Universities Press.

———. 1984. *The Foundations of Psychoanalysis: A Philosophical Critique*. Berkeley: University of California Press.

———. 1971. "Free Will and the Laws of Human Behavior." *American Philosophical Quarterly* 8: 299–317.

Haji, Ishtiyaque. 1994. "Autonomy and Blameworthiness." *Canadian Journal of Philosophy*. 24: 593–612.

Hare, Richard. 1992. "Weakness of Will." In Lawrence Becker and C. Becker, eds., *Encyclopedia of Ethics*. New York: Garland.

———. 1981. *Moral Thinking*. Oxford: Clarendon Press.

———. 1963. *Freedom and Reason*. Oxford: Oxford University Press.

———. 1952. *The Language of Morals*. Oxford: Oxford University Press.

Harman, Gilbert. 1993. "Desired Desires." In Raymond Frey and C. Morris, eds., *Value, Welfare, and Morality*. Cambridge: Cambridge University Press.

———. 1986. *Change in View*. Cambridge, Mass.: MIT Press.

———. 1976. "Practical Reasoning." *Review of Metaphysics* 79: 431–63.

Haworth, Lawrence. 1986. *Autonomy*. New Haven, Conn.: Yale University Press.

Heil, John. 1984. "Doxastic Incontinence." *Mind* 93: 56–70.

Hick, John. 1960. "Theology and Verification." *Theology Today* 17: 12–31.

Hill, Thomas. 1986. "Weakness of Will and Character." *Philosophical Topics* 14: 93–115.

Hobart, R. E. 1934. "Free Will as Involving Determinism and as Inconceivable without It." *Mind* 43: 1–27.

Honderich, Ted. 1988. *A Theory of Determinism*. Oxford: Clarendon Press.

Hume, David. [1739] 1975. *A Treatise of Human Nature*. Ed. Lewis Selby-Bigge. Oxford: Clarendon Press.

———. [1777] 1975. *An Enquiry Concerning Human Understanding*, 3rd ed. Ed. Lewis Selby-Bigge. Oxford: Clarendon Press.

Irwin, Terence. 1983. "Euripides and Socrates." *Classical Philology* 10: 183–97.

Jackson, Frank. 1985. "Internal Conflicts in Desires and Morals." *American Philosophical Quarterly* 22: 105–14.

———. 1984. "Weakness of Will." *Mind* 93: 1–18.

James, William. [1897] 1979. *The Will to Believe and Other Essays in Popular Philosophy*. Cambridge, Mass.: Harvard University Press.

———. 1907. *The Principles of Psychology*. New York: Macmillan.

Jeffrey, Richard. 1974. "Preference among Preferences." *Journal of Philosophy* 71: 377–91. Reprinted in Richard Jeffrey, *The Logic of Decision, 2nd ed.*. Chicago: University of Chicago Press, 1983.

———. 1965. *The Logic of Decision*. New York: McGraw-Hill.

Kane, Robert. 1989. "Two Kinds of Incompatibilism." *Philosophy and Phenomenological Research* 50: 219–54.

———. 1985. *Free Will and Values*. Albany: State University of New York Press.

Kant, Immanuel. [1785] 1964. *Groundwork of the Metaphysic of Morals*. Trans. Herbert Paton. New York: Harper & Row.

Kapitan, Tomis. 1989. "Doxastic Freedom: A Compatibilist Alternative." *American Philosophical Quarterly*. 26: 31–42.

Klinger, Eric. 1993. "Clinical Approaches to Mood Control." In Daniel Wegner and J. Pennebaker, eds., *Handbook of Mental Control*. Englewood Cliffs, N.J.: Prentice-Hall.

Koriat, Asher, R. Melkman, J. Averill, and R. Lazarus. 1972. "The Self-Control of Emotional Reactions to a Stressful Film." *Journal of Personality* 40: 601–19.

Kunda, Ziva. 1990. "The Case for Motivated Reasoning." *Psychological Bulletin* 108: 480–98.

———. 1987. "Motivated Inference: Self-Serving Generation and Evaluation of Causal Theories." *Journal of Personality and Social Psychology* 53: 636–47.

Lamb, James. 1993. "Evaluative Compatibilism and the Principle of Alternate Possibilities." *Journal of Philosophy* 90: 517–27.

Lewis, David. 1989. "Dispositional Theories of Value." *The Aristotelian Society* (supp. vol.) 63: 113–37.

———. 1986. *Philosophical Papers*, vol. 2. New York: Oxford University Press.

Lindley, Richard. 1986. *Autonomy*. Atlantic Highlands, N.J.: Humanities Press.

Logue, Alexandra. 1988. "Research on Self-Control: An Integrating Framework." *Behavioral and Brain Sciences* 11: 665–79.

Lütkenhaus, P., M. Bullock, and U. Geppert. 1987. "Toddlers' Actions: Knowledge, Control, and the Self." In Frank Halisch and J. Kuhl, eds., *Motivation, Intention, and Volition*. Berlin: Springer-Verlag.

McCann, Hugh. 1995. "Intention and Motivational Strength." *Journal of Philosophical Research* 20: 283–96.

———. 1986a. "Intrinsic Intentionality." *Theory and Decision* 20: 247–73.

———. 1986b. "Rationality and the Range of Intention." *Midwest Studies in Philosophy* 10: 191–211.

Marcus, Ruth. 1980. "Moral Dilemmas and Consistency." *Journal of Philosophy* 77: 121–36.

Marks, Isaac. 1969. *Fears and Phobias*. New York: Academic Press.

Maugham, W. Somerset. 1915. *Of Human Bondage*. New York: Penguin Books.

Mele, Alfred. 1993. "History and Personal Autonomy." *Canadian Journal of Philosophy* 23: 271–80.

———. 1992a. *Springs of Action*. New York: Oxford University Press.

———. 1992b. "Intending for Reasons." *Mind* 101: 327–33.

———. 1992c. "Intentions, Reasons, and Beliefs: Morals of the Toxin Puzzle." *Philosophical Studies* 68: 171–94.

———. 1992d. "*Akrasia*, Self-Control, and Second-Order Desires." *Noûs* 26: 281–302.

———. 1992e. "Recent Work on Intentional Action." *American Philosophical Quarterly* 29: 199–217.

———. 1991. "Akratic Action and the Practical Role of Better Judgment." *Pacific Philosophical Quarterly* 72: 33–47.

———. 1990. "Errant Self-Control and the Self-Controlled Person." *Pacific Philosophical Quarterly* 71: 47–59.

———. 1989a. "Motivational Internalism: The Powers and Limits of Practical Reasoning." *Philosophia* 19: 417–36.

———. 1989b. "Akratic Feelings." *Philosophy and Phenomenological Research* 50: 277–88.

———. 1987. *Irrationality: An Essay on Akrasia, Self-Deception, and Self-Control*. New York: Oxford University Press.

———. 1985. "Aristotle on *Akrasia, Eudaimonia*, and the Psychology of Action." *History of Philosophy Quarterly* 2: 375–93.

————. 1984a. "Aristotle on the Roles of Reason in Motivation and Justification." *Archiv für Geschichte der Philosophie* 66: 124–47.

————. 1984b. "Aristotle on the Proximate Efficient Cause of Action." *Canadian Journal of Philosophy* (supp. vol.) 10: 133–55.

————. 1984c. "Aristotle's Wish." *Journal of the History of Philosophy* 22: 139–56.

————. 1983. "*Akrasia*, Reasons, and Causes." *Philosophical Studies* 44: 345–68.

————. 1981. "Choice and Virtue in the *Nicomachean Ethics*." *Journal of the History of Philosophy* 19: 405–23.

Mele, Alfred, and P. Moser. 1994. "Intentional Action." *Noûs* 28: 39–68.

Mill, John Stuart. [1865] 1979. *An Examination of Sir William Hamilton's Philosophy*. Ed. John Robson. Toronto: Routledge and Kegan Paul.

Mischel, Harriet, and W. Mischel. 1983. "The Development of Children's Knowledge of Self-Control Strategies." *Child Development* 54: 603–19.

Mischel, Walter. 1981. "Metacognition and the Rules of Delay." In John Flavell and L. Ross, eds., *Social Cognitive Development: Frontiers and Possible Futures*. Cambridge: Cambridge University Press.

Mischel, Walter, and N. Baker. 1975. "Cognitive Appraisals and Transformations in Delay Behavior." *Journal of Personality and Social Psychology* 31: 254–61.

Mischel, Walter, and E. Ebbesen. 1970. "Attention in Delay of Gratification." *Journal of Personality and Social Psychology* 16: 329–37.

Mischel, Walter, E. Ebbesen, and A. Zeiss. 1972. "Cognitive and Attentional Mechanisms in Delay of Gratification." *Journal of Personality and Social Psychology* 21: 204–18.

Mischel, Walter, and B. Moore. 1980. "The Role of Ideation in Voluntary Delay for Symbolically Presented Rewards." *Cognitive Therapy and Research* 4: 211–21.

————. 1973. "Effects of Attention to Symbolically-Presented Rewards on Self-Control." *Journal of Personality and Social Psychology* 28: 172–79.

Mook, Douglas. 1987. *Motivation: The Organization of Action*. New York: Norton.

Moore, Bert, W. Mischel, and A. Zeiss. 1976. "Comparative Effects of the Reward Stimulus and Its Cognitive Representation in Voluntary Delay." *Journal of Personality and Social Psychology* 34: 419–24.

Nagel, Thomas. 1986. *The View from Nowhere*. New York: Oxford University Press.

Nisbett, Richard, and L. Ross. 1980. *Human Inference: Strategies and Shortcomings of Social Judgment*. Englewood Cliffs, N.J.: Prentice-Hall.

Nowell-Smith, P. H. 1948. "Free Will and Moral Responsibility." *Mind* 57: 45–61.

Nozick, Robert. 1993. *The Nature of Rationality*. Princeton, N.J.: Princeton University Press.

————. 1981. *Philosophical Explanations*. Cambridge, Mass.: Harvard University Press.

Oakley, Justin. 1992. *Morality and the Emotions*. London: Routledge.

O'Neill, Onora. 1989. *Constructing Reason*. Cambridge: Cambridge University Press.

Parfit, Derek. 1984. *Reasons and Persons*. Oxford: Clarendon Press.

Peacocke, Christopher. 1985. "Intention and *Akrasia*." In Bruce Vermazen and M. Hintikka, eds., *Essays on Davidson*. Oxford: Clarendon Press.

Pears, David. 1984. *Motivated Irrationality*. Oxford: Oxford University Press.

Perry, John. 1980. "Belief and Acceptance." *Midwest Studies in Philosophy* 5: 533–42.

Pettit, Philip, and M. Smith. 1993. "Practical Unreason." *Mind* 102: 53–79.

Pink, Thomas. 1991. "Purposive Intending." *Mind* 100: 343–59.

Plato. *Cratylus*. In Benjamin Jowett, trans., *The Dialogues of Plato*. Oxford: Clarendon Press, 1953.

————. *Laws*. In Benjamin Jowett, trans., *The Dialogues of Plato*. Oxford: Clarendon Press, 1953.

————. *Protagoras.* In Benjamin Jowett, trans., *The Dialogues of Plato.* Oxford: Clarendon Press, 1953.

————. *Republic.* In Benjamin Jowett, trans., *The Dialogues of Plato.* Oxford: Clarendon Press, 1953.

Price, Henry. 1954. "Belief and Will." *The Aristotelian Society* (supp. vol.) 28: 1–26.

Pugmire, David. 1994. "Perverse Preference: Self-Beguilement or Self-Division." *Canadian Journal of Philosophy* 24: 73–94.

Putnam, Hilary. 1973. "Meaning and Reference." *Journal of Philosophy* 70: 699–711.

Quattrone, George, and A. Tversky. 1984. "Causal versus Diagnostic Contingencies: On Self-Deception and on the Voter's Illusion." *Journal of Personality and Social Psychology* 46: 237–48.

Rachman, Stanley, and R. Hodgson. 1980. *Obsessions and Compulsions.* Englewood Cliffs, N.J.: Prentice-Hall.

Rickert, GailAnn. 1987. "Akrasia and Euripides' *Medea.*" *Harvard Studies in Classical Philology* 91: 91–117.

Rorty, Amelie. 1983. "Akratic Believers." *American Philosophical Quarterly* 20: 175–83.

————. 1980a. "Akrasia and Conflict." *Inquiry* 22: 193–212.

————. 1980b. "Where Does the Akratic Break Take Place?" *Australasian Journal of Philosophy* 58: 333–46.

Salmon, Wesley. 1984. *Scientific Explanation and the Causal Structure of the World.* Princeton, N.J.: Princeton University Press.

Schiffer, Stephen. 1976. "A Paradox of Desire." *American Philosophical Quarterly* 13: 195–203.

Schlick, Moritz. 1962. *Problems of Ethics.* Trans. David Rynin. New York: Dover.

Schoeman, Ferdinand. 1978. "Responsibility and the Problem of Induced Desires." *Philosophical Studies* 34: 293–301.

Schrödinger, Erwin. 1983. "The Present Situation in Quantum Mechanics." In John Wheeler and W. Zurek, eds., *Quantum Theory and Measurement.* Princeton, N.J.: Princeton University Press.

Searle, John. 1984. *Minds, Brains, and Science.* Cambridge, Mass.: Harvard University Press.

————. 1983. *Intentionality.* Cambridge: Cambridge University Press.

Shapiro, David. 1981. *Autonomy and Rigid Character.* New York: Basic Books.

Skinner, B. F. 1953. *Science and Human Behavior.* New York: Macmillan.

Slote, Michael. 1982. "Selective Necessity and Free Will." *Journal of Philosophy* 74: 5–24.

Smart, J. J. C. 1961. "Free-Will, Praise, and Blame." *Mind* 70: 291–306.

Smith, Michael. 1992. "Valuing: Desiring or Believing?" In David Charles and K. Lennon, eds., *Reduction, Explanation, and Realism.* Oxford: Clarendon Press.

Snell, Bruno. 1964. *Scenes from Greek Drama.* Berkeley: University of California Press.

Solomon, Robert. 1980. "Emotions and Choice." In Amelie Rorty, ed., *Explaining Emotions.* Berkeley: University of California Press.

————. 1973. "Emotions and Choice." *Review of Metaphysics* 27: 20–41.

Sorabji, Richard. 1980. *Necessity, Cause, and Blame.* Ithaca, N.Y.: Cornell University Press.

Spinoza, Benedict. 1955. Letter to G. H. Schaller [1674]. In Robert Elwes, trans., *On the Improvement of the Understanding; The Ethics; Correspondence.* New York: Dover.

Strawson, Galen. 1986. *Freedom and Belief.* Oxford: Clarendon Press.

Strawson, Peter. 1962. "Freedom and Resentment." *Proceedings of the British Academy* 48: 1–25.

Swanton, Christine. 1992. *Freedom: A Coherence Theory.* Indianapolis: Hackett.

Suppes, Patrick. 1970. *A Probabilistic Theory of Causality.* Amsterdam: North Holland.

Taylor, Richard. 1966. *Action and Purpose*. Englewood Cliffs, N.J.: Prentice-Hall.
———. 1963. *Metaphysics*. Englewood Cliffs, N.J.: Prentice-Hall.
Taylor, Shelley, and S. Fiske. 1978. "Salience, Attention and Attribution: Top of the Head Phenomena." In Leonard Berkowitz, ed., *Advances in Experimental Social Psychology*, vol. 11. New York: Academic Press.
———. 1975. "Point of View and Perceptions of Causality." *Journal of Personality and Social Psychology* 32: 439–45.
Taylor, Shelley, and S. Thompson. 1982. "Stalking the Elusive 'Vividness' Effect." *Psychological Review* 89: 155–81.
Teitelbaum, Philip. 1977. "Levels of Integration of the Operant." In Werner Honig and J. Staddon, eds., *Handbook of Operant Behavior*. Englewood Cliffs, N.J.: Prentice-Hall.
Terr, Lenore. 1991. "Childhood Traumas: An Outline and Overview." *American Journal of Psychiatry* 148: 10–20.
Thoresen, Carl, and M. Mahoney. 1974. *Behavioral Self-Control*. New York: Holt, Rinehart and Winston.
Thorp, John. 1980. *Free Will: A Defense against Neurophysiological Determinism*. London: Routledge and Kegan Paul.
Tice, Dianne, and R. Baumeister. 1993. "Controlling Anger: Self-Induced Emotion Change." In Daniel Wegner and J. Pennebaker, eds., *Handbook of Mental Control*. Englewood Cliffs, N.J.: Prentice-Hall.
Toates, Frederick. 1986. *Motivational Systems*. Cambridge: Cambridge University Press.
Tooley, Michael. 1987. *Causation*. Oxford: Clarendon Press.
Tversky, Amos, and D. Kahnemann. 1973. "Availability: A Heuristic for Judging Frequency and Probability." *Cognitive Psychology* 5: 207–32.
Uleman, James, and J. Bargh. 1989. *Unintended Thought*. New York: Guilford Press.
Unger, Peter. 1984. *Philosophical Relativity*. Minneapolis: University of Minnesota Press.
van Inwagen, Peter. 1992. "Reply to Christopher Hill." *Analysis* 52: 56–61.
———. 1989. "When Is the Will Free?" *Philosophical Perspectives* 3: 399–422.
———. 1983. *An Essay on Free Will*. Oxford: Clarendon Press.
Velleman, J. David. 1989. *Practical Reflection*. Princeton, N.J.: Princeton University Press.
Waller, Bruce. 1990. *Freedom without Responsibility*. Philadelphia: Temple University Press.
Watson, Gary. 1977. "Skepticism about Weakness of Will." *Philosophical Review* 86: 316–39.
———. 1975. "Free Agency." *Journal of Philosophy* 72: 205–20.
Williams, Bernard. 1981. "Internal and External Reasons." In Bernard Williams, *Moral Luck*. Cambridge: Cambridge University Press.
———. 1973. "Deciding to Believe." In Bernard Williams, *Problems of the Self*. Cambridge: Cambridge University Press.
Wilson, George. 1989. *The Intentionality of Human Action*. Stanford, Calif.: Stanford University Press.
Wolf, Susan. 1990. *Freedom within Reason*. New York: Oxford University Press.
Yates, Gregory, M. Yates, and C. Beasley. 1987. "Young Children's Knowledge of Strategies of Delay of Gratification." *Merrill-Palmer Quarterly* 33: 159–69.
Young, Robert. 1986. *Personal Autonomy*. New York: St. Martin's Press.
Zillman, Dolf. 1993. "Mental Control of Angry Aggression." In Daniel Wegner and J. Pennebaker, eds., *Handbook of Mental Control*. Englewood Cliffs, N.J.: Prentice-Hall.

# Index